French Finance in Transition:

Designed for Europe?

by

Carlos Pardo

of

Fédération pour la Recherche Economique et Financière

English translation by Isadore Ryan

Published by Lafferty Publications Ltd

Lafferty Group International Customer Service Centre:

Lafferty Publications Ltd,
The Tower, IDA Centre,
Pearse Street,
Dublin 2, Ireland.
Tel: (+353-1) 718022 Fax: (+353-1) 718240

Contents

Contents

Pensions and Taxation

Appendices   229

Executive Summary

From the end of the Second World War until the late 1980s, France's financial industry was strictly regulated, with competition stifled and strictly delineated financial sectors. Faced with international trends like disinflation and financial deregulation, the public authorities belatedly abandoned restrictive practices and liberalised the financial system. Credit controls were abolished in 1986 and exchange controls were relinquished — first, in 1986, for corporations and then for individuals — while interest rates became the main instrument of monetary policy.

By the early 1990s, the government relied largely on money supply variations, leaving the market freer to regulate interest and exchange rates. To ensure the success of this new direction, the government reformed the existing markets and, when necessary, organised the creation of new financial markets and instruments. Important institutional and regulatory reforms were also carried out. A peculiarity of French deregulation is that innovations generally emanate from the public authorities.

Reforms and innovations in a climate of consensus

Modernisation of techniques for funding state needs through the creation of *obligations assimilables du Trésor* (OATs — Treasury bonds) and *titres de créances négociables* (TCN — marketable debt securities), as well as the "restoration" of the transferable securities market served as the basis for new markets like the MATIF, the MONEP, and the market for warrants. These markets enable dealers to offer economic instruments for hedging against variations in interest and exchange rates.

France also equipped itself with a new Banking Law

in 1984 and modified its Insurance Code in 1989. In parallel, the financial and monetary markets were decompartmentalised and stock market structures were overhauled to increase the capabilities necessary to withstand competition from other centres, most notably London.

Exceptional political consensus surrounded the modernising and deregulating process. While there was some political conflict — over the privatisation issue, for example — this had more to do with the pace and the means than the actual content of the reforms.

Close links between the state and financial intermediaries

In France, the banking and insurance industries retain close links with the public authorities. Not only is the state the main shareholder in both, but also ties have long been woven between the heads of financial institutions, the monetary authorities, the Treasury and high-ranking civil servants, although it is not always easy to understand the actual level of influence wielded by the public authorities. The autonomy of state and semi-state institutions was noticeably greater by the early 1990s than before.

Nevertheless, in terms of its foreign competitors, the French system is marked by the continued existence of invisible barriers which stem from the particular nature of relations between the state and economy. Yet, French institutions are noted for their aggressive approach to foreign acquisitions.

A French market that is difficult to penetrate ...

With a highly international capital market, France

appears to be one of Europe's most interesting financial centres. However, opportunities for foreign investors to buy branch networks (whether bank or insurance) are limited.

Institutions arousing the interest of potential acquirers belong either to the co-operative/mutual sectors or public sectors. The capital of private sector companies has been carefully "put under lock and key", making the buying of important stakes very difficult. The building up of *noyaux durs* (core shareholders) to ensure "political control" of institutions privatised by Finance Minister Edouard Balladur is proof of this. The eviction of Assicurazioni Generali during the takeover of Compagnie du Midi by AXA is another prime example in insurance.

But large French companies are less protected by the locking up of capital than by the effective network of alliances — both explicit and implicit — existing between public and private institutions and which come into play to offset external attacks. In fact, by studying the French economy's main financial hubs, one sees the intertwining of interests. Side by side with private sector companies are the giants of the public sector which, despite some inclination for independence, have built formal and informal ties with each other.

... and aggressive French groups abroad

However, it will not be easy for French institutions to avoid acquisitive thrusts by foreign investors, not least because French financial groups themselves spend large amounts abroad (some $12 billion in 1990), which cannot but irritate both potential investors and allies for French banks who find themselves cut off from any real access to the French market. The "one-way" flow of acquisitions is a source of tension. French banks and insurers appear to be protected while at the same time maintaining a relatively free hand to invest in foreign markets.

It does not appear that the desire of French financial institutions' for foreign acquisitions has been quenched. But one should look to the insurance companies rather than the banks for the next large deals: the healthy cash flow situation of the former — especially the mutuals — contains a potential for foreign growth that still has been little exploited.

A new wave of privatisations?

While the French market arouses much interest, foreigners find it difficult to access. Will the launch of a programme of partial privatisations change this? Such a programme, involving a number of important financial institutions, may at least have the merit of loosening the constraints on buying into state-owned groups even if it is not able to lift the invisible barriers. Such a programme should allow foreign institutions at least to take minority stakes in the institutions subject to privatisation.

The eminently political doctrine of *ni privatisations ni nationalisations* (neither privatisations nor nationalisations) has enshrined the predominance of public companies, casting their ownership structures in stone. Caught between this doctrine and pressure from the growing public deficit which became apparent in the second half of 1991, the Minister of Finance announced plans to move towards the partial privatisation of a number of companies rather than increase the tax burden. While the government's stated objective was to use the money taken in to solve the budgetary deficit problem, in the long term this is really a way of supplying oxygen to state companies that lack own capital on condition that the state maintains majority control.

This new wave of privatisations again casts a shadow on the sacrosanct *ni-ni* doctrine. But the relaunch of the privatisation programme was not the first attack on the presidential dogma that dates back to 1988 and which was designed both to dispel investors' fears of a socialist government's policies and to reassure the left-wing faction — President Mitterrand's supporters.

Other measures had already eaten away this policy by the early 1990s: the decree at the end of 1989 to open up to the public 25 percent of insurance companies' capital (which benefited UAP, AGF and GAN); the share swap agreements between banks and insurance companies (BNP/UAP, GAN/CIC, AGF/BFCE); the decree of April 1991 which stimulated "co-operation" between public and private sector companies and established guidelines for share swaps between credit institutions and industrial groups (BNP/Air France, Crédit Lyonnais/Usinor-Salicilor etc;) the opening up of the capital of Crédit Local and its listing on the stock market; etc.

The large groups will continue to dominate

Deregulation, financial innovation, technological developments and the decompartmentalisation of markets all proved to be powerful factors in loosening the shackles that bound French financial institutions. They have also helped to change the environment in which credit institutions carry out their business, which in turn affects the nature of competition. But although a number of standardised services may now be offered by "non-network" banks or even "non-bank" organisations, branch networks have lost none of their importance in retail banking. And the same holds true for the powerful sales networks in personal insurance.

Bancassurance *and the global service offer*

Liberalisation of banking legislation in France and modernisation of the capital markets have helped to erode the traditional divisions between the various professions within the financial industry.

The forging of bank-insurance links — one of the main events of the 1980s which was instigated primarily by the banks (thanks to disintermediation) — will probably remain a major factor in the 1990s: after 10 years of operations, the banks' insurance subsidiaries were already selling about half of all new premiums. In addition, the emergence of important strategic "alliances" provides a foretaste of large pan-European groups and the foundation of a new financial services industry. The most important of these alliances are between UAP and BNP, and the link established between BNP and Dresdner Bank.

The French banks had at least two motives for forming closer links with insurers: first, to utilise insurance resources in their attempts to strengthen capital, and, second, to diversify business to offer complete management of customers' savings.

Whatever form *bancassurance* takes, the global service offer is, above all else, a strategic choice made by intermediaries. While new services and investment vehicles are being introduced, consumers are increasingly inclined to make choices based on maximum utility. In short, the relationship between intermediary and consumer has been completely turned round. From being a passive seller, very

rapidly the intermediary has had to become an active one: products are no longer bought by clients, they must now be sold to them. In addition, the old distinctions between insurance and banking products is breaking down — both bankers and insurers are becoming financial advisers.

Europeanisation

The single European market, even if merely symbolic in its attempts to create a parity of conditions between the financial services sectors of the EC countries, and the signals coming from financial centres abroad (especially London) have been powerful factors in modernising French financial institutions. French financial institutions very quickly made a strategic choice in favour of "Europeanisation", which has meant diverting attention away from markets outside Europe. Ninety-five percent of international business conducted by French insurers and 90 percent of that done by French banks is concentrated in Europe, mostly within the EC.

Paradoxically, at the same time as this trend towards Europeanisation is taking place, an increased defensiveness among financial institutions around Europe is also arising. While competition has increased, banks and insurance companies have urgently been consolidating their national networks, either by acquiring complementary operations or by dropping unprofitable businesses. But the objective remains clear: to secure uncontested control of decision-making centres at home. Within this context, France occupies a relatively favourable position thanks to the size of its banking and insurance distribution networks and its leadership in the area of collective investment schemes.

The financial markets

The French public authorities have undertaken wide reforms of the regulations governing the capital markets. The impetus given by financial centres abroad (in particular, London) has speeded up this process. As a result, in the space of a decade, Paris has become an international financial centre.

Dealing conditions and market accessibility have been improved on several counts. Particularly significant was the opening up of the primary markets to foreigners in 1984 and the ending of fixed commissions on bond and share brokerages. Also, a second market was created in 1983, geared towards companies that wish to raise capital without having to satisfy all the conditions imposed on those seeking an official listing.

A highly liquid public debt market ...

Numerous technological and financial innovations helped the growth of Paris as a financial centre, while unarguably the greatest success has been the revolution in the bond market.

While the volume of issues doubled between 1982 and 1992, the volume of French bond transactions increased more than 50-fold thanks to the state's search for capital on the markets. The introduction of the technique of "assimilation" which facilitates state borrowing (*obligations assimilables du Trésor* — OAT or Treasury bonds), together with the creation of a network of Treasury security specialists, has increased liquidity and allowed greater accessibility to the French market to outside investors. The rapid rise of the MATIF, in direct and fierce competition with London's LIFFE, is a result of the quality of the state debt market.

... and an equity market that lacks liquidity

Despite successful restructuring, the market for equities continues to be relatively weak. With share capitalisation 10 times larger than it was at the start of the 1980s, French corporations' low recourse to public share offerings has handicapped development. And the relatively low level of public offerings is reflected in the lack of liquidity of certain types of share options traded on the Paris MONEP, for example. This is in contrast to the MATIF, which benefits from the high liquidity of the public debt market.

A significant proportion of French shares are traded on the SEAQ-International in London. "Excessive" transparency on the Paris CAC (Compagnie des Agents de Change) and a turnover tax on traders have played a part in this phenomenon.

French transferable securities portfolios

Modernisation of the stock market and the Chirac government's privatisations helped increase the number of people who held transferable securities: by 1991, more than one Frenchman in five held a securities portfolio, compared to one in 10 in 1984, and over 8 million people held transferable securities indirectly through the mechanism of collective investment schemes (OPCVM).

The policy of maintaining a strong franc and the French economy's excellent performance — especially in curbing inflation — explain foreign investors' rush to buy French securities. Foreign-owned securities were by 1991 worth an estimated FF800 billion ($141 billion), of which over FF500 billion ($88 billion) was in the form of bonds. This was just below twice the value of foreign securities held by French residents (FF500 billion). Such figures give a good idea of the international flavour of the Paris market. Naturally, such internationalisation is a little risky for the market's equilibrium, making it more dependent on institutional investors abroad.

A collective investment market that prospers but is causing some concern

The role of the Paris Bourse was strengthened by the spectacular growth in French OPCVMs, which now account for half of all net assets under management in Europe. Nevertheless, the inordinate growth of this market — which is dominated by the banks — is largely due to regulations limiting, and indeed prohibiting, the remuneration of bank deposits at market rates. Much in demand from individuals and institutional investors, *SICAV monétaires* (short-term money market funds) account for over half of all assets invested in SICAV (open-ended investment companies) and worry the authorities as much as the banks. For the former, the concern essentially stems from the short-term nature and volatility of these investments, while for the latter it is the increase in the cost of funding caused by the flight from traditional banking deposits to these investments, which pay interest rates approaching those available on the money market.

Deregulation of deposit interest rates would bring the OPCVM market back to a more "normal" pattern. The trends in competition would then probably lead away from a market offer largely based around "monetary" or short-term products towards more long-term, sophisticated ones or even to products not yet authorised in France. Thus, French financial institutions have been demanding more favourable tax treatment, especially for collective share products.

The cost of modernisation

There has been sweeping modernisation of the Paris

Bourse. It has been reformed on a number of levels: technologically — continuous trading, the RELIT settlement and delivery system, etc; regulatory and institutional — ie increased powers for the regulatory Commission des Opérations de Bourse (the stockmarket regulatory body); the separation of functions of the old Chamber of Stock Brokers, the establishment of the new *sociétés de bourse*, and the opening up of their capital.

Modernisation has profoundly affected the dealers. Although the Paris stock market possesses a more modern structure, most dealers are in a precarious situation. Heavy investment in technology, sharp competition between the new *sociétés de bourse* and the poor climate which prevailed on the stock market have proved to be formidable challenges to a number of dealers. The banks' entry into the capital of *sociétés de bourse* has also played a part in the dealers decline by reducing the volume of business on which brokers have first call. The subsequent general reduction in brokerage fees sealed the fate of many intermediaries. The number of people employed by the industry has fallen by a third, from 6,000 to 4,000. Additionally, savers' confidence in the market was sorely tested by the collapse of the Parisian stock broker, Tuffier, and the Lyons-based Girardet.

Necessary reforms

Several factors have brought into question the future of the French financial markets. Most serious is the lack of an appropriate tax framework to encourage development of the equity market. In terms of volume, it is too small compared to key rivals like London. In addition, the sheer size of the state and semi-state sectors deprive the market of a large volume of equities in which to deal while a large proportion of private sector companies continue to avoid making public share offerings. Moreover, the continued predominance of "pay-as-you-go" pension schemes has deprived the financial markets of a basic institutional investor.

And yet, taking into account the public authorities' willingness to reform, the outlook is relatively promising. The French financial markets are well equipped technically and have at their disposal a ready supply of highly competent professionals. But the fact remains that further measures — mainly related to the mechanics of the market — are necessary to complete modernisation. Systems for quoting

blocks of shares need to be perfected to enable the French market first to stop the flight of some of the more significant French securities towards the SEAQ in London, and then to entice them back to Paris.

Banks

From the end of the 1960s to the middle of the 1980s, only partial reforms were carried out in the French banking system. Despite efforts in the second half of the 1960s (most notably the Debré reforms), the banking system remained highly compartmentalised and suffered from legal balkanisation with each bank governed by a different set of regulations.

An ambitious set of reforms

Following the change of direction in the government's economic policies in 1983, a number of important reforms were implemented. The 1984 Banking Law equipped the banking system with a single regulatory and statutory framework. As part of the principle of universality, all credit institutions (with the exception of La Poste, the Caisse des Dépôts et Consignations and the Treasury) are now subject to a common banking law, although legislation for centrally-organised institutions has not been revised. The Banking Law undertook to overhaul the supervisory authorities and promulgated rules for the protection of depositors and lenders.

In parallel, credit controls were lifted and successive left and right wing governments applied a series of measures aimed at decompartmentalisation and so put banks on an equal footing. Also, the special interest rates some institutions could offer were modified and reduced. The abolition of exchange controls on individuals became the final part of liberalising capital movements.

Differences between banks persist

If one takes the broad definition adopted in the 1984 law, there were almost 2,000 credit institutions in France in 1991. But different classes of institutions fit within this definition. Apart from the 800 "network" banks with a total of 26,000 permanent outlets, there were about 1,000 finance companies active in specialised funding. Despite the principle of universality enshrined in the Banking Law, the network banks still maintain unique features. But the continued existence of "specificities" has less to do with the actual nature of a bank than with the maintenance of certain privileges related to deposit-taking and lending. This is the case with the savings banks' *Livret A*, Crédit Mutuel's *Livret Bleu* and Crédit Agricole's last privilege — the deposits of rural notaries. Thus, certain divisions are still evident in the French banking market.

A fall in the number of intermediaries

In France, the overwhelming share of business (around 80 percent) is conducted by about nine banking groups (BNP, Crédit Lyonnais, Société Générale, Crédit Agricole, Paribas, Suez, CIC, CCF and Crédit du Nord) which together control over 100 small and medium-sized banks. Few small and medium-sized banks are independent, but rather have a large institution as their main shareholder.

Since 1984, the French banking system has become highly concentrated and the process has intensified since 1988. The time was ripe for a reduction in the number of banks, whether through internal mergers or regional absorptions. In under 10 years, the number of mutual and co-operative banks (particularly those belonging to Crédit Agricole) has been halved, while the number of savings banks tumbled from 488 in 1984 to 184 in 1990. These were expected to fall to under 40 by 1995.

Banks: a public service?

Banking in France developed originally as a public service. The perception that the banking system was often a component of the government's social policy was reinforced when it was used to finance public housing. It was also the government which ensured that cheques were cost-free to encourage the opening of bank accounts, though the absence of charges continues to be resented by banks. But in 1987, faced with the hostility of users and the media and an impending general election, the liberal government had to defer the introduction of cheque charges.

"Non-price" competition

In a tightly-regulated environment, the French banking system is still distinguished by the strong competition that exists between the large banks. The main aim of French banks, however, is to capture market share, so that profitability has played only a small part in bank strategy. Faced with numerous regulatory constraints which hinder price competition, the French banks have traditionally adopted a strategy based around quality and the creation of wide networks in France and abroad.

Increasing the number of traditional high street outlets and of automated teller machines (ATMs) has been at the heart of French banks' commercial policies. While growth in the number of retail bank accounts continued, such a policy made sense. But by 1991, when the retail market was saturated and 95 percent of the adult population maintained a bank account, the policy of opening new outlets as quickly as possible had reached its limits in terms of profitability. Also, the banks' rush for standardised, mass-market products no longer seems justified, due mostly to the steady increase in the cost of funding which has hit margins and profitability. In addition, an organic growth strategy such as this may provoke an important negative reaction. For example, the establishment of a new interbank ATM network, for example, that is of necessity co-operative, risks paving the way for new competitors.

Restricted as they were by credit controls at home, French banks have been no less active abroad and they have managed to build up a wide international network. But during the 1980s, French banks were to appear somewhat handicapped compared to their Anglo-Saxon competitors.

Apart from Banque Lazard and, in certain respects, the Paribas Group, the French are still weak in merchant banking businesses like M&A, advisory services, asset and securities management — that is, large value-added type businesses.

One could say that while overall, the strategy adopted in these past decades by French banks has been successful, they presently find themselves faced with major upheavals. These are leading to a change in the nature of banking.

A vicious circle

Rationalisation of operations to counter the difficulties caused by lack of competitiveness has been slow. This is due to a vicious circle that has a lot to do with the banks' insistence on achieving closer customer contact.

Despite large investments in data-processing and cards, resulting in France being equipped with an advanced payments system and one of the world's densest ATM networks, the pace of restructuring and staff reduction is slower than what senior bank officials would like. In addition, industrial relations are on a knife-edge. Conflict is possible between staff and management over the collective agreement that was rejected in 1991 after failure to agree on its terms. Pressure is also coming from the banks' own pension funds which, from an actuarial point of view, no longer seem able to cope.

Apart from general expenses, the maintenance of vast branch networks is all the more detrimental in that they exert further pressure on banks to diversify into areas where it is difficult to see the rationale for them to do so.

Cheques remain the main means of payment...

What is more, rapid development in the area of cards has not taken anything away from the public's enthusiasm for cheques, entailing large administrative and staff costs for banks. This cost has weighed even heavier since non-interest bearing sight deposits (the reverse side of free cheques) have been falling as a proportion of overall bank funding.

...followed by bank payment cards

The development of *cartes bancaires* (bank payment cards) can be considered a technological success. The fact that they are free and compatible between banks (something without equivalent in the industrialised world) helps to explain their wide distribution. But despite the volume of transactions, the card — just like the cheque — is viewed by many as a failure in terms of profitability given the huge administrative costs involved. Banks are becoming increasingly restless about the fact that card transactions are free and beginning to constitute an enormous burden.

A set of regulations which remains incomplete

Given that the volume of commissions taken in by the banks is limited because there are no charges on basic bank services, profits very much depend on income from interest margins. On average, French bank commissions represent only one-quarter of net banking income, compared to over one-third for their European rivals.

So long as the banks remain reluctant to pay interest on current accounts (forbidden by law anyway), then this situation will persist. However, whether under mounting pressure from the growing sophistication

of savers, or from the rise of the 'non-network' banks such as Compagnie Bancaire, or from foreign competition, things are set to change. Failure to do so will mean the major banks risk losing some of their customers to these competitors. If the preference of economic agents for assets paying the best rates of interest (such as the short-term mutual fund) continues, the banks will be faced with an ever heavier financial burden and, as a consequence, a cut in net banking income.

Low profitability...

Towards the end of the 1980s, French banks embarked upon a new development phase. The capital requirements imposed by the Cooke ratio led banks to focus on the profitability of their operations.

For a long time, profitability was not fundamental in the strategic choices of French banks: between 1981 and 1986, profits were around one-third those of the British. But in 1989, an improvement began, especially among the private sector banks which now occupy a middle ranking position — far behind the Spanish banks and just behind Abbey National, but ahead of the Germans, some British establishments like NatWest and Barclays, and Italian banks like Cariplo and San Paolo.

...and the capital weaknesses of the public sector banks

As for capital, the four main French banks will meet the 8 percent rule set down in the Basle Concordate, but will be behind the Germans, British and the Spanish, especially in terms of "core" capital. In addition, the public sector banks manage to reach the ratio by making use of a wide variety of financial instruments and techniques. They use the issuing of hybrid securities as well as the transfer of some businesses to separate subsidiaries that then become limited companies to raise funds on the stock market. *Bancassurance* in the form of share swaps between public institutions is another weapon at the disposal of banks wishing to strengthen own capital.

The greatest paradox is that the state-owned banks appear to enjoy a relative advantage over private sector ones when it comes to bolstering capital since the stock market slump has made raising funds more difficult. But this situation may just be transitory while the problem of capital funding for public sector institutions will remain.

The government's plans for a programme of partial privatisations of various state-controlled institutions, including banks and insurers, is designed to strengthen their own funds. This exercise is made all the more urgent because French public sector companies still appear not to have reached their objective of building up networks in Europe outside of France.

A European strategy that irritates rivals

For the wider European market, French banks apply a two-pronged strategy; protection of market share within France and conquest of market share in other parts of Europe. This strategy has aroused the criticism of rivals, especially the British. These rivals point to measures taken to protect the French market, even though French institutions can act freely abroad.

The sheer verve of French acquisitions abroad contrasts strongly with the relative imperviousness of the French market to foreign banks. The latter come up against invisible barriers that make attempts at acquiring a sizeable bank almost impossible. Factors such as the low profitability of retail banking and market saturation further explain the comparatively weak presence of foreign banks in France despite regulations that these institutions find none-too-restrictive.

But while foreign banks may find it hard to position themselves in the retail market, the same does not apply to investment banking. Apart from the subsidiaries and branches traditionally operating in France, some other foreign banks occupy an enviable position in this business thanks to the stakes they hold in stock broking firms and the links established with their operations in other parts of Europe. This is the case with J P Morgan and VVV, both specialists in Treasury securities, and with Warburg-France which is the main dealer in French equities in London. And then there are the numerous foreign institutions working in the area of M&A and even in privatisation advice.

Diversification of bank business

We have seen in the introduction to this section the important role *bancassurance* plays in bolstering the capital of public sector banks in France.

Overall, the need to diversify is more pressing for the banks than for the insurance companies. First,

banking seems to have exhausted its potential for growth. Practically everybody has a bank account and in some cases several. Second, the fact that companies, as the main motors of the economy, have direct access to the money market means that they no longer need the intermediation of banks. Last but not least, as a result of the fierce competition in the loan market, margins are declining fast. But the insurance market is not so saturated, and there are still markets that have not been exploited. What is more, insurance stands to benefit in the coming years from the crisis in the welfare state.

Put differently, after having opposed each other for a long time, French bankers and insurers now see that their professions are complementary, especially in the area of savings management. Both aim at the same customer base with products that are increasingly similar such as SICAVs, PEPs (*Plan d'Epargne Populaire*), life insurance and even loans. Insurers are also able to sell their mass retail products through bank networks.

Industrial shareholdings

Following Crédit Lyonnais' initiative, the major deposit-taking banks have been filling out their portfolios with shareholdings in industry since the late 1980s. Crédit Lyonnais alone holds a portfolio valued at over FF25 billion ($404 billion).

The trend among banks towards becoming "shareholders" is part of a strategy aimed at revitalising relations with companies that have turned away from bank credit to direct funding. In the view of some banks, taking stakes in industry will allow them to attain a privileged position when it comes to offering these companies other banking services, especially in the areas of M&A and financial engineering where the commissions are high.

But this strategy entails huge risks because the banks' dual role as shareholder and creditor or provider of services can give rise to serious conflicts of interest if the company fails. That such a strategy should have been adopted betrays a certain ambiguity on the part of French banks searching for a future role. While following in the footsteps of German banks, they seem not to have noticed that, for some considerable time now, the German banks have been pulling out of activities that could endanger their own business.

Insurance

As in the case of banking, French insurance has experienced an unprecedented growth in business volume and, at the same time, a profound structural transformation. From being a protected industry, insurance has in a few years become extremely competitive.

The French insurance market is characterised by the variety of legal statutes governing companies, although the state's role remains significant. One-third of the market is controlled by four large state-controlled companies and the rest is shared between private sector and mutual ones. The latter are particularly strong in non-life business.

Reforms and innovations

Insurance has been shaken by a genuine "cultural" revolution. Product innovations continue apace while the supervision of companies has changed drastically: the need to obtain a visa to work in general insurance has gone and rules on commissions have been steadily liberalised. A new supervisory structure has been introduced, inspired by the model adopted in the Banking Law. In terms of consumer protection, there has been noticeable improvement, especially concerning prior information, risk description, changes in contracts etc.

Given the sheer scale of changes afoot, the Insurance Code dating back to the 1930s has to be modified. A new code, completely recast, is due to make its appearance in 1992.

Dizzy growth

Thanks to the dizzy growth of life business, insurance (with an average annual growth rate of 22 percent since 1980) has managed to become one of the most dynamic parts of the French economy. By the end of the 1980s, France had improved its international ranking significantly, accounting for 5 percent of all world premiums. France is the third largest market in Europe behind Germany and the UK in volume of premiums taken in. But despite these remarkable performances, French life insurance is still comparatively weak: the French have a long way to go before they have the same level of insurance cover as their counterparts in Switzerland, Japan, the UK and the US.

Market concentration

Within 10 years, over 80 percent of the market — more so in life than in general insurance — has become concentrated in the hands of 15 to 20 of the largest groups. The biggest of these (UAP, Victoire, AXA GAN) are also major players elsewhere in Europe. Over the long-term, such concentration will continue, especially in general insurance.

Heightened competition and new channels of distribution

These changes come at a time when competition for market share has been heightened by a price war and the complexities of making product offers in a more mature market. The various companies and banks fight each other in a war sometimes defined as "suicidal" so as to gain market share and strengthen their positions on the eve of the single European market. New entrants to the market, especially bank subsidiaries (and, further down the road, even the Post Office) are also making life difficult for the established companies.

The agents généraux *(tied agents) are in a difficult position*

The sale of insurance products through tied agents is in crisis. Considering this sales channel costly and inefficient, companies have been turning increasingly towards new forms of distribution. This, of course, has not left the agents indifferent and is the basis of conflict between them and the insurance companies that give them their mandates. Thus, the closer bonds between banks and insurance companies (cross-shareholdings, the opening of bank subsidiaries and sales agreements) is hardly reassuring for tied agents. Already bank outlets sell around half of all new life premiums and they are waiting their turn to penetrate the general insurance market, largely with products directed at personal customers (cars, health etc).

Unless they want to see their share of the insurance policies market further eroded, the tied agents must be more flexible and adapt to the new requirements for productivity set down by the companies. Otherwise, it is possible that companies will forge even stronger links with bank and non-bank channels of distribution. These would then fulfil the role of brokers instead of the tied agents.

The banks' hold on the life market will be further strengthened...

In the first half of this decade, banks will probably continue to invest in the life and capitalisation markets. The market share held by banks and bank subsidiaries in most products will soon be over one-quarter of the market. But this depends on the bank subsidiaries making a radical shift in their sales policies: "fewer savings products and more real insurance products" would seem to be the motto for these subsidiaries, whose takings fell sharply in 1990.

...although this is unlikely in general insurance

The technical particularities of general insurance business may discourage some banks already involved in life insurance that wish to enter this market, unless they buy medium-sized companies that can ensure balanced growth of such operations. The market is made even more problematic by the fact that the customer segments targeted by the banks are already close to saturation. The highly competitive non-intermediary mutual companies are also making it difficult for new entrants to make a breakthrough.

General insurers still have a lot to fear, though, from the incursions of these new rivals, especially when it comes to the markets for simple, standardised products that are easy to manage. The involvement of the Post Office in the selling of general insurance seriously risks destabilising the market and stirring the flames of price competition still further. While the consequences of such competition are serious for the existing market participants, users should be the main beneficiaries.

New channels of distribution

Quite apart from the institutions they already have to confront, intermediaries will also face tougher competition from "newer" channels of distribution. By these are meant the wholesale introduction of direct marketing techniques, such as direct mail and marketing through department stores or retail chains which may carve out 10 percent of the personal insurance market for themselves. Here, the non-intermediary mutual companies are more vulnerable. Some Anglo-Saxon companies that have previously mastered this technique, such as Norwich Life, may carve out a niche for themselves in the French markets.

Restructuring the industry

In the past few years, French insurance groups have been particularly active acquirers in France and elsewhere. This trend has undoubtedly been stimulated, if not actually motivated, by the prospect that barriers to national markets will be raised when the single market comes into force.

Consolidation

In France, regroupings, mergers and absorptions have been the order of the day. These have led to the consolidation of major groups like AXA (after its takeover of Compagnie du Midi) and Victoire (whose financial position after its acquisition of Colonia was strengthened by Suez becoming a majority shareholder). There were other successful regroupings in 1990: the Athéna and Allianz (France) groups consolidated their insurance businesses and entered the ranks of France's top 10 general insurers.

Is the French market impenetrable to foreigners?

A certain asymmetry characterises French insurers' acquisitions and shareholdings. Outside France as well as in, French companies are extremely active in this area. For example, Victoire took over the second-largest German insurer, Colonia, in 1989 and the following year AXA gained a foothold in the US market by buying Equitable Life after its bid for Farmers Insurance Company had failed. Acquisitions in the UK, Spain and Italy have been no less significant.

But while French companies make prodigious acquisitions abroad, their home market appears to be difficult to penetrate for foreign investors. First and foremost, this is because a considerable part of the market is in the hands of state-controlled or mutualist companies. In addition, private sector companies are often linked through shareholdings to other groups and, if not, "marketplace solidarity" helps counter any hostile takeover bids. Generali's abortive attempt to take over Midi is a prime illustration. But it is also true that Allianz was able to obtain 50 percent of Navigation Mixte's insurance business, thus allowing it to build up a group that controls 2.5 percent of the French market.

The main focus of international development is incontestably Europe. Over 90 percent of French insurers' international business is located in Europe. For state-controlled companies, the US is virtually excluded because of regulations forbidding entry by foreign, state-backed companies. As for the private sector insurers, apart from AXA, they all have a clear preference for European investment so as to be prepared for the single market.

Groups that are highly internationalised

One can expect further increases in the share of total new premiums originating outside France. For the major public and private-sector companies (UAP, AXA, Victoire etc), this should be over 50 percent within a few years. The current spate of foreign acquisitions in Europe and the US confirms this.

While the actual rate of share purchases and acquisitions of foreign companies slowed somewhat in 1990, it may pick up again. In fact, the trend towards internationalisation may spread and intensify once the process of knocking down national barriers within the EC is complete.

Employment remains stable

Unlike banking, the employment situation in the insurance industry — which accounts for 1 percent of the nation's work-force — has remained remarkably stable since the beginning of the 1980s: indeed, there has even been an annual 1 percent increase in the numbers employed. This stability can be attributed to the buoyancy in personal insurance.

But behind this one can actually detect some conflicting changes in employment trends: the numbers employed in certain grades is increasing (salaried employees of brokers and claims inspectors), while there is a significant drop in others because of industry concentration (tied agents). As for the salaried employees of companies themselves, the tendency is towards a modest fall in the numbers of purely administrative staff alongside growth in the sales and marketing departments. Such trends will continue in the next five years. Viewed globally, everything seems to indicate that employment numbers will be maintained in the insurance industry.

Conflicts between management and workers, most notably over the contents of collective work agreements, together with a souring of relations between companies and tied agents, risks disrupting the industry's modernisation process.

Penal taxation

Even as it is going through a period of rapid deregulation, French insurance has also managed to adapt to strong competition in the newly decompartmentalised home market and to the opening up of the single European market. But a major factor in competitiveness is taxation. French tax rates are still penal and no harmonisation with rates elsewhere in Europe is planned. This is despite numerous measures to lighten the tax burden of policies, especially life insurance. But it is mostly in general insurance (ie car insurance) that France finds itself at a disadvantage. Competition for policies is distorted, first by rivalry between French and foreign insurers and, second, between French insurers themselves (due to the continued existence of unequal tax regulations for different types of institution).

It would therefore seem both logical and probable that the tax environment will converge towards that pertaining among its most "dangerous" European rivals. However, it is unlikely that there will be very much foreign competition for mass risk (*risques de masse*) although competition for large scale risks (*grands risques*) business will intensify.

Contrasting prospects for growth

The potential for growth in French insurance is far from exhausted. Although the French population has long been introduced to banking, it is still underinsured. Life insurance, however, still has a larger degree to manoeuvre than general because growth in the latter is more closely tied into economic growth.

Life insurance: renewed growth?

Growth in life insurance should take off again, depending on two factors: first, the outcome of discussions concerning the future of the pensions system. And second, new legislation authorising the creation of supplementary capitalisation-based pensions managed by insurance companies and offering tax benefits to individuals. From now to the end of the century, one can expect growth in life and capitalisation to be in the range of 5 to 15 percent per annum with wide variations for individual types of business.

One can probably reckon on higher rates of growth (around 15 percent per annum) for group insurance which offers a good return on savings. Life and capitalisation policies denominated in units of account (collective investment schemes) are likely to advance at a rapid rate (10 to 15 percent) thanks to the public's concerns about the future of existing retirement schemes.

When one considers that expenditure on pensions (both private and public sector) is among Europe's highest, then a shift towards funding through capitalisation will have a beneficial effect on life insurance companies. However, this market is bound to show signs of maturity. Its growth is based on the introduction of personal products that everybody finds easy to understand. Of all life products, those targeted at groups are set to increase the most rapidly.

General insurance: more modest growth

The prospects are less auspicious for general insurance than they are for life. The sector will grow by one or two points a year in real terms. But, as in the case of life insurance, growth for different property and casualty products will vary.

Car cover will grow at anything between 3 and 8 percent a year. Industrial fire insurance will find it difficult to beat the estimates of 5 percent per annum in the first half of the 1990s because it is a product that is adversely affected by the present recession. More generally, one can spot two trends in industrial risk. First, the rise in self-insurance will continue among large companies. Second, one can expect strong growth - if not actually an explosion - in sales of policies to small and medium-sized enterprises which now have barely any cover at all. Most growth will come in insurance against trading risk. This particular market could triple within five years.

Much more favourable are the forecasts for insurance cover of certain personal and wholesale risks (personal risk and health insurance, group accident cover etc). Growth rates will be between 10 and 15 percent. The market for health insurance is likely to undergo a revolution between now and the end of the century. This will come about as the state begins to disengage itself and the level of supplementary cover required by companies grows.

Conclusion

The French government has taken a number of steps to introduce European Community directives on freedom in the provision of services into French law

so as to enable institutions to deal with the challenge of free capital movements. Thus, reform of the Insurance Code will allow the industry to make up lost ground and will soon make it possible to cut the need for congruence in areas like foreign currency-denominated policies etc. A proposal to introduce an insurance version of the 1984 Banking Law is also being examined.

Banks and insurance companies have adapted very quickly to the opening of the single market and to lively competition in the newly decompartmentalised and deregulated home market. That being so, French financial institutions still face a dual challenge:

- Rapid change in financial services and in customer needs. Bankers and insurers are both becoming more and more like "financial advisers" and the distinction between insurance products and bank savings products is disappearing. One can now expect changes in sales channels and the products on offer in France.

- After having been sheltered for a long time, the French financial services industry may well be "challenged". In other words, institutions now risk being assailed from abroad.

Nevertheless, invisible barriers still exist largely due to cultural differences and these tend to discourage foreign competitors, especially in mass risks business and retail banking.

Finally, while France is today faced with a growth crisis similar to that in other countries in the developed world, it still has a number of trump cards typical of a relatively healthy economy and a wide political consensus on extending the policies of liberalisation and deregulation. The plan for partial privatisation of certain state-controlled companies, as well as the decision to place on the agenda the delicate question of supplementary capitalisation-based pensions — just to name those presently being debated — confirms once again the firm desire of the public authorities and the economic agents to transform the French financial system from top to bottom.

Section I

Introduction

Chapter 1

The Development of Financial Services in France

The postwar years in France were marked by a far-reaching shift in the relationship between the financial system and the state. How this complicated relationship developed has had — even up until the present day — a lasting impact on new economic policies and on the development of financial services, themselves largely dependent on this relationship. Initially, when the state began to finance directly the rebuilding and development of core industries from 1945 until the end of the 1950s, the Treasury and the institutions within its sphere of influence occupied a central role in funding the economy. In the 1960s and 1970s, the banks took over as the primary source of funding for the private sector, with the government's decision to accord priority to budgetary concerns. From the end of the 1970s onwards, when public debt began to be financed in line with market conditions, France went through a process of wide-ranging financial and monetary reforms that radically changed financial services in the country. Despite such reforms, deregulation remained incomplete by the early 1990s.

Reconstruction and growth (1945 to 1960)
In 1946, in an era when contemporary thinking favoured state intervention, the De Gaulle government undertook some determined and audacious economic policies — policies rooted in a programme of large-scale nationalisation. This resulted in an expansion of central planning in the French economy. The need for this policy of nationalisation resulted mostly from a number of factors affecting France's economy at the time: long-term investments in infrastructural development, distribution of Marshall Aid for purposes of reconstruction, and repairing the weaknesses of the financial institutions.

A particular brand of "Keynesianism"
As in the UK and the Scandinavian countries, this new economic vision found its most direct inspiration in the "Keynesian Revolution". However, France distinguished itself from other Keynesian laboratories due to the fusion of sorts that occurred between an "anti-capitalistic", or rather "statist" ethic, and high-ranking civil servants who were consecrated as an élite. This triggered the move toward centralisation.

The Banking Law of December 2 1945 left intact the corporatist-type institutions set up by the banking law of 1941: the Association Professionnelle des Banques and the Association Professionnelle des Etablissements Financiers as well as the Commission de Contrôle des Banques. The 1945 law also maintained the traditional distinction between *banques de dépôts* (the deposit-taking banks) and *banques d'affaires* (merchant banks). The law forbade the former from accepting deposits of over two years duration, while the latter were forbidden from transforming deposits of less than two years duration into loans for industry. A new law of May 17 1946 sanctioned the creation of medium and long-term *banques de crédit* that could extend loans for over two years, though they were not allowed to collect deposits of under two years without the authorisation of the Commission de Contrôle des Banques.[1]

The consequences of the reforms for the financial system
Overall, these measures served to create a banking system that was compartmentalised according to the duration of funds maintained within each bank and the business conducted by the bank. Likewise, the nationalisation of the Bank of France and of the four

big deposit-taking institutions reinforced state control over commercial banking.

The insurance companies suffered a similar fate, with their role severely diminished due to the intervention of the public authorities. The establishment of a social security system in 1946 had a major impact: industrial accident insurance, which made up one-third of the industry's business in 1946, was transferred to the government's social security division, as was health insurance. And when the pay-as-you-earn pension system was established, the life insurance companies lost yet another huge share of their market.

Who oversaw and implemented the reforms?

Several public bodies (the Bank of France, the central planning body and the Treasury) under the control of the Ministry of Finance could in theory have claimed the authority to oversee the reforms and to implement the laws passed by parliament. In practice, however, a major obstacle hindered this authority because the French state, despite its professed aim of broad-sweeping centralisation, was far from being unified. In effect, authority was divided into a number of semi-autonomous sub-systems, each pursuing its own political objectives and each with its own "clientele".[2]

In this period of reconstruction, punctuated by a power struggle at the heart of the state, the Treasury quickly established its leadership and authority to the point where its development and that of the French economy became inextricably linked.

As a result, the financing of the French economy from the postwar years to the middle of the 1960s was dominated by *le circuit* — ie, the state Treasury and its correspondents. In addition, funding of the public deficit occurred through non-market mechanisms such as *planchers d'effets publics* (bottom prices for government stock), a policy which would not be wholly changed until the mid-1970s.[3] From these elements stemmed direct supervision of wide sections of the financial system.

The means of financing growth

The financial markets, which had been very lively in the inter-war years, collapsed after the Second World War due to a combination of galloping infla-

tion, the establishment of the social security system and the nationalisation of large corporations (electricity, the railways, banks and insurance companies). The state fuelled growth, either directly through the *Fonds de Modernisation et d'Equipement* (the modernisation and capital goods fund, under the authority of the Treasury, which in 1955 became the *Fonds de Développement Economique et Social* — FDES), or controlled non-bank financial institutions through the fund — the most important of which was the Caisse des Dépôts et Consignations.

In the 1950s, the Treasury and the non-bank financial institutions mentioned provided between 40 and 50 percent of all credits to the economy and 80 percent of all investment loans, half of which ensued from the Treasury. This method of financing, while accelerating France's economic recovery, failed to satisfy the growing funding needs of the private sector.

The re-organisation of the financial services sector and the control that state bodies exercised over the sector undoubtedly compensated for the weak level of direct funding available after the war. And, over time, indirect funding generated serious imbalances, with the offer of long-term credits proving insufficient to meet companies' capital resource needs. As a result, these companies were forced to seek and accept short-term loans not suited for sustaining long-term growth. The situation forced a retrenchment in the government's central control of funding by 1961-62, resulting in a boom in investments.

The reduction in public deficits and intermediated funding (1960-1980)

At the end of the 1950s, a new foundation for France's economic policy was ratified in the Rueff Plan. The plan was intended to cut the public deficit, which resulted from the inflationary effects of printing too much money. This plan was the first postwar policy advocating a contraction of central planning and control. In developing new conditions governing the involvement of banking institutions in the activity of private sector funding, the state indicated its desire to progressively dismantle its role of primary investor.

For the next two decades, economic policy was marked by efforts to maintain balanced budgets. In place of the chronic public deficits of the postwar years, which lasted until the government opted to decentralise some of its activities by 1960, a series of surpluses arose that were magnified in the years 1970 to 1973. From 1974 until 1980, France encountered budget deficits due to the oil shock. This forced the government to use all instruments of monetary policy at its disposal to try to re-establish budgetary equilibrium. In any event, the other industrialised countries were faced with the same situation.

A highly compartmentalised banking system and protected banks

The separation of *banques d'affaires* from *banque de dépôts* and the establishment or sponsorship by the state of a constellation of specialist funding bodies resulted in increased compartmentalisation and anti-competitive practices within the French financial system. The *banques de dépôts*, which had the greatest access to funding sources, were partially excluded from financing investment needs: the state required that they "voluntarily" limit themselves to short-term investments. From 1945 to 1967, this policy ruled out any visible sign of competition within the banking sector. The *entente bancaire* covered everything: loan conditions were the same in every single case and banks sold the same products at the same price, and the opening of new outlets had to be authorised by the Conseil National du Crédit.

For the most part, state intervention to help manufacturing and the funding of public works came in the form of direct loans or subsidies granted to state-controlled bodies (Crédit National, Crédit Agricole, Crédit Hôtelier and the Caisse des Marchés etc — the last two becoming the Crédit d'Equipement des PME). The subsidies allowed these quasi-state institutions to distribute loans at reduced rates of interest for agriculture, housing, and the infrastructural needs of local authorities.

Against a backdrop of complicated and multifarious procedures for the allocation of loans, these institutions enjoyed numerous privileges, namely: tax exemption for the savings banks' Livret A passbook savings accounts and Crédit Mutuel's Livret Bleu, as well as for public issues of Treasury bonds; exemption from tax on profits and from the licensing tax (*la patente*) for Crédit Agricole; and a state

guarantee and exemption from withholding tax for loans issued on the bond market by the main non-bank financial institutions. Clearly, the few remaining elements of a private banking sector had little hope of competing in this environment.

The first wave of deregulation and the revival of interbank competition (1966 to 1974)

In 1967 and 1968, the Minister of the Economy, Michel Debré, launched a package of reforms aimed at freeing banks from the administrative shackles put in place in 1945. These reforms took account of the banks' new involvement in, and the state's progressive disengagement from intermediation, as initiated under the Rueff Plan. These reforms also encouraged the mobilisation of households' liquid assets — deposits taken in by the banking system and savings that might be utilised in capital markets investments.[4]

The financial reforms undertaken by Debré were in accordance with other new policies geared towards boosting the economy, which had shown signs of slowing down under the 1963 stabilisation plan instituted by the Minister of Finance, Valéry Giscard d'Estaing. A notable feature of these corrective policies was a series of tax incentives intended to benefit companies that made investments and companies that adopted profit-sharing plans for their employees. The policies resulted in a wave of innovations linked to particular tax schemes and aimed at improving the range of savings products offered to the small saver.

The first and undoubtedly most important of the Debré reforms was the ending in 1968 of the separation between *banques de dépôts* and *banques d'affaires* instituted under the 1945 Banking Law. *Banques de dépôts* were henceforth allowed to engage in conversion activities, financing medium or long-term loans through the use of short-term deposits. The intent of this policy, besides the obvious one of liberalising banks' business, was to spur deposit-taking activities and (given the risks inherent in conversion activities) to allocate the deposits among the liabilities held by the *établissements de crédit.*

To boost deposit-taking, the reform introduced two important measures: first, it granted banks the right to open new outlets, and second, it overhauled the banking system by facilitating consolidations among banks, for example, the 1967 merger of Banque Nationale pour le Commerce et l'Industrie and the Comptoir National d'Escompte de Paris to form Banque Nationale de Paris (BNP). Similarly, the three large state-controlled insurers — UAP, GAN and AGF — were born of these reforms.

To strengthen banks' resources, the following measures were taken:

- Remuneration of sight deposits was banned;

- Privileges attached to Treasury bonds were abolished;

- New tax-free products to be distributed by the banks were created (the home savings account followed later by the home savings plan);

- The possibility of selling off long-term debts arose, due to the establishment of an outstanding mortgage loans market; and

- The market for funding was broadened, and the money market was opened up to non-bank financial institutions. Institutional investors (the insurance companies and the Caisse des Dépôts et Consignations) were thus enabled to lend a portion of their huge liquid assets.

A second series of reforms concerned the operation of the financial markets. As with the preceding reforms, the objective was to mobilise new sources of financing. From 1959 to 1965, while gross household income increased by 77 percent and consumption by 70 percent, savings grew at a still faster rate: 110 percent. At the same time, only 7 percent of these savings were invested in transferable securities.

To encourage long-term financial savings and investments among households, the authorities undertook several measures, including the adoption of a system of tax credits for equity dividends,[5] a standard tax rate and tax exemption for income from bonds, the creation of tax-free savings products for the financing of housing, etc.

While these reforms did help to modify the manner in which household wealth was structured, the intent of the reforms was not adequately met. It was, in fact, tax-free liquid instruments that absorbed the brunt of household investments, while the demand for stock decreased.

The upswing in competition; consequences and limitations

The Debré reforms caused major upheaval in the French banking and financial worlds. Within less than two years, the sector was transformed from being an overprotected one, to one that was relatively exposed to competitive forces. The stimulus afforded by competition was seen in the battle between Suez and Paribas for control of Crédit du Nord between 1968 and 1969. Such heated rivalries presaged the bitter takeover battles of the 1980s.

The commercial banks were the first to profit from the revival in competition. Their growth was spectacular: in the years 1967 to 1974, the number of banking outlets increased threefold, the number of sight deposits twofold and the number of term deposits fivefold. They surpassed the savings banks — their main competitors — in terms of new savings products and new home savings accounts and plans. In addition, they were better placed to diversify the application of funds. Short-term loans, which had made up the lion's share of credit in the early 1960s, gave way to non-realisable medium and long-term loans and declined to below 50 percent of the total. The banks became particularly involved in leasing, which underwent rapid growth after it was authorised in 1967. Likewise, banks quickly took over the funding of the economy from the (direct and indirect) financing that had been provided by the Treasury.

But differences between the commercial banks and the "privileged"[6] institutions persisted. The commercial banks' share of deposit-taking activities decreased from 42 percent in 1950 to 36 percent in 1970 and 33 percent in 1980. Moreover, while the savings banks and non-bank financial institutions grew at quite an acceptable rate, the mutual and co-operative networks developed rapidly in power. This was particularly true for Crédit Agricole, which virtually cornered the rural and small town markets where people's familiarity with banks was still low. In 1973, it amassed 21.4 percent of sight deposits, compared with 15 percent in 1967, and thus became one of Europe's largest banks.[7]

In the period 1967 to 1980, the French economy

benefited from the features associated with an "economy run on indebtedness". The leverage effect of indebtedness was turned to advantage by companies investing in production facilities in the same way as it was by those investing in real estate or spending on consumer durables. The average annual funding needs of companies increased from 3.8 percent of GDP in the years 1960-1969 to 4.6 percent of GDP in the years 1974 to 1980 (see Table 1.1). This situation would rebound at the beginning of the 1980s with the increase in net interest rates, although funding needs should show a tendency to rise again in the 1990s.

The strengthening of credit controls: the return in force of state regulation

The late 1960s and early 1970s were marked by the spirit of the Debré reforms and the relative retreat of the state. But the oil shock of 1974 and increasing inflation — coming at a time of worldwide economic recession — broke the momentum. Facing a budget deficit, state authorities renewed their influence over the banking system.

In February 1958, for the first time the monetary authorities resorted to credit corsets. Further limits on growth in outstanding loans were implemented between February 1963 and June 1965, at a time of inflationary tension, and again from November 1968 to October 1969.

Credit controls were again introduced in December 1972, following an EC conference where member states were advised to ensure that money supply

growth did not outstrip expected growth in GDP. During the stagflation of the 1970s (a stagnant GNP and high inflation), different credit restrictions, of varying flexibility, were in turn introduced. Complete dismantling of these controls did not take place until 1986.

The perverse effects that credit corsets had on banking operations have tended to be somewhat exaggerated. By freezing market shares, such a provision could have penalised the most dynamic, aggressive and innovative banks. More generally, it could have diminished competition between banks and created an oligopolistic banking system. The reality, however, was not as dire as the predictions. While some merger and acquisition agreements were forged, competition between the banks remained healthy, as shown by the race to open new outlets (the growth in the *banque de proximité* concept) and the considerable increase in advertising and marketing.

Naturally, the increased competition infringed on the banks' profitability. In addition, there were distortions, arising from the fact that certain institutions which specialised in areas of funding that were not covered by credit corsets (exports, real estate, etc) enjoyed a competitive edge over financial entities which were restricted.

The results of two decades of economic growth and social conflict

While growth in France can hardly be qualified as 'miraculous', the three decades that followed the end of the war (1939-1945) are still known as the

---

Table 1.1

The balance between savings and investment by institutional sector in France, 1960-1990

(a) Funding capacity (+) or need (-) (in percentage of GDP)

	1960-1969	1970-1973	1974-1980	1981-1983	1984-1986	1987-1988	
Non-financial companies	-3.8	-4.4	-4.6	-3.8	-1.6	-1.6	-1.9
Individuals	+3.5	+3.6	+4.3	+4.5	+3.2	+1.6	+1.7
Public authorities	+0.4	+0.8	-0.7	-2.6	-2.8	-1.7	-1.3
Other sectors (b)	—	+0.1	+0.4	+0.6	+1.3	+1.3	+1.5
Rest of the world	= +0.1	= +0.1	= -0.6	= -1.3	= +0.1	= -0.4	—

(a) The base date is 1970 for data from the '60s and '70s and 1980 for data from the '80s.

(b) Financial institutions, insurance companies and private sector authorities.

Source:National accounts, INSEE (national statistics office), Ministry of Finance estimates for 1989-1990.

'Glorious Thirty'. The average annual growth rate in these years, at 5.5 percent, was higher than the average recorded for the OECD countries (4.2 percent). While growth was higher in both Germany and Italy in the 1950s, economic development was most intense in France in the '60s and early '70s (see Table 1.2). GDP per head of population also moved ahead fast until the middle of the 1980s.

Table 1.2

Growth in GDP in six industrialised countries, 1960-1989 (in volume)

(a)	1960-1968	1968-1973	1973-1979	1979-1989
US	4.5	3.2	2.4	2.8
Japan	10.2	8.7	3.6	4.1
Germany	4.1	4.9	2.3	1.9
France	5.4	5.5	2.8	2.2
UK	3.1	3.3	1.5	2.1
Italy	5.7	4.5	3.7	2.5
Group of Seven (b)	5.0	4.4	2.7	2.9

(a) Average percentage variation between the two years in question

(b) The Group of Seven largest industrialised nations:(the six included in this table plus Canada)

Source: OECD, back-dated statistics, 1989; Conseil National du Crédit, 1989

The strength of this growth is all the more remarkable given that it took place against the backdrop of a society still disrupted by a number of blockages. There was still considerable social conflict compared with countries like the Federal Republic of Germany which benefited from a consensus born out of social partnerships and social-democratic governments. The activities of French companies were stalled by numerous strikes, particularly during the *événements* of 1968. In addition, the growth in the power of the state — indispensable if the twin needs of the baby-boom generation and economic growth were to be met — threw up a new bone of contention between the private sector and a public sector dreaded as being technocratic and inefficient (see Chapter 10).

The willingness to put liberal policies in place

Apart from an interlude of reflation under Prime Minister Jacques Chirac (1974 to 1976), French economic policies took a more liberal turn under Presidents Georges Pompidou (1969 to 1974) and Valéry Giscard d'Estaing (1974 to 1981). Central planning was steadily abandoned, financial intervention by the state reduced, and budgetary equilibrium sought after (the Barre Plan). The Treasury manifested a certain willingness to extract itself from its central role, especially through attempts at de-budgeting. For its part, the Monory Law of 1978 served as a shot in the arm for SICAVs (unit trusts) and the stock markets. At the same time, the privatisation of state-controlled banking institutions was begun and the government had geared itself up for the deregulation of the banking system by the end of the 1970s following on from the recommendations contained in the Mayoux report.

The 1980s: deregulation of the financial system

Paradoxically, while the socialist victory in the 1981 presidential elections signalled an end to the privatisation process, the re-nationalisations occurred separately from the trend towards financial deregulation. Deregulation began in 1983, at a time when other western economies had fully embarked upon privatisation. Henceforth, the historical cleavage between left and right centred more around political and social questions and the primary concerns related to financial matters were limited to the means and pace of deregulation.

The nationalisations of 1981 and 1982

Given that nationalisation was closely linked to the economic policies of the party in control, the country's new leaders came up with a strident sales pitch. The overall objectives set for nationalisation were crystallised as: the reinforcement of state control over credit — the sole means of effectively mastering inflation — and the bolstering of investments, which had slowed considerably. To reach these objectives, two main instruments were employed: first, loans were granted selectively and in accordance with priorities outlined in the State Plan; and second, the relatively high external rates of interest for non-residents (designed to defend the franc) were separated from a lower, internal rate of interest operating independently of the international money markets and designed to maintain the cost of credit at a reasonable rate.

The socialists also pushed to the top of the agenda new banking policies favouring the establishment and growth of small and medium-sized companies, traditionally disadvantaged as a result of bank lending policies. The same line was taken by Prime Minister Edith Cresson, ten years later.

Criticism focused then, as now, on several points. First and foremost, opposition leaders insisted on the pointlessness of strengthening the state's role at a time when it already controlled almost 80 percent of the banking system, either through direct shareholdings, or indirectly through the power to nominate senior management.[8] Another criticism was that the decision to opt for maximum control over the banks already or soon to be nationalised (of which some had been well on the road to partial privatisation by the late 1970s) was more like the imposition of state-socialism (*étatisation*), far exceeding any accepted definition of mere nationalisation. In addition, the critics argued that the stated policies of decentralising economic control and introducing prioritised loans were illusory rhetoric. Last, but not least, was the argument that public authorities were incapable of correctly managing financial institutions.

Going for a radical option
The February 11 1982 Law on nationalisations had a huge impact. It affected every non-state bank maintaining a registered office in France which had liabilities totalling over FF1 billion ($176 million) in short-term deposits. This meant that 36 of the 171 private sector banks were nationalised in 1982.

This law also hit the two *compagnies financières*, Paribas and Suez. The *trois vieilles* (Banque Nationale de Paris, Crédit Lyonnais and Société Générale) were also re-nationalised and half of the three banks' capital had to be sold to small investors following the January 1979 Law.[9]

As a result, if one just looks at the banking sector (excluding the Caisse des Dépôts et Consignations, the postal chequeing accounts and the savings banks), by the end of 1982, the nationalised banks accounted for 86.8 percent of credits and 81 percent of deposits. To the three established state banks (49.1 percent of credits and 58.6 percent of deposits) and the newly nationalised banks (30.7 percent of credits and 27.5 percent of deposits) must be added small institutions controlled by the nationalised banks and other banks controlled by state firms — for example, state-controlled insurance companies.

Taking stock of the nationalisations
Opinions obviously diverge on the results of nationalisation. Some prominent financial personalities believe that, given their legal standing, the nationalisations fractured coherent financial structures and destabilised financial channels. To illustrate the argument, the critics refer in particular to the second nationalisation of Banque Indosuez. Precious time was lost in structural reorganisations at a time when, internationally, financial systems and practices were undergoing rapid modernisation. However, the same critics have recognised the positive aspects of this period as well, especially the (eventual) success of Suez in finding a modern, rational style of management after it had been brought under public control. Overall, the results proved positive for Suez and for the majority of nationalised financial institutions. From 1982 to 1987, the consolidated balance sheet for Suez increased by 40 percent.

What is more, management at the nationalised banks has been subjected to the increased demands placed on banks in general by international competition and overall they have emerged from the 1980s quite well, with their competitiveness intact. Other countries, on the other hand, and most notably the UK, argue that the international expansion of the French banks and their ability to compete would not be possible but for government intervention. These countries argue that the state "subsidies" give the French banks an unfair advantage. However, continued state involvement for the long term cannot be guaranteed, as exemplified by the fact that the state, and particularly the Treasury, has come up against more pronounced, more visible opposition from the Bank of France.[10]

The socialist reform offensive
Despite the reforms introduced since the late 1960s, the French financial system remained rigidly compartmentalised and ill-suited to the changes taking place. But the change in economic policy in 1983 under Prime Minister Laurent Fabius was to result in a recommencement of the reforms begun, however timidly, at the end of the 1970s. The first developments were the modernisation of the financial markets and the changes in the legal framework governing banking activities.

The unification of capital markets and stock market reform

The astonishing progress made in establishing a French financial marketplace was no doubt favoured by the political consensus (at least over the content of reforms) that had prevailed since the end of the 1970s, except during the period of the nationalisations. A profound change in mentality was necessary to move the French from the paternalistic ideology of the De Gaulle era (which found expression in the faith held in real estate investment) to accepting the whims of the financial markets advocated by the new generation of liberals. The 1978 Monory Law on the removal of taxes on income invested in equity is often quoted as the first initiative designed to pull the capital markets out of their lethargy. Several reports put together by top financial and academic personalities were largely behind the reforms undertaken and therefore also contributed to the growth of the financial markets.[11]

Until the middle of the 1980s, the various capital markets were kept separate. Since reform, capital has been able to move from one "compartment" of the market to another. There are no longer any insuperable borders between the interbank monetary market (reformed in 1985 and covering a wide range of maturities from the straight "day to day" type to the seven-year one), the bond market and even the mortgage market. The latter, too narrowly-based as it was to satisfy the non-state aided housing sector, was reformed in 1985.

As a result, funding companies, particularly the Caisse de Refinancement Hypothécaire (CFH — the mortgage financing fund), set up in the same year, can issue bonds on the money market similar to the securities that they buy (of over 12 years maturity).

Deregulation of the stock market consisted of exploding the old corporative professional structures. The new stock market law put an end to the monopoly held by the *agents de change* (stock brokers); shares trading, which before this had almost become a purely administrative function became a commercial activity like any other; and brokerage commissions were no longer fixed (see Chapter 10).

The new Banking Law

In the wake of practically all the major western countries that had already updated their banking legislation (mainly at the beginning of the 1970s), the French government decided to draft a new banking law once the nationalisation process had been completed. The main objective of the 1984 Banking Law was to encompass all banks in one common legal framework. Impending EC banking directives undoubtedly inspired the new law, as the Treasury Director, Jean-Claude Trichet, stated several times. Previous legislation had been somewhat disparate: besides the laws of 1941, 1945 and 1946 for registered banks and financial institutions, the constitutions establishing the Caisses d'Epargne (savings banks) in 1885, the Banques Populaires in 1917 and Crédit Agricole in 1920, were all still in force.[12]

The French financial system was, in the words of Daniel Lebègue, former Treasury Director, characterised by a large degree of legal and professional "balkanisation". Until the Banking Law, there was no single overall regulatory and supervisory authority.

A peculiar sort of liberalism

Although the economic liberalism flaunted by Pierre Bérégovoy and Edouard Balladur (Minister of the Economy, Finance and Privatisation in the Chirac government [1986 to 1988]) was actually put into practise through wide-sweeping deregulation and privatisation measures, the role of the state, and particularly the Treasury, remained predominant through the early 1990s. However, one has to recognise that it is not always easy to assess the actual scope and influence of the banking authorities. While the liberalism inherent in French monetary policy is comparable in some ways to other western countries (abolition of credit and exchange controls, total freedom in the movement of capital, etc), the extent to which it resulted from central state planning is not.

Financial innovation propelled by the public authorities

In France, financial innovation comes from the public sector — at the initiative or under the close control of the monetary authorities, generally the Treasury.[13] Innovations result either from the need to respect state budgetary constraints (in the circumstances, the need to make the non-monetary financing of budgetary deficits easier),[14] or from the need to bend to external forces (pressure on the competitiveness of the banking system and pressure on Paris as a financial marketplace). Such pressures are all the more acute because of the progress being made towards a single European financial space.

The generic term "financial innovations" essentially refers to just three closely connected phenomena. First, there is the innovation that stems from the creation of new financial products. This interests private sector savers and institutional investors (new financial assets), as well as the Treasury and monetary authorities (diversification in money market securities) and borrowers (new methods for managing liabilities). Second, financial innovation can encompass the establishment of new financial markets (like, for example, the MATIF, the MONEP and the unlisted securities market in France). Finally, the development of new technologies — expert systems, plastic money — is a third source of innovations (RELIT, continuous trading etc).

The greatest irony is that the state may sometimes take the initiative in financial innovation in order to get around its own regulations. The frequent recourse to complicated financial engineering in order to increase the capital of state companies without infringing the *ni nationalisations ni privatisations* rule applied by the socialists since 1988 would seem to be a case in point. However, one has to ask whether this system of cross-shareholdings between institutions often belonging to different economic sectors does not end up reinforcing the state's role as main shareholder.

One should note the very positive effect these innovations have had on the way the Treasury is funded: medium and long-term OATs (Treasury bonds), ORTs (renewable Treasury bonds) and short-term negotiable Treasury bonds (see Chapter 9). Without the former, the establishment of the *marché à terme d'instruments financiers* (MATIF — the futures market) would have been impossible.

ORTs have proven useful, if not indispensable, in institutional treasury management. Likewise, the state prompted the various economic agents (banks, insurance companies, manufacturing and service companies, local authorities) to issue negotiable instruments on certain markets (most notably the money market).

On the other hand, by paralysing private sector innovations in other markets, the state also plays a negative role. In particular, the regulation of bank savings deposits (LEP, LEE, CODEVI, PER, PEP [see Chapter 3]) and the narrow definition applied

(in terms of duration, ceilings, etc) by the monetary authorities obliges the banks to engage in a very expensive form of competition which involves diversifying their promotional materials. From this springs a competitive inflexibility, with large retail networks possessing distinct advantages. Price competition, at least on the retail market, is illusory: the interest rates offered on over half of banking deposits are determined by the public authorities (see Chapter 2).

Generalisation and the increased availability of financial products

Despecialisation of the big network banks was one of the main objectives of the 1984 Banking Law. Yet, movement in this direction actually predates 1984 and was continuing during the early 1990s. Widening of activities (universal banking) has particularly hit the Ecureuil group of savings banks, the sole mission of which until the late 1960s was to take in deposits. This process is an ongoing one, and in 1983 the savings banks were recognised as fully-fledged, though non-profit making banks (see Chapter 4).

A greater availability of financial products developed in tandem with the broadening of business and represented a form of compensation for the specialised banks following the extension of their scope of activities. The creation in 1982 of the *Livret d'Epargne Populaire* (LEP — the people's savings account) and of the CODEVI in 1983 allowed the banks to compete for deposits on an equal footing with the Ecureuil and the Post Office's Livret A or with Crédit Mutuel's Livret Bleu. There has also been a greater availability of government-subsidised loans which were previously accessible only through specialised banks. It has been the same story for new products like the *Plan d'Epargne Retraite* (PER — the retirement savings plan), and its successor, the *Plan d'Epargne Populaire* (PEP — the people's savings plan), which are available through all the banks and insurance companies.

The growing availability of products has not left bank deposits unaffected. The spread of the various special accounts, together with the lightning effect of liquid SICAVs (mutual funds) and a greater discernment among French people when it comes to their investments, has had a negative impact on the deposits of institutions that previously had been the only authorised deposit takers (the Ecureuil and the Post Office). The difficulties these institutions experienced has led to new concessions to strengthen their deposit base.

The 1987 privatisations: continuity or break?

In 1986, the Chirac government questioned the previous socialist administration's nationalisation programme. Indeed, the "slimming down" of the public sector through privatisation was intended to be the centrepiece of the Chirac government's strategy. The Chirac privatisations from 1986 to 1988 were not to be overturned when a new socialist prime minister came along. Quite the contrary; deregulation, modernisation and financial innovation gained a new momentum under the socialists, with a lifting of all exchange controls, the reform of the insurance code, the introduction of securitisation techniques, the ending of fixed commissions in stock market and insurance brokerage etc.

Liberal heterodoxy on the question of privatisation

In the view of Edouard Balladur, Minister of the Economy, Finance and Privatisation under the Chirac government, there were at least five objectives that justified the privatisation of both those financial institutions nationalised in 1982 and the three big national banks transferred to the public sector in 1945:

- The development of a shareholding population, with subscription preference given to small orders (maximum 10 shares);

- The development of employee stock option schemes with 10 percent of share transactions automatically reserved for employees (this objective also involved preferential subscription conditions and an allocation of free shares);

- The transparency of transactions and the protection of private interests through the establishment of a Privatisation Commission made up of independent, qualified persons. Protection would also be ensured through an audit of accounts and an estimate of the value of the companies concerned by specialist auditing firms;

- The protection of national interests by way of a

20 percent limitation being placed on the investment of any foreigner or nonresident in any share disposal; and,

- The setting of the pace and conditions of the privatisation process by the Ministry of the Economy, Finance and Privatisation.

The fifth objective is not an example of orthodox liberalism, as the state explicitly reserved for itself a "piloting" role in the privatisation process. Likewise, the state's freedom to build up as it saw fit a series of *noyaux durs* (core shareholdings) in privatised companies using non-market mechanisms also contradicts classic liberalism.

A privatisation programme left unfinished

An idea of how it was envisaged that the 65 privatisations would proceed is contained in the laws of July 2 and August 6 1986. The former fixed a deadline of March 1 1991 for the sell-off of the 42 banks and financial groups and 23 manufacturing companies. The latter laid particular emphasis on determining the advantages to be granted employees and small investors and it also authorised the establishment of a Privatisation Commission. The programme was, however, halted by the stock market collapse of October 1987 and subsequently by the socialist victory in the 1988 presidential elections.

What assessment can be made of those privatisations that took place? Twenty-two of the 42 state-controlled banks and financial groups were transferred to the private sector during 1987. Among them were Société Générale, Crédit Commercial de France (CCF), Paribas and Suez plus their subsidiaries, and two small independent banks, Banque Industrielle Mobilière Privée (BIMP) and Banque du Bâtiment et des Travaux Publics (BTP). These privatisations proved very successful with employees and the public at large. On average more than two-thirds of employees subscribed to their own company's shares.

Taking stock of the 1980s

The state's decision to disengage from the financial services sector was due to a combination of factors including: the wide range of reforms that took place in the 1980s, as described above; the steady loosening of ties linking it to quasi-state financial institutions (the failure to obtain "appropriate gains" from the greater sophistication of financial products, the loss of direct control over institutions because of the privatisations, as well as the mutualisation of the Caisse Nationale du Crédit Agricole and of insurer Mutuelles de Mans in 1988); and the trend towards contractual procedures as a result of the setting up of the Comité des Usagers (Users' Committee) within the Conseil National du Crédit (appointed as part of the Banking Law).

The Comité des Usagers played a leading role in paving the way for a revolution of sorts, giving preference to agreements and contracts over purely regulatory solutions: The Commission Bancaire, after the Banking Law, took over responsibility for supervising the activities of banks operating in France from the "Comité de Réglementation". And, more flexible instruments aimed at supporting business were made available.

Disintermediation

Financial deregulation caused a sharp fall in financial intermediation (see Figure 1.1). While banks incorporated in France accounted for almost three-quarters of the economy's funding requirements in 1980, by 1989 they accounted for only 46 percent. Since they were created in 1985, marketable debt securities, most notably commercial paper and Treasury bonds, have come to represent almost one-third of all funding disintermediated. The downward spiral in funds intermediated (some 36 percent of the

total in 1986), was checked by the stock market collapse of 1987. With this trend ebbing, it appears possible that the rate of intermediation will stabilise in the 40 to 50 percent range in the early 1990s.

Disintermediation has been at the expense of banking business *strictu sensu* (the transformation of deposits into loans), but not that of the banks themselves. The banks, it seems, anticipated the growth in the capital markets, basing around them a large part of their services and activities. As a result, the dealing rooms of the major banks, together with the brokerage firms and interbank market agents which they took over, handle a large part of stock market transactions. By 1991, they controlled practically 90 percent of the French mutual fund market — the largest share anywhere in Europe (see Chapter 11).

Rising risks
International financial deregulation has produced large-scale fluctuations in the interest and exchange rates applying between different currencies. This has resulted in transactional risks for banks. In the present climate there is a growing risk of default among clients (such as debt-ridden countries and financial market speculators) that have been destabilised by interest rate movements over recent years.

In addition, banks are now more exposed to liquidity risks due to changes in funding mechanisms. As funding now is carried out by means of Dutch auctions (whereby the price is lowered gradually until it meets a responsive bid and is sold), there is no longer anything "automatic" in the granting of tenders.

With the growth of off-balance sheet operations, rendered possible by deregulation, compensation risk seems another hazard that will grow in importance in the future.

Deregulation remains incomplete
Several important regulations continue to limit the banking system's autonomy. Paradoxically, the main defender of the ban restricting interest payments on current accounts is the Association Française des Banques (AFB). The AFB originally favoured payments on interest in return for deregulated pricing of bank services. But after its campaign to charge fees for cheques failed, the AFB dug its heels in on the issue of current accounts. Nonethe-

Figure 1.1

Changes in the rate of financial intermediation

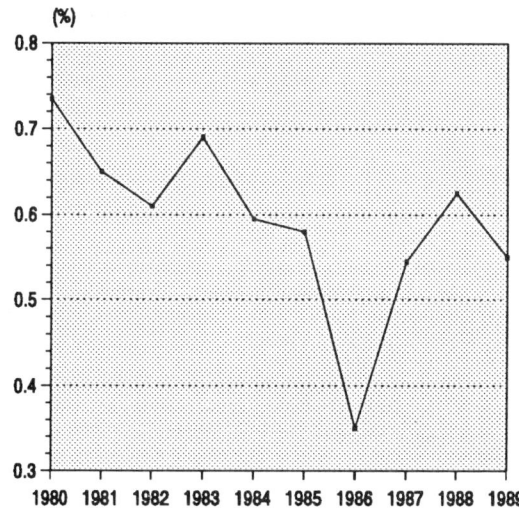

Source: Conseil National du Crédit

less, interest-bearing current accounts seem both inevitable and necessary: France and Belgium are the only European countries where such a ban exists, and the approach of a unified European market cannot but hasten a final decision on the issue. Also, payment of interest may even become necessary because the growth in sight deposits has slowed dangerously in the years leading up to 1992 because of the rise in SICAVs *monétaires* (short-term money-market instruments) and investments remunerated at market rates. The result has been that bank liabilities have become more expensive as institutions increasingly have had to fund themselves at or near money-market rates.

Loans at preferential rates is another feature of the state's intervention in the banking system, though these were declining dramatically in light of the increased availability of products mentioned above. Nevertheless, new loans granted at preferential rates of interest grew by 5.9 percent in 1989, reaching FF240 billion ($42 billion), which represents a break in the trend between 1986 and 1988 when they declined at an average annual rate of 8.5 percent.[15]

Though the asset side of banks' balance sheets has been deregulated, the same is not true for the liabilities side. A considerable proportion of the funds taken in by banks (apart from bonded debt) pays interest at rates fixed by the authorities: 55.5 percent of funds in 1989, as opposed to 64 percent in 1985 (70 percent in 1980).[16]

Major tax disparities persist between different products, such as the tax exemption on income from accounts held at the savings banks or Crédit Mutuel, or between the rate of compulsory levies on household financial assets (bonds, time deposits, short-term securities, the people's savings plan, etc). In this area, the AFB has campaigned for a level playing field arguing in particular for the creation of tax-free accounts that would be available through all bank networks.

The insurance sector is also affected by the continuance of "privileged" networks. These latter can either be insurers or in a sector close to insurance and include such entities as La Poste. They are "privileged" in the sense that they are state controlled and, therefore, exempted from the normal rules and regulations pertaining to banking and insurance.

Insurers have, in fact, already complained to the European Commission of unfair competition from the Post Office. But the latter still intends to begin distributing general insurance products, although it is part of the public service rather than a commercial company. A new law in 1991 affirms the Post Office's right to engage in general insurance activities. However, its request to be allowed to grant loans has been rejected.

The European Community syndrome
Do foreign institutions find the French market attractive?

The mutual recognition of all EC institutions has forced the French banks to become more competitive and, while the number of foreign institutions has increased, their actual market share has not changed to any great extent (see Figure 1.2).

The Banking Law of 1984 significantly relaxed the regulatory barriers that limited the ability of foreign banks to operate in France. Now, the only barriers to entry are "initial financial strength, the character and competency of the intended managers and the financial standing of its shareholders". These regulatory barriers are of a technical and economic nature: but the profitability of French banking is low and quality networks are hard to find, or do not interest the foreign banks because of the exorbitant costs of acquisition.[17] What is more, the French market is a difficult one to penetrate because of the close links between the banks and the public authorities. Despite this, foreign institutions have been very active in the financial markets, being particularly successful in picking up the best broking firms. On the other hand, French banking groups are particularly active on the European and international M&A markets, reflecting the lack of expansion opportunities on their over-banked home ground.

Foreign insurers have only a small presence in France (2 percent) and entry into the market is proving difficult.

The growing role of the European Commission
Running parallel to the relative retreat of the public authorities, banking has witnessed growth in the European Commission's influence with a widening in the scope of EC regulations. The single European

Figure 1.2

Foreign banks with a presence in France (as % of total in various fields of activity)

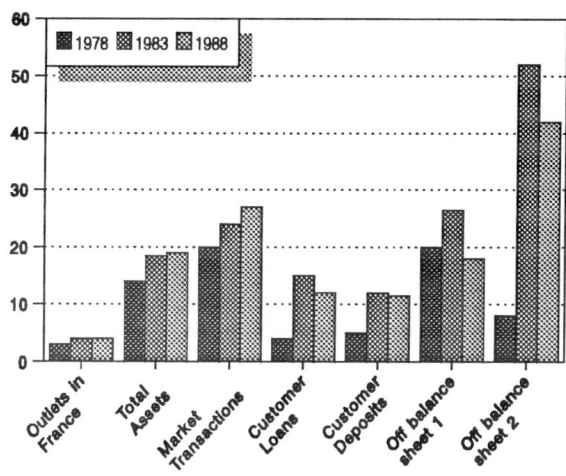

1. Off Balance Sheet Commitments to Credit Institutions
2. Off Balance Sheet Commitments to Clients

Source: Commission Bancaire, 1988 Report

market and the prospect of a single capital and financial services market is forcing the French authorities to liberalise the financial system. The French government, it must be noted, has never really been in profound disagreement with the Community's financial policy as forged by the Commission President, Jacques Delors.

A single currency?
One imponderable remains: what would be the effects of European monetary union? The establishment of a European central bank and a single currency would shatter state control over financial and monetary affairs. Such a goal, outlined in the Delors report, has enjoyed a wide consensus among French politicians, at least with regard to the first stage of the three-stage plan, which was approved by a majority at the Madrid Council of Ministers in June 1989.

The savings habits of the economic agents
After 1983, the share of value added, which had shifted in favour of individuals in the previous 15 years, became more propitious to company profits. The result was a marked decline in both the funding needs of companies and the funding capacity of individuals. The growth of public authority funding needs also encountered these changes. The shift greatly favoured the financial institutions on account of the rise in real interest rates.

These developments exemplify how necessary it became to change the way the French economy was funded. First of all, the internationalisation of capital movements and the growth in corporate investment led to the establishment of competitive financial instruments and of broad, high-performing markets. Next, the priority given to the fight against inflation meant preference being systematically accorded to funding of the public deficit by means of securities issues. After that, the need to reduce costs — all the more pressing as interest rates rocketed — encouraged competition between different forms of funding and between different financial institutions. The steering of investments towards the financing of the budget deficit was another indispensable element. Finally, the instability of exchange and interest rates necessitated the setting up of mechanisms for hedging (interest rate swaps, the MATIF, the MONEP, etc).

A fall in the personal savings rate
The transformation of the French financial system took place against the backdrop of a fall in the personal savings rate (see Figure 1.3). This decline can be attributed chiefly to trends in real income, deflation and developments in property investment. In addition, the drop in the savings rate came at a time when cash loans to individuals were increasing, thus enabling them to maintain their levels of consumption. On the other hand, the stock market boom and the rise in the private assets/income ratio in the

mid-1980s would appear not to have had a significant influence insofar as households did not consume the resultant value gains. While the rise in real interest rates on credit failed to counterbalance this, it did actually play a role in the overall changes in the way individuals structured their financial assets, giving additional encouragement to equities and savings products (see Table 1.3). One can also detect a long-term trend towards holding personal wealth in the form of financial instruments. Thus, financial instruments as a share of total personal assets rose from 29.5 percent in 1975 to 32.5 percent in 1983, and then to almost 40 percent in 1990. As further proof of the increasing financial sophistication of individuals, while the ratio of "private wealth to income" was 3.95 in 1975, by 1990 it had risen to 4.2.

Personal financial investments
Personal investment habits have undergone a pro-

Figure 1.3

The household savings rate in France, 1970-1991
(as % of gross disposable income)

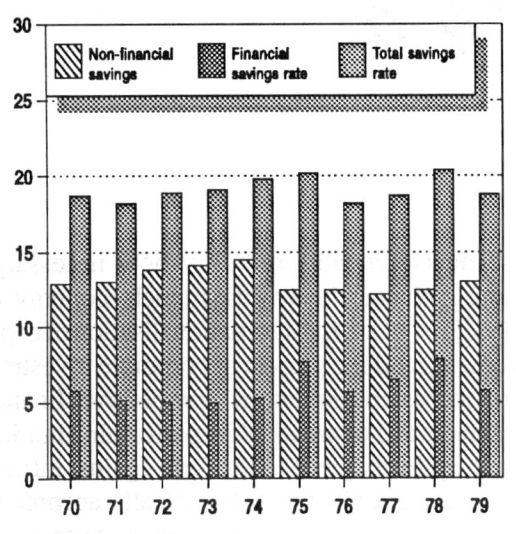 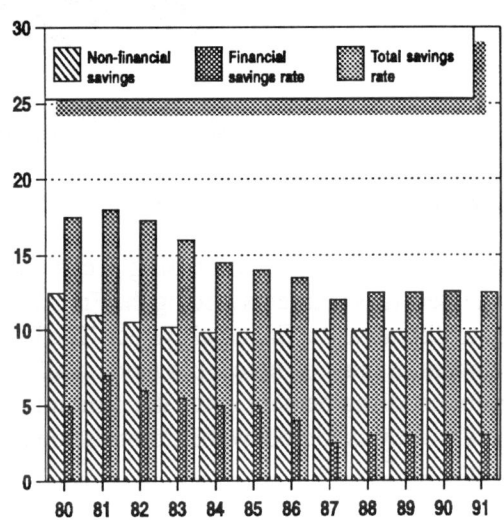

Table 1.3						
The make up of personal financial assets (in %)						
At year-end	**1983**	**1984**	**1985**	**1986**	**1987**	**1988**
Means of payment	16.4	16.1	15.4	14.3	14.6	13.3
Other liquid assets (excluding contractual savings)	36.1	34.7	32.7	28.2	29.6	26.2
Contractual savings	3.9	4.2	4.4	4.8	5.8	5.8
Bonds	10.7	9.3	8.9	7.3	7.2	5.1
Shares and other participations	17.3	22.0	25.5	33.0	30.0	36.6
(of which OPCVMs)	(n/a)	(5.8)	(7.7)	(9.5)	(9.2)	(11.7)
Loans	8.1	5.5	4.6	3.6	2.5	2.2
Insurance technical reserves	7.5	8.2	8.5	8.8	10.3	10.8
Total	**100.0**	**100.0**	**100.0**	**100.0**	**100.0**	**100.0**
Source: Comptes de la Nation						

found change: within 10 years, from a general preference for liquid assets (accounting for a little under 70 percent of annual investment flows) a switch has occurred where three components — liquid assets, stocks (including OPCVMs) and insurance products — have an almost identical share in personal investments. Parallel to all of this has been a perceptible decline in the flow of transferable securities investment since the stock market collapse of 1987 and the growth in the demand for insurance products (see Figure 1.4).

Figure 1.4
Breakdown of annual personal investment flows

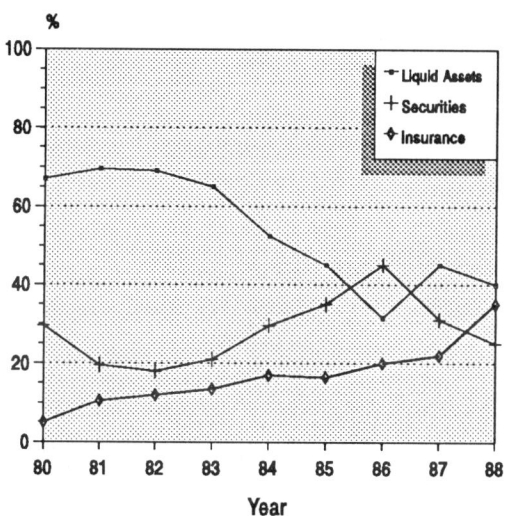

The growing impact of personal indebtedness

The attitude towards personal indebtedness has also changed, as seen by the ratio of "total liabilities to income" which rose rapidly from 0.58 in 1970 to 0.62 in 1980 and 0.76 in 1988. Individuals are taking on more debt, especially for housing financing, which now makes up 60 percent of all household indebtedness. However, cash loans to private individuals are the fastest growing form of debt (see Table 1.4), due in part to the removal of credit restrictions in 1986 and to an increased offer of loans from the banks. It is also attributable, at least temporarily, to a drop in individuals' real income. Three elements, all of recent origin, typify the sort of credit offered to individuals: the growth in variable rate loans, the growing use of sureties at the expense of mortgaging and the arrival of "securitisation" — the changing of non-negotiable debts into securities that form part of a fund that can be placed with investors.

While indebtedness is not a new phenomenon for most French people, over-indebtedness among some was so acute by the early 1990s that it was worrying the monetary authorities as much as the financial intermediaries. According to a report by the consultative committee of the Conseil National du Crédit published in 1989, 200,000 individuals drawn from the top 20 percent of France's population in terms of wealth were sustaining monthly repayments that exceeded 60 percent of income. As a consequence, to obviate the difficulties experienced by private individuals, the Neiertz Law was promulgated (named after the minister responsible). The aim of this was to handle personal indebtedness in a systematic and concerted way. But one of the effects of the Neiertz Law appears to have been to depress the market for consumer credit. In fact, the specialised credit institutions have put a brake on their loan offers since the law came into force.

The consumer movement

The consumer movement made an abrupt entry into the area of bank-customer relations during the fee-charges-on-cheques affair in 1986. It thwarted the measures envisaged by the Ministry of Finance and the AFB by launching campaigns aimed at paralysing cheque processing. They were abetted in their efforts by a large well of sympathy in press circles, or at the very least by the antipathy of that same press towards the banks.

The banks' attitude was, and is, far from uniform, with four distinct stances emerging:[18]

- The "aggressive" banks which emphasise quality and thereby justify the billing of services (Cortal, Crédit du Nord, Crédit Commercial de France, Lyonnaise de Banque);

- The *trois vieilles* (Banque Nationale de Paris, Crédit Lyonnais and Société Générale) and the AFB banks, which demand the right to be able to bill for services but attempt to negotiate this right in a relatively low-key fashion;

- The savings banks (represented by CENCEP) and Crédit Agricole, which have been markedly reticent on this issue, adopting a wait-and-see policy to preserve and maybe even benefit from an improved public image that comes from not being associated with the commercial banks;

Table 1.4

Developments in loans to the economy in France, 1979-1988 (as a percentage of GDP)

	Company cashflow	Exports	Investment	Cash loans to individuals	Accommodation and property developers	Others	Total
1979	11.7	2.8	25.8	2.3	26.1	2.1	70.8
1985	11.2	2.0	28.3	2.8	27.7	3.2	75.2
1986	9.7	1.6	28.0	3.6	27.9	3.9	74.7
1987	10.0	1.3	28.9	4.6	29.4	4.4	78.6
1988	11.5	0.9	29.6	5.3	29.8	5.3	82.4
1989	13.1	0.7	32.0	6.5	31.3	5.8	89.4

Source: Banque de France

- The Crédit Mutuel of the South West, which has taken the consumers' side in this matter, denies that there is any justification for service charges or for the practice of *jours de valeur* (floats) and instead advocates the remuneration of deposits. As a result of this stance, it has gained market share in its region from another mutual bank, Crédit Agricole.

The attitude of the authorities has not been (and still is not) any more coherent, with an equal number of distinct positions: (i) the liberal position adopted by a deputy governor of the Bank of France, Philippe Lagayette, who advocated the substitution of two prohibitions with two liberties (the right to remunerate sight deposits and the right to bill services); (ii) the pro-consumer stance of the Secretary of State for consumer policy (part of the Ministry of Finance) who, in the wake of the consumer movements' protests, declared his opposition to the idea of billing for services; (iii) the opportunistic position of the Budget Minister who chose to emphasise that services are provided free by *comptables du Trésor* (chartered accountants), where any individual can open an account; (iv) the flexible position adopted by heads of the Treasury and the Minister for Finance, who have tried above all else to avoid losing control over the banks, even if it has meant contradicting themselves as events have unfolded.

One cannot deny the growth in power of the consumer movement. Whether they like it or not, the banks (and increasingly the insurance companies) cannot afford to ignore consumer groups without running the risk of being plunged into fresh image-damaging controversies. In point of fact, the AFB, anxious to improve its image, mounted a four-year publicity campaign aimed at establishing a form of dialogue with bank customers.

Users' attachment to a concept of banking as a public service

The belief that banking is a public service has been particularly evident in consumers' reactions to various measures taken by the banks in terms of service offering. Since the new Banking Law, access to a bank account has been recognised as a right. The heavy-handed way in which some banks have chosen to close small accounts has had a deep effect on public opinion and revived the negative image of the banker. The obvious risk of social discrimination in terms of banking services worries French people almost as much as discrimination in hospital care. Such feelings seem largely to have prevailed over any desire to have "up-market" financial services at their disposal. Thus, while most French people (97 percent) are still satisfied with their banks, especially in terms of how their accounts are managed, 90 percent oppose charges being placed on cheques and other services. Nor are they any more enthusiastic when it comes to interest on sight deposits.

The reasons for equating banking with a public service are deep-rooted and varied. First, there is the whole development of the French banking system since the 19th century in which the savings banks and the mutual networks have played a central role. These institutions enjoy a large degree of support among the populace. Second, the policy adopted since the late 1960s of introducing the population to banking in order to curb the risk of tax fraud through the creation of a paper trail, and to lessen the opportunity for theft (through widespread use of cheques and/or bank cards) is equated with genuine social conquests.

Thus, the banks do not have complete freedom of manoeuvre.

The nature of banks' activities is of such fundamental importance to the economy as a whole that it would be difficult even for a state steeped in good intentions and of particularly liberal outlook to consider financial services in the same way as any other branch of the economy.

The state's future role in financial services

The announcement made by the French president in September 1991 that partial privatisations would be allowed revived the thorny problems of rights of ownership and the state's disengagement from certain companies. The actual intentions of the public authorities have still to be revealed: whether it is to open up the capital of financial intermediaries to strengthen state funds, or whether it is simply to lighten the budget deficit, as some members of parliament would like the public to believe.

Whichever the case, it is clear that this "transgression" against the sacrosanct policy of *ni privatisations ni nationalisations* is a subtle warning of things to come. Nonetheless, it seems to be taken for granted that the government will reserve the right to set its own terms for these partial privatisations. This, as much as the politics at stake, is important in view of the approaching election deadline.

Endnotes

(1) These institutions have survived up to the present time under the respective names of Association Française des Banques (AFB), Association Française des Etablissements de Crédit and Commission Bancaire.

(2) For each of these sub-systems there is a "Grande Ecole" (élite training college) such as the Ecole Polytechnique and the Ecole Nationale de l'Administration (ENA). The latter, set up in 1945, has supplied fresh generations of *trésoriens* (high-ranking Treasury officials).

(3) Through use of *planchers d'effets publiques*, banks were required to intervene as acquirers of Treasury bills, for up to 25 percent of their source of funds.

(4) These reforms were not very fruitful because the capital markets were still highly compartmentalised and the possibilities for arbitrage between the short and long term practically nonexistent.

(5) This measure enabled investors to increase the pre-tax return from equities by 50 percent.

(6) The mutual or co-operative banks, the savings banks and other financial institutions.

(7) Crédit Agricole underwent two decades of spectacular growth. It distributed 23 percent of all credits and took in 28.6 percent of all deposits (excluding sight deposits) in 1979, as opposed to 9.8 percent and 19.8 percent respectively in 1960. By 1979, one bank outlet in four belonged to the *banque verte's* network.

(8) The newly-nationalised banks then represented 20 percent of the banking system's deposits, while 41 percent was held by the Caisse des Dépôts et Consignations, the Caisses d'Epargne et de Prévoyance and other quasi-state institutions, and 18 percent by the mutual sector.

(9) In 1982, 16.5 percent of BNP's capital, 12.9 percent of Société Générale's, and 9.3 percent of Crédit Lyonnais' was in the hands of private investors.

(10) In October 1981, following the adoption of the Mauroy Plan, the Governor of the Bank of France, Renaud de la Genière, refused to grant the Treasury funding for a much larger loan (FF40 billion [$7 billion] instead of the usual FF10 billion).

(11) The Pérouse Report on the feasibility of new financial techniques (1980); the Dautresme Report on a new policy for long-term savings (1982); the Tricot Report on the cost of financial intermediation (1985); the Pastré Report on the modernisation of French banks (1986); the Lebègue Report on the taxation of savings (1988).

(12) The law is not universally applicable however, as it does not include the financial services provided by the Post Office or those of the Caisse des Dépôts et Consignations. In addition, preceding legislation and regulations specific to the different types of bank have not been rescinded.

(13) Jean-Claude Trichet, Treasury director, tended to downplay this fact, pointing out that modernisation was sought as much by financial industry specialists as by the public authorities.

(14) The reform and opening up of the money markets, together with the creation of negotiable Treasury bills and the flotation of market-rate OATs (Treasury bonds) are two complementary facets of deficit financing policy that have contributed to the modernisation of the financial markets.

(15) Housing accounts for two-thirds of the loans granted at preferential rates, and agriculture (with FF37 billion — $6.5 billion) for 15 percent.

(16) Interest paid on more than 80 percent of liquid deposits is state-regulated.

(17) In 1989, NatWest's protracted negotiations to buy L'Européenne de Banque broke down. The price demanded seems to have been one of the reasons for the British bank's withdrawal. At the beginning of 1991, Barclays took over the bank for a price in the region of FF1.5 billion ($265 million). Other banks (including Deutsche Bank) have been looking for a "suitable" bank (both in terms of quality and price) for some time.

(18) The "static warfare" waged over the billing of services versus paying of interest issue is still not over, with all sides more or less clinging to the positions described here.

Section II

Banking

Chapter 2

The French Banking Sector

Between the late 1960s and the mid-1980s, French banking experienced only partial reform. The strict divisions between the different banks and between banks' activities, the proliferation of reduced interest rate schemes, credit restrictions, controls on currency movements and the prospect of large-scale nationalisations, conspired to stifle dynamism within the banking system.

The French banks came up with a dual response to this array of constraints:

- Domestically, the banks increased the number of branches and ATMs (DAB-GAB) to offer increased convenience and enlarge market shares. But such a strategy, which gave rise to fierce competition, soon reached its limits in terms of profitability. In addition, it had a perverse "economies of scale" effect because the establishment of an interbank system (of necessity co-operative) opened the door for newcomers. Even the smallest institutions could thereafter access the latest technological innovations;

- Abroad, the banks succeeded in establishing large networks that allowed them to circumvent credit restrictions. Although this approach enabled French banks to rank themselves among the largest in the world based on size of international networks, the effectiveness of such a strategy was brought into question in the wake of changes in funding mechanisms on the national and international markets which took place in the 1980s. In the course of that decade, the French banks appeared somewhat handicapped compared with their Anglo-Saxon competitors in some of the more specialised and profitable areas such as

commissions, M&A, divestments, market-making and securities management.

From 1984/85 onwards, France joined the movement towards liberalisation which had begun in the Western economies in the middle of the 1970s. Liberalisation triggered far-reaching deregulation, restructuring and modernisation. On a domestic level, the changes have been many: the lifting of credit restrictions, privatisations, a progressive levelling of the playing field in terms of the businesses banks are authorised to engage in and in terms of distribution of subsidised loans, the lifting of currency controls, the creation of the forward negotiable options markets and the banks' entry into the capital structure of broking houses.

Modernisation of the French banking system was also distinguished by more intensive efforts towards diversification on the part of financial institutions, entailing mass re-entry into areas which had previously been the preserve of specialised operators. The banks may now carry out practically all activities either directly or through subsidiaries. From this stems largely the dynamism of French *bancassurance* and, more recently, *banquindustrie* whereby the banks are directly investing in industrial corporations. In addition, banks are now facing increased competition on the corporate and retail markets due to the expansion of non-bank entities in the financial services arena. Sometime in the future they will also face competition from other parts of Europe and, perhaps, from the financial services section of the Post Office.

Abroad, the French banks have become extremely active, especially in acquiring stakes in foreign institutions. They have also conducted a successful strategy of co-operation agreements and alliances aimed at building Europe-wide banking networks.

Both the overhaul of domestic operations and the feverish level of acquisitions abroad have posed problems for those institutions' restructuring, notably for the state-owned banks. Rarely has profitability lived up to ambitions.

While the building of a single Europe undoubtedly helped increase the speed of modernisation, at the root of the vast movement towards reform (still alive in the early 1990s) was the new Banking Law of 1984 and the deregulation of the financial markets under the impetus of the public authorities.

A new regulatory framework

The new Banking Law redefines and widens the concept of a bank

The Banking Law of January 24 1984 which addressed the activity and inspection of credit institutions, completely altered the legislative framework of banking and financial operations, replacing laws dating back to the period between 1941-45. In Article 2, the new law defines credit institutions as "legal entities which carry out banking operations as part of their normal business, which includes the taking in of funds from the public, credit transactions and the placing at the customers' disposal of, and administration of, the means of payment".

Compared to the 1941 Law and to the First EC Banking Directive, this definition of banking operations contains a number of distinctive features:

• It broke the link between the liabilities side of the balance sheet and the assets side (as per the EC Directive). This means that only loans or receive deposits which are covered by the Law need be granted;

• It defined the role of banks in money circulation. This is a peculiarity of French law and derives from the rapid growth in new payments systems and, in particular, electronic-based ones. Hitherto, as the issuance of the means of payment was not considered a banking activity, any company could develop its own payments system;

• The new legislation tended towards universality. Although certain institutions remained subject to a special legal status, they were henceforth required to submit to the Banking Law and were encompassed within the definition of the *établissements de crédit* (credit institutions).

Activities recognised by the Law

Credit institutions are authorised to carry out both direct and indirect transactions: banking operations and connected activities, non-banking activities and the taking of participations. The right to engage in some of these businesses is reserved for institutions that have been given special authorisation and are subject to particular forms of supervision (see Table 2.1 and 2.1b).

Given that they are subject to the Banking Law alone, the Association Française des Banques (AFB) banks or banks formerly members of the association, enjoy the widest freedom. The operations of the mutual and co-operative banks, the savings banks and the Crédit Municipal banks are restricted, on the other hand, by express authorisations and restrictions included in legislation specific to these institutions and their activities (although this, in practice, does not prevent them from carrying out all commercial bank-type business). As for the other categories (finance companies, securities houses and business organisations), the main restraint on their activities is the ban on accepting sight deposits of less than two years duration.

Not all financial services are covered by the Banking Law. Some — especially off-balance sheet activities — are subject to special regulations and "do not justify authorisation under the terms of the Banking Law". Among these are "market dealing", advisory activities and activities that are not part of the normal business of credit institutions as defined in the Banking Law, including exchange transactions, transferable securities operations, dealings on the MATIF etc.

Another notable provision is that all financial institutions, without exception, must obtain special authorisation from the Comité de la Réglementation Bancaire whenever they wish to take stakes in non-financial or financial companies.

Table 2.1

Nature of the activities open to institutions subject to the Banking Law and to other commercial companies

Type of activity	Commerical banks	Co-operative, mutual, savings and Crédit Municipal banks	Finance companies	Specialist financial institutions	Securities houses (art.99)	Commercial companies
I — Balance sheet operations						
1.1 *Activities appearing on the assets side of the balance sheet*:						
Customer loans(i)	Yes	Yes(ii)	Yes(iii)	Yes(ii)	No	No(iv)
Purchase of transferable securities and marketable debt securities (v)	Yes	Yes	Yes	Yes	Yes	Yes
Interbank operations	Yes	Yes	Yes	Yes	Yes	No
Participations in the financial sector	Yes(vi)	Yes(vi)	Yes(vi)	Yes(vi)	Yes(vi)	Yes(vi)
Participations in non-financial sectors	Yes(vii)	Yes(vii)	Yes(vii)	Yes(vii)	Yes(vii)	Yes
Investments in the real estate sector	Yes(viii)	Yes(viii)	Yes(viii)	Yes(viii)	Yes(viii)	Yes
1.2 *Activities appearing on the liabilities side of the balance sheet*:						
Customer deposits of less than 2 years duration	Yes	Yes(ii)	No(ix)	No(ix)	No	No(x)
Deposits of over 2 years duration	Yes	Yes	Yes	Yes	Yes	Yes
Funds received for special uses(xi)	Yes	Yes	Yes	Yes	Yes	Yes
Issue of transferable securities	Yes	Yes(xii)	Yes	Yes(xii)	Yes	Yes
Issue of marketable debt securities	(certificates of deposit)	(certificates of deposit)	(Specialist finance company bonds)	(Specialist finance company bonds)	(Specialist finance company bonds)	(Commercial paper)
Interbank operations	Yes	Yes	Yes	Yes	yes	No

Notes:

(i) Including both leasing and rental with purchase option activities

(ii) As stipulated in the institution's statutes and, should the case arise, the rules of territoriality

(iii) Subject to these activities being compatible with the approval granted or statutes

(iv) Excluding credits linked to some sales and loans to some companies belonging to the same group

(v) In the form of transactions or investments

(vi) According to the conditions and limitations set down in Regulation No.84-07 and modified by Regulation No.87-08

(vii) According to the condititions and limitations set down in Regulation No.85-16

Table 2.1b

Type of activity	Commercial banks	Co-operative, mutual, savings and Crédit Municipal banks	Finance companies	Specialist financial institutions	Securities houses (art.99)	Commercial companies
II — Off-balance sheet operations						
2.1 Services encompassed by the Banking Law						
Guarantees and endorsements in favour of third parties	Yes	Yes(ii)	Yes(iii)	Yes(ii)	No	No
Placement guarantees on transferable securities	Yes	Yes(ii)	No	Yes(ii)	Yes(iii)	No
Issuing of payment or credit cards	Yes	Yes(ii)	Yes(iii)	Yes(ii)	No	No(xiii)
Remittance of cheques	Yes	Yes	Yes(iii)	Yes(iii)	Yes(iii)	No
2.2 Financial services subject to special regulations						
Foreign exchange transactions	Yes	Yes	Yes	Yes	Yes	No(xiv)
Transferable securities trading	No	No	No	No	No(xv)	No
Marketable debt securities trading	Yes	Yes	Yes	Yes	Yes	No
Trading and clearing of MATIF contracts	Yes(xvi)	Yes(xvi)	Yes(xvi)	Yes(xvi)	Yes(xvi)	No
Management and safe custody of transferable securities	Yes	Yes	No	Yes(xvii)	Yes	No
Services of receptor and depository of SICAV and FCP assets	Yes	Yes	Yes	Yes	No	No
Marketing of transferable securities	Yes	Yes	Yes(xvii)	Yes	Yes	No
Marketing of deposits and credits	Yes	Yes	Yes(xvii)	Yes	No	No
Presentation of insurance contracts	Yes(xviii)	Yes(xviii)	Yes(xviii)	Yes(xviii)	Yes(xviii)	Yes(xviii)
Financial advice and financial engineering	Yes	Yes	Yes	Yes	Yes	Yes
Non-banking assets	Yes(xix)	Yes(xix)	Yes(xix)	Yes(xix)	Yes(xix)	Yes

(xiii) Except cards designed for the purchase of determined goods from the companies concerned

(xiv) With the possible exception of manual foreign exchange transactions

(xv) Except in the case of sociétés de bourse

(xvi) Subject to having been authorised by MATIF SA

(xvii) Subject to these operations being connected to those specified in the authorisation

(xviii) According to the terms defined in the Insurance Code

(xix) As stipulated by Regulation No. 86-21 of November 24 1986 relative to carrying on non-banking operations

Source: Comité des Etablissements de Crédit

Bringing the various authorities together
The universality that was evident in the 1984 Banking Law — although somewhat strained by the continued existence of the "special status" banks — was cemented by the unification of the various regulatory and supervisory powers operating in the banking and financial sectors. The authorities' powers are divided as follows: decision making (Comité de la Réglementation Bancaire and Comité des Etablissements de Crédit); supervision (Commission Bancaire); consultation (Conseil National du Crédit and its off-shoot, the Comité des Usagers).

Another of the institutional particularities of the French banking system is that all "professional associations" or "central bodies" without exception are required to adhere to a sort of confederation — the Association des Etablissements de Crédit (AFEC) — which represents the different institutions to the public authorities.

The structure of the banking sector
To use the phrase coined by Daniel Lebègue, Treasury Director and managing director of BNP, the aim of the 1984 Banking Law was to end the "legal balkanisation" that had characterised the French banking system. Most financial institutions are subject to the law, with the exceptions of the Treasury, the Bank of France, the Caisse des Dépôts et Consignations and the financial services of the Post Office.

The establishment of a system posited upon the principle of universality was not intended to stifle the particularities which distinguish one financial institution from the other. On the contrary, the idea was to create an environment in which banks could best exploit their specific strengths and specialise in their chosen areas through the creation of a parity of conditions for all financial entities. "Making conditions more equal for all" was understood to mean a reduction in disparities in legal standing that might impede bank competition.

While it respects the identity of each bank, the Banking Law distinguishes six types of credit institution: the AFB-member banks, the mutual or co-operative banks, the savings and provident banks (Caisses d'Epargne et de Prévoyance), the Caisses de Crédit Municipal, the finance companies (*sociétés financières*) and the specialist financial institutions (see Figure 2.1).

Since 1984, the French banking scene (which in 1990 was made up of over 2,000 credit institutions and securities houses [see Table 2.2]) has undergone important changes, especially regarding the number of authorised financial institutions, their degree of concentration and their internal organisations.

Table 2.2

Changes in the number of credit institutions encompassed by the Banking Law

Metropolitan France and overseas *départements*	1984	1989	1990
I AFB-member banks	349	404	406
II Mutual or co-operative banks	195	176	173
of which:			
Banques Populaires	(42)	(33)	(33)
Crédit Agricole	(95)	(92)	(90)
Crédit Mutuel	(23)	(23)	(22)
III Savings and providence banks	468	224	186
IV Crédit Municipal banks	21	21	21
V Finance companies	875	1,062	1,047
VI Specialist financial institutions (IFS)	28	32	32
VII Securities houses	65	144	62
Total	2,001	2,063	2,027
Monaco			
I Banks	9	14	13
II Finance companies	7	7	7
III Securities houses	0	1	1
Total	16	22	21
Overall total	2,017	2,085	2,048

Source: Banque de France

Ongoing restructuring within the profession
The growth in the number of banks and finance companies is partially attributed to the strong push by foreign institutions to establish presences in France (see Table 2.3). Likewise, the setting up of banks and specialist finance companies by manufacturing and trading companies and by insurance companies, as well as the creation of new subsidiaries by existing banks, has also contributed to this increase. The status of *société financière* (finance company)

Figure 2.1

Organisation of the French banking system

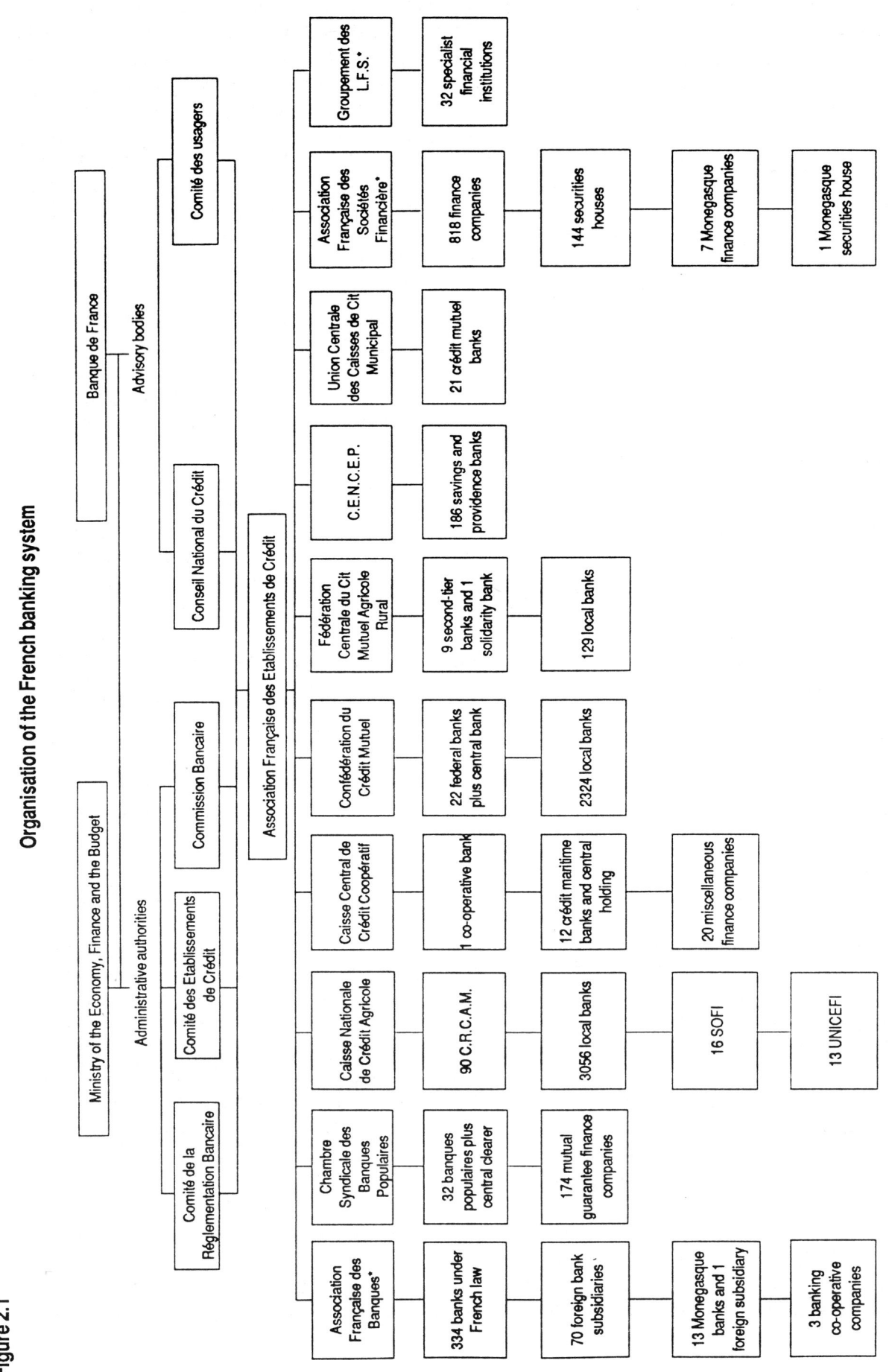

Banque de France

Advisory bodies

Comité des usagers

Ministry of the Economy, Finance and the Budget

Administrative authorities

Conseil National du Crédit

Commission Bancaire

Comité des Etablissements de Crédit

Comité de la Réglementation Bancaire

Association Française des Etablissements de Crédit

Association Française des Banques*	Chambre Syndicale des Banques Populaires	Caisse Nationale de Crédit Agricole	Caisse Central de Crédit Coopératif	Confédération du Crédit Mutuel	Fédération Centrale du Cit Mutuel Agricole Rural	C.E.N.C.E.P.	Union Centrale des Caisses de Cit Municipal	Association Française des Sociétés Financière*	Groupement des L.F.S.*

334 banks under French law

32 banques populaires plus central clearer

90 C.R.C.A.M.

1 co-operative bank

22 federal banks plus central bank

9 second-tier banks and 1 solidarity bank

186 savings and providence banks

21 crédit mutuel banks

818 finance companies

32 specialist financial institutions

70 foreign bank subsidiaries

174 mutual guarantee finance companies

3056 local banks

12 crédit maritime banks and central holding

2324 local banks

129 local banks

144 securities houses

13 Monegasque banks and 1 foreign subsidiary

16 SOFI

20 miscellaneous finance companies

7 Monegasque finance companies

3 banking co-operative companies

13 UNICEFI

1 Monegasque securities house

*Entries marked with an * are professional organisations; the rest are central bodies*
Source: Comité des Etablissements de Crédit

Table 2.3 Foreign presences in France						
	Banks		Finance companies		Securities houses	
	1985	1989	1985	1989	1985	1989
UK	12	14	4	6	2	1
Germany	5	7	7	12	1	2
Italy	7	10	1	5	—	3
Spain	8	11	—	2	—	—
Portugal	6	7	—	—	—	—
Other EC countries	18	17	7	12	2	10
EC total	**56**	**66**	**19**	**37**	**5**	**24**
Switzerland	5	8	6	6	2	—
Other European countries	3	5	3	6	—	1
European total	**64**	**79**	**28**	**49**	**7**	**25**
US	22	26	8	12	1	10
Other American countries	9	7	—	1	—	—
Near and Middle East	32	27	—	4	—	—
Japan	4	9	—	—	1	4
Others	15	19	1	1	—	2
Overall total	**146**	**167**	**37**	**67**	**9**	**41**

Source: Comité des Etablissements de Crédit

is of interest particularly to the co-operative or mutual banks, which can circumvent the special restrictions imposed on mutual institutions through the establishment of a finance company subsidiary.

On the other hand, for Crédit Agricole and more so for the savings banks, rationalisation through regional mergers developed as the key strategy by the early 1990s. As a result, the number of "central clearers" was expected to fall to about one-third of the 1991 level — or approximately 30 regional banks per banking group. These institutions will thus ultimately be more competitive.

Banking business is becoming concentrated
In 1991, almost four decades after the period of amalgamation in the banking sector began, approximately three-quarters of total loan transactions were concentrated in the hands of eight large banking groups — BNP, Crédit Lyonnais, Société Générale, Crédit Agricole, Paribas, Suez, CIC and Crédit Commercial de France. This group controlled more

than 50 percent of the finance companies and 110 banks in total, with few small and medium-sized banks remaining independent: almost all had an *actionnaire de référence* (shareholder of reference). Apart from the 167 foreign-controlled banks, 20 banks were controlled by a mutual bank, a specialist financial institution (IFS) or by the state; 18 were controlled by French insurance companies; 27 were controlled by manufacturing or trading groups; and 18 belonged to "diversified financial groups" (Commission Bancaire).

The concentration of control in the banking sector resulted from several key elements, including the costs entailed in new technology (computers and telecommunications) and the development of strategies to ready the French banks for Europe-wide competition.

Banking's changed legal framework has not entirely eliminated features that continue to distort competition. The French market remains relatively compartmentalised and the continued survival of "specialisations" has less to do with the specifics of various institutions than with the maintenance of a number of privileges in terms of the taking in and distributing of funds. Such is the case with the savings banks' Livret A, Crédit Mutuel's Livret Bleu, Crédit Agricole's rural notaries and deposits (see Chapter 4). The structure of customer deposits held by the different categories of banks thus remains strongly marked by these privileges, both past and present (see Table 2.4).

Non-price competition is distorting banking structures
For at least three decades, and for reasons mostly linked to the strict regulation of banking activities, the French banks have based their growth strategies almost exclusively around competitive advantages other than pricing. So as to gain market share, the credit institutions first engaged in ferocious competition by capitalising on their local presences and by offering free payment services to stimulate the use of cheques. This, however, changed at the beginning of the 1980s with the introduction of automatic banking services (DAB-GAB [ATMs]), which are characterised in France by universal interoperability between the banks.

While such innovations have placed France at the

Table 2.4

Breakdown of customer deposits in 1989 (in %)

	The *trois vieilles**	Crédit Agricole	Banques Populaires	Crédit Mutuel	Caisses d'Epargne
Ordinary accounts	40.9	34.1	38.4	17.4	n/a
Time deposit accounts	11.0	5.5	9.8	6.1	n/a
Special status savings accounts	27.2	38.0	26.8	63.2	93.3
of which:					
Livret A and Livret Bleu	—	—	—	41.3	58.6
Plan d'Epargne Logement and Compte d'Epargne Logement	17.2	23.9	16.8	15.7	n/a
Others	10.0	14.1	10.0	6.3	n/a
Certificates of deposit	6.7	17.9	4.2	4.8	0.1
Negotiable bills	14.2	4.5	20.8	8.5	0.1

*BNP, Crédit Lyonnais, Société Générale
Source: Commission Bancaire

forefront of technological progress in the areas of payment systems management and *la monétique* (plastic money), the French banks face problems of low profitability as a result of over-saturation of the market and an excessive number of employees.

Despite efforts at rationalisation, the overall number of outlets remains high

Branch openings is one area where the strategy of French institutions appears to run counter to foreign developments. While in other developed countries, banks began restructuring their branch networks in the 1970s leading to a cut in the total number of outlets, the French banks have failed to apply a similar policy in any consistent way (apart from the mutual banks [see Table 2.5]). Such a strategy seems even more aberrant in light of the fact that the French banks have created one of the densest ATM networks in the world.

In 1981, to slow the unbridled growth in the number of bank outlets, the authorities introduced special checks on openings. But such restrictions did not prove effective and the freedom to open outlets was re-established in 1987 (Regulation no. 86-22) for commercial, private sector banks and in 1991 for co-operative and savings banks. Despite such a limitation, the latter have continued opening outlets in

cities and regions where they had a weak presence during the 1980s.

As a result, the rate of rationalisation occurring in the early 1990s was slower than the banking authorities would have liked. On the one hand, there was a firm wish to improve productivity and cut operating expenses, a policy which demands banks to rationalise the number of outlets. But on the other, there is the obvious importance of having a network to build up a relationship with customers: the density of a network may be a "winning card" and banks find it hard to downscale their presences. This latter point becomes even more compelling to the banks as analysts discuss the imminent return of intermediation — a development which could not help but reinforce those institutions possessing a strong network.

The French banks are aware that the maintenance of a vast network of branches carries with it a number of drawbacks that outweigh the advantages:

- As branch networks weigh heavily on operating expenses, banks without such networks have a comparative advantage;

- They constitute an additional pressure on banks

Table 2.5

Change in the number of banking outlets (Metropolitan France, Monaco and overseas French *départements* and territories)

	Banks	Institutions affiliated to central bodies						Total
	Total	Crédit Municipal banks	Banques Populaires	Crédit Agricole	Crédit Maritime and Crédit Coopératif	Crédit Mutuel and Crédit Mutuel Agricole et Rural (CMAR)	Savings banks	
end-1981	9,953	—	1,494	5,309	97	3,716	3,733	24,302
end-1982	10,113	—	1,541	5,587	102	3,753	3,892	24,988
end-1983	10,160	—	1,547	5,644	103	3,815	4,136	25,405
end-1984	10,166	—	1,560	5,657	134	3,757	4,216	25,490
end-1985	10,213	45	1,568	5,657	138	3,762	4,399	25,782
end-1986	10,209	47	1,580	5,688	141	3,759	4,391	25,815
end-1987	10,251	50	1,598	5,726	142	3,753	4,395	25,915
end-1988	10,270	64	1,609	5,723	144	3,663	4,324	25,797
end-1989	10,160	72	1,611	5,706	145	3,618	4,322	25,634
end-1990	10,212	75	1,620	5,689	145	3,596	4,307	25,644

Source: Comité des Etablissements de Crédit

to adopt diversification programmes, the rationale for which is not always obvious;

• In some ways, they slow down the drive towards modernisation at branch network banks. It is, in fact, difficult to see how home banking can really grow while banks continue to give priority to establishing a type of intimate contact with their clientele based on the density of the branch network.

One important reform remains to be carried out: most banks are still subject to a 1937 decree which strictly regulates opening hours even though the pace of life of the working population has changed profoundly over the past half century. In addition, Saturday opening is a huge commercial advantage which Crédit Agricole alone possesses, a situation which penalises the other banks.

The restructuring of human resources

Since 1987, there has been a fall of around 1 percent of the number of bank employees (see Table 2.6). As with the number of outlets, the situation varies between institutions. Staff numbers at the AFB banks (which registered the largest increases in the 1970s) as well as at the Banques Populaires and the specialised financial institutions tended to fall in the second half of the 1980s, while other banks — like Crédit Agricole and Crédit Coopératif, whose operations expanded — experienced erratic staff levels. The *trois vieilles* (Banque Nationale de Paris, Crédit Lyonnais and Société Générale) started rationalising staff at the beginning of the 1980s.

Only the savings banks and the finance companies experienced any real increase in personnel: the former because of diversification (credit, insurance, securities) and the latter because of the rapid increase in the number of companies.

"Excess staff" is a phrase commonly used to describe the problems of French banks. But, while recruitment has stabilised, the real problem is how to equip the workforce for the technological changes that are transforming banking. French banks, in general, have a labour-intensive and not very highly-skilled front office and an inefficient back office.

Table 2.6

Number of personnel employed by the main credit institutions, 1980-1989									
	1980	**1981**	**1982**	**1983**	**1984**	**1985**	**1986**	**1987**	**1988**	**1989**
AFB-member banks (including Banque Française pour le Commerce Extérieur from 1988 on)	243,668	243,918	247,674	250,390	251,498	252,613	254,409	252,187	249,260	244,275
Crédit Agricole	60,932	62,496	65,494	69,004	69,804	68,599	67,456	67,024	66,486	66,665
Banques Populaires	26,700	27,000	27,600	28,500	28,800	28,748	28,575	28,445	27,953	27,435
Crédit Mutuel and CMAR	14,687	15,501	16,365	17,756	18,830	19,787	20,191	21,043	21,549	22,104
Caisses d'Epargne	20,034	21,139	22,525	24,672	25,700	26,500	27,162	27,705	28,215	29,346
Specialist financial institutions	—	—	—	—	11,393	11,411	11,422	11,231	11,020	11,027
Finance companies	13,410	13,400	13,750	14,100	14,570	16,000	19,500	20,200	21,200	21,300
Total	—	—	—	—	422,280	425,418	430,604	429,788	427,644	424,102
Annual change (in %)	—	—	—	—	—	+0.74	+1.22	-0.19	-0.50	-0.82

Source: Comité des Etablissements de Crédit

Some fundamental changes have occurred in recruitment: in place of the retention of low-qualified staff as was the practice in the 1970s, came the selective recruitment of graduates in the 1980s. In 1986, 40 percent of employees hired by banks had higher education backgrounds, as against 10 percent in the 1970s. According to an AFB study of 37 banks which collectively account for 75 percent of the market, there has been a shift in the share of overall staff numbers in favour of the "executive" and "officer" categories. These have gone from 50 percent and 14 percent respectively of staff in 1985 to 60 percent and 19 percent in 1990, while "clerks" (meaning personnel with few or no qualifications) have dropped by 15 percent to 21 percent. But this policy of employing better educated staff has the negative effect of raising the cost of salaries.

In addition, staff turnover in French banks is low (2 to 4.5 percent of staff per annum), compared to the German (4 to 6 percent) and the British or American banks (where it can reach 15 percent and is never less than 10). Such a low turnover is an important factor sustaining structural rigidity as French banks attempt to overhaul their operations.

Until the early 1980s, the banks enjoyed an "industry consensus" which was quite atypical for France: salaries were relatively protected and in return industrial disputes were limited. But as conditions changed, industrial relations became a time bomb by the early 1990s. Conflicts between management and staff risk seriously damaging the reforms begun by the French banks, a risk which increased in 1991 when the AFB opted not to renew the trade union's collective agreement which dated back to 1954.

In the recession-ridden years of the early 1990s, labour-management conflicts could increase should banks' profits decline and salaries stagnate. In addition, banks and trade union representatives have been negotiating problems surrounding the industry's retirement schemes to stave off impending imbalances in the banks' own complementary pension funds. Forecasts estimated that from now through the year 2005, the contributions that will have to be paid into the funds will rise from 17 percent of wages to 27 percent (see chapter 12).

These negotiations still had not reached a conclusion by mid-1992. But, conscious of the seriousness of the situation, the unions have accepted the principle of a link to the general complementary scheme for executive staff (AGIRC) and of an increase in subscriptions to the ARRCO complementary pension fund. However, one obstacle stands in the way of integration — the banks have one overall group agreement for the profession but not a unified pension system.

There is no mechanism in place for the 15 existing schemes to compensate one another. In addition, the AGIRC is looking closely at the integration of the banks' pension funds to ensure that such a move does not affect the equilibrium of the scheme. It is demanding that solidarity towards one another be shown by the bank pension schemes.

La monétique and the French payment systems

In the 1980s, management of the payment systems became a crucial matter for the banks as a result of the concomitant problems posed by an explosion in the number of cheques and the arrival on the scene of *la monétique* (plastic money). What is more, management of the payment systems was raised to the status of "bank operation" under the terms of the Banking Law. Linked to banking intermediation, it encompasses the execution of customer payment orders, interbank transfers and the keeping of accounts linked to these transactions.

In the late 1960s, the first *distributeur automatique de billets* (DAB — cash dispensers) were put into service by the Banques Populaires (1968). A long series of innovations followed: first was the decision in 1983 to launch the *Système Interbancaire de Télécompensation* (SIT — the interbank clearing system), the real backbone of the French cards world. Then there was the formation of the Groupement Cartes Bancaires (interest grouping incorporating bank card issuers in France) in 1984, which made possible interbank compatibility and which helped spread the heavy investment costs among the banks.[1]

Within a few years, payment cards became the second most important means of payment in terms of number of transactions: the proportion effected by means of cheques receded by 20 percent, principally in favour of payment cards but also in favour of direct transfers (see Table 2.7).

Cheques still dominate in France

While the introduction and subsequent development of payment cards made possible a cut in their share of non-cash payments, cheques retained their lead, comprising 56 percent of all transactions in 1990. Although far behind the US, France is the world's second most cheque-oriented country by number of inhabitants and by absolute value.

The preference for using cheques results from several factors: first, their legal status (cheque books are free, there exists a central file on unpaid cheques and

Table 2.7		
Changes in the use of non-cash instruments (in % terms)		
	1979	1989
Cheques	76.7	56.4
Transfers	9.5	11.0
Interbank payment orders	6.7	7.9
(Truncated) bills of exchange	4.0	2.2
Carte Bancaire	3.1	22.5
Total	100.0	100.0
Source: AFB		

a legal guarantee for cheques of under FF100 ($17), etc) and second, the economic benefits (free cheques, etc). What is more, the use of cheques is closely linked to the rush to open new outlets and the increasing familiarity with banking among the French: 95 percent of French adults have a relationship with at least one bank, compared to less than 40 percent in the 1960s.

The handling of cheques poses huge problems for institutions because of the associated economic and labour costs — about FF4 (70 cents) per cheque. The encouragement given to use cheques plus the fact that they are free has resulted in large numbers of cheques being written for declining average amounts.[2]

At present, certain banks like Crédit Agricole — anxious to improve the profitability of their payments systems — are trying to rid themselves of customers who write cheques for small amounts and whose current account balances are of no commercial interest. In reality, the cheque problem, like that associated with accounts which are managed free of charge, can only be "resolved" by imposing a fee, which the law does not allow. The issue is also linked to the introduction of interest-bearing current accounts, which is vehemently opposed by the major banks.

The payment cards and ATMs

From 1985 to 1990, the French, who hold almost 20 million payment cards — increased sixfold the value of all transactions conducted with cards, while their total expenditure only rose by 14 percent (Table 2.8).

Free card use and interbank compatibility (through the grouping together within the GIE Cartes Bancaires interest grouping of new institutions: Visa, Mastercard and Eurocard) are two major factors contributing to the spread of payment cards in France. Table 2.9 gives an approximate idea of the density of the French banking groups' networks.

Cards are a failure in terms of the inherent administrative expenses. While the cost of a cheque hovers around FF4 (70 cents) for banks, according to a CIC study the cost of a card-linked payment is FF6.70 ($1.18) per electronic payment and FF9.60 ($1.21) per manual transaction. Given that these costs are not totally offset by the commissions received from retailers and the holders' annual fee, the same study estimates that cards are responsible for a bank deficit of some FF2 billion ($353 million).

Table 2.8
Bank cards

	1985	1987	1989	1990
No. of cards (million)	11.7	17.0	18.7	19.5
Withdrawals				
No. of transactions (million)	186.0	300.0	425.0	446.0
Volume (FF bn)	80.0	170.0	192.0	202.0
Total payment operations				
No. of transactions (million)	194.0	530.0	1,040.0	1,178.0
Volume (FF bn)	59.0	160.0	320.0	380.0

Source: Groupement des Cartes Bancaires

Table 2.9
Cards and ATMs

	No. of cards ('000)	No. of ATMs
Crédit Agricole	8,800	4,100
Caisses d'Epargne	3,145	2,323
Crédit Lyonnais	2,827	1,868
Société Générale	2,300	1,408
Crédit Mutuel	4,000	1,350
Banque Nationale de Paris	2,516	1,115
Banques Populaires	1,280	846

Source: Bank annual reports

However, according to the CIC study, when account is taken of the different means of billing and of the use of interbank mechanisms, the situation varies from one institution to the next. Some, like Crédit Agricole, Société Générale, Crédit Mutuel and to a lesser degree the savings banks, appear to record a profit while Crédit Lyonnais, Banque Nationale de Paris, the Banques Populaires, the Post Office, Crédit du Nord and Crédit Commercial de France (CCF) are clearly losing money. Such imbalances challenge some of the efforts being made to cut the cost of card operations.

Beginning in the 1980s, the banks encountered a growing challenge from specialist institutions and retailers that became increasingly active in an area which the banks had totally neglected — credit cards (revolving credit). In fact, the success of payment cards has run parallel to the growth in private label cards being circulated by these non-bank competitors, which were more credit-oriented and distributed by specialist companies (Cofinoga for the Aurora card, Creg for the Pluriel card, by chain stores, hypermarkets and direct mail companies).

The specific nature of these two types of card can pehaps be understood by looking at the tactical thinking behind each of them: for the banks, the *carte bancaire* seemed like an alternative to the hypertrophy caused by cheque payments (with the controversy over charging for cheques acting as a catalyst), while private label cards on the other hand are the concern of retailers who see in them a vehicle for new sales strategies.

Likewise, the growth in payment cards would have been inconceivable without the rise in the number of ATMs, which increased from 3,000 in 1982 to 13,500 in 1990.[3]

There were 120,000 Point-of-Sale (POS) terminals in France in 1991, placing it at the top of the world ranking, with 464 inhabitants per terminal.[4] Half a million retailers are affiliated to the cartes bancaires network.

Despite the increasing popularity of *la monétique*, the relentless competition between credit institutions in this area has created a situation where cards are far from profitable. Thus, as with cheques, that card transactions may be conducted at no expense to

Figure 2.2

Structure of AFB-member banks' customer funds

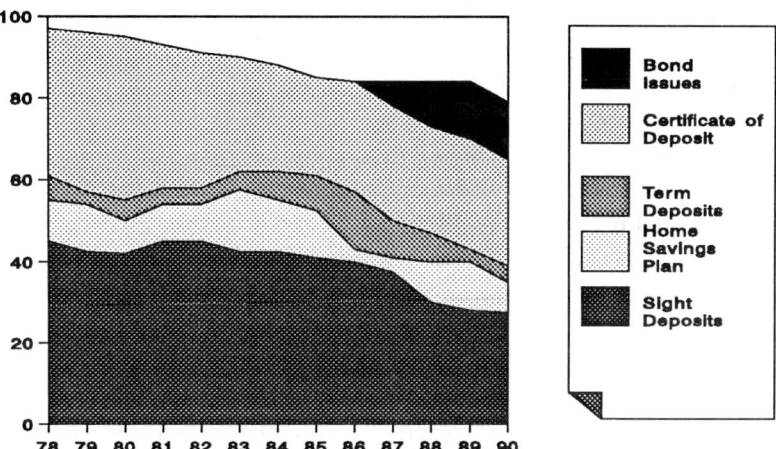

Source: Banque de France

the consumer is an issue hotly contested by banks for whom the burden is becoming too heavy.

Other innovations

France is a pioneer in the field of microprocessors, which should result in widespread availability and use of the carte à puce (smart card) by 1992. This development will reduce the level of fraud which currently accounts for FF450 million ($80 million), or 0.1 percent, of all transactions.

It is difficult to know with any degree of precision who loses the most from fraud — the retailer or the bank. However, the development of smart cards should improve relations between the parties.

The new technology, however, requires that all terminals be upgraded by the time the card is released on the market. In an environment where bank competition has become so exacerbated, agreement to spread the use of the smart card and to alter the existing bank card network to provide compatibility for the new card is far away. This in turn has created uncertainty regarding the continuation of interbank operability in the technological arena.

La banque à domicile (home banking) received a boost from the free distribution of Minitels (videotex terminals) by France Télécom (the Post Office's telecommunications subsidiary) in a move designed to replace telephone directories. By 1991 there were some 5 million terminals in operation, which was

expected to increase by another 50 percent in 1992, with 15-20 percent of the terminal owners subscribing to a home banking service. (However, according to a SOFRES study, most users turn to home banking for very basic transactions, such as obtaining account statements.) And in another development, France Télécom was expected to begin distributing smart cards which can be linked to the Minitel, allowing holders to make payments while guaranteeing an acceptable level of security.

Trading and clearing channels are likewise being adapted to developments in payments services, especially in the realm of *la monétique*. The increasing influence of the *Système Interbancaire de Télécompensation* (SIT — interbank automatic clearing system) will enable real-time clearing of payments. Already partially in service in 1990, all card transactions will pass through the SIT by 1992, which in turn will mean that each individual institution will be directly responsible for authorising and clearing payments. Prior to this, all transactions were batch processed through regional clearing computers at the Bank of France.

The functions of this new clearing network — primarily a system for transmitting information — could be widened and it is not inconceivable that it might be used to transmit stock market orders. Important economies of scale are thus expected of the SIT. Apart from the SIT and the Swift system for international transfers, two other specialised trade systems (*Sagittaire* and the regional *Images-Chèques*) complete the range of payments processing in France.

While considered one of the strengths of French banking, *la monétique* is faced with a substantial challenge. The form that Europe-wide interbank compatibility will take is still a matter for speculation. Networks like eurocheque and Eurocard are among the main adversaries of the French, and this opposition is likely to grow following the merger of eurocheque and Eurocard in 1991.

As a result, it is difficult to foresee what place French plastic money will have in the single market. The *cartes bancaires* interbank system will have to demonstrate that it has unique advantages over competing systems.

Credit institutions' freedom is handicapped by one-sided regulations

Following the example of other industrialised countries, France has made efforts to deregulate its financial markets and intermediation channels. Nevertheless, the French situation appears unique insofar as deregulation of intermediary business has been somewhat one-sided. While terms for interest rates on loans are more or less freely negotiable between banks and their customers, interest rates on deposits are still largely subject to strict regulation.

Put another way, liabilities-side items — still regulated — account for 40 percent of balance sheet totals or around two-thirds of liquid investments, while on the assets side, retail loan interest rates (in particular, housing loans) result in less than 15 percent of balance sheet totals. And this amount is declining.

Another particularity of France is the general absence of charges for banking services, something which obviously compensates for regulated interest rates on deposits. However, while most banks are in favour of charging fees, they are markedly less enthusiastic, if not downright opposed, to paying interest on current accounts.

The position of and prospects for the French banks

The international "Top 1,000 by capital" rankings produced by *The Banker* in October 1990 placed the French banks in an excellent position. Crédit Agricole came out as the fourth largest bank in the world, while two other French groups (BNP and Paribas) fell within the top 20. Within Europe, the seven largest French banks were even better placed among the top 20 (see Table 2.10).

But despite such ratings, comparatively speaking the French banks still have capitalisation and profitability problems. At the same time, maintaining growth rates for domestic banking activities and the desire for external growth places still greater demands on banks' funds.

A comparative "undercapitalisation"

Efforts to meet the Cooke Ratio has compensated for the impression given by international comparisons (based on the own-funds-to-total-assets ratio) that the French were weak in capital terms. Such apparent weakness was due to the preponderance of interbank transactions among Japanese banks compared to the French.

But while the four main French banks reached the 8 percent threshold as established in the Basle Concordat by the early 1990s, they were still behind the levels attained by German, British and, most notably, Spanish banks — especially in terms of hard core own capital (Tier 1) (see Table 2.11). What is more, the French banks have preferred to meet the 8 percent ratio by issuing hybrid securities (for example, *titres participatifs* — participating securities) which have a weak leverage effect on profitability.

The high average rate of sovereign risk provisions (around 50 percent) has mitigated this comparative weakness, but nevertheless these have remained well below the provisions made by the British and American banks and even further below those made by the Japanese banks. However, provisioning rates are gradually converging, demonstrating that the French banks have made extra efforts to strengthen their financial bases. On the other hand, the huge efforts poured into diversification and expansion by certain banks like Crédit Lyonnais could have an unfortunate effect on the level of provisioning made by subsidiaries (both in France and abroad).

Table 2.10

French banks — October 1990

Rank			Bank	Capital ($ million)	Assets ($ million)
France	Europe	World			
1	1	4	Crédit Agricole	11,802	241,992
2	6	12	Groupe Paribas	7,962	138,668
3	7	19	BNP	6,177	231,463
4	9	23	Crédit Lyonnais	5,617	210,727
5	10	24	Société Générale	5,528	164,741
6	13	29	Caisses d'épargne	5,180	152,722
7	—	—	Compagnie Bancaire	2,630	38,149
8	39	81	Banques Populaires	2,570	64,701
9	49	105	CIC Group	1,898	74,725
10	50	109	Banque Indosuez	1,838	55,316
11	57	132	CCF	1,512	45,603
12	76	174	Société de Banque Thomson	1,111	3,806
13	94	210	Crédit Mutuel	923	15,512
14	98	216	Crédit National	876	20,427
15	119	271	Sovac	653	8,144
16	115	363	Crédit Mutuel Bretagne	471	8,785
17	202	491	Compagnie Parisienne de Réescompte	309	9,505
18	253	593	UBAF (France)	240	7,824
19	264	628	Banque Worms	221	10,192
20	271	648	BFCE	212	41,023

Source: The Banker

Table 2.11

Structure of capital

	Tier 1	Tier 2	Tier 3
Crédit Agricole	—	—	8.4
BNP	4.5	4.3	8.8
Crédit Lyonnais	4.2	4.1	8.3
Société Générale	4.6	4.2	8.8

Source: IBCA

Efforts to lift profitability

For a long time, profitability was not fundamental to the French banks. They had launched themselves into a fierce "branch war" to win market share, and had no immediate concern for profitability. Competitive advantage rested essentially on the quality of services provided and this resulted in relatively weak profits. According to OECD data, the average profitability of French banks (return on assets) between 1981 and 1986 was about a third that of their British counterparts.

These particularities of the French banking system pose another problem: France is the only large European country where strict regulation of banking liabilities is maintained and where credit institutions' profits are so dependent on spreads. On average, commissions only represent about a quarter of banks' net banking income, as opposed to almost a third for other European competitors. This situation is bound to change, as supported by a July 1991 review of the impact of the 1984 Banking Law. In that review, the National Assembly's Finance Commission asserted that charges for banking services were inevitable, as was the payment of interest on sight deposits.

For some senior bank officials like François Henrot, director general at Compagnie Bancaire, the maintenance of controls on deposit interest rates is incongruous. While banks are paying for an increasing share of their funds at money market rates (negotiable money market instruments and OPCVMs [unit trusts]), they could just as easily offer interest on deposits to their customers at rates below those prevailing on the money market and at the same time bring part of their funding back onto their balance sheets.

The longer the delay in finding solutions to these problems, the greater the risk for the financial well-being of French banks. In effect, in the absence of further deregulation, the preference among economic agents for investments offering better rates of interest will grow. This in turn is likely to increase the banks' financial burden by eroding their income. In addition, the arrival of "non-branch" competitors in the market for high-net-worth customer deposits (to whom they offer very favourable terms for cheque accounts) could well remove the large banks' most valuable customer segment. These new competitors include Compagnie Bancaire, Sovac, Caixabank and retail chains like Leclerc, Lafayette and Printemps.

From the late 1980s to the early 1990s, with market saturation and shrinking margins, the banks made major efforts to improve the profitability of their operations with some success, most notably in 1989.

Figures relating to return on equity (ROE) in 1989 supplied by *Euromoney* demonstrate an actual improvement in the French banks' performance placing them in a median position: behind the Spanish banks (whose profits are atypically high) and Abbey National, but ahead of the Germans and certain British banks like NatWest and Barclays and Italian banks including Cariplo and San Paolo (see Table 2.12). In 1990, French banks' ROE figures fell to below 10 percent, and the banks continued to face a difficult operating environment in 1991.

Table 2.12		
French bank profitability (1989)		
	Return on Equity	Return on Assets
Société Générale	16.10	0.41
Crédit Lyonnais	14.02	0.30
Paribas Group	13.67	0.72
Banque Indosuez	13.29	0.44
Compagnie Bancaire	12.59	0.84
BNP	12.82	0.29
Crédit Local de France	10.34	0.45
Crédit Agricole	8.95	0.36
Groupe des Banques Populaires	9.12	0.36
Source: Euromoney		

It remains the case that certain big banks, especially some public sector ones, will continue to face a number of serious drawbacks: rising risks, the trend towards issuing "paper" as a way of funding the purchase of stakes in other state-owned companies or major acquisitions, the effect of the growing cost of deposits on profitability and the difficulty of cutting operating costs in any meaningful way. Finally, any extension in the financial services offered by the Post Office — something which is currently being debated — would cause additional hassles for the banks. With almost 17,000 outlets, La Poste would endanger the industry's overall equilibrium.

International business

Whether measured by size of network abroad or by the number of foreign banks in France, the French banking system is highly internationalised.

French banks already had a sizeable international network at the beginning of the century, but their foreign presence really expanded in the 1970s due primarily to the increasing constraints imposed by domestic credit controls and to the need to prepare for the single European market. With almost 40 institutions established in 110 countries, the French international network was by the early 1990s acknowledged as challenging the British for second largest worldwide presence after the Americans.

On the basis of figures supplied by the AFB, this international network accounts for 20 to 25 percent of industry business (as against 18.5 percent in 1980) and contributes 10 to 15 percent of all French bank profits. One should however note that, on the international level, French banks (apart from Banque Lazard and in certain respects Paribas) are still weak in merchant bank and market activities such as M&A, privatisation advice, asset and securities management, etc — precisely those areas where commissions are high and the Anglo-Saxons excel.

French banks apply what is essentially a twin-track policy towards Europe, consisting of protecting their French market and winning market share in Europe. Such a policy does not escape the criticism of foreign competitors, who are concerned about French protectionism — especially as French banks operate with complete freedom abroad.

Foreign institutions wishing to buy shares in French banks encounter hidden barriers which render any sizeable acquisition difficult if not impossible. As a result, in the recent past, excepting the Société de Banque Suisse (SBC) purchase of Banque Stern in 1989 and that of L'Européenne de Banque by Barclays in 1990, there have been no large acquisitions by foreign banks and even fewer examples of large-scale buying of equity in retail banks.

While foreign banks may have some difficulty in positioning themselves on the retail market, the same is not true for market activities. By acquiring broking firms in 1988, certain foreign banks gained entry into some very profitable niches. For example, Warburg, which holds a majority stake in the broker Bacot-Allain, has become the world's most important trader in French equities. Other banks, like Morgan, take part in the issuing and placing of Treasury securities under the guise of SCTs (*spécialistes en valeurs du Trésor*) which are responsible for bolstering the market. In addition, US and UK banks are among the most important providers of M&A advice to large corporates on the French market.

Banks and insurance companies draw closer

In strengthening their links to the insurance sector, the French banks may be motivated by three factors:

i)   the desire to utilise the resources of insurance companies to reinforce their own financial structures and/or

ii)   the desire to ensure the successful diversification of their range of business and savings management products and/or

iii) the desire to attain a competitive advantage through a wider range of services, thereby winning a larger market share.

The application of the Cooke ratio adds pressure to the French banks to maximise profitability. However, the adoption of a "dynamic" approach may also severely indent capital ratios without improving profitability if the pace of growth is maintained at the levels recorded from 1987 to 1989. It so happens that the need for capital has grown as foreign acquisitions have become more popular.

But the link-ups designed to strengthen own capital that have taken place appear to have resulted from constraints unique to the public sector banks, for whom the possibility of calling on the markets is somewhat limited by their very status. Of the four distinct *bancassurance* operations that had been established in France by 1991 (including the stake taken by AGF in Banque Française de Commerce Extérieur [BFCE]), three were between publicly-owned institutions. In addition, in order to bolster Crédit Lyonnais and BNP, the government arranged a series of asset swaps between state-controlled groups belonging to different economic sectors (see Chapter 4).

The 10 percent share swap between UAP and BNP — both publicly-owned — allowed the latter to increase its capital to the tune of FF5 billion ($88 million).

BNP issued new securities in return for UAP shares.[5] While such transactions do not violate the rules set down by the Bank for International Settlements (BIS), the idea that own funds can be "created" without capital actually changing hands leaves foreign, and especially Anglo-Saxon, banks perplexed.

Even more significant was GAN's acquisition of majority control of CIC, which should enable the bank to recapitalise and allow it to overhaul a regional network which has been lacking funds for a number of years. But given the dissimilar sizes of the participants, the coming together of CIC and GAN looks more like the "taking on of a burden" by the latter rather than a real *bancassurance*-type operation like that between BNP and UAP.

Although such transactions help to meet the overall Cooke ratio of 8 percent, as we have already noted it is still the case that "hard core" (Tier 1) capital is low compared to that of European competitors. Also, the extent to which such methods actually increase the competitiveness of banks is questionable, especially when it is known that they do not bring in any fresh money and entail "obligations" towards the purveyor of such capital — the state.[6]

The situation was quite different with Suez's takeover of Victoire because in this case the bank gained control of the insurance company rather than vice versa. In addition, as Suez is not a retail bank, there is no question of this being *bancassurance* in the pure meaning of the term, whereby the bank uses its branch network to distribute insurance products.

One could also argue that, after having opposed each other for so long, bankers and insurers now seem to perceive each others' profession as more complementary than appeared previously, especially regarding savings management. They each address the same clientele with increasingly similar products like SICAVs, life insurance and even loans. However, difficulties persist as to the best way of making this work. Among the various forms *bancassurance* takes in France — cross-shareholdings, takeovers and own growth — the last seems for the moment to be the most fruitful in terms of diversifying business connected with the taking in of household savings.

Own growth — in other words the development by a bank itself of insurance-related services through the creation of specialist subsidiaries using the distribution channels of the parent bank — seems much closer to the basic idea behind *bancassurance*. On the surface it is an attractive solution; the bank is thus able to offer a complete package of services to customers while holding full control of the company established. This is the way that almost all credit institutions have entered the life insurance market — resulting in almost one-third of all premiums

collected in 1990 going to *bancassurance* entities (see Chapter 5).

Banquindustrie

In the late 1980s and early 1990s, French banks developed an interest in industrial shareholdings. Beside the industrial participations traditionally held by the two merchant-bank oriented *compagnies financières*, Paribas and Suez, the large deposit-taking banks like Crédit Lyonnais, Société Générale and BNP together with smaller ones like CCF, began including such participations in their portfolios starting in the mid-1980s.

Among the deposit-takers, the trend was set by Crédit Lyonnais whose ambitions to become a great German-style universal bank (aiming to maintain a director on the boards of its main corporate customers) has been quite manifest and has formed the basis for its strategy for a number of years. In fact, taking its inspiration from the Germanic model, Crédit Lyonnais increased its industrial participations 18-fold in the space of four years.[7] Although BNP and even more so Société Générale have reserved judgment about such an approach, that has not stopped them from following the trend and leaping ahead with increases of over 500 percent in their participations over the same period. The total value of participations held by the main French banking groups in industry and commerce had reached almost FF160 billion ($28 billion) by 1991 (see Table 2.13).

Table 2.13	
French banks' industrial shareholdings (in FF bn)	
Paribas	53.4
Groupe Suez	48.0
Crédit Lyonnais	26.0
Société Générale	15.0
BNP	12.0
CCF	2.5

The motivations behind the banks' desire to become involved in this new activity are mostly economic and financial:

• Between 1985 and 1989, the robust health of the Paris Bourse and the subsequent improvement in corporate profits made investment in industry more attractive;

- Following the Chirac government's privatisations, corporates felt more secure in relying on powerful partners — such as banks — as their "hard core" shareholders;

- The approach of the single European market has made French corporates aware of the need to attain critical mass. Thus, since the mid-1980s they have been implementing an intensive external growth strategy to compensate for previous waywardness. This demands fresh funds for acquisitions abroad and an internal capital structure which is sufficiently strong to stave off counterattacks by foreign groups. The banks, conscious of the reciprocal advantages to be derived from such "solidarity" in international competition, have not hesitated to reinforce their links with industry;

- The shareholding trend among banks fits in with their attempts to revitalise relations with companies ("corporate finance business") which had turned away from bank credit in favour of direct funding on the capital markets. It is clear that non-intermediated corporate financing has forced the banks to seek other means of retaining their corporate customers: buying stakes, in the opinion of some bankers, should give them a privileged position in proposing other banking services to corporates, especially on the M&A market and when it comes to financial engineering where commissions are high.

But such a strategy of industrial participations is not without inherent dangers. Besides the conflicts of interest that may arise between the commercial and investment bank sides (cf. Crédit Lyonnais), the fact that the bank should be both creditor and investor in the same company could turn out to be disastrous if the company has problems meeting payments. Such was indeed the case at the end of the 1970s when Paribas was obliged by the government to intervene to save Générale de Fonderie; this deal resulted in a loss of FF600 million ($106 million).

And last, bank/industry alliances may turn out to be fragile because of their large reliance on market growth and especially on growth in industrial production, for which the outlook in 1991 was less than stable (INSEE forecasted a growth rate of 4 percent as against 13 percent in 1990).

Conclusion

Deregulation, financial innovation, the development of new technologies and the breaking down of market divisions are all factors that have contributed to loosening the constraints that bound French financial institutions. The same factors have also contributed to modifying the environment in which institutions work and how they carry out their business, thus affecting the way competition operates in France. Therefore, the cost of entry into certain traditional activities is falling and will continue to fall steadily. But while a certain number of standardised services can now be offered by "non-branch" banks or even "non-banks", branch networks have not lost their importance in retail banking.

In a highly internationalised capital market, France appears to be one of Europe's most interesting financial centres, though the possibilities for a foreign bank to buy a network on the French market are limited. The ones that might interest potential acquirers belong either to the co-operative/mutual bank sector or are publicly-owned.

Big private sector banks like Société Générale, Paribas and Indosuez or medium-sized ones like CCF and Crédit du Nord, all have capital structures which are largely closed to outsiders. But besides the fact that capital is tied up, the French private sector banks and the banking sector in general is "protected" by a very effective coat of mail made up of alliances, both explicit and implicit, between public and private-sector institutions. These alliances go into action to repulse any outside attack.

When one examines closely the main French financial constellations, one can spot this entanglement of interests. Shoulder to shoulder with private sector companies, one finds giants of the public sector and as often as not — despite their vague protestations of independence — they are tied to each other by informal and formal links of varying degrees of consistency. The French market, while it remains highly attractive, is still difficult for foreigners to penetrate. The partial privatisations announced by the government in September 1991 ought not really change this situation in the short term.

Endnotes

(1) The 10 largest branch-based credit institutions (including Crédit Agricole, the Banques Populaires and Crédit Mutuel) are responsible for over 90 percent of these investments.

(2) An individual holding a cheque account uses on average 120 cheques per annum for an average value of less than FF250 ($44) each.

(3) France has a relatively high density of ATMs per inhabitant — lower than that of Japan and the US, but higher than that of Germany and Italy.

(4) UK (one terminal per 2,346 inhabitants), Germany (7,106), US (5,614).

(5) Apart from strengthening both institutions' own funds, this exchange of capital also gives them a greater margin of manoeuvre in issuing *titres participatifs* (participating securities).

(6) Some state-owned banks see themselves "pressurised" into undertaking corporate rescues, as in the case of BNP which took over Banque de Bretagne when it collapsed.

(7) The investments made by Crédit Lyonnais and by subsidiaries such as Clinvest and Altus Finance are many and it is not easy to find a clear strategy behind them.

Chapter 3

A Description of Banking Products

To fulfil their role as intermediaries between economic agents, banks offer a wide range of services and products to different customer segments: administration of payment facilities and the collection of deposits on the liabilities side of the bank balance sheet; loans and financing on the assets side.

The management of payments services

The personal customer
In return for the funds (especially demand deposits) that are entrusted to it, a bank must provide cash services that fit in with the overall range of services available and allow for the use of the funds deposited. One of the features that differentiates French retail banking from that in other developed countries is the fact that account management-related transactions are free for personal customers. However, many other cash and cash-related services are heavily priced. (All prices quoted in this chapter are based on average prices quoted by French banks for 1991.)

Cheques
The 1986 Finance Law removed the obligation that individuals must pay for articles worth over FF10,000 ($1,767) by cheque, but cash payments above certain thresholds continue to be forbidden. Since 1979, cheque books (which are issued free of charge) are pre-crossed and non-endorsable. They are not payable to the bearer (not payable to whoever holds them), are not transmittable by endorsement and may not be cashed at bank outlets. They can only be cashed by a bank or an equivalent institution. Nevertheless, cash withdrawals by the account holder are allowed.

Uncrossed and endorsable cheques can be endorsed by a third person other than a financial institution and they are subject to a stamp duty (of FF4.5, $0.80 cents, per cheque) that the bank levies on behalf of the Treasury. This unusual procedure gives the authorities the right to inspect the user's identity.

What is more, to insure against the risk of bad cheques, a creditor can demand payment by certified cheque (*chèque visé* or *chèque certifié*) or by bank cheque (*chèque bancaire*). A *chèque visé* carries the drawee's attestation that cover does exist. A *chèque certifié* (the price of which varies from FF35, $6.20 cents to FF85, $15) offers more protection to the extent that the bank guarantees to block the funds necessary to cover the cheque until the deadline for cashing the cheque has expired. Upon the client's request and at his expense — FF50 to 80 ($8 to $14), depending on the bank — banks will issue bank cheques for the benefit of a named beneficiary. Responsibility for paying the amount of the cheque until it becomes void — one year and eight days after it is drafted — lies with the issuing bank.

Generally speaking, we can say that cheques are due on demand and have to be cashed within a certain period of time (eight days if the cheque is issued in France, 20 days elsewhere in Europe or in a country bordering the Mediterranean, 70 days in another country). Once this deadline has passed, the bearer has fewer means of recovery, although the cheque remains valid for one year — the limit of validity — after which it becomes void.

Postal cheques, on the other hand, are governed by different rules, though disparities appear to be diminishing. Thus, for example, the validity of a postal cheque has increased from two months to one year.

Free cheques, the processing of which costs the banks almost FF4 ($0.70 cents) per cheque, is a subject arousing fierce debate within the industry at a time when lowering operating expenses is fundamental to improving banks' profitability. On the other hand, the banks are still reluctant to offer interest-bearing current accounts, which is the most obvious compensation for account management charges.

Those opposing the introduction of cheque fees argue that the banks recuperate part of their expenses by charging heavily for other services and/or by demanding various penalties. For example, most banks impose a penalty of up to FF300 ($53) for cheques that bounce. Likewise, banks make wide use of the "float" (*dates de valeur*) — undoubtedly a source of income. Two to three working days pass before a cheque is cleared if it is one of the bank's own; five working days if the cheque is drawn on another bank; and in general, two days elapse before cheques show up in an account.

Forms of payment

Creditor demands have led to ways to ensure that payment will be made for commercial transactions. Certain means exist through which the creditor can reduce the attending risk as follows:

Direct debits

This system depends on the debtor circulating a double standing order: one to his creditor that authorises him to issue a debit advice; the other to his bank that authorises it to pay this debit advice. The amount to be paid and the attending deadline are rarely decided in advance, and the creditor is required to send notice to the debtor shortly before the deadline expires. The debtor can then inject funds into his account or, alternatively, refuse to authorise the debit transaction. Only creditors backed by certain guarantees are allowed to make use of this vehicle (the electricity and gas board (EDF-GDF), the state post, telegraph and telephone company (PTT), insurance companies, etc).

Le Titre Interbancaire de Paiement *(TIP — The interbank payment order)*

This is a means of recovering debts automatically and is used by networked companies and organisa-tions. It was set up in 1987 in response to the drawbacks associated with the *Titre Universel de Paiement* (TUP — the universal payment order), which the TIP is intended to replace over time. What distinguishes the TIP from the TUP is the former's integration of postal and banking procedures. This allows for real interbank co-operation by breaking down the divisions that separate recovery channels and it is provided free of charge to bank customers. Despite these advantages, this mechanism was still not well known by the early 1990s.

Remittance of funds at customer's request

Upon the request of the account holder, the bank sends funds of a given amount to a specified branch or to a correspondent bank. Such an operation can be in favour of the account holder, the receiving bank or a third party's account.

For occasional transfers, prices vary depending on whether they come with a *relevé d'identité bancaire* (RIB — banking identity record) which are either free of charge or cost as much as FF41 ($7.24), or without a RIB (price: FF10 to FF60). Up to FF8 ($1.41) is charged per transaction for standing orders.

The procedure for the remittance of funds is similar to the interbank payment order, the only difference being that the operation goes through the intermediary of the Post Office by means of an order issued by the bank in the beneficiary's favour.

Payment cards

Payment cards make possible withdrawals of cash from ATM terminals. The limit on such withdrawals is FF3,000 ($530) per week (or more, depending on the institution and card type).

There are several kinds of payment cards: bank cards, credit cards and private label cards. Bank cards, issued by GIE (Groupe d'Intérêt Economique) Carte Bancaire are the most widespread in France.

While most cards allow access to a system of personal loans which come in the form of a standing overdraft facility (with an upper limit), bank cards are, for the most part, used simply as debit cards. Banks have only recently realised this and are now faced with competition from specialist operators and retailers who have pioneered electronic funds transfer at the point of sale (Eftpos).

International cards are covered by foreign exchange legislation. The card remains the property of the bank which thus has the right to withdraw it without justification. This type of card is widespread in France. In essence, the banks offer two types of international card: immediate debit cards (the most common), the annual fee on which is FF135 to FF175 — $24 to $31) and deferred payment cards with annual charges of FF135 ($24) to FF180 ($32).

Companies

To facilitate companies' handling of funds, a bank offers them cash services in the same way as it does individuals. However, given the greater risk, applications to open an account involve more complex procedures (the firm or corporate name, its field of activity and its entry in the Registry of Companies are scrutinised).

The company account or the current trading account

Legally, what distinguishes this account is the intention of the parties concerned (a consensual contract) and the existence and reciprocity of trade discounts (a trade discount is a claim that can take the form of money, goods or commercial paper). Each amount lodged on a current account pays interest on the day it returns to circulation. Interest can be reciprocal (the same rates for loans and deposits) or incremental (calculated at different rates of interest depending on whether there is a credit or debit balance). While the company account has the same advantages as the deposit account for individuals, other credit transactions (such as discounted bills, overdraft facilities and cash advances) are granted in accordance with individual agreements reached between the account holder and his banker.

Cash transactions

Companies can benefit from specific services (over and above those offered to individual customers). Thus, a bank can take responsibility for collecting the bills that a company will have placed with it, for paying domiciled bills (a notice of domiciliation authorises the bank to pay by debiting the company's account: what is more, it happens frequently that the company will place a standing order for this operation), and for issuing letters of credit to other bank branches (after which the company can make withdrawals or lodgments in places other than where the account was first opened).

Deposits

The acceptance of deposits from the general public and, to a lesser extent, from companies, is one of the three basic activities carried out by *établissements de crédit* (credit institutions), according to the Banking Law. By virtue of the monopoly that the authorities grant them, banks have to submit to strict supervision. A bank offers various products designed to satisfy the numerous needs of savers, whether it be a fair return for savings, security or investment projects. These deposits are recorded in different kinds of account, the legal standing of which is closely regulated.

We will now briefly describe several of these accounts: ordinary accounts (sight deposits) and the other types of account (special status accounts, time deposit accounts), as well as certificates of deposit (*bons de caisse* and *certificats de dépôt* [see Table 3.1]). High liquidity products (apart from certificates of deposit) are dealt with in Chapter 9.

Ordinary accounts

Since 1978, current and chequeing accounts are defined as "ordinary accounts". Before 1978, a distinction was made between current accounts (reserved for merchants and which could either be in credit or debt) and chequeing accounts (which were available to individuals but could only ever be in credit).

Interest-bearing ordinary (current) accounts have been forbidden in France since 1967. To overcome this obstacle, for the past one or two years several institutions (most notably Cortal, AGF [Banque Phénix] and Caixa Bank) have been offering interest-bearing current accounts linked to mutual funds (OPCVMs) conditional on payment of a "membership fee" of FF400 to FF700 ($70 to $123) per annum. Such products are directed at upscale retail customers.

In the early 1990s, Crédit Commercial de France (CCF) began offering interest-bearing current accounts linked to mutual funds. The move stoked the ire of other banks because CCF offers this type of current account (net of taxes) to American Express card holders. The big banks reacted negatively, firstly, because of their fear that the status quo would be upset and, secondly, because such accounts could

Table 3.1

Structure of funds taken in by the banks (%)

	1980	1985	1989
Regulated interest rate investments	69.6	64.2	55.5
of which:			
Non-interest bearing sight deposits	34.9	33.9	27.7
Sight investments*	16.2	18.3	14.1
Time deposit accounts	0.5	1.0	0.3
Bons de caisse	9.8	2.7	2.6
Contractual savings**	8.3	8.3	10.8
Investments offering market interest rates	30.3	35.8	44.5
of which:			
Deposits in foreign currencies	0.7	1.1	1.8
Time deposit accounts	11.8	8.0	5.8
Securities transactions	—	2.3	3.2
Certificates of deposit	—	0.9	13.4
Bond loans	8.2	13.9	14.5
Total (in FF bn)	1,133.0	2,002.3	3,090.6

* Sight investments = The Livret A and Livret Bleu, savings accounts subject to tax, the CODEVI, the LEP, The CEL

** Contractual savings = the PEL, the LEE

Source: Conseil National du Crédit

serve as a sort of Trojan Horse for American Express, which had long been looking for a way into the French market. Nevertheless, it appeared inevitable that the large banks would follow CCF's route sooner or later unless they wanted to see this cheap source of income's share of their overall funding drop still further.

Passbook savings accounts

Anybody, including minors, can open (or have opened on their behalf) a passbook savings account in a commercial or savings bank (where it is called a Livret B).[1] The amounts deposited are available on sight and can be withdrawn without notice. The initial minimum deposit is FF100 ($17) and there is no upper limit. Interest is calculated every fortnight with capitalisation occurring annually at a (regulated) rate of 4.5 percent, the same as that for the Livret A. But unlike the Livret A, revenue from a savings accounts is subject either to income tax or to a levy at source (at a rate of 38 percent in 1990). Given the low level of interest offered, the amounts

held in these accounts is falling all the time (down 9.3 percent in 1990).

Special status saving accounts

These are accounts whose workings are defined by specific legislative and regulatory provisions. Common to all are fixed, regulated interest rates that benefit from tax breaks. Likewise, ceilings are placed on the amounts that can be placed in each account. The rigidity of interest rates available on special status accounts (which have not changed since 1986) serves to explain their loss of appeal among savers. This disaffection has grown with the availability of new, high liquidity products and high interest-bearing financial instruments such as money market mutual funds and the Plan d'Epargne Populaire (people's savings plan — PEP). With the exception of the *Plan d'Epargne Logement* (PEL — home savings plan), all deposits in this category declined in 1990 (see Table 3.2).

Livret A and the Livret Bleu savings accounts are viewed as current accounts paying interest or as temporary investments. There is an upper limit on the amount placed in these accounts of FF90,000 ($15,908) per person and each member of a fiscal household (*foyer fiscal*) can open a savings book account. The (regulated) interest rate is 4.5 percent and income is exempt from taxes. A Livret A savings account can only be opened in a savings bank or at the Post Office-run Caisse Nationale d'Epargne, and a Livret Bleu account at a Crédit Mutuel outlet. (For more information about Livret Bleu see Crédit Mutuel, Chapter 4). But such accounts are mutually exclusive, meaning the holder of a Livret A cannot open a Livret Bleu account and vice versa.

In the course of 1990, these deposit products came under a lot of pressure despite the ceiling increase from FF80,000 ($14,140) to FF90,000 ($15,908). By then, the amounts under management were falling by up to FF25 billion ($4.4 billion) per year and their share of the relevant banks' funding was also diminishing. The main reason for this decline is because banks must offer non-competitive interest rates. Accounts tied to the money markets were attracting more customers.

The *Livret d'Epargne Populaire* (LEP — the people's savings account), available from all banks, was created in 1982 for people on low incomes (paying less than FF1,560 ($275) in taxes in 1988).

Table 3.2								
Changes in deposits taken in (growth rate in amounts under management in %)								
	Sight deposits	**Taxable savings accounts**	**Livret A and Livret Bleu**	**CODEVI**	**CEL**	**LEP**	**Time deposit accounts**	**PEL**
1989	8.8	-3.0	-0.5	2.9	7.3	8.5	-2.1	10.1
1990	2.7	-9.3	-1.5	-2.5	-1.9	-0.1	-0.8	1.7
Source: Banque de France								

An initial deposit of FF200 ($35) is needed, while the maximum deposit allowed is FF30,000 ($5,300). A married couple can each open a savings account, but not their children. The interest rate is 5.5 percent per year, net of taxes. Savings from which no withdrawals have been made for at least six months benefit from a bonus interest payment when the consumer price index exceeds the interest rate payable on the account.

The *Compte d'Epargne Logement* (CEL — the home savings account) is designed to allow people to obtain loans for the acquisition of homes, holiday homes, rented premises, or for the conversion or renovation of real estate. The minimum initial deposit is FF750 ($132), and FF150 ($26) for further lodgements. There must be a minimum balance kept in the account of FF750 (otherwise one may be forced to close it) over the minimum eight month period that it is opened and a maximum of FF100,000 ($17,676) (not including interest). Interest is calculated fortnightly and is not taxable. The interest rate is 2.75 percent, to which is added a state premium equivalent to five elevenths of the interest gained, up to a maximum of FF75,000 ($13,257). The actual size of the loan granted depends on interest gained and on the length of repayment (total interest due cannot exceed one and a half times the total interest gained). The maximum loan is FF150,000 ($26,514) at a rate of 4.25 percent, with an additional charge if a whole life insurance policy is attached. Loans can last from two to five years.

The *Plan d'Epargne Logement* (PEL — the home savings plan) is a form of savings that allows people obtain a loan at a subsidised rate for the purchase or renovation of a main residence at the end of four years. Unlike the home savings account, deposits are of a contractual nature and withdrawals are not allowed while savings are being accumulated. The initial deposit is FF1,500 ($265) and further annual

lodgements are required, from a minimum of FF3,600 ($636) (with the possibility of making further lodgements at any time) to an upper limit of FF400,000 ($71,000). Interest received is not taxable and is three-quarters the responsibility of the institution where the account is held and one-quarter the responsibility of the state. The rate of interest is 6 percent, but once an interest rate ceiling of FF10,000 (plus FF1,000 per dependent) is reached, savings are remunerated at a rate of 4.62 percent. To obtain a loan, the PEL must be of at least three years standing. Interest on the mortgage loan is 6.32 percent (plus life insurance), is of two to 15 years in duration and can have a maximum value of FF600,000 ($106,000). As opposed to the CEL, interest is payable at the end of the contract, even if the holder of the account does not request such a loan.

Home savings schemes enjoyed dazzling success up until 1987 with average annual growth rates of 20 percent. Thereafter, a slowdown occurred and in 1990 growth was below 2 percent, although home savings products (CEL, PEL) remained the second most important source of regulated interest rate funds for banks with FF600 billion ($106 billion) under management in 1990. In April 1992 the government decided to modify the terms of the PEL in order to stimulate the real estate sector.

The *Livret d'Epargne d'Entreprise* (LEE — the company savings book), designed to encourage the establishment or the recovery of businesses, and with operating procedures identical to those for the PEL, allows holders to benefit from a preferential interest rate at the end of the savings period. Only one such savings book can be opened per fiscal household. What distinguishes these accounts is the stipulation of a minimum initial lodgement of FF5,000 ($883), with further minimum annual deposits of at least FF3,600 ($636). The maximum amount that can be lodged in these savings books is FF200,000 ($35,353) (capitalised interest not included). Interest is calculated fortnightly and the annual interest rate is 3 percent. LEE income is tax-free. To obtain a loan, savings must have accumulated over a minimum two years period. There is no upper limit to the loan that can be obtained and the interest repayable is either fixed (at 6.5 percent) or flexible (6 percent at present). The period of the loan lasts from two to 15 years. Finally, and not the least of its advantages, the person who requests the loan can pass it to any individual entity (*personne physique*) wishing to take over his company. Despite the much vaunted benefits of this product, by 1990 sums under management had reached a mere FF1.8 billion ($318 million), the equivalent of 0.1 percent of regulated interest rate investments.

The *Compte pour le Développement Industriel* (CODEVI) — the industrial development account) is available from all bank networks. It pays the same rate of interest as the savings banks' Livret A (4.5 percent); interest is exempt from tax and withdrawals can be made freely. A husband and wife can each have a CODEVI account, but not their children. The maximum deposit has been fixed by the authorities at FF15,000 ($2,650) per account as and from August 1991, or FF30,000 ($5,300) per fiscal household. Funds attracted to these accounts are invested in bonds issued by the banks or certificates issued by the Caisse des Dépôts et Consignations (CDC) and are used to supply industry with loans and small and medium-sized enterprises with reduced interest loans.

The maximum interest rate on CODEVI loans was reduced from 9.25 to 8.75 percent in 1991. But such loans were thereafter reserved for companies with turnover of less than FF100m ($17.6 million) (as opposed to FF500 million previously) or for subsidiaries of companies whose turnover does not exceed FF100 million.

Time deposit accounts

Being straight investments, time deposit accounts only allow for further injections or withdrawals of cash. In addition, while they give a better return than sight deposits or savings accounts, they offer only limited liquidity (otherwise their advantage is lost). To combat these constraints, since January 1 1991 no limit has been placed on the interest paid for deposits of over one month's duration, irrespective of the amount.[2]

Once remuneration has been agreed upon, the saver requests the bank to freeze an amount of money on account for a fixed duration. This amount has to be over FF5,000 ($883) (there is no ceiling) for a period that can vary from one month to a maximum of five years, with a rate of interest and tax treatment that does not change over time. Interest is paid at the end of the period in question. The holder of a time deposit account can choose between being taxed on income or a compulsory levy of 38 percent (starting in 1990).

Bons de caisse

Bons de caisse are instruments representing an interest-bearing loan made by the holder. They are not the equivalent of transferable securities and are not quoted on the stock market (with the exception of negotiable *bons* which bear similarities to short-term debenture loans).

The lowest value *bon de caisse* that can be issued is for FF1,000 ($176) (in practice this turns out to be FF5,000). The *bon* can be issued for a minimum period of one month and a maximum of five years. Interest paid can go from a bottom rate up to the money market rate. The interest — which is calculated according to the duration of the investment — can be paid in advance for the first two years or paid at maturity if beyond two years. The *bons* can be anonymous (made out to the holder) or nominal. Anonymous *bons* are transferable and interest obtained is subject to a tax at source rate of 52 percent, plus 2 percent on the face value of the certificate. In the case of nominal *bons*, the holder can choose between being taxed on income or a compulsory levy of 38 percent (starting in 1990).

Since 1986, banks have issued five-year *bons de caisse*, called *bons d'épargne* (savings bonds). They have similar characteristics to the (fixed term) *bons de caisse*, but apart from being redeemable at any time from the third month onwards, the interest payable increases according to the duration of the investment. Finally, interest payments are only made from the fourth month on, insofar as the saver can choose redemption from then onwards. This particular vehicle means the holder does not have to set a precise "sunset" for the period of his investment. *Bons de caisse* have been in decline since the beginning of the 1980s, with the regulated interest rate certificates more affected than the market-driven interest rate ones (see Table 3.2).

Certificats de Dépôt (*Certificates of Deposit*)

Instituted in 1985, certificates of deposit are fixed-term negotiable bills with a duration of between 10 days and seven years. They are issued in francs for residents and in dollars or Ecus for nonresidents by authorised intermediaries. They can be made out to the holder or to order. Their minimum value is FF1,000,000 ($176,765) and interest paid (which is not subject to any restrictions) approaches that available on the money market. As regards taxation, holders have the choice between declaring income or a standard deduction of 34 percent. Capital gains are classed as income.

Since they were introduced in 1985, they have become one of the main sources of funding for the banks. Of the FF850 billion ($150 billion) under management, almost 80 percent is held by the public (non-financial agents and mutual funds). In fact, certificates of deposit play an essential role in cash management, especially for companies.

The Plan d'Epargne Populaire (*PEP — the people's savings plan*)

This addition to the family of products offered by financial institutions dates back to December 1989. It is a savings plan lasting a maximum of 10 years. Minimum deposits are FF2,400 ($424) per year with a ceiling of FF600,000 ($106,059) (interest not included). Interest is tax-exempt and the guaranteed rate varies from institution to institution (from 6 to 8 percent). Income benefits from a tax holiday when PEPs are retained for at least eight years. To leave the plan before four years are up leads to a tax levy at source of 38 percent and of 17 percent if one leaves the plan between the fourth and eighth year. For people not liable to tax, an annual bonus is awarded, worth 25 percent of the interest payment up to a maximum bonus of FF1,500 ($265). This bonus disappears once the saver becomes subject to tax.

The launch of this highly tax efficient product has undoubtedly contributed to the fall in certain regulated interest rate investments, especially the Livret A and the Livret Bleu. In 1990, PEP deposits totalled FF105 billion ($18 billion) of which FF85 billion was taken in by the banks (see Table 3.3). The 1991 figures exceeded FF200 billion ($35.3 billion). Nine and a half million plans have been taken out, half by households which are not liable to pay tax.

Table 3.3		
The PEP in 1990		
	No. of plans (millions)	Funds taken in (in FF bn)
Crédit Agricole	2.2	40.0
Savings banks	1.0	19.0
AFB member banks	1.3	13.5
Other institutions	0.8	12.5
Total		
Banks	5.3	85.0
Insurance companies	1.5	20.0
Overall	6.8	105.0
Source: Notes Bleues, quarterly supplement, 1991/I		

The market for credit

Granting loans is one of French credit institutions' main business lines, while the relative weight of the different types of credit on the market varies from one type of bank to another.

As Table 3.4 illustrates, the AFB-member or commercial banks are especially strong in the areas of export credit, short-term loans for corporates and personal loans. The latter is also a market where finance companies are particularly strong, while the savings banks and the Caisse des Dépôts et Consignations (CDC) account for the greater share of housing loans. The market shares for investment loans is more or less proportionate to the size of the institution in question.

Given that the types of credit available are numerous, the following is merely a description of the main developments in products for personal customers and companies.

The personal market

Although neglected for a long time, by the mid-1980s the personal market had become one of the main battlegrounds between credit institutions trying to mitigate the effects of disintermediation and to improve margins. It would be opportune to examine the two most important sections of this market separately: the market for cash loans (consumer credit) and mortgage loans. Growth rates for both of these slowed drastically between 1988 and 1991, especially for cash loans (see Table 3.5).

Table 3.4

Market shares for the main types of credit

	Short-term loans (corporates)	Investment loans	Export loans	Housing loans	Short-term loans (individuals)
AFB-member banks	79.0	26.6	92.5	27.8	40.4
Banques Populaires	5.8	4.2	1.9	2.9	4.5
Crédit Agricole	10.1	20.8	3.7	20.4	14.6
Crédit Mutuel	1.2	2.6	0.2	4.1	6.0
Finance companies and broking firms	3.7	23.7	1.6	6.1	32.4
Savings banks and Caisse des Dépôts	0.1	22.1	—	38.7	2.1
Overall	100.0	100.0	100.0	100.0	100.0

Source: Banque de France, AFB

Table 3.5

Gross figures (in FF bn)			Changes in credits	Change over 12 months (in %)		
Dec. '88	Dec. '89	Dec. '90		Dec. '88	Dec. '89	Dec. '90
4,715.5	5,285.7	5,878.0	**Total credits**	11.8	12.1	11.2
2,161.1	2,507.1	2,907.0	**Corporates**	13.2	16.0	16.0
577.7	678.4	810.0	Corporate short-term	26.2	17.4	19.4
922.9	1,076.4	1,220.0	Corporate investment	9.8	16.6	13.3
394.4	416.4	443.0	Commercial property [1]	5.9	5.6	6.4
266.1	335.9	434.0	Other credits	11.3	26.2	29.2
1,982.1	2,165.2	2,327.0	**Personal**	11.7	9.2	7.5
320.2	369.6	405.0	Personal short-term	24.3	15.4	9.6
1,260.2	1,352.9	1,442.0	Personal property	8.7	7.4	6.6
401.7	442.7	480.0	Other credits	12.2	10.2	8.4
572.3	613.4	644.0	**Other resident economic agents**	5.9	7.2	5.0

[1] = Loans granted to building and house rental companies

Source: Banque de France

Personal cash loans and consumer credit

Today it is becoming increasingly difficult to distinguish between "cash loans" in the strict sense and consumer credit, as the former are used more and more to meet consumption needs.

(Short-term) credit facilities

Temporary facilities allow borrowers to cover short-term lags in cash flow by allowing their accounts to fall into debit balances for an amount and for a duration of time set by the bank. To use this type of loan, the beneficiaries' (individuals or companies) accounts should show frequent movement on the credit and debit side. The amount made available is calculated on the size of turnover or income and should not exceed the total of one month's activity. Sometimes, banks ask for personal guarantees (for example, the security of another person who takes it upon himself to pay in case the borrower defaults, or in the case of a company, the personal guarantees of its owners) and more rarely for collateral (depositing of transferable securities).

Advances against securities authorise the customer to go into debt on his account depending on the value and the type of security offered as guarantee. Interest due, as for overdrafts, is calculated in relation to the duration of the loan (at average monthly rather than annualised interest rates). Securities (shares, bonds, stocks) offered as guarantee are at the heart of an agreement on collateral that specifies their nature and quality. Generally, to be protected against the ups and downs of the stock markets, the loan granted is for a value lower than the value of the security.

A *crédit personnel* is a credit transfer into an account and is granted more by reference to the standing of the borrower than to the use to be made of the loan. The amount extended generally does not exceed three months income and is given for a period ranging from three to 36 months, at interest rates of around 14 to 19 percent (not including insurance or administrative charges). The conditions that the customer must meet in the case of default or early repayment are established at the outset. The Scrivener Law of January 10 1978 stipulates that the borrower shall have a one-week period after accepting a loan during which he can withdraw from the obligations undertaken.

Banks also offer standing or revolving loans, taking money market rates or the base bank rate plus 5 to 7 points as benchmarks. These involve making sums available which do not exceed three months of the customer's income. The customer can use these funds as he wishes. Credit lines are renewed as repayments are made. This type of credit is not covered by the Scrivener Law.

Consumer credit

These credits enable deferred payment of domestic consumer goods and are sold mainly by specialist firms (Cetelem, Sovac, Cofinoga, etc). They have the same features as personal loans but their cost is generally higher.

Instalment payments are playing less and less of a significant role in the personal cash loan market: from the period 1986 to 1991, they decreased from 50 to 25 percent of the total of such credits. On the other hand, *prêts personnels* (personal loans) and *avances sur comptes débiteurs* (advances on debit accounts) are increasing in popularity, accounting for over 50 percent of the total in 1991, compared to

30 percent in 1981. Inroads made by other, less straightforward, forms of credit such as leasing,[3] help to explain changes in the structure of such loans.

A market that is drying up

Cash loans to individuals made up 2.8 percent of personal disposable income in 1981 and thereafter grew to reach a high point of 6.4 percent in 1987. The trend then reversed and the figure fell to less than 4 percent in 1990.

Despite spectacular growth, the boom in consumer credit appeared to have ended by the early 1990s. First, for a variety of reasons (a slowdown in salary increases, rising unemployment), households cut their purchases of consumer durables, particularly cars. Second, specialist credit institutions became more selective in the personal loans they granted following the adoption of the Law on Indebtedness (the Neiertz Law).

The result was a severe downturn in activity which simply contributed further to margin erosion. The shake up in the market impacted negatively on small institutions, whether banking subsidiaries or not. It became more and more difficult for small banks to serve this market segment; only the larger groups (Cetelem, Sofinco, and — to a lesser extent — Sovac) appeared able to cope with the crisis.

Loans for housing

These loans constitute by far the largest contribution banks make to the funding of household expenditure (see Table 3.5).

The French mortgage market is one of Europe's most complicated because of the growing diversity of financial intermediaries, the variety of products and terms on offer and, more particularly, the co-existence of a strictly regulated public housing market alongside a free market for mortgage loans. In addition, these markets have always been precisely organised by the state through Crédit Foncier de France (CFF).

There are three overall classes of mortgage loan:

i)   Subsidised loans

   • *Prêts d'Accès à la Propriété* (PAP — home ownership loans) are financed directly by the

CFF and benefit from direct state budgetary aid in the form of relief on interest repayments. Properties have to be the borrower's main residence, must be used for home building, acquisition or improvement and must fulfil certain price criteria. What is more, to have access to *l'aide personnalisée au logement* (personalised home purchase assistance), the borrower's own financial resources must be below a stipulated ceiling.

- *Prêts pour la Location* (PLA — rental loans) are granted solely by the CDC and CFF and are restricted to HLMs (*habitations à loyer modéré* — council flats) and mixed economy companies having signed a contract with the state.

ii) Discounted property loans

- Discounted property loans (with no government assistance) are available from banks that have signed an agreement with the CFF. The ceilings established for these loans are published every six months by the CFF, to which is added the bank's margin (not exceeding 1.5 percent). Loans are made for the purpose of buying a primary residence, and the accommodation in question must fulfil certain price and size criteria. Construction and home purchase loans are of 10 to 20 years duration, while loans for home improvements last between five and 12 years and there must be a personal contribution of 10 percent of the total outlay.

Discounted property loans may be refunded by the CFF but, in practice, funding comes from available home savings resources or through the mortgage market. (See the sections on PELs and CELs.)

iii) *Prêts libres* (repayment-instalments-at-will loans) are generally discountable medium-term credits with a maximum duration of seven years. The Bank of France delegates to the CFF the power to authorise individual (discountable) loans of up to FF750,000 ($133,000), thus accounting for practically all loans of this type.

Whether subsidised, discountable or re-payable-at-will, banks will generally require the client to take out a life insurance policy and even unemployment insurance to cover the risks of non-payment.

Structural changes favouring repayment-at-will
The funding of housing, in which subsidised and discounted loans used to play such a significant role, altered radically in favour of commercial sector mortgage loans during the 1980s (see Table 3.6).

Table 3.6 Market shares for new housing loans		
	1981	1988
Banks and finance companies	48	69
Crédit Foncier	14	8
CDC and the savings banks	31	20
Others	7	3
Total	**100**	**100**
Subsidised loans	35	19
Non-subsidised loans	65	81
Total	**100**	**100**
Source: Banque de France		

What happened was that, after the abolition of credit corsets in 1987, the commercial banks began competing fiercely for a share of the repayment-at-will market. As a result, their market share of new housing loans increased to over 50 percent of the total by 1991.

The rapid increase in French housing prices undoubtedly had the effect of reducing the usefulness of subsidised loans (PAPs and PLAs) because the funds on offer are limited. Complementary loans have had to be added to make up the difference.

By the early 1990s, the government was examining the possibility of replacing the system of PAP home ownership loans with a single mechanism for individuals borrowing from the commercial banks. This way, the state would pay out of its budget a "single" premium to credit institutions granting this type of mortgage credit.

The volume of discounted property loans has been declining with low interest loans tending to yield ground before a tide of loans linked to PEL deposits. The slowdown in housing construction has played a role in this change too, because PELs are much more adaptable to types of financing other than for main residences.

The large retail banks (the *trois vieilles* and Crédit Agricole) have dominated this market. Together, they have been granting almost two-thirds of new personal mortgage loans.

The "sudden" appearance of the commercial banks on the mortgage scene and their growing penetration bears similarities to the trend observed among British clearing banks at the beginning of the 1980s. In France, however, in the absence of vibrant competition from other sources as is the case with Britain's building societies, the large commercial banks alone have pushed forward the "privatisation" of home funding.

Finally, the continued financing of low-cost housing was experiencing deepening crisis up to the end of 1991 because of the fall off in Livret A deposits taken in by the savings banks that were specifically designed for funding such housing. These trends highlighted the hold repayment-at-will loans had on the housing market.

The corporate market
Since 1988, corporate loans have been growing strongly. In 1990, only investment loans experienced a downturn in growth (from 16.6 to 13.3 percent) while other types of corporate loans continued to advance rapidly (see Table 3.5).

Short-term loans
A bank grants short-term loans to companies to allow them to overcome temporary capital shortfalls. These last less than two years with repayment coming out of the company's current operations. In contrast to investment loans, their growth has accelerated. An increasing proportion of loans whose use is not defined ("miscellaneous") are in reality cash flow loans or *crédits globaux d'exploitation* (global operating loans).

There are three main forms of short-term credit: i) transactional loans; ii) loans for financing trade or occupational debts, and iii) diverse.

i)   *Crédits par caisse* (transactional loans) encompass many different types of loan, of which the most popular are *facilités de caisse* (overdraft

facilities for occasional cashflow needs), *découverts* (overdrawn balances) for cashflow needs on a more periodical basis and *crédits de campagne* (seasonal loans), of use particularly in supporting seasonal business. The latter provide exceptionally large outlays of funds.

These loans involve no trading guarantee and they finance general or specialist needs. On the other hand, they often do require a personal guarantee or collateral (the securing of a mortgage, a *nantissement* [pledge] and, most frequently, *cautions* [sureties]).

ii)   Loans for financing trade or occupational debts: forms of credit available to companies to surmount the frequent time lag between sales and payment. These include:

L'escompte (discount bills). These were particularly popular through the mid-1980s, but by 1991 they accounted for only one-fifth of corporate cashflow loans (as opposed to almost 40 percent in 1985). When a bank grants a discount bill, it provides its client with a loan that will be paid on the due date by a third party. The bank has to be sure of the client's standing (the grantor) and of that of the party paying the bill (the grantee) by consulting the Bank of France's central files of instances of non-payment. To avoid tying up capital, the bank can realise discount bills on the money market that will then be taken up by other banks or by the Bank of France.

The *crédit de mobilisation des créances commerciales* (CMCC — commercial debt discount loans) are instruments introduced by the Bank of France in 1967 to mitigate some of the drawbacks of discount bills (a lot of paperwork and high administrative costs). These have not encountered the success expected of them. They still represented less than 1 percent of short-term credits by 1991. Apart from being more expensive and less flexible than discount bills, the CMCCs in use do not allow banks to transfer discounted assets to their own advantage and thus constitute credits without collateral.

Dailly loans, ensuing from the Dailly Law of 1981 and modified in the 1984 Banking Law, work by transferring business debts to credit institutions. They were developed in order to facilitate access to CMCCs.

iii)   Banks also offer other forms of (all-purpose) credit, of which the most important are *crédits/avances sur marchandises* (loans/advances against merchandise), *crédits par signature* (loans endorsed by the bank) and *crédits sur commandes publiques* (public sector contract credits — used to discount debts arising out of contracts signed with public bodies.)

The *crédit global d' exploitation* — which aims to simplify funding of the operating cycle — has been on the market for the past two or three years and is growing rapidly in popularity. It can be denominated both in francs and in other currencies, lasts one year and is available at money-market-linked rates.

Directed primarily at small and medium-sized enterprises (SMEs), banks demand a complete set of figures to evaluate the soundness of the company in question (which must have been in existence for at least two fiscal years).

Finally, the importance in France of *crédits inter-entreprises* or *crédits fournisseurs* where the creditors actually fulfil the role of financial intermediary in place of the banks, must be noted. Loans of this type, which have their origin in the length of payment delays, amounted to FF1,800 billion to 2,000 billion ($318 billion to $353 billion) in 1991, or around two and a half times the amount of short-term bank loans granted to companies.

Investment financing

Since 1985, there has been a strong desire on the part of the authorities to reduce to the minimum their involvement in the investment financing of companies. Nonetheless, almost FF40 billion ($7 billion) in new loans at preferential rates were granted in 1990.

Medium-term bank loans

These are extended by banks working on their own or working in tandem with a specialist financial institution for a period of two to seven years, depending either on the life of the asset being financed, the type of guarantees offered or the financial capacity of the company (before, during and after the loan operation). These loans can either be re-discountable (in which case debts may be realised) or not, but in all cases loan financing does not cover the total value of the investment (but generally from 50 to 75 percent).

Non-discountable (and not officially regulated) medium-term loans offer some subtle benefits which explain their growth: most notably, the rapid processing of applications because the bodies responsible for re-discounting do not intervene.

Long-term bank loans

Lasting from seven to 20 years, these are issued by specialised bodies, such as Crédit National, Crédit Foncier, etc. Banks often simply act as a relay, sometimes taking on board some of the risk.

Prêts participatifs *(Subordinated debt)*

Set up in 1978, this is aid extended by banks or the state to small and medium-sized enterprises. Beyond a set rate of interest, the lender receives payment that varies depending on the borrower's performance or results. Use of this instrument means that all other creditors have priority if the company experiences financial difficulties. From the point of view of the borrower, this device is the equivalent to supplying capital for the entire length of the loan.

Multi-option facilities (MOF)

This loan instrument, developed in 1986, marries the techniques of spot and international loans. Expressed in dollars, Ecus, French francs or other Euro-currencies, MOFs have an exchange value of FF500 million ($88 million) to FF5 billion. They are generally of five years duration, with the possibility of extending them a further two. They can be used in two different ways on a revolving basis; by issues of a minimum of FF50 million ($8.8 million) (and subsequent multiples of this amount) and by unconfirmed lines of credit (the company can call upon other types of financing: Treasury bills, Euro-commercial paper, short-term advances). Advantages associated with MOFs are security, flexibility, and cost efficiency.

Endnotes

(1)   These accounts can only be used for a limited number of operations: the lodgement or the withdrawal of cash, the cashing of cheques or transfers to and from an ordinary account.

(2)   This measure is applied equally to term accounts and *bons de caisse* (certificates of deposit). Deregulation also permits automatic transfers from sight accounts to passbook savings accounts within the same institution but not the reverse.

(3)   These are largely rentals with a purchase option — most often of cars which account for 71 percent of all leases.

Chapter 4

The Main French Banking Groups

The 1984 Banking Law introduced considerable changes to banking regulations, with universality as the guiding principle. The Law aimed to bring all credit institutions, whatever their standing, under a common legal framework according to their business. However, the Law does not seek to abolish immediately all the distinguishing features of each institution. Instead, it defines a number of broad categories, depending on whether the institution is authorised to accept deposits and depending on a given bank's particular status and identity; the AFB banks (members of the French Banking Association), the mutual and co-operative banks, the savings banks, the Crédit Municipal banks, the finance companies and the specialist financial institutions. The main groups and networks belonging to each category are described in the following pages. Also considered will be the financial services of the Post Office, which are not subject to the Banking Law.

The banks were all faced with two major challenges during 1990: the first was the narrowing of interest rate margins resulting from increased competition and customers' demands that their savings give a better return; second was the sharp increase in risks, which meant that a growing share of gross operating income had to be allocated to provisions.

The main AFB banks

The AFB banks make up the greater part of the French banking sector. They had a 50 percent plus market share in deposits and credits in 1990, and accounted for 56 percent of the industry's assets (see Table 4.1). In 1986, the state-owned banks accounted for between 80 and 90 percent of the AFB banks' deposits and credits, but privatisation subsequently cut this to less than 50 percent of AFB banking operations and 30 percent of the total for all credit institutions.

The 418 banks in this category include a range of institutions varying considerably in size, but dominated by a few major ones. Six banking groups alone — BNP, Crédit Lyonnais, Société Générale, Banque Paribas, Banque Indosuez and Crédit Industriel et Commercial (CIC) — account for roughly 55 percent of the total assets of AFB banks. Some of these banks are numbered among the world's largest in terms of total assets, but are smaller when measured by own funds (see Chapter 2).

Banque Nationale de Paris (BNP)

Banque Nationale de Paris, which was nationalised in 1945, resulted from the merger in 1966 of two public sector banks (Comptoir National d'Escompte and Banque Nationale pour le Crédit Industriel) following the financial reforms introduced by Prime Minister Michel Debré. It was re-nationalised in 1982.

With assets of around FF1,480 billion ($261 billion) at the end of 1990, BNP was France's second largest bank behind Crédit Agricole and one of the main operators on the financial markets. In 1990, BNP had more than FF50 billion ($8.8 billion) in own funds (capital and reserves plus *titres participatifs* [participating securities]) divided almost equally between share capital on the one hand and *titres subordonnés* (subordinated notes) and *titres participatifs* on the other. Its Cooke ratio was in the 8.5 to 9.0 percent range. In 1990 BNP had a network of 2,000 branches throughout metropolitan France (equivalent to 7.9 percent of all permanent outlets), and 63,000 employees worldwide, with 45,700 lo-

Table 4.1					
Banks' market share in 1990 (in %)					
	Credits	**Deposits**	**Commitments to customers**	**Housing loans**	**Consumer credit**
AFB-member banks	51.5	53.9	68.1	29.9	42.9
Mutual and co-operative banks	21.9	27.2	9.5	28.7	23.4
Savings banks	4.3	13.7	0.8	11.8	2.9
Crédit Municipal banks	0.3	0.2	—	—	3.1
Finance companies	7.4	3.5	16.1	14.4	27.5
Specialist financial institutions (IFS)	14.6	1.4	5.5	15.2	0.2
Securities houses	—	0.1	—	—	—
Total	**100.0**	**100.0**	**100.0**	**100.0**	**100.0**
Source: Commission Bancaire					

cated in France. Staff levels, however, were being cut as the bank pursued a rationalisation policy.

BNP held over 20 percent of capital in 24 French financial institutions, 61 foreign financial institutions and 14 other French and foreign companies (insurance, property, computers, etc). Its industrial shareholdings were continually growing (to roughly FF15 billion [$2.6 billion]).[1]

Separate from its own branch network is BNP's strong international presence through its links with the ABECOR group (Algemene Bank Nederland, Banque Bruxelles Lambert, Banque Internationale à Luxembourg, Barclays Bank, Dresdner Bank, Hypo-Bank, Österreichische Landerbank) and other international commercial banks such as Banca Nazionale del Lavoro, Bank of America, etc.

A strong corporate client base, both in terms of small and medium-sized enterprises and large corporates, provides BNP with a distinct advantage. And in 1990 BNP was the leader in discounted bills with a market share of 16 percent. In the area of traditional banking activities it handled 13 percent of real estate and 9 percent of personal loans. It was also market leader along with Crédit Lyonnais in the term deposit market, with a 14 percent market share. Its subsidiary, Natio Vie, was the tenth largest French life insurer, not including the cross-shareholding arrangement between BNP and France's largest insurer UAP (see Chapter 7).

BNP, either directly or through one of its specialised subsidiaries, is one of France's leading OPCVM (collective investment schemes) managers behind Crédit Agricole and the CDC-Poste-Caisse d'Epargne group. While BNP's market activities are sizeable it is only midway down the rankings of French banks in this regard; it is fifth in terms of Eurobond issues and sixth in primary issues by French companies (see Appendix 4.2). Nonetheless, (in common with all the public sector banks), one of BNP's weak spots is the lack of "fresh" money (cash), a problem which neither cross-shareholdings nor the involvement of the state as shareholder, generous though it is, can resolve. While the bank has gone on a spending spree, the growth in the issue of hybrid securities (*titres participatifs et subordonnés*), which take the form of quasi-share capital, may pose serious problems for the future.

BNP's subsidiary, Banexi, is ranked second behind Lazard Frères in the French mergers and acquisitions market and the bank has played a substantial role in some important deals: Lyonnaise des Eaux, Stafor-Facon, UTA-Air France etc.

Despite its impressive standing in the market, BNP experienced a steady decline in gross operating results in the period 1987 to 1991, with operating costs increasing faster than net banking income (34 percent versus 21 percent). In addition, its average return on assets was one of the lowest among the major banks, mainly as a result of its policy of pursuing market share. In the midst of the decline occurring during this period, 1989 was the only exceptional year for BNP — with steady growth in profits, an improvement in the rate of return on capital (13.8 percent, although the objective was 15 percent), and a strengthened capital structure despite the extra provisioning made to offset worsening conditions in certain subsidiaries (BIAO, BAII etc) (see Table 4.2).[2]

Table 4.2					
Consolidated figures for BNP **(FF bn under management)**					
	1986	1987	1988	1989	1990
Total assets	916.0	975.0	1,193.0	1,340.0	1,486.0
Customer deposits	364.0	387.0	479.0	553.0	662.0
Customer loans	375.0	432.0	540.0	675.0	759.0
Own funds	18.2	20.4	23.1	28.8	41.0
Participating securities	7.6	7.3	17.2	17.6	n/a
Net banking income	29.5	29.7	31.9	34.9	35.9
Gross operating profit	10.0	9.3	9.6	11.2	9.7
Provisions allocated to reserves	5.1	4.4	4.3	6.8	7.2
Net profit after minority interests	3.0	2.8	3.1	3.4	1.6
ROE (in %)	16.5	13.7	13.4	13.8	9.7[e]
[e] = estimate					
Source: BNP					

In 1990, the bank again suffered from poor market conditions, as well as from factors unique to BNP. The factors included the liquidation of its Banque Internationale de l'Afrique Occidentale (BIAO) subsidiary and the cession of its African network; the constitution of large provisions when Banque Arabe et Internationale d'Investissement (BAII) was taken over; and a strike by BNP staff. As a result BNP's 1990 profits were only 50 percent of the 1989 level.

Market conditions which affected BNP's standing in 1990 included: continued reduced banking margins — counterbalanced by the growth in credits — often granted at rates of interest that were considered "barely viable"; the growing availability of banking products with the resultant frenzied competition between banks; and, the rapid increase in outstanding loans, forcing the bank to raise additional funds on the interbank market.[3]

Heightened competition in the lending market is a relatively new experience for the French banks and, in an attempt to remedy matters, René Thomas, chairman of BNP, launched an "appeal to reason" to the other banks (*Agefi*, 12/10/90) suggesting that they all "stop quarrelling with each other over credit terms like fishwives", alluding to the suicidal competition over rates between credit institutions. This statement was all the more significant as it recalled certain practices (which could almost be termed dumping), which had enabled some organisations, like BNP, to increase their share of the market in earlier years.

Added to this was an open battle between BNP employees and management, which led to a seven-week strike at the beginning of 1990. It was a reminder that growth and modernisation would have to be accompanied by more forward-looking strategies for staff. The strike had a very detrimental effect, costing the bank around FF600 million ($106 million).

BNP's strategic aim in its attempts to turn around the 1990 performance has focused on strengthening the capital base, improving productivity and profitability, instituting a company plan and strengthening both its operations in Southern Europe and its positions in capital markets in Northern Europe. Its *bancassurance* link-up with UAP and its plans for a partnership with Dresdner Bank are at the heart of this strategy.

To facilitate a link-up between UAP and BNP involving a share swap of 10 percent, in April 1990 BNP opted to increase its capital by FF5.3 billion, which was taken up entirely by the state. A second, supplementary, operation in the pipeline would be equivalent to a capital increase of FF4 billion and would increase UAP's shareholding in the bank's capital to 20 percent.

Its cross-shareholding with UAP, besides strengthening its capital base, has enabled BNP to continue its strategy of diversifying activities into the insurance sector, first in France and perhaps later elsewhere in Europe. Similarly, the acquisition of equity in the car company, Pechiney, resulted in an additional capital increase of FF1.34 billion for BNP. Such capital injections, plus the placing into reserves of FF1.7 billion of undistributed profits and the consolidation of FF4.6 billion worth of minority interests, has enabled BNP to increase own funds by 42 percent.

BNP's international strategy is built around a network of approximately 500 branches in 76 countries. More than 15,000 employees, roughly a quarter of its workforce, work abroad. While BNP's activities, according to its president and chief operating officer, Jacques Wahl, are mainly Europe-based, the North American and Pacific markets are no less important.

In preparing for the integration of Europe's markets, BNP's objective is to strengthen group structures around the continent. Its strategy of external growth by means of acquisitions, shareholdings and alliances, bears witness to this.

Within the framework of its European strategy, BNP was quick to take a 2 percent shareholding in Credito Romagnolo in Italy, increasing it to 10 percent during 1991.

Its acquisitions on the Spanish retail market, where it maintains a network of 75 branches, and its foray into the German mergers and acquisitions market (the alliance between subsidiary Banexi and Partner Gmbh), are two more success stories in its European strategy.

The link-up between BNP and Dresdner Bank, which was given a boost by the plan for partial privatisations in autumn 1991, could lead to the formation of one of Europe's leading banking groups.[4] Without relinquishing their right to compete in the marketplace, the two agreed, as a first step, to co-operate together in the event of stockmarket assaults and to assist each other if one or other wants to acquire a company in a third country. As part of these agreements, BNP handed over to Dresdner half of the 60 percent stake it held in Turkish bank, AkBank, to enable the Germans to gain a foothold in that market.

The alliance seems to benefit both banks. BNP has a sizeable European and international network which Dresdner can take advantage of while Dresdner can offer BNP the benefits of its prime position in Germany, facilitating access to the financial markets in particular. Dresdner is also an ideal partner for a bank seeking to increase its activities in what was East Germany and throughout Eastern Europe. Discussions between the two banks are ongoing and they appear to have agreed to a 10 percent share swap, plus a cash payment to UAP which is of greater size.

In 1990, two attempts to further develop a Europe-wide network failed. The first concerned a branch swap deal between BNP and Spain's Banco Bilbao Vizcaya (BBV). BNP was to trade the 85-branch Crédit Universel (in which the group has an 85 percent stake) for branches of Banco de Crédito y Ahorro[5] and some additional BBV outlets. But the negotiations broke down over the values of these subsidiaries. The other failure occurred when BNP and Dresdner lost their joint bid to take over the ninth largest British bank, Yorkshire Bank, to an Australian rival.

As a state-owned bank, BNP's attempts to extend its operations across the Atlantic are considerably hindered by the regulatory obstacles erected in its path by the American authorities. As a result, the bank is barely represented in the US.

In France, BNP bought the Banque de Bretagne in 1989. As of 1990, this bank had 75 branches in Brittany, assets of FF8 billion and own capital amounting to FF330 million (which takes into account the state's contribution of FF140 billion to encourage the takeover). According to BNP's president and chief operating officer (and former director of the Treasury), Daniel Lebègue, the takeover of an institution experiencing serious profitability difficulties was justified by BNP's efforts to strengthen its branch network in certain regions of France such as Brittany, traditionally dominated by the mutual banks. But this particular rescue appears more likely to have stemmed from the desire of the public authorities to bail out this institution.

In 1990 the state, with 75 percent of BNP's capital — including the 10 percent UAP shareholding — was the majority shareholder, with the remaining 25 percent held in the form of nonvoting shares (*certificats d' investissement*) by "private" shareholders. It had a Price Earnings Ratio (PER) of between seven and eight, and its stock market capitalisation was around FF4 billion. 1991 was a good year and profits rose again despite increasing sovereign risks. For example, it was expected to provide almost FF1 billion in loans to the former Soviet Union states. How the "partial privatisation" turned out would undoubtedly have (and was already having) an impact on BNP's earnings and on other state-controlled banks like Crédit Lyonnais.

Crédit Lyonnais

Founded in 1863, Crédit Lyonnais is one of France's oldest commercial banks. Nationalised in 1945 and again in 1982, management had high hopes that the bank would be re-privatised in 1987, but those hopes were never fulfilled.

It is a universal bank and one of the largest in terms of personal and business customers, corporate banking, the capital markets and investment banking.

In 1990, it had a network of 2,300 branches in metropolitan France, while its almost 1,500 ATMs handled 60 percent of cash withdrawals. It employed 61,000 people with roughly one-quarter working abroad. Training accounted for 4.5 percent of its wage bill.

With total assets of FF1,463 billion in 1990 (up 20 percent on the previous year[6] [see Table 4.3]), Crédit Lyonnais was France's third largest bank by volume of business and the ninth largest in Europe in terms of own funds. External growth policies partly explain this increase.

In 1990, for the first time in several years, deposits collected grew faster than loans (up 25 and 20 percent respectively). This was due particularly to the strong advance of certificates of deposit (up 113 percent) while sight deposits (offering officially regulated rates of interest) were subject to strong pressure from investments paying market rates. However, the retail market still contributed 60 percent of deposits.

On the assets side, corporate loans made up over 70 percent of all credits and this figure was increasing, with property development loans in particular rising sharply (up 27 percent in 1989). Although Crédit Lyonnais has a high profile in large projects financing, it is somewhat weaker in the specialist credit market. In 1990, over three-quarters of the backing

Table 4.3

Consolidated figures for Crédit Lyonnais (FF bn under management)

	1986	1987	1988	1989	1990
Total assets	837.0	899.0	1,048.0	1,220.0	1,463.0
Customer deposits	330.0	359.0	412.0	464.0	580.0
Customer loans	369.0	430.0	505.0	575.0	692.0
Provisions	26.9	31.8	36.2	37.5	41.6
Own funds and equivalent	20.2	24.6	33.8	39.0	61.6
Net banking income	26.1	26.9	29.8	33.2	28.3
Gross operating profit	9.0	8.8	8.2	10.2	11.7
Provisions allocated to reserves	6.2	5.3	6.4	6.3	6.5
Net profit after minority interests	1.8	2.2	2.1	3.1	3.7
ROE (in %)	14.8	13.9	10.9	15.2	11.3

Source: Crédit Lyonnais

given to individual customers was for housing purposes.

With 8.5 percent of the market in OPCVMs, Crédit Lyonnais was in fourth place behind BNP. The group managed OPCVM assets worth FF290 billion both in France and abroad in 1990. Crédit Lyonnais was equally active on the capital markets and in merchant banking.

The bank was the second largest issuer on the primary markets in France and third largest bank issuer of Eurobonds (see Appendix 4.3). The bank also established an intermediary arm for bourse and market trading, structured around Altus Finance. Through Altus Finance, Crédit Lyonnais has developed a very ambitious strategy which has involved acquiring broking houses (see Chapter 10). The strategy has been implemented to attain a commanding presence in the Paris market over the long term.

Crédit Lyonnais was in third place by volume of M&A deals in 1990. But while the total number of deals was high (61), their average value was only one-fifth that of merchant banks such as Lazard or its Anglo-Saxon peers (see Appendix 4.4).

In 1990, while the results of the other big banks took a sharp downward turn, Crédit Lyonnais' net profits increased by 19.4 percent reaching a record level of FF19.4 billion ($3.4 billion). Such a performance was partly due to the relatively low provisions made, despite the general increase in risks and the fact that the bank concluded a large number of acquisitions both at home and abroad. One of the distinguishing marks of this bank is a provisioning policy which is less consistent than others.

As proof of this, in September 1991, Moody's decided to downgrade the long-term debt (almost FF40 billion — $7 billion) rating of the bank and its subsidiaries, including Altus Finance, from Aa1 to Aa2. The reasons given were the increased risk profile of the group's activities, including its aggressive expansion into areas other than traditional banking business.

The bank's strategy for the 1990s focuses on three main areas: building up own funds, improving profitability, and conquering the European market.

Own funds reached FF61.6 billion ($10.8 billion) in 1990, up 58 percent on the previous year. According to the bank itself, the Cooke ratio was almost 9 percent. This spectacular increase was largely the result of a number of cross-shareholdings, of which the main ones in 1990 brought in; i) FF6.4 billion, subscribed by Thomson CSF by way of the 65 percent stake taken in Altus Finance; ii) FF1.7 billion from the French state through stakes taken in Rhône-Poulenc; iii) in the same manner, Crédit Lyonnais picked up around FF5 billion through issues of conditional return *titres subordonnés à intérêts progressifs* (perpetual annuities — TSIP) and the integration of Altus Finance. (TSIPs have no contractual redemption date and are only refundable if the issuer so decides or if the company goes into liquidation.)

These capital increases changed the voting rights of the main shareholders. In terms of voting rights, the French state's direct stake in Crédit Lyonnais fell from 94.26 percent to 69.43 percent, and that of the Caisse des Dépôts et Consignations from 5.74 percent to 4.67 percent. Two new partners, Thomson CSF (5.4 percent) and Société de Participation Banque Industrie (20.46 percent) thereafter completed the list of shareholders.

While Crédit Lyonnais succeeded in broadening its financial base in 1990, the recapitalisation problem has not been entirely resolved because almost half of the bank's funds are made up of hybrid securities, the quality of which is questionable because they come largely from stakes in French manufacturing companies.

The bank has been attempting to find acceptable returns not only by lifting productivity in traditional businesses, but also by making increased efforts in value-added businesses, especially high finance. However, only a quarter of net banking income is derived from commissions. The long-term objective foresees that 50 percent of net banking income should come from interest rate business and 50 percent from commissions.

One of the main strategic aims of Crédit Lyonnais in the 1990s is to become a Europe-wide universal bank. Consequently, it has concentrated on three markets: the financial, corporate and retail. To achieve its objectives, it adopted a strategy of open attack on the markets for mutual funds, insurance and finance houses (leasing, factoring, etc).

However, Crédit Lyonnais seems to be experiencing some difficulty in turning its dreams into reality and several aspects of its strategy are proving hard to realise.

To start with, it has made some poor acquisitions. The losses sustained by its London acquisition, Alexander Laing (renamed Crédit Lyonnais Capital Markets), and Crédit Lyonnais Nederland — where losses have been made worse by the Parretti scandal — may cost it some FF5 billion. And then there are the group's plans to diversify into the insurance sector, for example, which remain unclear.

Indeed it is hard to foresee who will be its partners either in France or abroad. In fact, its plan to link up with Commerzbank by means of a cross-shareholding arrangement was put "on the back burner" after the privatisation programme was halted in 1987. Though subsequent negotiations failed to resolve the deadlock, a return to the negotiation table is not impossible, especially if partial privatisations occur in France.

The bank's international strategy is focused primarily on Europe, where growth is both organic and through acquisitions. Crédit Lyonnais has opened about 50 new branches around the continent since 1989. It maintains a network of 1,000 branches in 70 different countries with 530 branches located in Europe outside of France, making it the French bank with most non-domestic branches. One-quarter of its workforce (15,000 people) is employed outside its home country.

In 1989, to further build up its European network, it acquired 49.5 percent of Credito Bergamasco in Italy, took control of Chase Banque de Commerce in Belgium (merged with CL Belgium in 1990) and became shareholder of reference in Woodchester in Ireland.

Spain is at the centre of its growth by acquisitions strategy. In 1990, It acquired an 83 percent holding in Banco Commercial Español and bought a 40 percent stake in brokers Iberagentes, while awaiting the approval of the Spanish authorities to take up the entire capital of the company. With a protocol agreement signed in 1991 to acquire Banca Jover, the number of Crédit Lyonnais-affiliated outlets in Spain increased to 230 — the largest French bank presence there.

In 1990, to better assert its position and at the same time attract additional capital, the bank's chairman, Jean-Yves Haberer,[7] decided to create a holding company — Crédit Lyonnais-Europe — to co-ordinate all its commercial banking activities. All European operations were brought under the control of its new holding company, while its merchant banking operations have been centralised within the bank's industrial business department and Clinvest, its M&A subsidiary.

The merchant banking side of the business was valued at around FF12 billion ($2 billion) in 1990, representing one of the largest capitalisations of any French commercial bank portfolio. The bank holds FF26 billion ($4.1 billion) worth of equity in manufacturing and trading companies.

To keep pace with developments in the markets and increased competition, changes have taken place in the internal organisation of Crédit Lyonnais. Customer services have been divided into different categories: large, small and medium-sized commercial and manufacturing companies (PME/PMI), and per-

sonal and professional customers. Also, a transfer of the branches' administrative responsibilities to central processing units have occurred, giving the branches more time to devote to service customers. At the beginning of September 1991, in line with this policy, Crédit Lyonnais inaugurated its latest service innovation: a new "free access" branch along the lines of American "financial centres" that is open to consumers without obligation to open an account or "buy" a service. This centre represented a breakthrough in the thorny issue of banking hours, because it remains open six days a week (including Saturdays) from 07:30 to 20:00.

For all its strengths and weaknesses, Crédit Lyonnais was by 1992 one of the most high-profile banks in Europe because of its ambitions to be a universal bank and its acquisition of stakes in industrial and financial concerns, etc. But the fact remains that its strategy includes elements of high risk, especially since funds and their use depend increasingly on the financial markets. Stock market capitalisation is of the order of FF4 billion ($700 million) and PER is between five and six billion.

Société Générale

Established in 1864 and nationalised in 1945, Société Générale was re-privatised in 1987, thereby becoming the largest private-sector banking group and the fourth largest French bank by total assets.[8]

The breakdown of shareholders in 1990 was: French institutional investors: 24.9 percent; French industries: 20.4 percent; foreign interests: 15.8 percent; employees: 7.0 percent; *autocontrôle* (ownership of its own shares): 5.4 percent; state: 1.0 percent; Société Générale pension fund: 1.3 percent. 24.2 percent of its capital is placed among the general public.

Its property portfolio, half of it in the Paris region, measured in excess of 1 million square metres for an estimated value of FF23 billion ($4 billion).

Customer deposits, which failed to grow as fast as total assets, stood at 73 percent of credits outstanding in 1990 compared with 90 percent in 1986. One of Société Générale's distinguishing features is the importance of specialist credit-type activities. Individuals account for 42 percent of customer deposits.

Société Générale has had the best profitability and

productivity ratios on the French banking scene. With a return of 19.3 percent (net profit over own funds) in 1989, it compared favourably with its Anglo-Saxon counterparts. One of its main strengths is its solid capital base. Be that as it may, that return declined considerably to 9.6 percent in 1990 due to a drop in profits as well as to an appreciable strengthening in own funds (see Table 4.4).

Table 4.4					
Consolidated figures for Société Générale (FF bn under management)					
	1986	**1987**	**1988**	**1989**	**1990**
Total assets	749.0	817.0	942.0	1,017.0	1,120.0
Customer deposits	285.0	296.0	330.0	362.0	399.0
Customer loans	315.0	349.0	412.0	475.0	546.0
Provisions	29.0	32.2	35.1	36.1	37.0
Own funds	21.7	25.0	29.5	32.0	36.4
Net banking income	28.0	28.6	31.0	32.2	32.5
Gross operating profit	10.4	9.2	9.8	10.2	9.0
Provisions allocated to reserves	7.2	5.1	4.7	4.8	6.8
Net profits after minority interests	2.4	2.4	3.1	3.6	2.7
ROE (in %)	16.8	14.0	15.1	15.3	9.6
Source: Société Générale					

In 1990, it had a total workforce of 45,000, a network of 1,800 offices and subsidiaries and 1,000 ATMs throughout France. After the first oil crisis, Société Générale became careful about the number of new staff it recruited, which accounts for the smaller size of its branch network and workforce compared with BNP and Crédit Lyonnais.

Société Générale, with net profits of FF3.56 billion in 1989, was ahead of BNP (FF3.4 billion), despite the fact that it suffered badly from the poor state of the bond market, where it has a high profile. However, profits fell by 25 percent in 1990. Société Générale's results were affected firstly, by the strong rise in general expenses (which depressed net banking income) and secondly, by provisions allocated to reserves, up 41 percent in the light of increased risk in all lines of business. On a more

positive note, the make-up of net banking income shifted with commissions accounting for an increased percentage (39), thus rendering the bank less sensitive to changes in interest margins.

One of its strategic aims is to buy into the industrial sector. Its 1990 portfolio of industrial holdings was valued at around FF15 billion with possible capital gains of some FF3 billion and it had shares (generally less than 1 percent) in several of France's major companies such as Accor, CGE, Canal Plus, La Générale des Eaux, Havas, La Redoute, Navigation Mixte, Les Nouvelles Galeries, Perrier, Peugeot, Le Printemps and Rhône-Poulenc. It also had a 10 percent share in Société Parisienne d'Entreprises et de Participations (SPEP), the Schneider holding company.

Traditionally, it has considered itself a *banque d'entreprise*. It has business connections with 85 percent of France's top 250 manufacturers and does business with some 300,000 companies. Nevertheless, according to its chairman, Marc Viénot, the bank has been careful not to get involved in financing companies on terms which might adversely affect returns on shareholders' equity especially at a time of shrinking margins. Leasing is a prime example of an area where the bank has been determined to hold onto its market share.

Another primary target of the bank is the personal sector, especially the middle and upper-ends of the market which have been relatively neglected in the past.[9]

The bank has adopted a global approach towards clients, offering products to match customer profiles. Its *Convention Galaxie* contract, introduced in 1989, offers current account holders cash loans, a bank card, and an insurance product. Always intent on achieving maximum profitability, it is active in the market for private asset management with 60 agencies handling this type of business.

Société Générale has a domestic and foreign expansion programme which is limited in scope but carefully nurtured. It is in the process of restructuring its branch network and its various activities to meet the challenge of 1993.

At home it has set up a company called Franfinance

to group together subsidiaries specialising in personal lending (CREG and CALIF) and has also launched a successful takeover bid for Sogenal. There have been moves to create specialised subsidiaries within the group "along the lines of Compagnie Bancaire".

In 1988, as part of its restructuring programme, it handed over control of Banque Internationale de Placements (BIP) to Dresdner Bank.

As for international operations, it had a network of 500 branches in 64 countries in 1990. It has a presence in all EC countries except Ireland (although this did not prevent it from arranging the takeover of Irish Distillers by the Pernod Ricard group), and is also the only French bank to have outlets in every Eastern European country.

Either directly, or through its subsidiary, Société Générale Elsäische Bank, it holds seats on the Amsterdam, Frankfurt and Zurich stock exchanges and has financial departments in New York (Sogen Securities), London (Société Générale Merchant Bank and SGST Securities), Sydney and Hong Kong.

Despite all this, it still lags behind significantly in the international field. To rectify this situation, it has earmarked a number of areas for development. To strengthen its European position, Société Générale has adopted a niche strategy, becoming one of the largest players in European leasing with a network of over 30 companies, according to the British magazine *Asset Finance and Leasing Digest*. It also ranks as France's number one lessor.[10]

Another development has been its establishment of a strong presence in the European fund management and SICAV markets. It has aimed to corner 1 percent of market share in this sector in four countries — Spain, Italy, Germany and the UK. To this end, in April 1989 it acquired Touche Remnant, one of Britain's leading fund management companies managing almost FF30 billion ($5.3 billion) worth of assets. Together with this company, Société Générale set up *Realvalor*, the first co-managed Franco-British SICAV. It hoped to extend its fund management operations to Japan and the USA through the intermediary of Société Générale Touche Remnant Asset Management (SGTR), a holding company set up in 1989 to co-ordinate the group's fund management activities. With assets of around FF230 billion ($40 billion), SGTR is now a leader in collective investment funds (OPCVM) in Europe.

Société Générale has a full range of products at its disposal around Europe. In Italy, it has taken a 20 percent stake in a real estate investment company which it co-manages along with Cassa di Risparmio di Verona. In Spain, it has 100 percent ownership of a fund management company, whose products are sold through local Société Générale agencies, and it has concluded an agreement with the German insurer, Kölnische Leben-Berliner Verein, to market corporate funds.

Another target is stock market business, as demonstrated by its taking control of Dutch stock brokers, Ingwersen & Co., in which it had a 55 percent shareholding in 1990. In the UK, it overhauled brokers Strauss Turnbull to set up a new company, SGST Securities. Among French banks in 1990 it was the second largest issuer of equities, fourth largest issuer of bonds on the home market and third largest issuer of Eurofrancs. It ranked second for market flotations, while its M&A activities remained less significant.

Although Société Générale is not opposed to alliances, it is consolidating its position gradually and does not want to become a Europe-wide universal bank, as is the goal of Crédit Lyonnais. In fact, chairman Marc Viénot has said that, at least in the foreseeable future, Société Générale has no plans to link up with any other banking establishment, much less an insurance company. His refusal is based on a sceptical view of the merits of *bancassurance* and his confidence that the bank can secure capital by other means. His bank's strategy is defined in terms of profitability rather than size (total assets).

With a PER ratio of between 9 and 10 and stock market capitalisation of some FF30 billion ($5.3 billion) in 1990, Société Générale would appear to have a bright future because of its consistently healthy returns and because of its position as the largest provider of specialist credit.

The mutual and co-operative banks

This sector is made up of six networks: Crédit Agricole Mutuel, Crédit Mutuel, Banques Populaires, Crédit Mutuel Agricole et Rural, Crédit Coopératif and Crédit Maritime Mutuel. The first three banks on this list are among the most important institutions on the French banking scene.

These groups have complex tiered structures. Put simply, regional or "departmental" banks and local banks (which are called *caisses* in the case of Crédit Agricole, Crédit Mutuel and Crédit Coopératif), coexist with central institutions, which act more or less as "clearers".

In contrast with the AFB banks, they are theoretically non-profit making, their status being based on the following principles: no restrictions apply regarding becoming "a company member" — a company member, also called a *sociétaire*, has just one vote irrespective of the number of shares held; and, there is neither distribution of dividends nor capital gains on shares held (as a result, these banks have large reserves of capital as there is no distribution of profits).

In the past, these banks benefited from numerous legal privileges, leading to the formation of large and powerful groups. The principles of co-operation and mutuality are undoubtedly an advantage, although in practice the scope of these principles varies from bank to bank. It is a very important advantage for Crédit Mutuel, a moderately important one for Crédit Agricole and a purely commercial one for the Banques Populaires.

Many customers are also *sociétaires*; at Crédit Mutuel, for example, a customer cannot obtain a loan if he is not a company member.

The mutual and co-operative institutions were traditionally subject to numerous restrictions in return for the legal advantages they enjoyed, and they were specialised by type of activity and customer. However the restrictions no longer apply and all of these institutions without exception have engaged in a process of restructuring and modernisation.

This, together with the public's increased familiarity with banking, has brought the mutuals ever closer in line with the manner in which other banks function. Consequently, they have extended their range of products and services and they increasingly re-

semble the AFB banks, particularly in retail services. The mutual and co-operative banks are also very active on the capital markets and are formidable competitors for the banks in OPCVM business.

In 1990, the number of individual outlets was very large. At 11,000 branches (Crédit Agricole — 5,600, Crédit Mutuel — 3,700 and the Banques Populaires — 1,600), they outstripped the 9,800 branches of the combined AFB banks.

The mutual and co-operative banks are France's largest banking institutions by size. But while their market share in 1990 was 28 percent of deposits and 22 percent of credits, they accounted for only 16 percent of total assets in the French banking sector, due to the fact that their interbank operations are comparatively smaller.

Crédit Agricole

Crédit Agricole was established by the Méline law of 1894 to facilitate agricultural modernisation. Today, it is France's largest banking group.[11]

The privatisation of Caisse Nationale de Crédit Agricole (CNCA), which was decided upon in 1986 and carried out in 1988 under the Chirac government, took place through a process of *mutualisation*.

Upon completion of the privatisation process, 90 percent of the capital of CNCA was handed over by the state to the regional banks (based on a calculation of the number of local *caisses* over total assets). The remaining 10 percent was set aside for civil servants and employees of the whole network and the CNCA.

Crédit Agricole consists of three tiers: local, regional and national. As of 1990, there were over 3,040 local banks or *caisses locales* spread throughout France. These are designated as *sociétés coopératives à capital variable* (floating capital co-operative companies). Their function is to collect deposits which they pass on to the regional banks (to which they are affiliated) and to place the group's certificates and bonds. The operations of the *caisses locales* are far from autonomous: the deposits which they receive and the credits they grant are not included on their balance sheets.

Banking operations are in fact the prerequisite of the *caisses régionales*, which alone are regarded as credit institutions. These regional banks must in turn deposit cash surpluses as well as all savings products (deposit savings book accounts, contractual savings, bonds and loans) with the Caisse Nationale, which they take in on its behalf. As of May 1991, there were 87 regional banks (as against 94 in 1988), operating within areas roughly corresponding to a *département*, thus theoretically eliminating any "intra-*caisse*" competition. As their sizes varies greatly, (some regional banks group together a dozen local *caisses* while others cover over 100), a process of rationalisation was underway in 1991 to bring their number down to around 75 by 1992, and to 40 or 50 by the year 2000.

The Caisse Nationale de Crédit Agricole (CNCA) has a dual role in the group. As the central clearer, it centralises savings and liquid funds and manages services common to the whole group as well as the group's subsidiaries. CNCA also carries out banking operations either directly or through the regional banks.[12] As the central body, it supervises accounts and approves new directors. Placed at the head of the group, the CNCA is also in charge of international development.

The CNCA coexists with the Fédération Nationale du Crédit Agricole (FNCA) which is purely a consultative and representative body for members of the Crédit Agricole network and has no financial functions.

Considering total assets and own funds as the sole indicators, Crédit Agricole was France's largest bank in 1991, and ranked as the world's fourth. With 17 million customers (almost one in three of the French population), 5 million *sociétaires*, 15 million accounts and over 6 million *carte bancaire* holders, a huge network of 9,300 outlets (of which 5,600 are permanent) and 4,091 ATMs, Crédit Agricole is essentially a mass-market bank. Staff numbered 74,500 in 1990 — a figure which is relatively stable.

Crédit Agricole's growth has been triggered by two concomitant developments: a broadening of its range of businesses in return for a reduction in its privileges. Privatisation of the CNCA has undoubtedly accelerated the growth of the "Green Bank". Originally established for the sole purpose of financing agriculture, and small farmers in particular, Crédit Agricole has gradually broadened the scope of its activities, initially to the rural community as a whole (including trade and industry outside towns), then to all agro-food industries, all personal customers including urban dwellers, and to all retailers and craftsmen. Recently, Crédit Agricole has been allowed to open branches in towns without restriction and without prior authorisation. Since 1989, in return for the gradual removal of its monopoly on the distribution of subsidised loans to farmers, the bank has had no limits placed on its activities.

Because of its numerous fiscal privileges, Crédit Agricole grew to become the leading French bank during the *trente glorieuses* (the 30 years of economic growth after the Second World War). The gradual removal of these fiscal privileges began in the early 1970s:

1971 — the ending of Crédit Agricole's exemption from the trading licence, *la patente,* (replaced by the professional tax);

1979 — the abolition of Crédit Agricole's tax exemption financial operations (replaced by Value Added Tax);

1983 — Crédit Agricole became liable for corporate tax, with the group thereafter becoming the largest contributor of taxes among credit institutions.

While Crédit Agricole lost its monopoly in the distribution of subsidised loans to farmers in 1989 and the discounting of ONIC (Office National Interprofessionnel des Céréales) bills, it has succeeded in retaining one privilege: managing the deposits of rural notaries (in towns of fewer than 30,000 inhabitants), which function it shares with the Caisse des Dépôts et Consignations (CDC).

However, the preservation of this privilege was proving costly by the early 1990s due to the authorities' insistence that the financial burden of heavily indebted farmers be alleviated.[13] Crédit Agricole managers expressed concern that this would require that the institution underwrite this troubled sector. Consequently, deposits from rural notaries (approximately FF1 billion — $176 million in 1990) which help to balance the bank's books, have become a double-edged sword, in the long term threatening Crédit Agricole's profitability.

To recompense its loss of privileges, Crédit Agricole's scope of operations has been altered radically in practically every area of banking activity. Originally set up as the farmers' bank, Crédit Agricole's share of this market fell from 50 percent in 1980 to less than 20 percent in 1990, while its share of the personal market grew from 33 percent to 55 percent in the same 10 year period.

The group is dominant or among the market leaders in many products and sectors. In 1990, it accounted for 16.8 percent of all deposits, 15.0 percent of SICAVs, 45 percent of PEPs, and 8 to 10 percent of life insurance premiums. The bank controlled 14 percent of the total market for credit and distributed 27 percent of new loans to professional people, 8 percent of personal loans, 6.7 percent of corporate loans and over 40 percent of housing loans to individuals.

Other indicators (see Table 4.5) show that the group is financially sound. Own "resources" — nearly 15 percent in *titres participatifs* — was the highest of any French bank and its Cooke ratio (falling slightly) stood at 8.5 percent in 1990. Productivity (gross operating profit over staff) in 1990 was 2.4 times better than in 1986; operational expenses represented 64 percent of net banking income, as against 75 percent in 1985 and return on assets increased

from 0.22 percent in 1986 to 0.34 percent in 1989 before falling to 0.31 percent in 1990.

However, Crédit Agricole is a complicated organisation and behind these figures lie serious problems concerning the profitability and management of the majority of regional banks, which means that more than half of the group's earnings come from the CNCA and its subsidiaries alone.

With only 24 units, for the most part small, in 21 countries, the group is aiming to increase its international presence, especially in Europe. Progress during 1990 included:

Southern Europe: Having acquired a 12 percent holding in the Italian group Ambroveneto,[14] and having made several acquisitions in Spain (Configasa, stockbrokers ABA), Crédit Agricole was attempting to penetrate Greece where it has a 25 percent stake in Eteba (FF3.5 billion ($618 million) in loans), a subsidiary of the National Bank of Greece;

Northern Europe: Through Unico (an international umbrella organisation for mutual banks), Crédit Agricole had co-operation agreements with DG Bank in Germany, Cera in Belgium, RZB in Austria and OKO Bank in Finland.

On the international capital markets, the group has increasingly capitalised on its experience in portfolio management by establishing SA-Crédit Agricole Luxembourg, which is a depositary and distributor of *SICAVs à compartiments* (umbrella funds). Cash and asset management activities for higher-income retail customers (both French and foreign), and an increased involvement on the derivative markets (options and futures) are also envisaged.

To finance its foreign growth programme, Crédit Agricole has been able to utilise funds secured by the opening of the capital of some of its important subsidiaries (Prédica, Segespar, Unicrédit, UEI). However, its "hesitant" foreign acquisition policy is partly due to the fact that the prices of what has come available have been too high. According to Philippe Jaffré, chief executive of CNCA since 1988, banking saturation and deregulation will have a disastrous effect on some institutions. It is then that Crédit Agricole will be able to increase its investments in

Table 4.5

Consolidated figures for Crédit Agricole

	1986	1987	1988	1989	1990
Total assets	997.0	1,145.0	1,302.0	1,400.0	1,554.0
Customer deposits	588.0	649.0	710.0	772.0	885.0
Customer loans	555.0	634.0	731.0	837.0	937.0
Own funds	27.8	31.7	47.0	53.5	60.5
Participating securities and subordinated notes	2.5	2.7	7.0	7.8	10.0
Net banking income	34.4	39.3	43.8	48.7	51.6
Net profits after minority interests	2.1	2.5	3.9	4.5	4.7
ROE (in %)	7.6	7.9	8.3	8.4	7.7

Source: Crédit Agricole

banks experiencing financial difficulties, paying more reasonable prices (*Agefi*, January 1991).

Despite this explanation, Crédit Agricole's international network has remained limited, apart from its hesitant expansion policy, in part because the effort required to make the bank more competitive on the French market and to restructure the regional banks appears to be consuming all the energies and financial resources of the Caisse Nationale — a sign of the times.

The transformation that Crédit Agricole has undergone is both striking and paradoxical. Striking because it had become the leading bank for housing loans (which far exceeds lending to agriculture) by the early 1990s. Paradoxical, because while enjoying the status of a "mutual", Crédit Agricole has become a commercial bank. In fact, the *caisses régionales* have increasingly entered the mainstream of commercial banking. Likewise, there has been a rapid increase in provisions because of the huge growth in outstanding loans. The regional banks enjoyed a PER of between five (for the smaller among them) and 10 (for the Caisse de l'Ile-de-France).

The Banques Populaires

The Banques Populaires group is the second largest mutual banking group (see Table 4.6). It was established under the Second Empire and structured under the law of March 13 1917 to cater for small and medium-sized manufacturing, trading and craft businesses. The Law of July 24 1924 created the Chambre Syndicale des Banques Populaires and

other laws have subsequently been passed to strengthen the legislation covering the group.

The Banques Populaires grew rapidly in the 1950s and 1960s. They too benefited from the progressive extension of its sphere of activities, first of all into the liberal professions (1955) and then into retail banking (1962).

Of all the mutual banks, the Banques Populaires resemble most closely the universal-type commercial banks. They conduct the full range of banking operations, and have no special privileges. The distribution of subsidised loans to small businesses (previously an oligopoly of the Banques Populaires, Crédit Agricole and Crédit Coopératif), has been open to all institutions since 1985 and channels for the distribution of these loans are now chosen by tender.

Nevertheless, the Banques Populaires differ from the AFB banks in that they have a central body and a specific legal status. By law, the Banques Populaires are a group of proper mutual banks because they can conduct credit operations only through their *sociétaires* (though there are no restrictions on becoming a *sociétaire*). In addition, the Banques Populaires group has co-operative status, with the exception of the floating capital Banque Régionale d'Escompte et de Dépôts (BRED).

The Banques Populaires have a two-tier structure: regional and national. At the base of the organisation are the Banques Populaires. These banks are proper regional banks, not only because they operate within certain delineated geographical areas, but also (and more importantly) because their decision-making bodies are composed of members residing in that area. For example, the chairman of the board of directors is generally not a banker but is involved in another field of business, while the chief executive is a professional banker.

The number of regional banks continues to fall. There were 31 in 1990 as against 40 in 1985. The process of mergers should in theory reduce the number to 21, corresponding to the 21 economic regions of France.

In addition to the regional banks, there are two

| Table 4.6 |||||||
| The Banques Populaires (FF bn under management) |||||||
	1986	1987	1988	1989	1990
Total assets	250.00	287.00	338.00	374.00	399.00
Customer deposits	139.00	156.00	181.00	209.00	227.00
Customer loans	103.00	125.00	149.00	172.00	193.00
Own funds	9.30	10.90	13.10	14.70	15.70
Gross operating profit	2.50	2.80	3.30	3.50	3.70
Net profits after minority interests	0.70	0.87	1.18	1.12	1.16
Source: Banques Populaires						

Banques Populaires which operate nationally. These are the Caisse d'Aide Sociale de l'Education Nationale (CASDEN Banque Populaire, which specialises in banking services for the staff and for mutual and professional bodies under the wing of the Ministry of Education), and the Banque Populaire Fédérale de Développement (BPFD), which supplies the regional Banques Populaires with support services for corporate clients. The latter administers the group's shareholding (36 percent in 1990) in Crédit d'Equipement des Petites et Moyennes Entreprises(CEPME).

The Caisse Centrale des Banques Populaires (CCBP), which has credit institution status, heads the network. It acts as a clearing house for operations between the Banques Populaires. It also centralises and manages their liquid resources, supplements the operations of the Banques Populaires either through direct assistance or by participating in large-scale financing deals, organises services common to all the regional banks (ie SICAVs, FCPs, etc) and administers some subsidiaries. Its chairman is also the chairman of the Chambre Syndicale.

In 1929, the Banques Populaires created a central body called the Chambre Syndicale des Banques Populaires which has various functions. It is the Populaires' representative at the Association Française des Etablissements de Crédit (AFEC), and regulates and supervises the network. It also issues recommendations and sanctions and oversees large loan operations. As the Banques Populaires supervisory body, it determines the group's general direction.[15] The Chambre Syndicale des Banques Populaires is administered by a board of 15 elected members whose chairman must be approved by the Ministry of Finance. Activities are similar to those of the commercial banks and have traditionally been less regulated than those of Crédit Agricole. Their particular speciality is acting as banker for tradesmen and SMEs.

The Banques Populaires managed 3.6 million accounts and had 1.8 million "members" as of 1990. The network consisted of approximately 1,900 outlets, with a workforce of 27,500 people. As with the AFB banks, there was a falling trend in staff numbers (a decrease of 5 percent between 1985 and 1990). Training accounted for 5 percent of the wage bill.

Apart from the slowdown in growth in deposits and loans, the Banques Populaires faced the prevailing problem of rapidly increasing funding costs in the early 1990s. The portion of resources on which there was little or no interest paid continued to decline. In 1990, it was less than 60 percent of the total as against 74 percent in 1987, although growth in net banking income outstripped that of general expenses, largely due to the moderate growth in personnel costs.

Nonetheless, the increase in risks forced the group to increase provisioning for doubtful loans substantially and this led to an almost 20 percent fall in net operating income. But profits from exceptional items meant that net profits grew 2.9 percent (see Table 4.6).

The Banques Populaires' strategy, which the mergers between the regional banks has served to reaffirm, is to attain a critical mass in the French market to meet the challenge of 1992. In addition they have sought to increase their share of deposits in France, which stood at less than 4 percent in 1990.

This group maintains only a small presence on foreign markets, with small operations in Barcelona, Frankfurt, London, Luxembourg, Madrid, Monaco and New York. The conclusion of a co-operation agreement with the Italian group, Arca Nordest, at the beginning of 1991, by the new chairman of the Banques Populaires, Jacques Delmas-Marsalet, who appears to have a more aggressive approach than his predecessor, was only the first step in the group's expansion into Europe. It now aims to extend the scope of its product and service offer to small and medium-sized commercial and manufacturing companies (PME/PMI) throughout Europe, and has lately concluded an agreement with the German co-operative bank, DG Bank, to this end.

Insurance, particularly life insurance is also one of the group's strategic axes. Fructivie, a Banques Populaires subsidiary, with premium income of FF2.8 billion ($494 million), ranked 27th among French life companies in 1990, but sixth in terms of productivity (with FF61.7 million ($10.9 million) managed per employee) and 10th in terms of net profits.

The restructuring and indeed the mergers taking place within the Banques Populaires are likely to increase their competitive edge, given their firm entrenchment in the regions. Nevertheless, the group produces low returns, which make the problem of own capital even more acute at a time when outstanding loans are still progressing rapidly. The problem is, the Banques Populaires can have only limited recourse to the market due to their mutual status. On the other hand, one of the group's strengths is the way in which it has managed to keep operating expenses under control.

Crédit Mutuel

Crédit Mutuel's origins date back to the end of the 19th century, when it was modelled on the banks set up in Germany by Raiffeissen. Its modern legal framework was formalised in the Order of October 16 1958. Apart from the normal regulations governing mutual banks (the requirement that one must be a "member" of the bank to qualify for a loan), there are no geographic or professional limitations on the activities of banks belonging to this network. Nevertheless, Crédit Mutuel appears to be strongest in retail operations (housing, consumer durables, the needs of professional people) and local administrations.

Even if Crédit Mutuel's three-tier structure is similar to that of Crédit Agricole, there are differences between the two organisations, particularly concerning the autonomy of each tier.

In contrast to Crédit Agricole's local *caisses*, the 3,000 local banks within the Crédit Mutuel network have legal and financial autonomy and are fully responsible for their own deposits and loans.[16] They are set up in the form of *sociétés coopératives à capital variable*. Crédit Mutuel's regional structure is also slightly more complicated than that of Crédit Agricole. First, there are 21 federal banks covering one or several *départements*. While leaving the greater part of operations to the local banks themselves, the networks do manage their cash surpluses and ensure absolute security for the depositor through a system of solidarity. Side-by-side are regional federations which represent the local banks and have administrative, technical and financial control. These are, in fact, semi-central bodies.

The Caisse Centrale du Crédit Mutuel is in charge of finances. It centralises and manages capital on behalf of the federal banks and seeks funds on the

markets (by the issuing of debenture loans and certificates of deposit). Through its own guarantee fund, it also serves as underwriter for the deposit guarantees offered by the regional banks to local Crédit Mutuel depositors.

The Confédération Nationale is the supervisory and representative body. It keeps a list of local banks and benefits from some prerogatives in its role as a public institution.

Although there are Crédit Mutuel outlets throughout France, the highest concentration occurs in Alsace-Lorraine, Brittany and central France. While lacking any international representation, Crédit Mutuel has, since 1989, been planning to set up operations and partnership agreements in the EC and outside Europe.

As of 1990, the Crédit Mutuel network was made up of 4,253 outlets (of which about 3,000 were local banks, 1,358 were offices and 77 were branch offices) and counted over 7 million customers, of which two-thirds were *sociétaires*. It had 1,100 ATMs and 2.1 million card holders. Staff employed stood at 21,600, though it was decreasing.

The financial year 1990 at Crédit Mutuel was distinguished both by the slowdown in growth in credits outstanding and by modest growth in deposits. There was also a trend towards short-term products in preference to passbook savings and other more traditional forms of deposit account (see Table 4.7).

Table 4.7		
Crédit Mutuel **(FF bn under management)**		
	1989	1990
Total assets	319.800	345.800
Customer loans	156.700	177.500
Customer deposits	220.300	244.700
Own funds	20.400	21.700
Net profits	0.951	0.891
ROE (in %)	4.800	4.200
Source: Crédit Mutuel		

In 1990, new funds collected through the network proper or the group's specialist subsidiaries reached

FF6 billion ($1 billion) in PEPs (7 percent of the total), and FF7 billion in term deposit savings. OPCVMs under management (SICAVs and FCPs doubled between 1989 and 1990) reached FF12 billion, and Crédit Mutuel collected almost FF5 billion in revenues from insurance premiums.

For a long time, Crédit Mutuel benefited from being the sole authorised collector of Livret Bleu funds (which are tax free). But this source of income is gradually drying up. In fact, Livret Bleu deposits have diminished both in absolute terms (down FF6.9 billion in 1990) and in relative terms, with the amount under management (FF87.5 billion at the end of 1990) accounting for only 39.3 percent of customer deposits as against 43.8 percent in 1989. Competition from other products offering higher returns such as the PEP and the *SICAV monétaire* would appear to have got the better of the Livret Bleu. In addition, in 1991 the government decided to withdraw Crédit Mutuel's last privilege, largely because there will be a shortfall (of FF5 billion) in funds from the savings banks' Livret A in 1991, earmarked to finance the FF35 billion government housing programme. Political pressure is being brought to bear on Crédit Mutuel by a Finance Ministry which envisages making up this deficit by way of the Livret Bleu.

This has not left the Crédit Mutuel much room to manoeuvre and discussions led to an agreement in March 1991, whereby Livret Bleu deposits were henceforth to be allocated progressively, over the space of 10 years, to the funding of public housing. This involves channelling funds through the CDC in return for a fixed rate of remuneration of between 1.3 percent and 1.5 percent. This decision will have serious consequences for the group's profitability, as it will shortly have to forego this "cheap" source of funding.

Les Caisses d'Epargne —
The Savings Banks

There are two savings bank networks in France: The Caisses d'Epargne et de Prévoyance (Ecureuil) and the Caisse Nationale d'Epargne (CNE). The latter will be dealt with in the section on the Post Office's financial services. Their legal statutes differ in the sense that the Ecureuil operates according to the terms of the Banking Law, while the Caisse Nationale d'Epargne is an administrative unit of the PTT (Posts and Telegraphs) and is not subject to banking regulations.

The Caisses d'Epargne et de
Prévoyance (Ecureuil)

Originating in the early nineteenth century (1818) and receiving formal legal standing in 1835, the savings banks, from the outset, channelled funds to the Treasury and later to the Caisse des Dépôts et Consignations (CDC).

Since the Law of July 1 1983, the savings banks have been authorised to undertake most banking operations. Under the terms of this law, the group was given a three-tier structure: at local level the group consists of just under 200 Caisses d'Epargne et de Prévoyance (as of 1990); at regional level there are 21 Sociétés Régionales de Financement (SOREFIs); and at national level there is the Centre National des Caisses d'Epargne (CENCEP). However, a 1991 reform completely changed the structure of the savings banks.

The savings banks are non-profit making credit institutions administered by a board of directors or a chief executive operating under the control of an advisory and supervisory committee made up of depositor representatives (elected by drawing lots), employees, and officials of local councils. They share a monopoly over Livret A deposits with La Poste, and these account for most of their deposit business. A large portion of the savings banks' funds are channelled to the CDC: Livret A — 100 percent, LEP (the people's savings account) — 85 percent: CODEVI (the industrial savings account) — 56 percent.

As of 1990, there were 21 Sociétés Régionales de Financement (SOREFIs) with capital constituted on a par with the CDC, though they are destined to disappear as the reduction in the number of *caisses* no longer justifies the existence of these regional bodies.

As the central body for the savings banks group, the Centre National des Caisses d'Epargne et de Prévoyance (CENCEP) has many different functions: it represents the banks as a whole; it negotiates and concludes national and international agreements for the group; it manages the network's finance companies; it organises the network and pilots the establishment, merging and closing-down of savings banks; and it supervises the operations of the *caisses*. But CENCEP's role is more complex than it first seems, due to the omnipresence of the CDC. For example, CENCEP may not undertake financial operations on behalf of the savings banks, as these are handled by the CDC. In 1990, CENCEP's capital was 50 percent held by the savings banks, 15 percent by the SOREFIs and 35 percent by the CDC.

Originally restricted to savings, the scope of the savings banks activities has gradually broadened to include financial services and investments, which has resulted in fierce competition for the commercial banks given the extent of the savings banks' network, their strong presence in the regions and their low cost of funds.

In 1968, the savings banks received authorisation to offer products with broad appeal, including the Livret B and SICAVs. In 1970, the Ecureuil was authorised to grant home-savings loans as well as personal loans to private individuals and the self-employed, while funding itself through issuing savings bonds. And in 1979 the savings banks were able to issue customers with cheque books.

The banks' diversification is virtually complete. Since the June 17 1987 Law on Savings, they have been authorised to grant loans to trading and manufacturing companies (with the exception of publically-quoted manufacturers). However, to counterbalance this business expansion, the banks are now subject to corporate tax.

Despite this extremely rapid diversification, the main activity of the savings banks remains centred around the Livret A, whose receipts are channelled to the CDC.[17]

The savings banks account for 7 percent of the assets of the French banking industry. In 1990, their market shares (following a pattern of decline), were about 4.3 percent of credits and 13.7 percent of deposits (15.6 percent in 1989). The network had over 4,300 offices and branches throughout France in the same year. Taken as a whole, it employed 35,535 people (up 2.8 percent on 1989) of which 29,346 worked in the local *caisses*.

The savings banks rated as the second largest collector of liquid savings in 1990 with total deposits in hand of FF886 billion ($156 billion). However, since 1985 there has been a fall in growth in Livret A deposits — the banks' main source of income. This particular savings vehicle, which in 1989 accounted for 52.5 percent of deposits, produced only 48 percent of deposits in 1990. During 1991, Livret A deposits continued to decline, with withdrawals reaching FF19 billion ($3.3 billion), compared to FF8 billion a year earlier.

New loans in 1990 came to FF69 billion ($12 billion), 6 percent less than in 1989. This decline was mainly due to contraction in MINJOZ loans, ie loans to local authorities backed by funds from the Livret A. However, there was also a marked change in the structure of savings banks' loans: retail customers who received 63 percent of loans in 1989 (for housing) only accounted for 48 percent in 1990, while direct loans to local authorities (backed by more widely-available funds) and to a lesser extent to professional people and companies rose from 13 percent in 1989 to 29 percent in 1990.

The group has become particularly sensitive to competition from other products which offer more attractive tax incentives, with savers favouring products offering much higher returns, such as high-liquidity SICAVs and PEPs. The savings banks themselves have encouraged their customers to invest in PEPs, which has further contributed to the "cannibalisation" of the Livret A.[18]

However, the collapse of the Livret A serves to remind us that the customer base of the *caisses* is made up of not just small savers. More than one-third of customers have reached the "ceiling" of FF90,000 ($15,900) — the maximum balance allowed per Livret.

This customer segment is now prepared to spend more time looking for good deals on the various products offered by the savings banks or rivals.

The outflow of funds from the Livret A accounts into other products is a cause for concern for the authorities due to the growing deficit in the funding of public sector housing.

Competition between the large French banks in the early 1990s, plus the opening of opportunities on a European scale, has led the savings banks to seek to optimise the size of their organisations. The savings banks' network is composed of institutions of varying sizes spread throughout France whose very density, while convenient for the public, is an obstacle to further development.

The restructuring of the banks began in 1985, when the number of savings banks stood at 468, and picked up again in 1989 and 1990 along the lines of a plan of action drawn by management consultants McKinsey. Consequently, the total number of institutions decreased by 77 in 1989, dropping from 301 to 224 local *caisses* and to 200 by the beginning of 1991, with much of the reduction occurring as a result of takeovers and mergers.[19] The goal was to cut the number of banks to between 30 and 40 by 1992.

This restructuring and rationalisation process occurred in tandem with an increase in the strength of specialised subsidiaries linked to the holding company, Ecureuil Participation.[20] In 1989, this holding company concentrated on setting up FCPR Epargne-Développement and CDE-Ecureuil Immoblier, which provides real estate companies with capital.

Until the early 1990s, the French savings banks were practically absent from the international scene. Since then, numerous co-operation agreements with European savings banks have been concluded with the aim of gaining access to the international marketplace.[21]

In Spain, agreements have been finalised with several savings banks (the main one being with La Caixa de Barcelona); in Italy, with the association of Italian savings banks; in Sweden with the national federation of savings banks; in Germany with the local savings banks and federations as well as with the national federation of German savings banks; and in Belgium with ASLK-CGER bank.

Despite these advances, growth through the acquisition of banks seems to be ruled out, at least for the foreseeable future, in view of the efforts being poured into restructuring and consolidating the *caisses*.

In 1991, the Minister for Finance gave his approval to a bill designed to reform the savings banks, with the subsequent debate centering on the maintenance of links between them and the CDC. This bill, by modifying the Law of July 1 1983, supports the banks in their restructuring and modernisation plans. The reform is intended to accelerate the re-grouping process and turn the *caisses* into fully-fledged banks. As a consequence, each *caisse* is meant to cover a maximum of one region, or a minimum of two *départements*, which is one or two *caisses* per region.[22]

Three salient elements are contained in the proposed reform. First, the bill seeks to simplify the savings banks structure by relieving the SOREFI of the function of centralising regular sources of income (excluding the Livret A), which reached about FF450 billion ($79 billion) under management in 1990. The SOREFIs' (in which CDC has a 50 percent holding) legal status is thus to be abolished and the *caisses* will have direct links with CENCEP. However, this transformation does not at all mean that the savings banks will be "emancipated" from the CDC, with the relationship between the two remaining highly complex.

Second, the financial functions of central clearer, currently in the hands of the CDC, will pass to two finance companies: one for the management of liquidities, in which CDC will have a 65 percent holding and the savings banks 35 percent; and the other (in which the central clearer will have 35 percent and the savings banks 65 percent) for bond issues, large credit operations and the domestic capital market. This split of functions and shareholdings is supposed to reassert the close financial association between the CDC and the *caisses* while, in principle, the latter will retain a degree of autonomy.

Third, CENCEP's role will be strengthened, thereafter having authority to appoint management at the *caisses* and to decide on mergers. The composition of CENCEP's capital will probably change in the *caisses*' favour because the SOREFIs' stake will probably be redivided.[23]

Other measures are to be introduced to change the system of management at the *caisses*. One of the most important of these is the proposal to limit directors' mandates to four to six years (there is presently no limit), according to the legal statutes of each *caisse.*

While the savings banks are potentially serious competitors in the banking market, the ambiguities that exist in the definition of their powers and the unforeseeable results of the restructuring process leaves the future of these banks uncertain. It should be noted, however, that interpenetration with the CDC is far from being dissolved.

The financial services of the Post Office

The Post Office's financial services have existed since 1817.[24] For historical reasons, they benefit from an incomparably dense and convenient network of approximately 17,000 PTT offices. Before the 1970s, the Post Office played a major role in introducing banking to the countryside and to the less sophisticated sections of the population. (The Caisse Nationale d'Epargne (CNE) shares a monopoly over the Livret A with the Ecureuil). In addition, the Post Office has a large "captive" institutional clientele, among public companies and government departments in particular. However, the Post Office's inherited position as a large deposit-taking institution has been crumbling under the impact of ever-growing competition and the decline of the Livret A.

Even though the Post Office is one of France's largest financial institutions, its peculiarities have often relegated it to the background. The Post Office's financial services do not include the right to grant loans and it was excluded from the reform of credit institutions (the Banking Law of January 24 1984, Article 8). Due to its status as a public service, the Post Office encounters strong resistance from the credit institutions when it expresses an ambition to extend its activities into lending.[25] The Post Office's plans are audacious, calling for the transformation of its 17,000 offices into outlets offering every kind of product and financial service (by the early 1990s, the Post Office had already gained a strong foothold in the insurance market).

The Post Office is the third largest deposit-taker after the Ecureuil savings banks and Crédit Agricole. Its hold on the deposits market is a great advantage and included in 1990: 17.4 million Livret A and 3 million CODEVI, LEP and Livret B accounts (funds collected are centralised at the CNE), as well as 8.5 million Post Office current accounts (Chèques Postaux — CCP).

The extent of the PTT network in 1990 accounted for 40 percent of all banking outlets in France, and took in 11 percent of all demand deposits.[26] But this market advantage is counterbalanced by several weaknesses: its image is too much that of a public service, its outlets must undertake a variety of tasks (telecom transactions and mail as well as finance), and the outlets have little expertise in money matters. In addition, its outlets are predominantly in rural areas and it finds it difficult to combine the ethos of financial institution with that of a public service.

In the 1970s, the increasing power of the commercial (and mutual) banks signalled relative decline for the CCP. While the number of bank accounts doubled during the decade, the number of CCPs only increased by 5 percent. Likewise, in the space of 15 years, the Post Office's market share of demand deposits fell from 30 to 11 percent. Moreover, like the Ecureuil savings banks, the CNE is confronted with the serious problem of maintaining stability in Livret A accounts. Over time, the Livret A risks being drained of funds due to pressure from other financial products offering more attractive tax arrangements.

Leaving aside the tax-exempt Livret A, the Post Office in 1990 accounted for only 6 percent of CODEVIs and 17 percent of LEPs. The Post Office has only 6 percent of the market for home savings products and it is clear that in terms of other common banking products, the Post Office does not have an impact proportionate to its large customer base nor to the size of its network.

Long protected by the absence of any real competition and also by its Livret A privilege, the Post Office has been forced to renew its marketing drive as a provider of financial services in a very competitive environment.

Since the beginning of the 1980s, the Post Office has been attempting to recover its share of the retail market by extending the range of products it offers. Consequently, in the 1980s, the Post Office developed its customer retail services by establishing an ATM network. It also joined the SIT (Système Interbancaire de Télétransmission) interest grouping in electronic clearing and the GIE-Carte Bleu interest grouping in 1983, which saved it from becoming "marginalised". Since 1985, travellers cheques have been available to its customers, and its outlets are authorised to handle foreign exchange transactions.

In addition, at a time when stock market business is of growing importance and in order to bolster its financial standing, the Post Office has been putting an extra effort into securities-linked savings products, increasing the number of SICAVs and FCPs it offers (managed by the CDC).[27] In 1984, the Post Office set up the Centre National des Valeurs Mobilières (CNVM — National Centre for Transferable Securities) which allowed it to manage share accounts and related services directly. And the Post Office usually participates in the placement of government loan issues.

The Post Office also looks after the investment of Caisse Nationale de Prévoyance policies (life insurance and pension schemes) and occupies a relatively important position in the market for PEPs. At the end of 1990, deposits collected as part of this scheme came to around FF8 billion ($1.4 billion), representing 7 percent of funds taken in.

All of these innovations and activities accurately convey the Post Office's current strategic aims: to regain market share and to assert its position as an important financial institution on the personal customer market.

But the financial world takes a dim view of the Post Office's ambitions, alleging that it is using its protected public service position to pursue a policy of "bankification". The banks accuse the Post Office of unfair competition as its cost of funding (interest rates which are partly subsidised) is very low, allowing it to sell financial services at minimal cost. In addition, the Post Office is not subject to the same supervision and solvency requirements as are the banks.

While the Post Office is not authorised to grant loans, it is actually very flexible over small, short-term overdrafts, another fact which greatly irritates the banks. Thus, it is essential to find a solution which will align law with practice.

As opinions vary widely on how the Post Office's financial services should develop, the Finance Minister asked the general secretary of the Conseil National du Crédit, Yves Ullmo to prepare a report on the question at the beginning of 1991. The resulting Ullmo report, presented in September 1991, argued against granting an extension to La Poste's financial services. The government's response to the report, however, was unclear at the time of writing due to parliament's preoccupation with La Poste's new plan to launch an interest-bearing type account linked to a mutual fund and with the level of interest to be paid for Chèques Postaux accounts.

While awaiting reforms which would bring the Post Office's financial services closer in line with those offered by the banks, steps have been taken to modernise marketing and management. For example, Jacques Lenormand, ex-head of retail at Crédit Agricole and noted bank marketing expert, was appointed assistant chief executive in charge of financial customers. This recruitment "offensive", together with a huge advertising campaign, did not go unnoticed in the banking world. For the chairman of the Post Office, Yves Consequer, this recruitment drive is a sign of the Post Office's intention to become part of the financial world.

As proof of this, and following in the line of banking institutions like Cortal and Caixabank that have managed to get round the official prohibition of interest-bearing sight deposits, the Post Office has plans to remunerate sight deposits indirectly. To this end, it created an account (called *Libertitude*) linked to an investment fund. But this product has encountered resistance from the Minister of Finance before its launch, as well as predictable opposition from the majority of banks. Whether this product is authorised or not, the bold initiatives being undertaken by the Post Office are sure to continue irritating its competitors.

Finance companies

Numbering 1,069 and accounting for 7.4 percent of total credits in 1990, the finance companies are a mixed bag of institutions. However, despite their different origins and activities, almost all these companies come under the umbrella of the Association Française des Sociétés Financières (ASF), similar in function to the AFB.

The finance companies can only carry out those

banking operations specifically authorised by legislation or regulations. So they may not, except in rare instances, accept deposits from the public of less than two years duration — a peculiarity of the French banking system. These institutions mainly turn to the banks for funding, from which they receive resources at favourable rates due to their access to the interbank money market. Most of the companies are themselves bank subsidiaries.

The finance companies play an important economic and social role, particularly in the funding of corporate investments, home improvement and housing loans. They are specialist institutions (subject to the Banking Law as well as to specific legislation and regulations) whose main activities entail granting loans and related operations, particularly leasing, rent-to-buy and consumer credit. There are also institutions which specialise in the issuing or management of payment systems such as cards or travellers cheques.

Under the terms of Article 18.2 of the Banking Law, there are two main categories of finance company:

First, there are those whose activities are strictly limited by specific legislation and regulations. These are Sociétés de Caution Mutuelle (mutual guarantee companies), Sociétés de Crédit Différé (deferred credit companies), Sociétés de Crédit Immobilier (property loan companies for local authority housing agencies), Sociétés de Crédit Outre-mer (overseas loan companies), SICOMI (commercial and industrial real estate companies), SOFERGIE (telecommunications finance companies) and the Caisse Nationale de l'Energie (National Energy Bank).

Second, there are those companies authorised to carry out very specific activities. These are classified according to their main fields of operation; funding of sales on credit, housing loans, housing and property leasing, rent-to-buy, factoring companies, industrial and commercial loan companies (venture capital) and others (see Table 4.8).

i) Rent-to-buy:

Although there are about 100 such companies, the five market-leaders handle over half of all business.

Table 4.8 Finance companies: key figures (in FF bn under management)		
	1989	1990
Corporate and occupational financing[1]	169.0	190.1
of which:		
Straight loans	37.7	39.3
Leasing of movables and other equipment rental transactions	131.3	150.8
Financing of individuals	184.7	197.7
of which:		
Straight loans[2]	136.2	162.1
Rent to buy	48.5	35.6
Financing of commercial property	226.1	297.8
of which:		
Straight property loans	67.5	103.3
Property leasing	158.6	194.5
Housing finance for individuals[3]	165.8	180.2
of which		
Straight property loans	146.6	156.7
Loans for council housing	19.2	23.5
Financial and miscellaneous services	65.9	60.6
of which:		
Factoring	13.3	17.2
Miscellaneous	52.6	43.4

[1] *Excluding property*

[2] *Appropriated loans, standing accounts, personal loans*

[3] *Excluding state-assisted property loans*

Source: Association Française des Sociétés Financières

The market share of each of these is over 10 percent and they are all subsidiaries of the main credit institutions: UFB-Locabail (Compagnie Bancaire), BNP-Bail (BNP), Bail-Equipement (CIC), Slibail (Crédit Lyonnais), Unimat (Crédit Agricole).

ii) Property leasing:

Even though property leasing experienced steady growth between 1980 and 1990, profits are falling as competition becomes keener, with the number of companies growing from 60 in 1987 to around 100 by 1990, while personnel costs have increased more quickly than turnover. The high rate of provisioning also accounts for the low profits (and even losses) of some companies in this sector.

The property leasing company market depends mainly on the level of investments made by small businesses and the professional classes as well as personal consumption levels. These three categories are the largest "consumers" of property leasing in France.

iii) Real-estate leasing:

One must differentiate between SICOMI and non-SICOMI companies, which together account for 150 companies.

SICOMIs (*Sociétés Immobilères pour le Commerce et l'Industrie* — commercial and industrial real estate companies) benefit from tax breaks and specialise in renting office buildings. The main companies are: Locindus, Interbail, Locabail, Bail Investissement and UIS. The non-SICOMI houses, on the other hand, do not benefit from any tax breaks.

Since January 1 1989, SICOMIs may operate abroad. Nevertheless, the very uneven tax situation in Europe constitutes a hindrance to the development of international real estate leasing.

The French real estate leasing market is second in Europe after the UK and the activities of French real estate leasing companies are currently enjoying a period of strong growth abroad. Société Générale has the densest international real estate leasing network controlling 29 foreign companies for a total turnover of FF2 billion ($353 million). The SICOMI Locindus has expanded into Spain, establishing a subsidiary called Euroleasing Immobiliario in conjunction with Caixa de Barcelona. UCA-Bail is also developing a presence in Portugal.

iv) Consumer credit companies

The main institutions in this category (Sofinco, Cetelem, Crédit Universel) have bank status and others are subsidiaries of industrial groups such as Renault and Peugeot. Three-quarters of turnover is made up of car loans and revolving credit, but since the market for this type of credit has stagnated, companies have been going through difficult times.

v) The market for factoring, though expanding, is still small. There are 14 companies whose turnover has been increasing rapidly (annual growth of 20 to 25 percent) — roughly FF45 billion ($7.9 billion) in 1989 as against FF37 billion in 1988.

vi) The 49 companies specialising in venture capital are still in their infancy and have a combined turnover of FF15 billion. This market is very concentrated: four companies account for two thirds of business.

vii) The situation is very similar in the financing of cash needs business. Of the 71 companies in this sector, the three market leaders account for three-quarters of business. Companies in this sector are experiencing serious profitability problems.

Endnotes

(1) BNP's *banque d'affaires*-type activities are split up among subsidiaries as follows: Banexi handles the top-of-the-range *petites et moyennes entreprises* (PME — small and medium-sized enterprises) side of the business while BNP-Développement and Compagnie Internationale de Paris deal with larger corporates.

(2) Where BIAO (Banque Industrielle de l'Afrique Occidentale) is concerned, BNP found itself virtually trapped in its role of "lender of last resort" in the region. In 1989, its losses amounted to FF1 billion ($176 million).

(3) In 1990, 42 percent of BNP's funds was sourced on the money market, although 37 percent of customer funds was still "free of charge"!

(4) BNP and Dresdner swapped directors in 1989 and are carrying through a number of joint operations in central Europe (eg the setting up of BNP-KH-Dresdner Bank in Hungary, a joint subsidiary).

(5) This bank has been taken over by the Spanish savings bank, Caja de Madrid.

(6) The integration of Credito Bergamasco accounts for the 12 percent increase in 1989 consolidated assets.

(7) Director of the Treasury from 1978 to 1982 and former chairman of Paribas.

(8) 800,000 shareholders and a market capitalisation of around FF30 billion ($5.3 million).

(9) Société Générale has 3.5 million personal customers, 1 million of whom hold stocks and shares.

(10) Sogebail is number one in the French property leasing market.

(11) Crédit Agricole can, in fact, be broken down into two unequal parts: the official Crédit Agricole network or Crédit Agricole Mutuel (regulated by Section 5 of the Rural Code), and the free Crédit Agricole network or Crédit Mutuel Agricole et Rural. The former, which is analysed here, represents over 95 percent of the total.

(12) The CNCA allocates advances to the regional banks and grants loans, in particular to farming co-operatives and farming groups.

(13) At the end of 1989, overall loans outstanding to agriculture had reached FF152.3 billion ($26 billion) or nearly 21 percent of total funding.

(14) The leading Italian private sector bank with total assets in the order of FF100 billion ($17 billion) and a network of 340 outlets, mostly in northern Italy.

(15) Even though it is not a financial organisation, the Chambre Syndicale manages a collective guarantee fund to which the banks in the group contribute. This allows it to intervene when banks encounter difficulties or to participate in special modernisation and development programmes.

(16) However, deposits of the local banks are subject to two legal requirements: half of the deposits must come from "company members" and the total sum of deposits may not exceed 5 percent of the company members' liability, which is set at 20 times the sum of the stock subscribed.

(17) Deposits taken in by the savings banks (including those of the Post Office) are used in funding government housing at below market rates; either the CDC provides this funding directly or funding takes place indirectly, which means that the CDC passes part of the funds back to the savings banks, which in turn fund the projects they wish to.

(18) In 1990, the savings banks took in FF19 billion ($3.3 billion) in the form of PEPs — in other words 18 percent of all such deposits and 22 percent of funds collected by all credit institutions.

(19) Two-thirds of the 121 banks involved in mergers in 1989 had own funds of less than FF50 million ($8.8 million).

(20) In 1989, CENCEP's holdings in the savings banks subsidiaries were transferred to Ecureuil Participations, a holding company set up in 1988.

(21) The potential of the savings banks movement with 53,000 outlets across Europe occupies a central position in Ecureuil's plans.

(22) One-third of these *caisses* will have over FF1 billion in own funds while the average will be FF600-800 million.

(23) In cases where there are still several banks in any one region, the SOREFIs (modified to become GIEs — interest groupings) will stay on, their sole function being issuing public bonds.

(24) The PTT administers two hugely-important financial services: Chèques Postaux and the Caisse Nationale d'Epargne (CNE). Funds collected by Chèques Postaux are channelled to the Treasury and those of the CNE to the CDC.

(25) The financial services of the Post Office are regulated by the Post and Telecommunications Code (Decree of 8/10/52).

(26) The tens of thousands of public service accounts represent close to 50 percent of current accounts taken in by the Post Office.

(27) The Post Office now accounts for almost 4 percent of the OPCVM market as against 3.2 percent in 1980.

Section III

Insurance

Section III

Insurance

Chapter 5

The Insurance Industry

Since the mid-1980s, French insurance has undergone a revolution, both in terms of products and of companies operating in the market. The industry has shown itself to be highly innovative, creating or adapting a broad range of new life insurance products. Some examples are: civil liability contracts for pollution, policies denominated in foreign currencies and non-exclusion of HIV-positive patients. These innovations have gone together with a process of market deregulation, the end result of which has been reform of the Insurance Code. Thus, supervision of companies has been substantially modified, the requirement of visas to operate in general insurance has disappeared, commission rates have been liberalised, etc. To adapt to the new situation, companies have undertaken various forms of financial restructuring either by means of external growth on the French market, by the acquisition of stakes in companies in other parts of Europe or by signing agreements with banks. Such moves have taken place in an environment of ruthless price competition and product diversification, an environment which has forced companies to become more service-oriented.

Such developments have been stimulated — if not directly motivated — by the impending unification of EC markets as part of the liberalisation of capital movements and the provision of services.

The world standing of the French insurance market

As late as the mid-1980s, the French insurance sector occupied a relatively lowly position in the world compared to that of its main trading partners. This was due to the lack of demand for personal insurance (life and health) and due to the reach of the social security system. In fact, unlike other developed countries, private pension funds hardly exist in France and French insurers are not very active in the retirement market.

But figures for the latter part of the 1980s show an appreciable improvement in world standing (see Tables 5.1 and 5.2). At least two factors account for

Table 5.1		
General insurance world ranking, 1989		
Country	Premiums	
	$ bn	% of world market
1 US	264.9	46.0
2 Japan	65.6	11.4
3 Germany	47.5	8.2
4 France	29.5	5.1
5 UK	27.8	4.8
6 Italy	17.6	3.1
7 Canada	14.9	2.6
8 USSR	12.7	2.2
9 Netherlands	10.0	1.7
10 Australia	9.7	1.7
11 Spain	9.1	1.6
12 Switzerland	6.8	1.2
13 Belgium	4.9	0.9
14 Sweden	4.8	0.9
15 Austria	4.8	0.9
Total world premiums	576.3	—
(EC total = $152.9bn)		
Source: Swiss Re (Zurich)		

Table 5.2
Life insurance world ranking, 1989

Country	Premiums	
	FF bn	% of world market
1 Japan	199.1	31.4
2 US	188.3	29.7
3 UK	48.7	7.7
4 France	33.7	5.3
5 Germany	29.0	4.6
6 South Korea	17.5	2.8
7 USSR	16.9	2.7
8 Canada	14.3	2.3
9 Australia	9.7	1.5
10 Switzerland	9.0	1.4
11 Netherlands	9.0	1.4
12 South Africa	7.4	1.2
13 Italy	5.8	0.9
14 Finland	4.5	0.7
15 Taiwan	4.3	0.7
Total world premiums (in US$ bn)	633.7	—
(EC total = $137.4bn)		
Source: Suisse Re, Zurich		

1989 and France jumped four places to rank twelfth in the world. In addition, life surpassed general insurance, even though their weightings were 1.8 and 2.8 percent respectively as recently as 1986. Also, there has been progress in the total value of premiums per inhabitant. France ranked 11th in 1989, while in 1986 it was 13th (see Table 5.3).

Table 5.3
Premiums per inhabitant in 1989 (in $)

	Total	General	Life
1 Switzerland	2,375.6	2,018.9	1,356.6
2 Japan	2,149.9	533.0	1,616.9
3 US	1,817.1	1,062.2	754.9
4 Finland	1,417.9	504.8	913.1
5 Sweden	1,384.8	563.2	821.6
6 UK	1,335.7	485.2	850.5
7 Netherlands	1,281.1	677.1	604.0
8 Germany	1,241.7	771.1	470.6
9 Australia	1,158.3	579.7	578.6
10 Norway	1,140.4	702.6	477.8
11 France	1,126.7	525.8	600.9
12 Canada	1,116.9	571.1	545.8
13 Ireland	1,105.4	412.8	692.6
Source: Suisse Re, Zurich			

this; first, annual growth rates of 25 to 30 percent in life insurance could not help but make up for lost time and second, adjustments in exchange rates led to an improvement in France's position.

France, which in 1987 accounted for 4.5 percent of all world premiums, increased its share to 5.2 percent in 1989. By 1991, France was ranked fourth by volume of life and non-life premiums (in dollar terms), ahead of both the UK and Germany. Within the EC, France was ranked second in non-life (19.3 percent of premiums) and in life (24.5 percent of premiums).

If one takes into consideration the economic impact of insurance, France's position has improved considerably when measured by premiums as a percentage of gross domestic product and by total value of premiums collected per inhabitant.

Premiums as a share of gross domestic product increased from 4.5 percent in 1986 to 6 percent in

Despite these changes, the French remained severely under-insured in the early 1990s compared to the Swiss, Japanese, British and American counterparts.

Structure and size of the French market

The number of direct insurance companies in France, both life and non-life, is growing. In life insurance, the number of companies rose from 89 in 1984 to 137 in 1990: 120 companies were authorised to operate in the life business and 85 in capitalisation. The reasons for this growth can be attributed to the dynamism of the market for capitalisation and pension savings. Around 50 new companies were approved between 1985 and 1990.

After a strong initial burst in 1985, the number of non-life insurance companies rose consistently to reach 456 in 1990. The greatest number sell property insurance (243), followed by bodily injury (204), transport (189), general civil liability (182) and car insurance (151).

The French insurance market is distinguished by the co-existence of companies governed by different statutes with *sociétés anonymes* (limited companies) including bank subsidiaries dominant in life and capitalisation, and the mutuals dominating general insurance both in number of companies (see Table 5.4) and in terms of premiums collected (see Table 5.5).

Table 5.4

Number of direct insurance companies, 1989

	Life and capitalisation	General	Total
State-controlled companies	4	3	7
Limited companies	103	121	224
Mutual companies	17	191	208
Branches of foreign companies	10	136	146
Miscellaneous (CNP, *tontines* etc)	3	5	8
Total	137	456	593

Source: Commission de Contrôle des Assurances, Le Journal de l'Assurance

Table 5.5

Breakdown of receipts by status of institution (1990)

	Life and capitalisation	General	Market as a whole
Limited companies	53.6	33.4	44.1
Mutual companies	8.9	40.9	24.1
State-controlled companies	26.3	21.3	24.0
Caisse Nationale de Prévoyance	9.1	—	4.6
Foreign companies	2.1	4.4	3.2
Total	100.0	100.0	100.0

Source: Commission de Contrôle des Assurances

The relative market position of the different life and non-life insurance companies as defined by legislation changed rapidly between 1980 and 1990.

In life insurance, the state-controlled sector (UAP, AGF and GAN) has been losing ground in relative terms (minus 22 percent). The slack has been picked up by the private groups linked to financial holding companies (Axa, Victoire-Suez, Athéna, Allianz) and the numerous offshoots of banks (which combined are up 24 percent). The web of insurance companies is completed by the mutuals (with or without intermediaries) which have gained market share at the expense of the traditional companies since the end of the 1960s. The mutuals now control a growing share of the general insurance market, notably car and household comprehensive insurance. Nevertheless, growth rates were faltering by the early 1990s.

Although the number of branches belonging to foreign companies had already reached high levels by 1990 (146, of which 136 operate in non-life), their market share was falling (3.2 percent of the total market compared to 6.4 percent in 1980).

The French insurance industry is highly concentrated. If one takes the share of total turnover of the top four, 10 and 20 groups, this concentration appears more pronounced in life than in non-life (see Table 5.6).[1] Given that most groups are made up of several companies, the top 20 groups' share of the market actually derives from 40 percent of all companies authorised to sell life insurance (53 out of 132). In general insurance, however, the figure is only 16 percent (73 out of 446), due primarily to greater specialisation in the general insurance market.[2]

Table 5.6

The degree of concentration in French insurance (in % of turnover, 1989)

	Non-life insurance	Life insurance
4 largest groups	36.5	42.2
10 largest groups	58.6	69.8
20 largest groups	82.1	87.3

Source: FREF

It should be noted that the French insurance market, especially the life market, was already highly concentrated by the mid-1970s: for the top four, 10 and 20 life companies, market shares were 62, 77 and 91 percent respectively. In the 1980s, the arrival of new companies led to a certain dispersion away from the four main companies (UAP, AGF, GAN and CNP) which lost 20 points to the other two types of insurance group (private companies and mutuals).

The growth of life insurance and the moderate progress of general

Since the beginning of the 1980s, French insurance had been growing at a steadier pace than national output. This trend became more pronounced in the second half of the 1980s before slowing down sharply in 1990. While the gap between growth rates in annual turnover registered by insurers and the growth rate in gross domestic product reached 11.6 percent in 1988, it narrowed to practically nothing by 1990.

Before 1990, turnover in French insurance (excluding foreign subsidiaries and reinsurance) was expanding rapidly: FF390 billion ($68 billion) in 1989, as against FF340 billion in 1988, an increase of 15 percent. This expansion can be ascribed to the advance of life insurance and capitalisation products where net revenues increased by around 26 percent (a yearly average of 24 percent since 1980), while general insurance grew at a much slower rate (5.3 on average between 1985 and 1990). At the end of the 1980s, life insurance was the industry's largest business line, while it stood at only 25 percent in 1980 (see Table 5.7).

The increasing importance of insurance companies can best be described, if not explained, by a growing desire for protection on the part of economic agents. This desire was in part spontaneous, arising out of changing consumption habits, and in part encouraged by tax breaks and other measures taken by the public authorities. Also, the proliferation of compulsory insurance schemes aided in increasing the importance of insurance companies.

Progress in terms of product offer has been relatively slower because insurers have traditionally adapted products only in response to demand. It is only recently that French insurers have developed an active approach to the market.[3] Now the technique of strategic marketing enables insurers to move beyond the old adage that "life insurance is sold, not bought".

But this new spirit was to run out of steam in 1990 when there was growth of just 2.9 percent in life insurance due to a steep decline in amounts taken in on capitalisation products (down 30 percent). Be that as it may, the insurance industry has managed to become one of the most dynamic sections of the French economy.

A change in the insurance-friendly environment?

The period 1980 to 1990 was marked by a consistently favourable environment for life insurance, especially pension savings products.

Compared to financial investments and to households' gross disposable income, technical reserves (covering 90 percent of life contracts) attributed to households have doubled their share of the total. Insurance in 1990 accounted for 40 percent of household investments, compared with under 20 percent at the beginning of the 1980s. This growth is notable as it occurred at a time when the savings rate dropped from 16 to 12 percent. Several factors might explain this enthusiasm for life insurance:

* The French were becoming more conscious of the problems associated with preparing for retirement given the uncertainties hanging over the present *répartition* or pay-as-you-go system;

Table 5.7

Changes in premiums taken in by insurance companies (in FF bn)

	1980	1981	1982	1983	1984	1985	1986	1987	1988	1989	1990
Life and capitalisation	29.5	35.7	43.9	48.9	59.4	75.2	95.8	118.1	159.8	200.7	206.3
Non-life	86.0	100.0	116.3	133.7	147.6	155.7	162.5	171.9	180.9	190.1	201.8
Total	115.5	135.7	160.2	182.6	207.0	230.9	258.3	290.0	340.7	390.8	408.1

Source: FFSA

• The introduction of tax measures favourable to life insurance (viewed rightly or wrongly by the authorities as a savings support) resulted in a high return on these products (2 to 4 points above that available on bonds);

• An appreciable improvement in loading rates (the ratio of commissions and expenses charged by life insurance sellers to total value of premiums paid in) occurred due to the rise of the bank subsidiaries in insurance. Within 10 years, the rate was halved and it stood at just 10 percent in 1990;

• A greater availability and improvement in product offer as a result of intense competition.

Between 1980 and 1990, premiums collected by the life and capitalisation branches of the industry increased sevenfold to reach FF200 billion ($35 billion) in 1989, representing annual growth of 24 percent. But growth in the different lines of business has varied (see Figure 5.1).

Capitalisation, which had been one of the main engines of growth, began to flag in 1988 and dropped by 30 percent in 1990 (as against average growth rates of over 50 percent between 1985 and 1989) due to the launch of the PEP (the people's saving plan) and, to a lesser extent, the *SICAVs de capitalisation* (capital growth funds). The share of capitalisation in the total amount collected, which increased from 13 to 27.5 percent in the space of 10 years, was down to 19 percent in 1990. The bank subsidiaries suffered most from this decline because funds taken in were based around activities linking them closely to the parent bank's customer base.

Life, on the other hand, registered a strong 15.4 percent growth rate in 1990, benefiting from exponential growth in "open group" contracts linked to savings and retirement products (subscribed to by individuals through savers' associations like AFER, a subsidiary of Victoire) and from a renaissance in personal contracts (up 31.9 percent in 1990).

As for families of products, the renewed vitality of personal contracts denominated in units of account deserves to be mentioned. Standing at FF12 billion ($2 billion) in 1990, these increased by 112 percent following a sharp fall in 1988 after the stock market collapse. By 1990, they accounted for a quarter of these contracts. One should also note that the pension savings side of personal contracts accounted for 95 percent of the total, while death insurance represented only a negligible fraction.

Figure 5.1

Premium income by class of business in life insurance (FF bn)

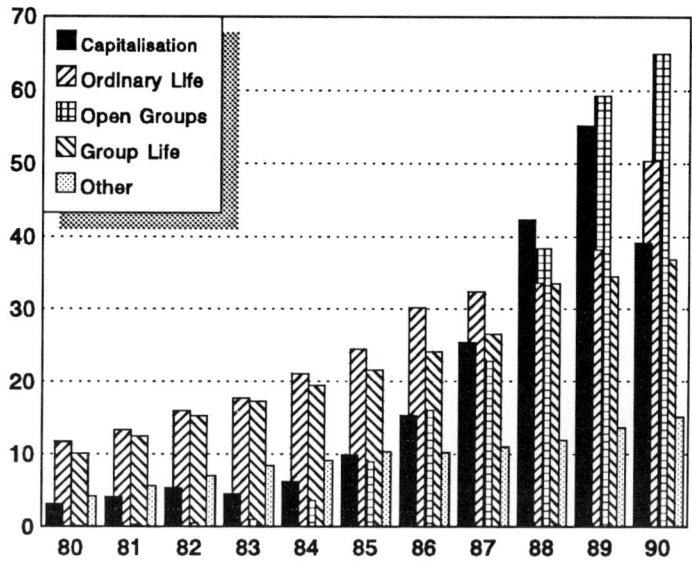

■ Capitalisation
▨ Ordinary Life
⊞ Open Groups
◧ Group Life
▦ Other

Source: GAP/FFSA

The slowdown in activity in 1990 hardly came as a surprise to insurers. First, the inordinate growth in premiums could not have continued forever because they were cumulative; second, competition coming from the PEPs was acute from the start, especially affecting the bank subsidiaries. Parent banks were paying increasing attention to this product to the detriment of their own "creations". The traditional insurance companies — which experienced no real downturn in capitalisation — were able to boast that their predictions were turning out to be accurate: they had foretold the shrinkage of bank subsidiaries whose activities were based, to a greater or lesser extent, around financial "techniques".

However, the shortfalls were largely made good by investments and capital gains. Life and capitalisation demonstrated a chronic deficit in terms of operating balance, a deficit which can be best explained by the size of the mathematical provisions made to cover long-term commitments and with-profits insurance.[4] However, with investment yields worth FF69 billion ($12 billion) and with FF7 billion in capital gains from sales of securities, balance sheet earnings came to FF8 billion in 1990.

Measured by percentage of premiums, on the other hand, 1990 results for this line of business were scarcely encouraging because they showed a decline in most of the elements that make up the trading account (see Table 5.8).

Table 5.8						
Life insurance results (in % of premiums)						
	1985	1986	1987	1988	1989	1990
Operating balance	0.7	-0.8	-0.5	-0.6	-0.5	-0.8
Balance sheet income	6.4	5.8	4.1	3.8	3.7	3.8
Claims and settlements	58.8	51.8	48.4	34.3	41.5	51.9
Operating expenses	17.7	16.2	14.9	12.5	11.7	12.3
Investment income	37.2	34.2	26.9	29.6	30.1	33.4
Source: FFSA						

Despite the slowdown in growth in life and capitalisation between 1988 and 1990, rates were expected to stabilise at between 5 and 15 percent by 1995. Apart from innovations in price and quality of pro-

ducts offered, other developments may have either a negative or a positive impact on these forecasts.

The introduction of new legislation authorising the establishment of supplementary capitalisation-based pension schemes (personal retirement packages and French-style pension funds) along the lines of Anglo-Saxon pension funds, to be administered by insurance companies and offering tax advantages to households, would provide new impetus to the life insurance industry.

However, while French taxation was relatively well-disposed towards life insurance up to 1990, this is changing in the light of existing and expected measures, including: tax breaks for liquid savings over and above those available on contractual savings (for example, capital growth funds); the lengthening of the duration of savings required to obtain tax exemption for income from insurance from six to eight years; a probable rise in the taxes levied on long-term capital gains that will have the effect of reducing the return from those products, etc. Given the very "fiscal" character of insurance products, such measures will undoubtedly lead to a slowdown in growth in this line of business.

General insurance: moderate growth

General insurance has not experienced the same boom as life insurance. Turnover growth remained unchanged at 5 to 6 percent a year between 1985 and 1990. Such minimal, albeit regular, growth can be attributed both to saturation of the personal market[5] and the importance of motor insurance in large industrial risks. Fierce competition for premiums, unleashed by the mutuals operating without intermediaries and countered by other insurers, especially in the car and comprehensive insurance market, would also seem to have had a long-term depressive effect on turnover (see Table 5.9).

Unlike the other branches, turnover in bodily injuries insurance, through 1990, has increased at a higher-than-average rate (9 percent is the average). New activities, such as litigation insurance (which showed a 20 percent increase in premium income in 1990) and credit insurance also appear to have a bright future.

Operating balances go into the red

Lax management and too much competition — something often decried by members of the profes-

Table 5.9 Distribution of direct general insurance				
	1987	1988	1989	1990
Damage to property	25.7	25.8	25.5	25.0
of which:				
Individuals	11.9	12.0	12.0	11.7
Professionals	10.7	10.7	10.5	10.3
Agriculture	3.1	3.1	3.0	3.0
Car	40.0	39.6	39.0	38.5
of which:				
Civil liability car insurance	18.5	18.7	18.9	18.9
Car damage insurance	21.5	20.9	20.1	19.6
Bodily injury	17.5	17.9	18.6	19.1
Other	16.8	16.7	16.9	17.4
Total (in %)	100.0	100.0	100.0	100.0
(in FF bn)	153.5	161.4	170.6	180.5

Source: FFSA, Commission de Contrôle des Assurances

sion — did not have an obvious effect on operating results overall, at least up to 1990. But in that year, operating balances, which had always been positive, went into the red and balance sheet earnings fell by 13 percent (see Table 5.10 — non-life results).

Table 5.10 Non-life insurance results (in % of premiums)						
	1985	1986	1987	1988	1989	1990
Operating balance	1.9	1.9	2.3	2.9	3.0	-0.2
Balance sheet income	3.9	5.0	5.3	6.0	5.7	4.7
Claims and settlements	61.2	62.6	62.1	62.1	59.9	64.6
Operating expenses	26.4	27.0	27.4	27.6	28.2	28.3
Invesment income	13.2	13.5	13.2	13.1	10.8	12.1

Source: FFSA

These are the fruits of a bad year and of claims accumulating over a number of years, combined with an increase in general expenses as a percentage

of premiums. The total loss experience increased by 5 points to reach 65 percent of premiums and investment income also fell.

Balance sheet earnings (profits) came to FF9.4 billion ($1.6 billion), 90 percent of which was monopolised by the top 20 companies.

Outlook
General insurance is evidently linked to economic performance. When economic activity is growing risks increase, thereby increasing the demand for coverage.

While growth is expected to remain slow until 1995 (growth in 1990 was a mere 2 percent), growth in demand for various property and casualty products will vary. Some areas, such as car damage insurance, will advance slowly — at most, 5 percent. Others, like fire insurance, might actually stagnate.

Yet, prospects look brighter for some personal and group risk coverage (personal accident and health, group accident cover, etc) where annual growth will be in the region of 5 to 10 points above gross domestic product. And it can be anticipated that the health insurance sector will experience a revolution by the end of the century.

The growth in health insurance will depend on the extent to which the social security system is able to continue to cover health expenditure. It is estimated that expenditure not covered by social security because of the state's disengagement and the increase in small risks — which are not covered by social security — could reach 30-35 percent of all health expenditure by 1995.[6]

Insurers will probably widen the coverage they offer and absorb between 15 and 18 percent of households' expenditure on health (compared to 9 percent in 1989); in other words, over FF110 billion ($19 billion).

In the long term, small and medium-sized businesses (which are claimed to be under-insured), local authorities (helped by decentralisation), and environmental and hazardous waste and other increasingly specialised types of insurance, may become strong growth areas.

The French personal sector remains under-insured

While there is an almost complete saturation of the French home and car insurance markets (where 95 and 90 percent respectively of households have at least one policy), only one-third of households held a life insurance policy in 1986 according to a survey of personal financial assets carried out by INSEE, the French statistical office (see Table 5.11). While official figures for 1991 are still pending, certain indicators point to an increase in the level of life insurance cover among certain socio-economic categories (pensioners, unemployed people), while for other categories it seems to have fallen (tradesmen, retailers, workmen, clerks) or stagnated (farmers, members of the liberal professions, various kinds of intermediary). Overall, the 1991 estimates reflects no overall change in the level of life insurance cover held by Frenchmen.

Table 5.11

The degree of insurance cover in France[1]

Farmers	38
Tradesmen, retailers, businessmen	53
Executives	45
of which	(60)
"Intermediary professions"[2]	40
Administrative employees	33
Manual workers	39
Pensioners	16
Other non-workers (students, people of private means, etc)	13

[1] *Among people that possess at least one personal life insurance policy*

[2] *Includes nurses, primary school teachers, health service workers, technicians, foremen, etc*

Source: INSEE, survey of personal financial assets, 1986

This is surprising in light of the fact that turnover in life insurance progressed by 30 percent every year since the 1986 survey, as did the number of personal policies. The paradox arises from the fact that companies have been much more selective in the risks they were willing to assume as compared to five or even 10 years before. Companies have freed themselves from most "bad quality" policies (eg industrial life).

Companies have continued to concentrate on growth in the personal insurance market (life insurance and capitalisation and bodily injury), which in 1990 accounted for two-thirds of premiums taken in, as against under 40 percent in 1985.

Reinsurance

The French reinsurance market developed very late. Although France is ranked fifth in the world and has 20 specialist companies, it is still well behind the large, traditional reinsurance markets like London, Switzerland and Germany.

By 1990, to make up lost ground, the industry was undertaking a process of corporate restructuring, merging operations to increase its influence on world markets. In 1989, SCOR (Société Centrale des Organismes de Réassurance) and UAP-Ré (14th and 19th respectively in the world rankings) merged into SCOR SA to become one of Europe's top reinsurers.[7] Two other important reinsurers — Société Anonyme Française de Réassurance and AGF-Ré — have also merged.

The numerous mergers and acquisitions by insurance companies do not make it easy for the reinsurers. In fact, formation of large insurance groups requires close inspection of the quality of risks underwritten. And the commitments taken on by direct insurers or by "captive" insurers are showing signs of increasing.

While the volume of business conducted by specialist reinsurers continued to rise (FF25.5 billion ($4.5 billion) in 1990, up 14.4 percent) because of the strong growth registered by a number of the larger companies, results for the industry as a whole are declining. In 1990, total profits for the top five fell by FF310 million, or 29 percent.

Insurance company investments

Insurers' investments are the reverse side of technical provisions — their commitments towards insured parties and victims — and own funds. The make-up of liabilities differs according to sector of activity: for life and capitalisation companies it is, on average, 90 percent of technical reserves and 5 percent of own funds; for general insurance companies it is 66 and 17 percent respectively.

In France, insurance company investments have always been strictly regulated. And in November

1990, new investment rules came into effect. De-crees Nos. 90-981 and 90-982 have changed the rules radically in harmony with changes in insurance Europe-wide (see Table 5.12).

The new regulation did not really change the manner in which companies invest their funds. Nonetheless, it was important because it abolished *l' obligation de l' obligation* (the obligation to invest in bonds) and forced insurers to publish an estimate of the market price of their real estate assets at regular intervals. Other measures introduced include: companies are authorised to grant loans to everybody, including individuals, on condition that they are nationals of an OECD country; and investments are no longer restricted to France, but extended to all OECD mem-ber states. But the congruency rule,[8] while it has been loosened, still limits the scope of investments that can be made outside of France.

From the early 1980s on, one notes a constant pro-gression in the relative share of life insurance invest-ments compared to general: of FF1,231 billion-worth ($217 billion) of investments in 1990, 70 percent could be attributed to life insurance, the rest to general. The proportion in 1983 was 54 to 46, for a total amount under management of FF351 billion ($62 billion).

The late 1980s and early 1990s saw significant growth in new investment in equity, mutual funds and money market securities (which together ac-counted for over half of investments), while bond

investments lost steam. But the structure of current investments, which reflects long-term price move-ments on the financial markets (see Table 5.13) has remained more than favourable to bond-type pro-ducts (including *titres participatifs* or participating securities, bond-linked SICAVs and FCPs), which are the most significant assets held by insurers: 54.4 percent in 1990. However, within this category, a downward trend in bonds and *titres participatifs* was evident, as was a rise in the proportion of bond-linked SICAVs and mutual funds (*fonds communs de placement* — FCPs), which accounted for 13.1 percent of the total in 1989 compared to 8.5 percent in 1985.

With FF600 billion-worth ($106 billion) of quoted bonds and mutual fund securities placed in bonds, insurers controlled 24 percent of the stock market capitalisation of French bonds at the end of 1990, as against 16 percent in 1985.

Investments in equities have gained in importance and the total amount under management (FF262 billion—$46 billion) was equivalent to 21.3 percent of all insurance company assets in 1989. This gain in market share is a result of the healthy state of the market and, more specifically, of the extent of indus-try restructuring in 1989. Also of note is the growing volume of equity investments made by foreign in-surance companies, opening the industry to interna-tional influences. Their investments increased from FF3.7 billion ($654 billion) to FF13.5 billion in 1989. Almost 15 percent of the stock market capi-

Table 5.12

Changes in rules on investments

	Old rules	New rules (1991)
Bonds (and OPCVMs invested in bonds)	Min. 34%	Abolished (same regulations as for marketable debt securities)
Shares (and OPCVMs invested in equities)	No upper limit (depending on availability apart from bonds)	Max. 65%
Real estate	Max. 40%	Unchanged
Loans, deposits, certificates	Max. 35%	Max. 10% (for loans only)
Deposits only	Max. 15%	Abolished

Source: FFSA

Table 5.13						
Breakdown of insurance companies' investments						
	1985	1986	1987	1988	1989	1990
Bonds and bond-linked SICAVs	54.3	54.3	54.9	56.6	54.8	54.4
Equities and equity-linked SICAVs	15.9	18.7	21.4	19.6	20.9	21.3
Property	17.0	15.8	14.5	13.4	12.5	12.3
Loans	5.7	4.6	3.4	2.5	1.9	1.6
Bills and deposits	4.1	3.6	1.8	2.2	2.9	3.2
Other	3.0	3.0	4.0	5.7	7.0	7.2
Source: *Ministère de l'Economie et des Finances*						

talisation of equities was held by insurance companies.

The share of real estate investments fell from 1985 to 1990, due to weak returns, while capital investments represented a mere 4.5 percent of total investments by 1990. Although not presently treated as a separate category in statistical analysis, capital investment appeared to be emerging as one of the most highly profitable forms of investment by the early 1990s.

The way insurance company investments are structured varies depending on whether the company operates in life or general insurance, as well as on the company's legal status.

Although the investment regulations are the same for life and property and casualty insurers, the differences in their businesses explain their different choices of investments. The perspectives are not the same: life insurers build up provisions for longer periods than property and casualty companies and must guarantee given rates of return for profit-sharing with their policy holders. From this standpoint, their preference for fixed return securities appears justified. In 1990, the percentage of such assets held was 59.3 percent, as opposed to 47.4 percent for general insurers. The fact that property and casualty insurers generally have a shorter-term perspective (three to four years) and are more sensitive to inflation because it leads to increases in the cost of claims, serves to explain why they usually hold a larger portfolio of share securities than their life insurance counterparts. The ratio for 1990 was 25.3 and 17.2 percent respectively.

Such differences are even more pronounced when one looks at the investments made by companies with different legal statuses. In life insurance, bonds represent an average of 70 percent of limited company investments as against 50 percent of state-owned company investments, while the mutuals are midway between the two with 59 percent. The position is the opposite for equity investments: they make up 14, 24 and 13 percent respectively of insurance company investments.

Significant changes in distribution

Since 1970, the "classic" insurance companies (and their sales networks) have faced competition from companies using innovative distribution methods. Two successive waves changed the way policies were sold: in the 1960s, the mutuals operating without intermediaries arrived on the scene, followed in the 1980s by the life insurer subsidiaries of banks.

Besides loss of market share, increased competition has resulted in a "distribution crisis" for the traditional companies (both state-owned and private), reflected both in the structure of their funding and in the conflicts with their tied agents. Insurance brokers appear to have been less hit by the crisis, but they were also facing a dual challenge from the growing regionalisation of their businesses and the arrival of foreign intermediaries.

In general insurance, distribution is mostly in the hands of tied agents, but their position is far from comfortable (see Table 5.14). Following the spectacular advances made by the non-intermediary mutual insurers (41 percent of car insurance turnover and 27 percent of comprehensive home insurance in 1990) whose market shares now appear to be stabilising, the companies and their intermediaries are now dealing with new forms of distribution and new

Table 5.14		
Sales channels in general insurance (in %)		
	Property and casualty	Car
Agents	48	44
Brokers	18	8
Non-intermediary mutuals	27	41
Salaried employees	4	5
Direct sales	3	2
Source: *CAPA/FFSA*		

competitors (the Post Office, the Ecureuil savings banks and the banking subsidiaries).

Traditional distribution methods — tied agents, brokers and own employees — are most threatened in the area of life and capitalisation. These channels fell from 76 percent of sales in 1980 to 52 percent in 1989, while banking outlets (including the Caisse Nationale de Prévoyance (CNP)) increased their share of premiums taken in from 17 percent in 1980 to 41 percent in 1989. Within a few years, banking subsidiaries became the main beneficiaries of this market growth. In 1989, according to a GAP[9] study, 58 percent of new premiums went directly to a financial institution. This development has caused considerable concern for intermediaries, especially tied agents which control around 10 percent of the market (see Table 5.15).

Table 5.15		
Sales channels in life and capitalisation in 1989 (in % of new business*)		
	Capitalisation	Life
Tied agents	6.3	16.7
Brokers	0.8	5.7
Salaried employees	28.2	19.7
Banking outlets	63.2	46.3
Direct sales	1.5	11.6
Total	100.0	100.0
* Out of a total FF110.9bn of premiums issued		
Source: GAP/FFSA		

The growth of other sales channels, like direct marketing and the sale of insurance contracts through retail chains, looms in the near future. But if their influence remains limited, certain institutions specialising in these forms of distribution may decide to extricate themselves.

Bancassurance — *a powerful factor in reshuffling the cards*

The blossoming of *bancassurance* covers a wide area, ranging from the establishment of insurance subsidiaries by banks to co-operation agreements between banks and insurance companies (BNP-UAP, AGF-BFCE) and even the taking over of an insurer by a bank (Suez-Victoire) or vice versa

(GAN-CIC). It is a powerful factor in the transformation of the French insurance world.

Their wide range of customers enables banks to attract buyers of life insurance or capitalisation products — buyers who normally would not take out contracts of this nature with traditional intermediaries.

Practically all the banking groups have one or several insurance subsidiaries and a number of them (CNP, Prédica, Cardif, Natio Vie), with over FF5 billion ($883 million) in premiums were among the market leaders in life insurance and capitalisation in 1989. The banking subsidiaries (of which there are around 30) were particularly active in capitalisation (63.2 percent of new business in 1989) and in personal and open life contracts (47 percent) up to 1990.

But the rise in the bank subsidiaries' turnover began to show signs of slowing by the early 1990s, especially since the launch of the PEP and the SICAV and the general slowdown in life business. The rise of the PEP in particular has shown up the much lamented weaknesses of the subsidiaries: first, as the products on offer have a very small pure insurance element, they can easily be substituted by other financial products; second, in some circumstances, the subsidiaries are in open competition with the parent bank, to their own detriment.

Henceforth, the real challenge these banking subsidiaries face is to gain market share in products such as life insurance and life products with a strong insurance element. The same holds true for non-life products. During 1991, efforts by the banking subsidiaries to penetrate a number of particular areas (car insurance, comprehensive home insurance and health insurance) failed to encounter any immediate success. Such was the case with Médicale de France (Crédit Lyonnais) and Pacifica (Crédit Agricole). Only Crédit Mutuel has managed to achieve success with its subsidiary ACM-Iard, which was set up 20 years ago (FF2.2 billion — $388 million — taken in, of which FF1.6 billion was in car and comprehensive home insurance).

The scenario is a bit different for *bancassurance* in the strict meaning of the term. It is intended to allow insurance companies to win back market share by giving them access to bank outlets through distribution agreements (UAP-BNP, GAN-CIC). But the formula does not appear to be working all that well, at least on present evidence.

Any sort of assessment of the current state of *bancassurance* would be misleading. Entry into the market, especially into non-life insurance, takes time and the protagonists involved are very discreet. Such discretion, which betrays a certain cautiousness, may also have its roots in a desire by large insurers to avoid antagonising the independent agents and competition from bank outlets.

Traditional distribution channels are in crisis

The insurance industry employed almost 1 percent of the French working population in 1990 — 216,000 people. But, since the mid-1980s, personnel growth has been below 1 percent a year. Only brokers and assessors have seen their sales forces grow rapidly. But for other intermediaries — with the exception of tied sub-agents[10] — and for the salaried employees of companies, the dawn of the 1990s brought cuts in numbers (see Table 5.16).

Salaried employees in insurance

The number of staff employed by insurance companies remained stable until 1987 after having increased rapidly through the 1970s. Then, up to 1990, numbers fell by 1 percent a year with administrative personnel particularly affected. This downturn in personnel can be ascribed both to the growth in automation and, in a more general sense, to rationalisation programmes that have been implemented throughout the services sector.

Stabilisation in the numbers employed in the industry is possible, especially in the light of a buoyant personal insurance market, which is far from reaching the end of its rapid growth phase. In addition, companies are turning increasingly to authorised agents, offering them performance-based salaries. These now make up about one-quarter of employees on companies' payrolls.

In fact, as with the banks, insurance companies have begun concentrating less on reducing numbers of staff (in absolute terms) and more on equipping personnel with relevant qualifications and bringing general expenses under control. To this end, insur-

Table 5.16				
Changes in employment in the French insurance industry				
	1980	1984	1989	1990
The companies' own workforce:				
Administrative staff	92,300	97,700	95,400	121,500[2]
Commercial staff	25,200	25,500	25,800	—
Caisse National de Prévoyance:	1,800	1,840	1,800	1,900
Independent agents:				
Licensees	26,000	23,200	20,500	20,800
Sub-agents	15,000	15,000	13,100	13,100
Salaried workforce	30,000	30,000	39,000	39,000
Brokers:				
Licensees	12,300[1]	1,700	2,000	2,400
Salaried workforce	—	10,000	15,000	16,000
Assessors:	3,000	3,200	4,150	4,200
Total	205,600	208,140	216,750	218,900

[1]Includes salaried workforce. [2]Includes commerical staff.

Source:Ministère des Finances and FFSA reports

ance companies have spent an average 3.5 percent of their wage bills on continuous staff training, with some of the large companies spending more than this, including: Mutuelles du Mans (6.8 percent), AGF (5.5 percent), UAP and GAN (5.4 percent).

The tied agents

The *agents généraux d'assurance* (AGA — tied insurance agents) are considered members of the liberal professions. They are more important in the provinces (90 percent are in towns of fewer than 200,000 inhabitants) but their numbers are falling. As independent workers, they represent the insurance companies for which they are, in principle, the sole authorised agents. Exclusivity of representation has as its counterpart territorial exclusivity, in non-life insurance, for example. The insurance company agrees to go through the intermediary of its authorised agent within a pre-determined geographical area. While the greater share of agents' activities is carried out as part of their mandate from a single insurance company, over one-third of their business was on behalf of third parties in 1990.

Given the AGA's low productivity, which the companies blame for their own high general expenses, the two sides have been in conflict for a number of years. This is particularly serious given that the agents are still one of the main channels of distribution for the major public and private sector companies (see Table 5.17). And it comes at a time when insurers are trying to make themselves more profitable to counter competition coming from the non-intermediary mutual companies and the banking subsidiaries which each have lower general expenses.

The AGAs are experiencing a consistent fall in their shares of the life and non-life markets. They also have to deal with low commission growth, the break-up and weak financial state of agencies and the widening gaps in different agencies' development.

Commissions on life insurance in 1990 were low: for 75 percent of tied agents, it was less than 10 percent with risks falling even further. The same was true for broking.

Table 5.17

Breakdown of companies' turnover by sales channel (in FF m)

Company	'89 turnover	'89 tied insurance agent turnover	'89 broker turnover	'89 salaried employees turnover	'89 other channel turnover
AXA	44,679	16,335	5,497	n/a	1,735
UAP	64,482	10,501	3,916	17,285	32,780
GAN	27,450	10,101	3,433	1,344	12,572
AGF	38,221	8,200	7,200	n/a	11,500
Mutuelles du Mans	16,158	7,639	4,354	n/a	4,166
Abeille	16,812	4,390	n/a	n/a	12,422
Groupe Athéna	9,113	3,338	2,792	2,925	58
Groupe Azur	3,166	2,691	n/a	n/a	475
Concorde	3,983	1,797	592	0	1,594
Le Continent	2,116	1,409	492	n/a	215
La France	4,663	777	838	n/a	3,048
Generali France	1,648	659	989	0	0
Total	232,491	67,837	30,103	21,554	80,565

Source: Le Journal de l'Assurance

Turnover for tied agents (FF13.5 billion — $2.3 billion) grew by 17.9 percent in 1989, while commissions went up by 3.5 percent. The average annual total of commissions received by agents varied from company to company (see Figure 5.2).

Figure 5.2

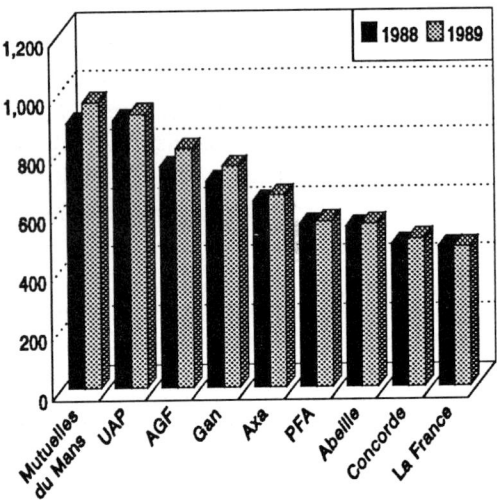

Source: FNSAGA

The AGA's clientele is essentially made up of individuals (unlike the brokers, 80 percent of whose turnover is linked to industrial risks). This explains their fear of existing and potential competitors targeting this market segment.

It is against this background of crisis that negotiations took place between representatives of the AGAs (the Fédération Nationale des Syndicats d'Agents Généraux d'Assurance — FNSAGA) and the insurers (Fédéation Française des Sociétés d'Assurance — FFSA) in November 1990. This ended with the signing of a draft agreement which proposed a new statute based on the following principles:

- Mandates were to be granted for set periods and reviewed every five years.

- Commissions were not to constitute the tied agents' sole remuneration — there could also be fees and profit-sharing schemes related to portfolio performances.

- If relations between the two parties were broken off after one of these reviews or if an agent decided to retire, compensation (the amount paid by the company to the agent whenever the latter hands over his portfolio) was to be calculated by reference to the agency's economic value — in other words, its productivity, profitability, etc.

- The principle of "exclusivity" of relations between agents and insurers was to be made more flexible. Henceforth, the tied agent was to be allowed to offer risk coverage which his own company did not offer while the latter had to provide compensation if it did not respect territorial exclusivity — in other words, if the company were to sell its products within a given agent's area through other channels. There was to be one important exception to this ruling: it was not to apply to life insurance products. However, it is precisely this domain which the mutuals and banking subsidiaries have targeted, making life very hard for the tied agents.

At the beginning of 1991, this agreement was rejected by an AGA general meeting.[11] However this impasse is resolved, one thing is certain: the AGA will have to adapt very rapidly to the new, more highly competitive conditions, as will the insurance companies, if they wish to maintain their respective market shares.

Ironically, the tied agents have become the objects of desire for insurers (mostly foreign) that wish to carve out a niche for themselves in the French market but do not have an effective means of distribution — and this despite the agents' low productivity which the companies so often complain about (see Chapter 7).

Insurance brokers

If the *agent général* is a company's authorised agent, then the insurance broker[12] acts as the customer's authorised agent. Like the tied agent, the broker receives a commission from the insurer. Their status, set down in Article 1 of the Code of Commerce, places them in the same category as retailers. They are predominantly active in the large cities and are particularly well-represented in large industrial risks.

French broking firms are extremely small: in 1990, total turnover for the top 75 firms together was 25 percent below that of the largest British broker, Sedgwick James (almost FF8 billion — $1.4 billion). The French subsidiary of Sedgwick James was ranked sixth in the country (see Table 5.18).

Table 5.18			
The main insurance brokers in France (1989)			
	Total turnover (in FF m)	Net profits (in FF m)	Staff
1 Faugère & Jutheau	646.6	n/a	1,376
2 Gras Savoye	545.0	n/a	1,215
3 Le Blanc de Nicolay	364.0	n/a	627
4 Assurances Verspieren	230.0	n/a	400
5 SGCA	215.8	9.73	428
6 Sedgwick James	190.4	n/a	381
7 CECAR	186.0	n/a	309

The profession's total turnover was some FF11 billion ($1.9 billion) in 1989, 10 percent up on the previous year. Figures relating to French insurance broking are few and far between. Profit figures are particularly scarce.

According to a SOFRES survey carried out among a cross-section of brokers in August 1990, new French entrants into the market rather than international competitors were the most cause for alarm: the big banks, the Post Office and the savings banks. As for their attitude towards the possibility of "understandings" or "alliances" with a foreign broker, only one-third declared themselves in favour, 43 percent said they would prefer not to enter such understandings and 23 percent did not express an opinion. The brokers surveyed also believed that concentration, often going hand in hand with specialisation, was inevitable; as proof, they pointed to the ongoing consolidation and mergers among firms.

Although they have previously been concentrated in France's three largest cities, some brokers, such as Faugère & Jutheau and Gras Savoye have attempted to conquer the personal market in the provinces as part of the "regionalisation" of their activities. Others (CECAR or, again, Gras Savoye and Faugère

& Jutheau) have also become very active in international brokerage.

As proof that nothing can be taken for granted in the French financial system, two major restructurings in French insurance broking took place in April 1992. First, the largest broking firm, Faugère & Jutheau, announced that it had been acquired outright by the American Marsh & McLennan, the largest insurance broking firm in the world. Second, Gras Savoye announced that there were changes in its shareholding structure: AGF, Athéna and UAP each took 5.7 percent of its capital (to be raised to 10 percent apiece in the near future, according to the agreement). But this deal has done nothing to disperse persistant rumours to the effect that brokers Johnson & Higgins will eventually take control of Gras Savoye.

Following these events, French brokers are more in doubt about their continued independence while they remain burdened by the same handicaps. For a start, capital often belongs to individual families (a structure that is obsolete given current international competition). In addition, their comparatively modest size prevents them from measuring up to the large British and American concerns. The recent link-ups show the inherent inability of French brokers to create large institutions and at the same time hold on to their independence.

Other sales channels
Other sales channels, which could either strengthen or weaken the traditional ones, include direct marketing, mail order selling and large retail chains.

In 1989, there were only about 30 insurance companies using direct marketing, and of these only half regularly made use of the technique. Insurers spent FF120 million ($21 million) on direct marketing in 1989, a figure which had probably doubled by the end of 1991 according to some analysts.

In the opinion of certain insurance and banking executives, the method has still not won its place among sales channels because of the high costs involved.

Legislation, too, plays a part in making direct marketing expensive. Contracts are, more often than not, marketed by companies that specialise in mail order business (eg La Redoute) which can only recommend but not sell. They can become involved neither in explaining the advantages of guarantees nor the collection of subscriptions. Therefore, their role is limited to that of a "pointer", as stipulated in Article R511.3 of the Insurance Code.

Direct marketing's share of total sales was around 3 percent in 1989 according to rough estimates, though the percentage was expected to grow as greater synergies were found with existing sales channels. Companies like Axiva (Axa), Rhin & Moselle and Norwich Life often use "mail order associations" (MOS), attributing policies worth FF1,100 million ($194 million), FF176 million and FF61 million respectively to use of this method in 1987.

Sales through retail chains (Carrefour, Leclerc, Habitat, etc) has also grown, albeit slowly. But this could turn out to be a formidable sales channel for personal insurance (life and health) given the increasing standardisation of contracts generally on offer. The establishment of this particular channel says much about the desire of a number of insurers to diversify their sales networks. This time it is not so much the "traditional" insurers as the non-intermediary mutual companies who find themselves in a vulnerable position (they both offer standard products to the same type of clientele).

Internationalisation and prospects for the insurance industry

Just like other economic and financial activities, the French insurance industry has not escaped internationalisation. First, one notes an increase in the percentage of turnover realised abroad — nearly 24 percent of premiums taken in by the early 1990s (of which 91 percent is within the EC and 4.2 percent in the US). Second, French insurers have shown a compulsion to make acquisitions or buy shares in foreign companies which bears testimony to their will to engage in activities outside France.

They appreciate that the dropping of restrictions on the provision of services across EC borders means there are 4,000 insurance companies with the potential to operate on the French market. Having been sheltered for a long time, the insurance industry can now be assailed from without.

To better appreciate the French insurance industry's

ability to compete in this changed environment, several key factors need to be reviewed. Some of these are specific to the insurance companies themselves, and others are tied up with the economic, financial and social environment in which they operate. As for factors specific to the insurance industry itself, the international strength of French groups appears proportionately greater than their strength on the home market, as seen by the growth in foreign compared to total turnover: the figure increased from FF74.7 billion ($136 billion) in 1988 to FF128.6 billion in 1990 an average annual increase of 30 percent (see Table 5.19).[13]

French companies' strategy for 1993

It is clear that January 1 1993 is as strongly etched in the minds' of French financial intermediaries — banks, insurance companies, brokers — as it is in that of the public authorities.

Over recent years, and especially in 1989, insurers have grown either through domestic expansion, through share acquisitions in other parts of Europe, or through *bancassurance* arrangements and co-operation agreements both in France and in other European countries (see Chapter 7).

It appears that most large French insurance companies have consciously decided to reach a certain critical mass on mainland Europe while small and medium-sized companies have found refuge in niche activities with consolidation not uncommon (Groupe Athéna, Via and Rhin & Moselle).

While there have been no large-scale operations carried out by foreign companies in France that have involved at least one French company, French companies have been lavish in other countries.

There is no formal discrimination against companies from other EC countries wishing to set up in France. However, Generali's experience (ie its attempt to take over Midi) indicates that entry by the acquisition route may not be that easy. There are more than 20 publicly-quoted companies, but as with banking, most of these are tied to other large groups through large shareholdings: it is therefore unlikely that a hostile takeover would be successful. Moreover, French insurance has tended to develop in isolation from the rest of Europe and a significant share of the market is controlled by state-owned companies or

Table 5.19

French insurers' international business (in FF bn)

	1987	1988	1989*	1990*
1. Direct insurance				
Through branches and offices	5.3	5.6	6.1	5.0
Through subsidiaries	38.0	46.8	79.6	101.1
Through underwriting of foreign risks in France	5.1	5.2	5.0	4.7
Total	48.4	57.6	90.7	110.8
2. Reinsurance (foreign risks)				
Through direct insurers	0.8	1.0	0.7	0.8
Through professional reinsurers	12.1	16.0	16.3	17.0
Total	12.9	17.0	17.0	17.8
3. Total foreign turnover	61.3	74.7	107.7	128.6
4. Share of foreign business in total turnover — % (Foreign turnover/overall turnover)	17.7	18.1	21.9	24.1

* = Estimates

** = or shareholdings (equivalences)

Source: FFSA

mutuals. The many foreign companies present in France have not made much inroad into the market.

Nevertheless, while they must await wider access to the capital of the large state-owned companies, some companies like Allianz have managed to carve out a niche in France.

The restructuring occurring throughout Europe has obviously not left insurance unaffected. The process of market concentration has gathered pace. In 1989, the top three companies in France held 34 percent of the life insurance market, compared to 20 percent for the top three in the UK and 25 percent in Germany. In non-life insurance, the figures were 22.2, 28.1 and 17.3 percent respectively. Compared to other European countries, the French life insurance market appears to be more concentrated than non-life.

Heightened profitability requirements
Companies still need to attain high productivity and gain an acceptable level of profitability in their own country before entering new markets. International expansion is costly and requires a huge input of own funds. As in any section of industry, the capacity for

international expansion is directly linked to levels of profitability.

Judged on the basis of certain common ratios such as "own funds over premiums" or "own funds over mathematical reserves" (see Chapter 7), practically none of the French insurers has any problem respecting solvency margins.

Environmental influences
Three basic elements comprise the environment in which companies operate: currency strength and how the financial markets and social security systems operate.

In the single market, currency strength has a particularly important role in the free provision of services, where anticipating currency movements can be part of the decision to take out a given insurance policy. Apart from the fact that the French franc has climbed among the ranks of the world's strong currencies, French insurers can now offer products denominated in foreign currencies. A currency's strength also becomes important when it comes to buying companies abroad. But its influence can also be negative when profits are repatriated or one decides to sell these foreign assets.

The financial environment plays an important role when one remembers that the loss experiences for insurance in most industrialised countries are negative. Profit margins derive primarily from financial operations. The state of the markets and the net returns after taxes from investments in part determine the competitiveness of companies. In this respect, French returns appear very attractive.

The social security system contributes in determining the actual size of a market: the more developed the social insurance, the less developed the insurance market. The French industry seems badly placed on this score given the importance of pay-as-you-go pensions, of sickness insurance and of the special-status mutual companies. French insurers do not manage the same amount of assets and do not take in the same level of premiums as their foreign rivals. The introduction of French-style pension funds may change this situation by introducing a "third pillar" to prop up the retirement system as has occurred in the UK and Germany.

Obviously, legislation and differential taxation are also competitive handicaps to be considered.

Reform of the insurance code

Historically, the French regulatory environment has been more restrictive and rigid than elsewhere in Europe. But since 1989 things have begun to change quickly.

The Insurance Code, based around two statutory orders going back as far as 1930 and 1938, regulated insurance companies for half a century. These orders assigned to the state a largely preventive role and were applied rigorously both to contract law and to the way companies controlled their finances. For example, all policy plans had to be passed to the supervisory authorities (the Direction des Assurances), which could prohibit the launch of a new product.

This capricious type of legislation dating back to the 1930s failed to meet the demands of an industry experiencing dizzy growth. The consumerism of the 1980s finally got the better of the Insurance Code, rendering many of its provisions obsolete.

Studies aimed at reforming the Code led to the adoption by parliament of the Law of December 21 1989 "concerning the adaptation of the Insurance Code to take account of the opening up of the Common Market".

The law brought national legislation in line with EC directives relating to the cross-border provision of non-life and legal protection services. The new law not only made explicit the difference between mass business risk (*risque de masse*) and large-scale (industrial) risk (*grand risque*), it also prescribed much less rigid supervision of companies operating within the framework of these directives. In addition, it authorised companies to sell life and non-life contracts denominated in foreign currencies.

The law included a definition of group insurance and specified the consequences of modifying contracts for the insured parties. Furthermore, it instituted a financial guarantee system for insurance broking and granted companies a degree of freedom to deal in securities similar to that available to banks. The law also abolished all controls over premium prices.

Among other innovations was the establishment of a mechanism to make the assets of life and capitalisation companies more transparent. First, parliament adopted a mechanism aimed at improving the quality of information provided to policy holders by means of an annual declaration on the realisable value of all assets including property. The mechanism was also designed to help determine policy holders' theoretical share of proceeds should a portfolio be sold. Second, a "reserve fund" was established for the benefit of policy holders in the case of effective portfolio transfer.

Additional legislative measures

The Decree of January 11 1990 abolished the restrictions placed on state-controlled insurance companies in distributing or selling shares, up to a limit of 25 percent of capital (Article 28). As for the remaining 75 percent held by the state, provisions were introduced to allow for indirect participations. It is predicted that such measures will allow the three main state-controlled companies (UAP, AGF and GAN) to raise almost FF50 billion ($8.8 billion) on the market through 1995.

The new law, which was drafted in accordance with

According to the group's chairman, Jean Arvis, it is unlikely that the group will want to make any large acquisitions in the short term, even on the American market where prices are attractive. On the other hand, share swaps have not been ruled out on the British market, for example, where Victoire is conspicuous by its absence. However, the group has a long-term interest in retaining its 51 percent holding in Colonia-Victoire, an interest shared by Victoire's own main shareholder, Suez. In 1990, Victoire acquired 50 percent of the Canadian company, Laurentienne, and 50 percent of Prudential Italia.

Victoire has a large property portfolio and a 4.2 percent holding in Compagnie Financière de Suez.

The AXA Group

AXA has had an eventful history under the chairmanship of Claude Bébéar. The group has been a pioneer in the area of growth by acquisition on the French market.

Until recently, part of the holding company AXA-Midi (controlled by Compagnie du Midi) was, as its name suggests, composed of two companies — AXA and Compagnie du Midi. These two were at times on the same side and at other times in conflict with each other.

AXA was originally made up of a group of medium-sized mutual insurance companies, whose origins dated back to the nineteenth century and whose turnover at the end of the 1970s totalled no more than FF4 billion ($707 million). With the changes that were taking place in the market, it was becoming increasingly difficult for these to survive. Consequently, the group was one of the first in France to recognise the need for organic growth as well as growth by acquisition.

To finance its organic growth programme (taking only the company's own resources into account as its status as a mutual company did not allow it recourse to the market), AXA early on established a company philosophy based on the intensive exploitation of profitability, competitiveness and innovation.

External growth was focused around partnership agreements with small-sized mutual companies, which resulted in the formation of Mutuelles Unies,

the core of the future AXA group, at the beginning of the 1980s.

The group's coming of age took place in 1982 with the takeover (after a stock market battle with Bouygues) of the privately-owned Drouot, a group twice the size of Mutuelles Unies. Other acquisitions followed, both large and small. With the takeover of the private insurance group La Paternelle in 1986, AXA doubled its turnover.

Midi, for its part, was a finance company with investments in industry, financial services and property, and had been used at the beginning of the 1980s to shield Assurances Générales de Paris (AGP) from nationalisation. In November 1987, the group's insurance operations broadened their scope with the takeover of Equity and Law, the sixth largest British insurance company.

The development of the group into its present form took about three years and involved the following steps:

- The link up between AXA and Compagnie du Midi in 1988 to ward off an attempt to take over Midi by Italian insurance giant Generali, which held 12 percent of Midi;

- The subsequent merger of the insurance operations of AXA and Compagnie du Midi completely altered the structure of AXA, which became AXA-Midi Assurances, a wholly-owned subsidiary of Compagnie du Midi. In return, AXA became the key shareholder in Compagnie du Midi with a 28.6 percent participation;

- In the spring of 1989, AXA took control of Compagnie du Midi, with its "ally-rival" Generali as minority shareholder;

- At the end of 1990, in a share swap, AXA-Midi merged with Midi. This merger resulted from an undertaking given by the group's chairman and chief executive, Claude Bébéar, to simplify the group's control structure, and to make its legal status correspond with its new business organisation. The newly established group was called AXA (instead of Midi), while the main holding company, Compagnie Financière Drouot (CFD), was called FINAXA (see Figure 7.2).

Figure 7.2

Structure of Mutuelles Axa

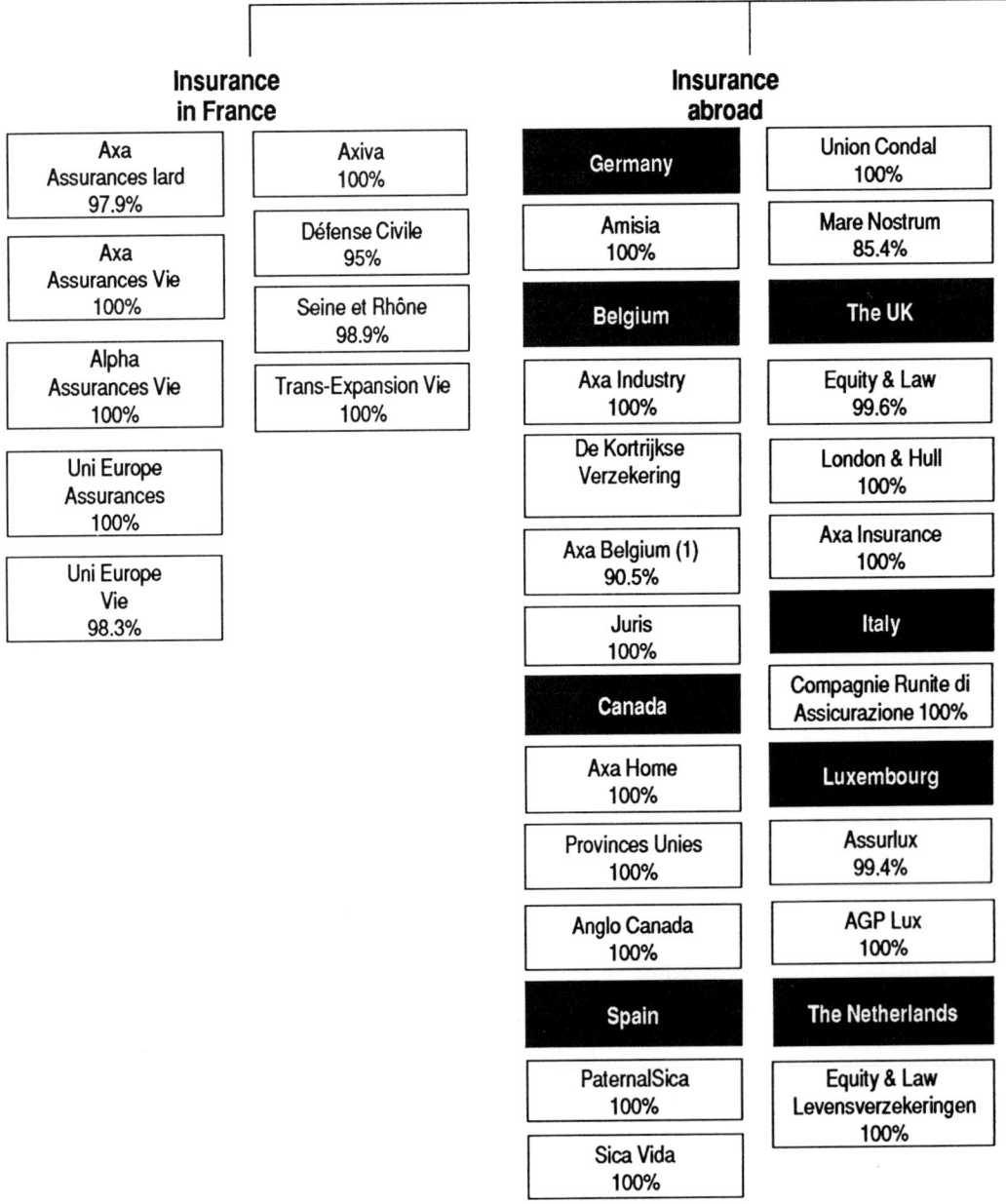

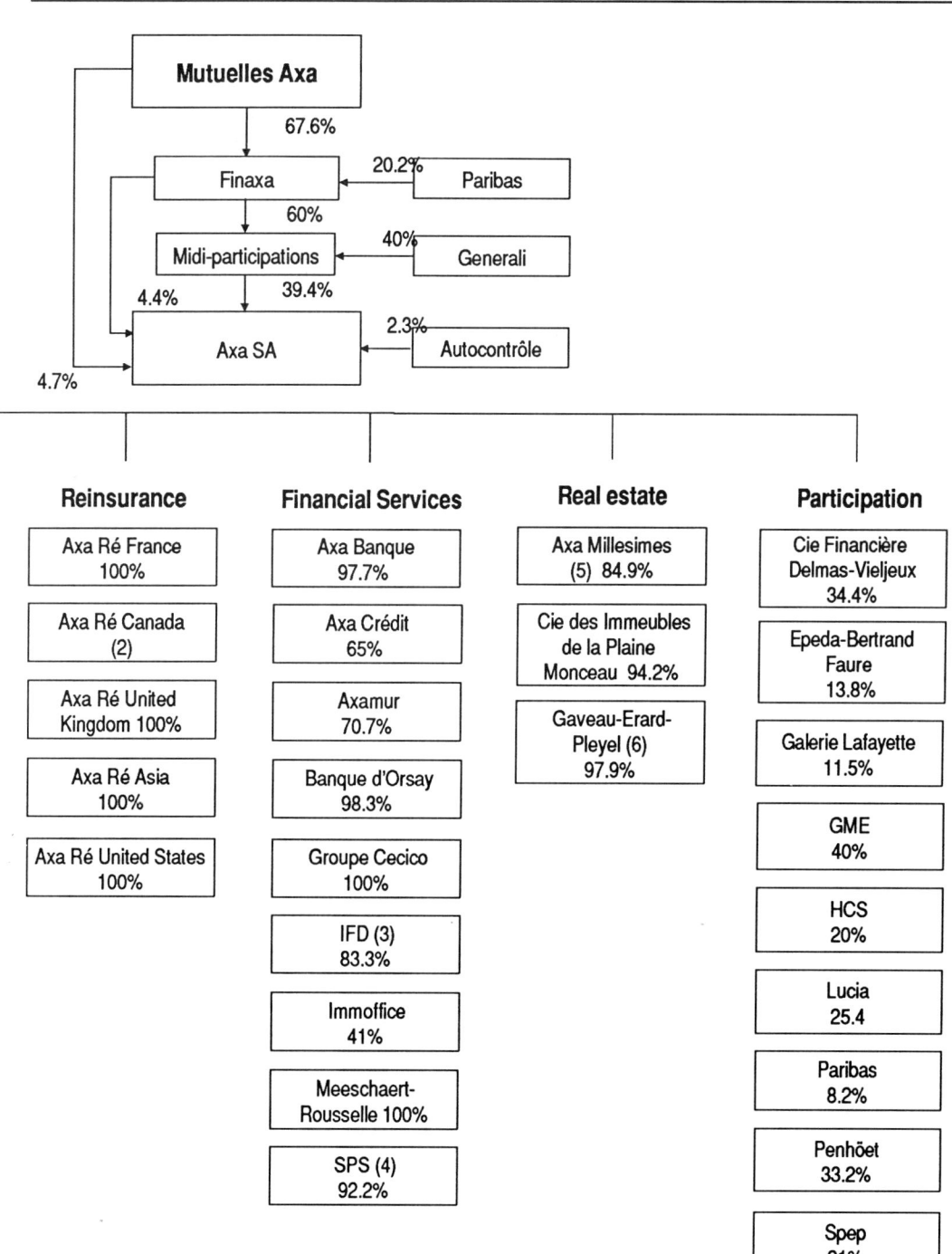

(1) Subsidiaries of Axa: 86.2%   (4) Axa and its subsidiaries : 51%
   Mutuelles: 4.3%   Mutuelles : 41.2%
(2) Branch of Axa Ré France   5) Axa and its subsidiaries: 72.5%
(3) Axa and its subsidiaries: 50.3%   Mutuelles: 12.4%
   Mutuelles: 33.2%   (6) Axa and its subsidiaries: 80.3%
   ANF: 0.3%   Mutuelles :17.6%

Source: Annual Report, 1990; Chart dated 31/3/91

The events which led to the formation of the AXA group are of interest in several respects. First, it highlights the viability of a mutual company taking control of a quoted company. Second, the stock market battle involving the Generali/AXA/Midi trio illustrates the difficulties that anybody making a takeover bid for a French company will encounter from "market solidarity". Finally, the current composition of AXA shareholders, (including Generali and Paribas), highlights the importance of alliances in the establishment of a Europe-wide group.

The new group controls 42 companies — 19 insurance companies in France and as many abroad — and four reinsurance companies. Since its involvement in the deal which saw the exchange of Ciments Français shares against Paribas securities, AXA has practically doubled its stake in its ally Paribas (to 8.3 percent of voting rights).

AXA is the leading private-sector French group in direct insurance, and in 1990 had a consolidated turnover of FF39 billion ($6.8 billion) — an increase of 6.7 percent on the previous year. Its net income from insurance suffered somewhat as a result of the restructuring, decreasing by 38 percent, while the group's profits increased by 2.8 percent. More than 80 percent of insurance profits came from France in 1990 (see Table 7.6).

Table 7.6		
Consolidated results for AXA (ex-Compagnie du Midi) (in FF bn)		
	1989	1990
Total turnover	43.87	47.99
of which:		
Insurance	36.61	39.40
Net profit	3.55	3.65
of which:		
Insurance	1.91	1.18
Total own funds	26.71	32.39
Source: AXA		

AXA's main target is to establish itself as one of the world's 20 leading insurance companies by the end of the century. The group's management has alluded to other strategic targets to accompany the race for size such as internationalisation, a greater focus on selected business lines and decentralisation.

AXA's international strategy is focused on three geographical areas: Europe, the US and Southeast Asia. Until the early 1990s, Europe was the group's main target. In 1989, nearly 90 percent of premiums earned outside France (FF12.5 billion — $2.2 billion) came from there. The UK alone accounted for half of the group's non-domestic turnover, followed by Belgium (16 percent), Spain (13 percent) and Italy (10 percent).

The British company, Equity and Law, with a turnover of FF5 billion ($883 million) and operations in the UK (95 percent of the total), the Netherlands and Germany, is one of the jewels in the AXA crown.

AXA has a sizeable war chest, estimated to be in the region of several tens of billions of French francs, available for further European acquisitions. For some time, the group has been seeking to buy a large company in a large market such as the UK, Germany or the US. Indeed, AXA's overriding ambition has been to gain a US foothold through a large acquisition. Around the middle of 1989, with this in mind, the group launched a bid to take over Farmers Insurance Company (the fifteenth largest US insurance company), a subsidiary of the British conglomerate BAT which previously had been the target of a £13 billion takeover bid by Jimmy Goldsmith.[7] Due to lack of success in convincing the US insurance commissioners, Goldsmith abandoned the deal in April 1990. But even though this operation was not a success, it had the beneficial effect of propelling AXA onto the forefront of the international scene.

In fact, the failure of its bid to take over Farmers did nothing to dampen AXA's enthusiasm. On the contrary, in 1991, AXA won the day when the American legislators allowed AXA to take a stake in Equitable Life. This, the third largest American insurance company, was on the point of collapse and had stated its intention to swap its mutualist status for that of a quoted company in December 1990.

With an injection of $1 billion (initially in the form of a loan), AXA has become the shareholder of preference in Equitable. The AXA loan was expected to be turned into a capital stake sometime in 1992, when Equitable's flotation is completed. At that point, AXA will control 45 to 49 percent of the company, although it cannot exceed this threshold for three further years unless another outside investor takes over 10 percent of the American company.

This deal, which fits in logically with the group's strategic objective of ranking among the world's top 20 insurers considerably changes its appearance: after consolidation, turnover will be equally divided between France, the rest of Europe and the US, going well beyond the original aim of realising 50 percent of turnover outside France.

Has AXA made a good acquisition? Industry sources remain sceptical of the quality of the company acquired and point to the critical state of the American market. But AXA chairman Claude Bébéar thinks this acquisition justifies itself on the basis of the reasonable price paid and signs that the US economy is recovering.

While AXA's US development strategy has resulted in the acquisition of a large company there, matters are different in the Far East, particularly in Japan where, according to AXA management, it is difficult to conclude reciprocal agreements. Nonetheless, the group is still continuing to prospect for a suitable company.

AXA has a relatively solid base in Canada where it holds 1.9 percent of the general insurance market through three subsidiaries.

In terms of what sort of business it wants to conduct, the group's strategy is clear — a renewed focus on insurance activities. This is shown by the fact that the group has now withdrawn from hands-on involvement in all industrial companies. As a minority shareholder, AXA is in the same position of any institutional investor: it holds and manages shares which can be acquired or sold in accordance with the normal workings of an insurance company.

Conscious of market globalisation, the group has opted for the idea of partnership, where each does his own job, rather than that of the conglomerate. (Through its links to Generali and Paribas, the company is a member of one of the most prominent

European financial constellations). *Bancassurance* does not fit in with AXA's strategy. Consequently, the group is very careful not to discourage its own network of tied agents.

In view of the changing behaviour of different customer segments, the group is also making distribution changes. AXA is undergoing a thorough structural transformation, which consists of tailoring products to the distribution channel being used. Three means of distribution have been devised and put in place:

- The main sales channel is Uni Europe, established in 1988 to serve brokers dealing in corporate and personal risks, both in France and in other markets. The AGF brokers are gradually linking up with Uni-Europe;

- The second consists of placing the group's network of 4,200 tied agents exclusively under the banner of AXA Assurances.[8] This company began operating in 1991;

- Finally, Franklin Assurances, which has been operating since 1989, uses all the other distribution channels. With the backing of Nouvelle Mutuelle Assurance and Cercle Français des Assurances, the company is exploring direct sales: mail order, coupon campaigns, sponsored customer forms, etc.

Decentralisation, the group's third strategic axis, is a concept which owes its origins to the structure of the original Mutuelles Unies (which was made up of independent mutual companies). The various companies are supposed to make their decisions independently, taking only the group's common principles into account.

Since January 1 1990, responsibility for distribution has been divided among 10 regional companies, each functioning as a profit centre and each totally responsible for its own results. The company is also contemplating moving some central Paris agencies to the suburbs.

Regionalisation certainly answers the desire to strengthen AXA Assurances, ensuring as it does a rapid and effective merging of the four component companies. In addition, this new structure is supposed to enable the regional companies to control more effectively their relations with the tied agents (ie increase profitability).

AXA's senior management has not escaped the group's wholesale reorganisation. Claude Bébéar has changed the structure entirely by appointing three managing directors in place of a vice-chairman (a post until recently held by Pierre Barberis who is leaving the group).[9]

As we have seen, AXA is unusual in its corporate structure, in its use of sales channels, in its expansion in the home market, in acquisitions abroad and in its relations with the trade unions (it introduced the *chèque syndical* for example).[10]

On the French market, this company represents "something different" with its inventiveness never ceasing to surprise partners and competitors alike.

Three powerful private sector groups

The Athéna group

The insurance group, Athéna, was formed in 1989 from the grouping of four medium-sized insurance companies (PFA, GPA, Proxima, Lilloise). It is 99.14 percent controlled by the Pechelbronn group, which in turn is majority-controlled by Worms & Cie. The four Athéna companies retain commercial independence, but are supposed to act in concert in three areas: health, assistance and legal insurance.

With turnover in 1990 of FF12.7 billion ($2.2 billion), group net share profit of FF752 million ($132 million — up 3 percent on the previous year) and own funds of over FF5 billion, the group ranks 10th in the insurance industry in France. General insurance predominates. Group operations doubled with the acquisition of an 85 percent stake in DAPA in Spain. Athéna also has a large property and finance division.

It is possible that Athéna will go into partnership with a large European group. However, there were rumours in 1991 of a possible sale of PFA which had run into problems in the life market. Not always healthy, the competition within the group between GPA and PFA products would serve as the basis for such a move.

The Allianz group

Until 1989, the largest European insurer had a disparate collection of French companies, resulting from the juxtaposition of its old branch with the companies of the La Protectrice group, itself a subsidiary of RAS, Allianz's Italian insurance acquisition.

Having taken control of the insurance activities of Mixte (Rhin and Moselle-Via) in September 1989, the following year the group organised all its operations around Allianz-Via (Holding France). The group's restructuring plan involves merging Allianz RAS and Via Assurances in several stages by 1993. The consolidated turnover of this "new" group (made up of 15 companies) will be over FF9 billion ($1.5 billion), thus placing it among the 12 leading French insurance groups.

The Generali group

In 1991, the subsidiaries of Generali, Europe's second largest insurance group after Allianz, earned nearly FF8 billion in insurance premiums in France. The group ranked 14th in both life and general insurance. Two companies within the group (Generali France and Fédération Continentale) earned FF3.5 billion ($618 million) apiece from life insurance. In general insurance, five affiliates, (in order of importance: Concorde, Equité, La Lutèce, Cie Continentale des Assurances and Européenne de Protection Juridique) took in FF4.1 billion in premiums.

Generali holds a minority shareholding (40 percent) in Midi Participations, and has AXA's Claude Bébéar on its board of directors.

It is possible that sometime in the future, La France Assurances, a company with FF4 billion in premiums, will be integrated into the Generali group.[11]

Groups which are subsidiaries of banks

Caisse Nationale de Prévoyance (CNP)

Established in 1959, CNP was born from the ashes of three specialist insurance companies, the oldest of which dated back to the end of the nineteenth century. In 1987, CNP became a state-owned commercial institution, under the supervision of the Finance Ministry. Although it enjoys relative autonomy, it is tied to the Caisse des Dépôts et Consignations.

In 1989, CNP began publishing consolidated accounts. With a turnover of FF29 billion ($5.1 billion) in 1990 (up 23 percent on 1989 despite a stagnant market), personal insurance policies represented almost half of its premiums, followed by group policies (one third of business). The group occupies third position in sales of life and capitalisation products in France.

The group's profitability record is poor and its net income for 1990 stood at FF870 million ($153 million), which is 2.9 percent of premiums received.

Though staff numbers at CNP are relatively small (1,900 people in 1990) and its own network is minuscule, it has numerous distribution channels. The CNP sells practically all of its personal insurance products through the Post Office and Treasury networks, while the Ecureuil savings banks distribute its personal and group products.[12]

In 1988, CNP set up three limited companies in partnership with the aforementioned three institutions to distribute capitalisation bonds: Préviposte, Investissement-Trésor and Ecureuil-Vie. It also established CNP-Internationale in association with the Caisse Centrale de Réassurance (which has a 20 percent stake).

It has other "privileged" sales channels at its disposal, such as provident and mutual institutions (for group and public sector providence), and local and national government bodies (statutory obligation to furnish providential cover). Moreover, its links to the pensions sector could prove to be a considerable asset if new legislation were to be introduced in relation to supplementary pensions by means of capitalisation.

Its personal insurance policies are biased towards products such as pension savings, policies in units of account (SICAVs) and "mass retail" products (PEP [people's savings plan] and capitalisation bonds). They are also characterised by their simplicity and practicality. For example, a new product called Prévaliance has been launched which in-

cludes a whole life insurance policy attached to a Livret A savings account.[13]

Although the group's international operations are in their infancy, they revolve around two main axes: investment in an international network and growth through local partnership agreements. According to the group's international director, Flavio Amoroso, CNP's target is to earn 10 percent of turnover outside France by 1992.

In Brussels in 1989, CNP signed a co-operation agreement establishing the Nexo network, bringing together 11 public sector insurance companies (local versions of the CNP). The same year, the group drafted a treaty with Cariplo and the British company TSB with the goal of establishing a life insurance company in Italy.

In view of the state of competition in Europe, CNP is fighting to obtain the status of *société nationale* (like UAP, AGF, etc) — a limited company with capital majority-controlled by the state. Such a transformation would allow it to expand into other markets because it would then be able to effect cross-shareholdings. It could also raise extra capital from shareholders and have increased recourse to the financial markets. Among its other long-term projects, CNP is contemplating breaking into the personal accident insurance sector with the Post Office as partner — a project which is vigorously contested by other insurance companies.

Prédica

Prédica is a life and capitalisation company established by Crédit Agricole in 1986. Crédit Agricole holds 96 percent of its registered capital and Groupama holds 4 percent.

Prédica is the result of Crédit Agricole's desire to deal directly with the insurance needs of its customers. Since its inception, it has benefited from its complete integration into the bank's regional network and support for its activities relies almost exclusively on the parent's financial strength. This explains its rapid growth up to 1989, as well as the collapse of 1990.

In 1989, after just four years of existence, Prédica ranked third in life and capitalisation (with a turnover of FF21.6 billion — $3.8 billion) and accounted for 18 percent of new business in that sector. Its strong point was sales of capitalisation products, which accounted for 60 percent of premiums and had a 24 percent market share.

In 1990, its net profit was FF403 million ($71 million) — an increase of 13 percent on 1989, while its turnover fell by 31 percent to finish at FF15 billion — $2.6 billion (see Table 7.7). Its share of the life insurance market decreased to 6 percent as against 11 percent in 1989. Its share of new business dropped to 11 percent.

Table 7.7				
Prédica's business				
	1987	1988	1989	1990
Turnover (in FF bn)	6.6	17.0	21.6	15.0*
Net profit (in FF m)	28.0	241.0	357.0	403.0
Own capital (in FF m)	219.0	1,177.0	1,959.0	—
Technical provisions (in FF bn)	n/a	24.5	47.6	63.0

*= Estimate

Source: Prédica

This fall was due mainly to capitalisation products which encountered strong competition from PEPs (marketed by all the banks and especially successfully by its own parent) and the arrival of capital growth funds.

Prédica's turnover in 1990 was composed of savings contracts (60 percent), group policies (30 percent) and individual pensions (10 percent).

Prédica's sales strategy is based on two simple principles. Products are classified according to their degree of complexity so as to rationalise and simplify the staff-customer relationship. Products are also closely tied to those of the bank and the available tax breaks are easily identifiable.

In strategic terms, the reduction by one-third in the group's turnover highlights the vulnerability of business plans based around savings products which can easily be replaced. Indeed, the priority given by Crédit Agricole to banking products once the PEP was launched, generated a massive transfer to bank savings and a sharp fall-off in premiums received by Prédica, particularly from capitalisation.[14]

By the early 1990s, Prédica was formulating plans to move into new niches in the retail customer market (whole life insurance and pensions). The professional and corporate market was also being targeted in its new sales strategy, but its implementation would require considerable time and funds.

Prédica was also considering establishing itself abroad, preferably in southern Europe, obviously with the help of the Crédit Agricole networks. Examples of foreign expansion through 1991 included: the agreement with Monte dei Paschi di Siena to set up Ticino Assicurazioni in Italy and the creation of Tranquilidade in Portugal, in which it has a 50 percent stake together with Banco Espirito Santo.

Other banking subsidiaries

Nearly all the banking groups own one or more life and capitalisation subsidiaries, of which there are about 30. The main ones belong to the big banking groups like CNP (controlled by the Caisse des Dépôts et Consignations), Prédica (Crédit Agricole), Assurances Fédérales (Crédit Lyonnais), Natio Vie (BNP) and Cardif (Compagnie Bancaire). The total premium income from these affiliates exceeded FF58 billion ($10.2 billion) in 1990.

After a spectacular rise to prominence, most of the banking subsidiaries were shaken by the 1990 results and they were losing market share to the traditional companies (see Table 7.8). As with Prédica, the reason for this is simple: subsidiary income is largely determined by the parent banks' policies toward deposits which, in 1990, shifted in favour of the PEP (see Table 7.8).

In general insurance, the compulsion to own companies is not as strong. Apart from ACM-Iard (Crédit Mutuel), which was established 20 years ago and is the only company to have had success in this sector, other projects to set up casualty and fire subsidiaries seem to be at a standstill. After a strong beginning, Pacifica, a subsidiary of Crédit Agricole,

Table 7.8

Ranking of the 20 largest bank subsidiaries (premiums in FF bn)

Insurance company	Bank	'90 turnover	'89 turnover	Growth rate(%)
1. CNP	CDC	29,200	23,435	24.6
2. Prédica	Crédit Agricole	13,198	21,625	-39.0
3. Assurances Fédérales	Crédit Lyonnais	5,601	5,932	-5.6
4. Natio Vie	BNP	5,182	5,071	2.2
5. Cardif	Compagnie Bancaire	4,791	5,376	-10.9
6. Sogecap	Société Générale	4,578	4,192	9.4
7. ACM Vie	Crédit Mutuel	3,396	3,524	-3.6
8. Socapi	CIC & AGF	3,278	3,127	4.8
9. Fructivie	Caisse Centrale des Banques Populaires	2,195	2,838	-22.7
10. Suravenir	Crédit Mutuel de l'Ouest	1,628	1,500	8.5
11. Erisa	CCF	1,337	1,321	1.2
12. Henin Vie	Groupe Suez	1,123	1,226	-8.4
13. Prepar	BRED	602	596	1.0
14. Assu Vie	BNP & GAN	398	512	-22.3
15. Avip	BIP	348	392	-11.2
16. Vie Plus	Sovac	329	297	10.8
17. Assurances Régionales de France Vie	Crédit Mutuel Artois-Picardie	269	399	-32.6
18. Sogenal Vie	Société Générale	243	166	46.4
19. Le Cap Ouest	Banque Populaire de l'Ouest	201	181	11.0
20. Hélios	Compagnie Bancaire	187	437	-57.2

Source: FFSA

seems to be lowering its sights and slowing down somewhat.

The mutual insurance companies

Assurances Mutuelles Agricoles (Groupama)

Groupama, which is the main general insurer in rural France, resulted from the 1986 fusion of Ama (Assurances Mutuelles Agricoles) and two limited companies: Samda (insuring all non-agricultural general risks — which Ama cannot accept) and Soravie (life insurance). Sorema, a reinsurance subsidiary, must also be taken into account. Their contributions to the

group's turnover by the early 1990s was 60, 12, 20 and 8 percent respectively.

Group turnover experienced poor growth between 1987 and 1990, while in 1990 it increased slightly for the various constituent companies: Ama (2.95 percent), Samda (6.5 percent), Soravie (0.3 percent), for a total of almost FF22 billion ($3.8 billion).

Despite such slow progress, Groupama's profit capability (on average FF1.9 billion — $335 million per year) was excellent and its liquidity margin rated as one of the highest of any French insurance group, with own funds (FF18 billion — $3.1 billion) reaching 80 percent of total premiums. Given this level of financial strength, large-scale acquisitions from this over-capitalised group may be in the offing.

The group is more active in general insurance than in life insurance (with market shares of 2.4 and 9.8 percent respectively) and it has an estimated 5 million policy holders.

Groupama's original target was to meet all the insurance needs of France's agricultural and rural community. Even though this objective survives in theory, developments outside the traditional framework are taking place.

Groupama is actively pursuing a strategy based on partnerships with a view to exchanging both products and sales channels.

In 1989, Groupama and two subsidiaries of Compagnie Bancaire (Cetelem and Cardif) set up two joint companies: Finama (a company specialising in retail lending), which offers Groupama's customers a range of financial services managed by Cetelem; and Union Européenne des Assurances (UEA), an insurance company which supplies the customers of Compagnie Bancaire with general insurance products, which is managed by Samda. A 10 percent cross-shareholding had already taken place between Cardif and Sovarie.

Other projects being explored include a potential link with the Carrefour supermarket chain (the aim being to distribute personal insurance products) and with C3D, a subsidiary of the Caisse des Dépôts et Consigations, the purpose of which would be to diversify into car-providence services.

Groupama's international operations date back to 1988. Included among its foreign subsidiaries are Sorema North America, Groupama-España and Groupama-Catalunya.

In 1990, the group concluded an important deal with the Fondiaria group (of which Italian conglomerate Ferruzzi and business mogul, Carlo de Benedetti, are the main shareholders) that gave it 1.2 percent of the Italian insurance market. The deal worked as follows: Groupama took a 5 percent stake in the Italian holding company, GAIC, which controls the Fondiaria insurance company (the number two private

sector Italian insurer) and in the process became a shareholder in two other Italian insurance companies.

In October 1990, Groupama signed co-operation agreements with ABB in Belgium, Interpolis in the Netherlands and R+V in Germany. Under the agreements each company, which controls over 5 percent of its domestic market, will establish its own insurance links in the other three countries.

The group's target through the 1990s is to corner 10 percent of the European insurance market. To achieve this, the new chairman of the group, Louis Bordeaux-Montrieux,[15] counted on the efficiency of the regional *caisses* which have recently been reduced from 64 to 15. Each *caisse* has a turnover of between FF1.5 billion and FF2 billion ($353 million).

At central direction level, Groupama is endeavouring to install structures to make financial and international deals possible. Since 1989, management and co-ordination of the subsidiaries has been handled by the Groupama Central *Groupement d'Intérêt Economique* GIE — "interest grouping".

Groupama has high hopes for growth in its banking division, set up under a holding company (Amacam) and established jointly with Crédit Agricole in December 1990. This holding company, whose share capital is held in equal parts by the two mutual groups, will control 40 percent of the existing and future companies set up by the two groups. With the formation of this alliance, the two groups signed a "peace treaty" whereby they undertook to avoid conflict with each other in the agricultural sector.

Mutuelles du Mans Assurances

Mutuelles du Mans, denationalised in 1987, is the leading French mutual insurer (with the exception of Mutuelles Agricoles which is part of Groupama) with intermediaries (1,200 agencies).

The group is more active in general insurance than in life and its turnover in 1990 reached FF13.7 billion ($2.4 billion). In France, the group consists of three mutual companies (Mutuelles de Mans Vie, Mutuelles de Mans Iard, and Défense Automobile et Sportive (DAS)) and four smaller subsidiaries. The group's reinsurance operations (FF1.3 billion — $229 million) are handled by Intercontinentale.

In 1990, Mutuelles de Mans turned in a consolidated net profit of FF537 million ($94 million), as against F1.15 billion in 1989 — a drop of 47 percent. At the root of this drastic profits cut was a combination of factors: a high total loss experience, the poor state of the financial markets which led to a fall in the capital gains realised, and, most importantly, fierce competition in the corporate risk market.

The group also has a financial services sector through which it distributes loans and leasing products. One of these finance companies — Cyril Gestion, its securities house — is a leader in fund management (for insurance companies), with a total of FF7 billion ($1.2 billion) under management.

Unlike other mutual insurers, Mutuelles du Mans is very international-oriented. With a presence in 23 countries, nine of which are in Europe, the group earned almost 20 percent of its turnover outside France in 1991, with the objective being that this figure would reach 25 percent in 1992. Priority is being given to growth in southern Europe to reach this target. It is the leading French insurer in Italy, which accounted for 60 percent of the group's operations abroad, followed by the UK (13 percent) and Spain (8 percent).

Mutual insurers operating without intermediaries

Famous for the speed with which they won market share in the motor and comprehensive insurance markets, there are 16 *mutuelles sans intermédiaires* (MSI — mutual insurers operating without intermediaries) and they are grouped together under GEMA (Groupement d'Entreprises Mutuelles d'Assurances). They continue to increase their market share to the detriment of companies operating through intermediaries.

In 1990, they had 11 million *sociétaires* (company members) or customers, FF40 billion ($7 billion) in premiums (90 percent in general and 10 percent in life), 19 percent of the general insurance market and 34 percent of the motor insurance market. In life insurance (where they had a market share of 2.4 percent), the MSI have yet to beat the competition from the dividend-paying insurance companies.

The following points help explain the success and financial soundness of these companies: they are non-profit organisations, they have no intermediaries to

Table 7.9				
Changes in direct business for the main non-intermediary mutual companies				
a. Direct turnover (in FF m)				
	1987	1988	1989	1990
MACIF	7,285	8,152	9,253	10,144
GMF	7,194	7,698	8,498	8,553
MAAF	5,753	6,058	6,667	7,224
MAIF	4,896	5,151	5,554	6,115
b. Balance sheet income (in FF m)				
	1988	1989	1990	
MACIF	215.2	274.5	103.1	
GMF	316.7	448.3	355.8	
MAAF	75.8	102.6	-111.4	
MAIF	276.0	272.9	589.6	
Source: L'Argus				

pay, they sell standardised products and they select risks rigorously (for example, some MSI give motorists existing no-claims bonuses of 50 percent).

Further proof of the financial possibilities of mutualist insurers can be seen in MAAF's decision to participate, along with other French (Altus Finance) and Swiss investors, in the "rescue" of the American company, Executive Life.

The following MSI accounted for over FF3 billion ($530 million) of their 1990 general insurance premiums: MACIF (5 percent of the market), GMF (3.7 percent), MAAF (3.5 percent), MAIF (2.9 percent) and MATMUT (1.8 percent).[16]

Given their concentration on the general insurance sector, GMF Vie (1.2 percent of industry premiums) is the only non-dividend paying mutual insurance company that figures among France's leading 20 life insurers.

Mutuelle d'Assurances des Commerçants et Industriels de France (MACIF)

Established in 1960, MACIF ranked fifth in the general insurance sector with 5 percent of the market in 1989.

In 1990, with over 3 million company members, MACIF was the leading French motor insurer (with 10.6 percent of the market as against 9.3 percent in 1988). It handled FF7.3 billion-worth ($1.2 billion) of motor insurance premiums (90 percent of its turnover). Pension savings and home loan policies completed its range.

To improve access for its customers, it has decentralised its operations to 11 autonomous regions. To gain exposure outside France, it has signed agreements with UNIPOL, the sixth-largest Italian insurer and a subsidiary of a major co-operative group.

Garantie Mutuelle des Fonctionniares (GMF)

GMF was founded in 1934. It ranked eighth among French general insurers in 1990, with FF6.3 billion ($1.1 billion) in premiums, and fourth in motor insurance. It has 2.6 million company members and 430 sales outlets.

To broaden its range of activities, GMF has established a number of companies; Sauvegarde, which is open to non-civil servants, GMF Vie (occupying 20th position in the life insurance sector with turnover of FF2.3 billion — $406 million), GMF Protection Juridique and GMF Ré. GMF is also involved in the banking (GMF Banque) and retail sectors (FNAC, La Redoute, etc). Insurance contributes one-third of the GMF group's turnover.

The group's product distribution plan will be a cause of concern to some members of the profession. The group has signed agreements with Renault (establishing Delta for motor insurance) and with retail chain FNAC for the distribution of personal insurance. It has bought a shareholding in La Redoute (leader in the mail order business) and signed another agreement with Elf (the oil company whose private label card for its 55,000 employees encompasses assistance products). Finally, an agreement with the Post Office[17] for the distribution of its general insurance products is in the offing.

In 1990, through its association with four European insurance groups,[18] GMF established a GEIE (Groupement Européen d'Intérêt Economique — interest grouping) called "Euro Safe", a collection of companies insuring civil servants in Europe. The GEIE represents 6 million insured civil servants and is receptive to other partners.

Foreign companies

There are 143 foreign companies operating in France, but details of these firms are not included herein for two reasons.

First, these foreign branches are, for the most part, small-scale. Taken together, they represent less than 4 percent of the total insurance market. Swiss companies account for just under half of foreign insurer premiums, followed by the British (15 percent) and the Germans (10 percent). They operate in the large risks sector: industrial, maritime and transport. The largest companies (branches) are: Swiss — Wintenthur, Société Suisse d'Assurance sur la Vie, Zurich — and British — General Accident and Norwich Union.

Second, foreign companies often operate as companies governed by French law. The largest among these are: Allianz and Generali, which have already been covered in the section on private sector groups, Commercial Union and Eagle Star France.

Endnotes

(1) The group's insurance division is responsible for around 80 percent of profits.

(2) Unlike GAN, UAP has opted for a long-term form of agreement with BNP and the insurer has no overall input into the actual running of the bank.

(3) GESA and UAP Assistance came together under a joint holding company, forming one of the main groups in this sector in Europe. However, the restructuring of GESA appears to have posed some difficulties as it has lost a lot of its "big" customers.

(4) Since 1984, AGF has been freezing prices for large industrial risks and has become more selective about its clients. Result: 10 percent of the market.

(5) AGF International conducts approximately three-quarters of its business in these countries.

(6) The managing director and head of the Suez group's *bancassurance* operations, Bernard Egloff, describes himself as Victoire's protector and UAP's link-man.

(7) For profile see The Power Brokers — An Insider's Guide to the French Financial Elite, Lafferty Publications Ltd, 1992

(8) AXA has broached the subject of tied agents by deciding not to question the existing mandates but instead is proposing to delegate authority based on the abilities and results of individual brokers. In addition, AXA will not be signing any product-distribution agreements with the banks and will be working exclusively with its agents. InterAXA has been the sole tied agents' trade union to approve the proposed FSA/FNSAGA agreement. But this has not prevented a deterioration in relations, most notably over the question of agents' retention of portfolios.

(9) Claude Tendil is in charge of insurance in France while Jean-Claude Damarval is responsible for insurance operations outside the country. Gérard de la Martinière, who is chairman of the stock broking firm Meeschaert Rousselle (a subsidiary of AXA), is in charge of financial services other than insurance (AXA Banque, Compagnie Financière de Paris, etc) as well as asset management.

(10) The *chèque syndical* is used to finance trade unions. Anonymous cheques are distributed to an insurer's employees, who may or may not designate a union as payee. This instrument is designed to strengthen the trade unions' role as negotiating partners and to prevent "wildcat" strikes. The idea has been adopted by several other companies in France.

(11) Banque Lazard, which has a 5 percent stake in Generali, is the main shareholder (80 percent) in the holding company La France Participations et Gestion. This in turn is attached to the holding company, France SA, in which Lazard has a 59 percent shareholding (AGF has 6.9 percent).

(12) This is despite lively opposition from the financial community to the development of an insurance division within the Post Office. In 1990, policies taken in by the Post Office insurance operations increased by 38 percent to reach FF10.2 billion ($1.8 billion) — 5 percent of the market.

(13) The Post Office, which is targeting Livret A savings book holders aged between 18 and 55 years in particular, estimates its potential customer base at 6 million.

(14) Such poor results have had an impact on the conflicts that have raged at top management level within Crédit Agricole and which have led to the departure of many managers including Prédica managing director, Roland Jolivot.

(15) The chairman of Groupama comes from the agriculture industry. He was formerly vice-chairman of the Caisse Centrale des Mutuelles Agricoles.

(16) This mutual made an effort two years ago to increase its share of the motor insurance market (3.8 percent), by discontinuing the practice of freezing the premium discounts for drivers whose vehicle is damaged while parked. It is thus held responsible for the reform of the no-claims bonus system — something other insurers did not wish to even contemplate.

(17) GMP's chairman, Pétriat, is also a member of the board of directors at the Post Office and at FNAC.

(18) The following are members of the GEIE: the German mutual insurance company Huk-Coburg Versicherungsgruppe, Association d'Assurances Mutuelles Belges (SMAP), the Spanish company Nueva Corporación, and the Luxembourg-based Assurances Mutuelles d'Europe (AME).

Section IV

Financial Markets

Chapter 8

The French Financial Markets

In an effort to encourage the development of Paris as an international financial centre, the French authorities have carried through a radical reform of capital markets regulations. These reforms have additionally provided an effective way of vigorously modernising the French economy. This process has been clearly aided by occurrences in other financial markets around the world and particularly in London.

Trading conditions and access to the markets gradually improved, notably from 1984 onwards, with the opening up of the primary market to international investors. The right to negotiate brokers' commissions on shares and bonds and bank commissions levied on bond issues was also established. A second market opened in 1983 for the benefit of companies wanting to raise capital without having to fulfil all the obligations imposed on companies listed on the official market.

A series of innovations has boosted the growth of the financial markets. Notable among these have been important new products on the equities market, investment certificates (preference and non-preference), participating certificates, and even more important products on the public debt market, (*obligations assimilables du Trésor* [OATs], equivalent instruments and negotiable Treasury bonds [BTNs], etc).

Other developments worth mentioning are the gradual establishment of various hedging instruments, of which the most important are the financial futures market (MATIF), the subsequent establishment of a traded-options market in Paris (MONEP) as well as the launch of a subscription warrants market.

In addition, the growth of the OPCVM market (*Opérations de Placement Collectif en Valeurs Mobilières* — collective investment schemes), which alone accounts for half of all such European investments, emerged to strengthen the position of institutional investors.

As far as the Paris Bourse is concerned, reforms have been both technological (with the creation of a *marché continu* or continuous trading, the RELIT settlement and delivery system, etc) and regulatory (increased powers given to the Commission des Opérations de Bourse — COB, the French stock market regulatory body), the break-up of the functions of the old Chambre des Agents de Change (the Stockbrokers' Association) and the establishment of *sociétés de bourse* (broking firms), etc.

The total removal of foreign exchange controls on individuals on January 1 1990 — in other words, free movement of capital — put the finishing touches to this period of reforms.

These huge changes have resulted in the establishment of vast, increasingly decompartmentalised financial and money markets and a progressively more competitive economy. But despite the ongoing easing in restrictions, the state's role in the process remains a decisive and complex one. Despite this highly competitive environment, the state has hardly relinquished any of its influence over the economy. The result is that the 1980s were marked by a tightening of the state's grip on the financial markets through the state-owned financial institutions, which are by far the most active participants.

Funding the economy by means of securities issues

Since the end of the 1970s, the role of the financial markets in funding the economy has continued to expand. The figures in Table 8.1 (showing on the one hand, the relationship between total net securities issues and gross domestic product and gross fixed capital formation, and on the other, the relationship between net corporate issues and the amount of investments in them), speak for themselves. Net securities issues contributed twice as much as in 1980 — and three times more than in 1976 — to the build-up of capital.

Table 8.1

	1976	1980	1986	1987	1988	1989	1990
Total net issues/GDP	2.5	4.1	8.0	5.8	6.8	7.2	6.4
Total net issues/gross fixed capital formation	10.7	18.8	41.6	29.7	34.0	34.6	30.3
Net corporate issues/corporate gross fixed capital formation	21.0	27.1	54.1	51.0	52.6	52.0	43.2

Source: Comptes de la Nation 1989, 1991 Finance Act

The meteoric rise of non-intermediated financing can be explained by the abnormally low level of recourse made by companies to the capital markets up to 1980. Other elements have also contributed to this phenomenal growth. First, the improvement in companies' capital positions reflects not only the growth in securities issues but also possible variations in rates of investment. Second, since 1986, the creation of *titres de créances négociables* (TCN — negotiable credit bills), which are included in "net issues", has artificially swollen this figure as these bills are mainly used to fund treasury needs rather than investments.

In any event, one thing is certain: the French economy is increasingly financed by means of securities issues rather than credits.

The growth in securities offers

Since 1982, the market capitalisation of shares has increased tenfold and the volume of issues sixfold. However, the market is still characterised by the rarity of public issues (*par appel publique à l'épargne*) and by the high concentration of market capitali-sation. In fact, it is in the bond market that France has been most successful. Not only has the volume of bonds issued and traded increased but, by creating a wide range of highly liquid risk management instruments (via public debt securities), Paris has become a financial centre of international standing.[1]

A weak market for equities

Since 1982, French corporates have increasingly resorted to financing capital needs through share issues. But despite an average annual growth rate of 22 percent, the market has remained relatively weak due mainly to the fact that most companies have continued to keep capital under tight control, only releasing a small percentage to the public. Only one-fifth are issues open to the general public while the rest is reserved for "relatives" (ie other, related companies) (see Table 8.2).

Certain tax measures have been introduced to encourage companies to open up their capital a bit more. Since 1989, there has been a sharp increase in equity issues resulting from the paying of dividends through the issue of equity or the exercise of warrant rights (see Table 8.3). French companies have been taking advantage of these procedures, which provide considerable tax savings and carry no intermediation costs.[2] Since 1989, they have accounted for almost 40 percent of all capital increases. This purely fiscal measure nevertheless contains certain limitations, ie only those companies subject to taxes on profits (*l'impôt sur les sociétés* — IS) can utilise the procedures.

In 1989, for the first time, equity issues on the primary market exceeded net issues of bonds. The rapid rise in corporate profits, allied with continued growth in economic activity and the stability of long-term interest rates, accounted for this development. In 1990, however, the climate became less favourable for equities.

Equity issues are made by a handful of big French companies. In fact, whether with or without public issues, capital increases of over FF1 billion ($17.6 million) were quite frequent between 1986 and 1991. In 1989, for example, 18 French companies completed transactions above this figure, thus accounting for one-third of all equity issues for a total value of FF84.6 billion ($14.9 billion). In 1990, on the other hand, only eight exceeded the FF1 billion mark.

Table 8.2								
Value of securities issues (1980-1990) (in FF bn)								
	1980	1982	1984	1986	1987	1988	1989	1990
Stock issues	24.2	38.6	48.5	137.4	148.2	150.6	239.0	218.0
of which:								
public issues	3.5	3.5	10.8	62.8	56.6	31.7	58.7	62.3
non-public issues	20.7	35.1	38.7	74.6	91.6	118.9	180.3	155.7
Debenture and government bond issues	111.7	154.7	249.9	351.5	296.5	344.5	392.8	339.0
Net amount (issues less redemptions)	89.7	116.3	199.3	275.6	174.8	235.6	276.1	207.0
Total issues	135.9	193.3	298.4	488.9	444.7	495.1	515.1	425.0
Net total amount	113.9	154.9	247.8	413.0	323.0	386.2	631.8	557.0
Source: Commission des Opérations de Bourse								

Table 8.3				
Issues by means of public share offerings				
	1989		1990	
	Total in FFbn	No. of issues	Total in FFbn	No. of issues
Capital increase:				
Cash, straight	38.9	105	34.9	93
Through equity issues	(36.4)	(98)	(34.1)	(87)
Through issues of *certificats d'investissement*	(2.5)	(7)	(0.8)	(6)
Arising out of the payment of share dividends	7.2	126	10.8	179
Arising out of the exercice of warrants	12.6	112	16.6	156
Total	58.7		62.3	
Source: Commission des Opérations de Bourse				

The monthly settlement market saw a tenfold rise in the volume of equity transactions between 1982 and 1990, reflecting the growing interest shown by French and foreign dealers (see Table 8.4).[3] But 1986 was without doubt a pivotal time in the development of the Paris Bourse. In that year alone, the volume of trading was equal to the volume of the three previous years.

The evolution in French share capitalisation reflects, and indeed amplifies, political events and decisions. As examples, there was a rise in prices after the 1978 general election, a sharp drop in prices with the coming to power of the socialists in 1981 and prolonged by the 1982 nationalisation programme, then a spectacular recovery in 1983 with the end of the period of austerity. Then, in 1986, the new privatisation programme brought about a strong increase due to the influx of investors. Later, share capitalisation, which had risen by 33.3 percent in 1989, fell back by 23 percent to FF1,688 billion ($298 billion) in 1990.

In France, stock market capitalisation is concentrated in just a few hands, a trend which was increasing in the early 1990s. In 1989, the 10 leading companies accounted for roughly 25 percent of total capitalisation and the 50 largest companies accounted for around 60 percent, compared with 19.4 percent and 54 percent respectively in 1985.

A stock market dominated by bonds

1982 marked the beginning of a relentless expansion in the bond market. While the volume of issues doubled, the volume of transactions increased 52 fold (see Tables 8.2 and 8.4).

The development of market offer has varied in accordance with the needs of issuers. From 1987 onwards, the state's recourse to bond issues as a means of raising funds slowed (as measured by net balance), as did that of non-financial companies. However, financial institutions' propensity to rely on bond issues has continued to grow. This slowdown in the government's use of the bond market can partly be explained by diversification into public debt instruments (negotiable Treasury bills issued on the money market).

As for the range of products offered, there has been a marked increase in OATs. These make up 35

Table 9.4								
The Secondary market (The Paris and provincial bourses, 1980-1990) (FF bn)								
	1980	**1982**	**1984**	**1986**	**1987**	**1988**	**1989**	**1990**
Transactions								
Shares	59.5	66.7	96.7	431.8	605.3	466.3	741.7	718.1
Bonds	64.3	158.3	426.7	1,718.6	2,582.1	3,506.5	3,385.1	3,090.1
Total	123.8	225.0	523.4	2,150.4	3,187.4	3,972.8	4,126.8	3,808.1
(percentage of which were foreign securities)	13.8	17.6	22.7	29.0	44.8	23.0	30.2	28.2
French securities capitalisation (year-end)								
Shares	257.5	210.6	431.5	1,150.0	967.7	1,538.0	2,193.7	1,737.5
Bonds	584.4	815.6	1,296.7	1,977.0	2,049.5	2,338.0	2,468.3	2,588.5
Total	841.9	1,026.2	1,728.2	3,127.0	3,017.2	3,876.0	4,662.0	4,326.0
Source: Commission des Opérations de Bourse								

percent of all bond issues and 100 percent of Treasury issues.

This market is also characterised by a noticeable predominance of fixed rate issues (more than 85 percent of the total in 1990), which principally reflects a "disenchantment" with variable and reviewable rate securities.[4] The reaction to the inversion in the return-on-investment curve provides little inclination for issuers to launch loans indexed against monetary reference points.[5]

Fixed rate issues are often matched by variable rate swaps.

France is also active on the Euromarkets. It makes numerous issues, which amounted to almost $17 billion ($3 billion) in 1990. The Eurofranc market continued to grow in 1990 with FF52 billion ($9 billion) worth of issues, representing an annual increase of more than 50 percent. However, the French franc only ranked seventh on the Eurobond market.

Since 1982, the volume of bonds sales has increased 52 times over. This is mainly due to the government funding itself on the markets and the establishment of public debt classification techniques by the Treasury. As a result, there has been a sizeable increase in OAT transactions, demonstrating to investors — particularly foreign ones — the excellent liquidity of the French bond market.[6] In addition, OATs are the most actively-traded securities on the listing.

Other factors have probably played a part in this

spectacular rise — a long-term drop in interest rates, the creation of the MATIF and the inauguration of continuous trading (*le marché en continu*). The latter, in particular, helped ensure growth in trading and the multiplication of bond operations carried out by OPCVMs.

However, bond capitalisation is affected by erratic movements in interest rates. It increased by 5.7 percent in 1989, only to fall by more than 5 percent in 1990. Since 1989, the bond market has been penalised by the inversion in the rates curve. This development favours money market securities due to the fact that short-term rates are higher than long-term ones.

The money market

Since 1985, the (short-term) money market has been open to all traders for issuing and buying securities. Since then, there has been a steady growth in issues, particularly of certificates of deposit and negotiable Treasury bills. But apart from the latter, trading in money securities on the secondary market is almost nonexistent and they tend to be short-dated, the majority of issues being of three to six months duration.

To guarantee market transparency, the Bank of France has been publishing a register of marketable debt securities since February 1991. This monthly publication contains information on each of the issuers individually: size of portfolios under management, market share, rating, and date of the latest information received. It is addressed particularly to managers of SICAVs so that they can ensure that

Table 8.5

Comparison between the volume of transactions on the regional and Paris bourses

(%)	Regional bourses/Paris Bourse	
	1989	1990
Official listing		
French equities	1.56	1.49
Bonds	2.37	2.44
Second market	14.22	16.03
Source: Société des Bourses Françaises		

their marketable debt securities portfolios do not go beyond the ceiling set down in the regulations. It also enables other investors and bodies made responsible for placing these securities to take positions in the market.

Who holds what?

The modernisation of the French financial markets has considerably altered the make-up of French (and to a lesser degree, foreign) transferable securities portfolios and has also affected foreign demand for French securities.

First, the number of people who own transferable securities has increased rapidly since 1987. In 1984, fewer than one French person in 10 held a securities portfolio, but by 1991 the proportion was one in five — over 10 million people. However, one must distinguish between "direct" and "indirect" investors. In the first category are 6 million shareholders and 3 million holders of debentures, while the second category — owners of units in OPCVMs — is made up of over 8 million people. In 1989, small investors accounted for 34.7 percent of market capitalisation (in shares), while 20.3 percent was held by institutional investors, 21.4 percent by industrial and trading companies and 23.2 percent by foreign investors.[7]

Second, by 1989, French investors held roughly FF450 billion ($79 billion) in foreign securities (54 percent in shares, 38 percent in bonds and 8 percent in OPCVMs) while the amount of French securities in the hands of non-residents[8] was valued at FF800 billion ($141 billion) (35 percent in equities, 63 percent in bonds and 2 percent in OPCVMs) which means a negative "trade balance" of FF350 billion

($61 billion); this underlines the growing interest foreign investors have in French securities. The high level of foreign ownership of French transferable securities could be seen as proof of the success of Paris in establishing itself as a financial centre of importance. Nevertheless, such a development has accentuated the dependence on foreign institutional investors, leading to increased volatility in an era when capital flows constantly from London to Frankfurt, from Frankfurt to Paris, and so on.

Turnover tax: a hindrance to the development of the bourse

Commissions and other transactional costs seem relatively fair to market operators because of increased competition between intermediaries since the deregulation of commissions (See Chapter 10). But the same cannot be said of the turnover tax levied by the government. This tax is a heavy burden on stock market business because it has to be paid twice on the same transaction, first by the buyer and then by the seller. Depending on the value of the transaction, two rates apply — a rate of 0.3 percent on transactions under FF1 million ($176,000) and a rate of 0.15 percent for trades above this threshold.

The debate surrounding turnover tax abolition is becoming more lively in the run up to the Single Market. But while nobody seriously disputes the need to abolish it, carrying this through at a time of budget cuts and when the tax brings in FF4 billion ($707 million) annually to government coffers is proving problematic. What is also apparent is that while turnover tax receipts are growing in line with trading, average commissions are stagnating if not falling, to the point where the volume of taxes taken in is currently 15 to 20 percent higher than the volume of commissions.

Several arguments militate in favour of the abolition of this tax, but the most convincing is the argument about the outflow, primarily to London, of a significant number of large French deals, especially in shares. Moreover, turnover taxes are in the process of being phased out in other European countries (from the beginning of 1991 in Germany and with plans well advanced in Switzerland and Sweden). Consequently, the French Budget Minister, Michel Charasse, thinks that a tax cut is inevitable as it is undoubtedly a handicap for the Paris market. In addition, the existence of this tax has created a curious, not to say ridiculous, situation whereby Paris has to bear the brunt of this tax while the regional bourses, which have little weight internationally, are exempt.

However, it seems unlikely that a straightforward abolition of turnover tax will take place before 1992, mainly because of the cost of such a measure to the budget. It is now expected that the first step will be a reduction of the two rates to 0.1 percent before the tax is finally abolished.

Reforms in the French financial markets

The 1988 reforms aimed at a total overhaul of the structure and functioning of the bourse[9] and the Law of August 2 1989 was aimed at completing the body of legislation governing the financial markets. Some reforms have already been implemented and several more are being so, while others will take effect as events dictate. It is against the backdrop of these reforms that the markets have seen the introduction of new technologies aimed at modernising structures.

Supervisory authorities

In France, supervision of the financial markets is carried out jointly by the Treasury, the Commission des Opérations de Bourse (COB — France's Securities and Exchange Commission), the Conseil des Bourses de Valeurs (CBV — The Stock Market Council) and the Conseil des Marchés à Terme (CMT — the Forward Markets Council) (see Figure 8.1). Undoubtedly, the new supervisory structure is far more workable than before, but it is also true that the extreme complexity of the regulations and the proliferation of rules, together with the juxtaposition of authorities, have meant their powers remain either too vague or too circumscribed and there has been an increase in the level of litigation. It is not unusual for some market officials to refer to the negative effects of "overtransparency".

While in principle the Treasury authorities do not intervene directly on the markets, in practice its role as guardian of the general interest means that its powers, under the new regulations, have been widened. Thus, for example, the post of chief executive of the COB — recently created to assist the chairman

Figure 8.1						
Authorisation, regulation, supervision and sanctioning of financial intermediaries						
	Sociétés de Bourse	Members of the forward market	Credit institutions (apart from their market activities)	Credit institutions (market activities). If they are members of the forward market, see corresponding column. If not for non-affiliated institutions	Collective investment schemes (OPCVM)	Portfolio managers
Authorisation	CBV	CMT	Comité des établissements de crédit		COB	COB
Regulation	CBV	CMT	Comité de réglementation bancaire	Comité de réglementation bancaire or the marketplace authorities	COB	COB
Supervision	CBV	CMT	Commission Bancaire		COB	COB
Sanctions	CBV	CMT	Commission Bancaire		COB and the OPCVM disciplinary council	COB

Key: CBV = Conseil des Bourses de Valeur; CMT = Conseil des Marchés à Terme; COB = Commission des Opérations de Bourse

Source: Commission des Opérations de Bourse

of this body — is automatically filled by an official from the Treasury (currently, Pierre Fleuriot[10]).

The COB, the market watchdog, managed by a body of individuals who are not state officials,[11] has, theoretically at least, been granted more autonomy under the new legislation. The COB's powers of investigation have been widened and it has acquired a power of injunction and of sanction, by way of fines, for infringement of its regulations. But such powers, which it "shares" with the courts, have had the effect of greatly increasing the number of legal proceedings lodged, thereby creating a backlog.

The French stock market's new structure

Since the mid-1980s, the stock market has been completely transformed by a sweeping programme of deregulation and technological advances. These changes are essential in the run up to the single market. The speed of this modernisation is fuelled by the ambition that Paris should become Europe's most important financial centre and also that it should rival London's dominance on certain markets such as the MATIF.

An electronic continuous trading system, CAC, and an electronic settlement and delivery system, RELIT (*règlement et livraison des titres*) are at the core of the new stock markets.

Continuous trading

The CAC electronic trading system,[12] set up at the beginning of 1986, initially to handle equities and then bonds, used to carry the bulk of transferable securities quoted in France and has handled them all since the beginning of 1992. Other computerised systems for transmitting orders (GAO, COCA) are in place to facilitate trading.

Electronic trading took off rapidly in France. The CAC system now quotes nearly all French securities on the *marché à règlement mensuel* (RM — the montly settlement market), and carries more than 2,400 bond trading lines as well as spot market and second market securities. And in April 1991, the Paris Bourse reached a new landmark by having 78 foreign securities quoted on the CAC system.

Trading takes place every day from 10:00 to 17:00 and is preceded by a pre-opening phase from 09:00

to 10:00 during which the "theoretical" prices are fixed. At 10:00, the system automatically triggers a market in all securities. The "theoretical" price at 10:00 then becomes the opening price. All "limit-buy" orders are executed. On average, 20 to 30 percent of transactions are executed at the opening price which can be close to that of the pre-market opening fixing.

On the continuous market, small investor orders used to pose a serious problem because they tended to clog up the system. After delicate negotiations, a compromise was reached on June 1 1988 and a two-speed system of orders was developed. For orders of less than FF30,000 ($5,300) for equities and FF50,000 for bonds, financial intermediaries offer their clients a choice: settlement in deferred time[13] or settlement in real time. As commission costs are higher for "real time", clients are "encouraged" to choose the deferred-time option.

There is an alternative solution. Some *sociétés de bourse* (broking firms) have set up *gestion assistée par ordinateur* (GAO — computer-aided management) systems. All small orders for which costs on the continuous market would otherwise be high can now be routed to the GAO system and dealt with at any time that a certain minimum lot is reached. With this system, the client can avail of the same advantages as if his order had been transmitted to the main market.

More recently, a computerised system has been developed to link broking firms' order books in real time to a software programme dubbed COCA *connexion à CAC* which feeds orders into the CAC system, thus avoiding double entries. Each firm is free to choose which type of order it wishes to pass directly through COCA and which type it wants to deal with manually. In this sense, COCA represents the final stage in the automation of order handling.

The settlement and delivery of securities

Another side to the modernisation of the Paris market has been the gradual introduction of a new securities settlement and delivery system (RELIT). RELIT's purpose is to put the back offices of dealers in the various markets on a par with each other. This is to guarantee the instantaneous execution (same account date) of transactions, by delivery against payment within the same time frame as exists on other international markets. This innovation was made possible by the elimination of physical certificates (*dématerialisation des titres*).[14] The RELIT system involves all share portfolio managers and brings together all securities accepted by the central depository authority SICOVAM (Société Interprofessionnelle pour la Compensation des Valeurs Immobilières).

With this system, investors are expected to observe a standard settlement deadline equal to J+3 (where J (*jour*) represents the trading day) for most transactions. For transactions on the RM monthly settlement market, the settlement deadline is L+3 (where L equals *liquidation*, the account settlement day). For over-the-counter deals (*opérations de gré à gré*), the settlement date is either imposed (as with the settlement/delivery date for transactions on the primary and grey markets) or negotiated between the parties, and falls between J+1 and J+30. The J+2 deadline is probably the one most frequently selected.

The outline structure of RELIT, which allows for the particularities of each market and dealer, can be broken down into several parts:

• The ISB system (*système inter-sociétés de bourse*) designed to facilitate trading between *sociétés de bourse*;

• The SBI system (*système sociétés de bourse intermédiaires*) — a system for adjustment and laying out the ground rules for negotiations between *sociétés de bourse* (dealers) and affiliated intermediaries (the principals);

• The over-the-counter system for the adjustment and preparation of transactions carried out between dealers;

• The final completion of deals (settlement day), by delivery against payment, is guided by the SICOVAM which keeps an account of the securities, and by the Bank of France, which clears the current accounts opened in its books.

The RELIT project links all operators trading on the market and involves over 300 different users of the service transmitting up to 600,000 transactions daily. To manage such a volume, two electronic transmission networks have been developed: the SIT/bourse network, which links all users with the SBI (for over-the-counter trades and settlements) and a separate, distinct, network designed to link *sociétés de bourse* to the ISB system. But setting up this system has been extremely costly for intermediaries already burdened by increasing competition and a drop in commissions.

The establishment of a unified market

Up to the beginning of 1991, in accordance with the principle of the uniqueness of each transaction, a security could only be traded on one of the eight French bourses. But since the end of January 1991, French equities can be traded on a unified market. The *sociétés de bourse* have thus acquired the right, nationwide, to negotiate all French and foreign securities quoted on the CAC. This decompartmentalisation has coincided with RELIT's extension to all French bourses.

But this is really only symbolic since in practice the Paris Bourse has always attracted most of the quoted companies. Most major French companies and, even more so, multinational companies listed on the major international markets would not even consider anywhere outside Paris for equity issues for the simple reason that the Paris Bourse is better known.

The disparity between Paris and the regional bourses has always been glaring. In total, the latter represent a mere 2 percent of all trades and 4 percent of total French market capitalisation (listed values), although they account for 15 percent of second market capitalisation. Moreover, there is an imbalance among regional exchanges themselves, with the Lyons Bourse alone accounting for half of all deals carried out on the regional bourses and almost two-thirds of regional capitalisation.

Putting the market in order

Over several years, various procedures have been put in place aimed at regularising the way the capital markets function and at protecting operators against erratic price variations.

(i) Where there is an imbalance between the offer and the demand price of a security, the stock market authorities resort to fixing the maximum divergence in prices that can be quoted from one trading session to the next. These divergences are, in principle, 2 percent for bonds, 4 percent for equities on the spot market and 7 to 10 percent for equities on the monthly settlement market.

(ii) In France, as elsewhere, a company or any person acting on his own or on behalf of a company is prohibited from buying its own shares. However, companies registered on the official listing (*la cote officielle*) or on the second market are authorised to do so if they want to regularise the market for their own shares. In this instance, they must follow very strict COB procedures.

(iii) As it challenges the notion of an "order-driven market", market-making (*la contrepartie*) is a controversial subject in France. Since 1972, the legal texts have had difficulty addressing the subject. French law sets out three types of market-making designed to "preserve the co-herence of an order-driven market". These are: ordinary market-making, block market-making and suspense/prepayment account-making.

According to Paris market professionals, ordinary and block market-making will only develop fully if two conditions are fulfilled — the abolition of turn-over tax and the ability of broking firms to procure liquid funds at a reasonable cost, either through securities issues or through the Euroclear system. For a variety of reasons, the illiquidity of securities and excessive market transparency play only a minor role.

French securities dominate the listing

The present organisation of the French bourses en-ables investors to buy or sell securities on the spot or forward markets. Until 1983, shares were quoted simultaneously at spot and forward prices. The re-forms of October 23 1983 introduced a rule whereby each security is listed on only one of the four mar-kets: the spot market, the monthly settlement market (both together are referred to as the "official list-ing"), the second market or the *marché hors-cote* (over-the-counter market).[15] French securities dominate the listing (see Table 8.6) while foreign ones have tended to be somewhat passive, with 148 of them remaining stagnant since quotation.

Although very different in purpose and in how they are accessed, the official, second and *hors-cote* mar-

---

Table 8.6

Make-up of the official listing and second market (1989)

	No. of issuers	No. of listings		
		Shares	Bonds	Overall
Paris	1,165	998	2,702	3,700
French securities	902	743	2,572	3,315
Foreign securities	245	243	117	360
French franc area securities	18	12	13	25
Provinces	373	269	531	800
(French securities)	(370)	(266)	(531)	(766)
Overall	1,527	1,267	3,233	4,500

Source: Société des Bourses Françaises

---

kets are supposed to complement each other. They are designed to attract to the bourse the widest range of issuers of whatever size, thereby building up the life of a security in successive stages. But movement upwards has given way to a certain degree of stag-nation.

The official listing corners the bulk of operations

The number of French companies on the official listing continues to decline (see Table 8.7), falling from 712 in 1982 to 571 at the beginning of 1991. There are two main reasons — first, the series of nationalisations begun in 1982 proved to be a great psychological shock to the market, and second, the second market had succeeded, between 1983 and 1989, in attracting a number of companies that would otherwise have been potential candidates for the *cote officiel*. The series of mergers and acquisi-tions which occurred in the late 1980s and early 1990s is a further reason for the drop. These have doubtlessly altered the number and size of large groups listed.

The volume of trading on the official listing alone accounts for almost 90 percent of total market activ-ity, while the importance of the second market has somewhat diminished (less than 7 percent of trading as against 10 percent in 1988). The rest is shared between the over-the-counter market and the re-gional bourses.

Table 8.7							
Number of companies quoted							
	French (official listing)			French (second market)			Foreign and franc area
	Paris	Provinces	Total	Paris	Provinces	Total	
1985	489	153	642	80	47	127	193
1987	481	152	633	169	89	258	207
1989	462	144	606	186	112	298	223
1990	444	134	578	186	111	297	219
Source: Société des Bourses Françaises							

The spot market (*marché au comptant*) assembles the least active securities on the official market — French and foreign securities and new equities, plus the majority of bonds (almost 4,000 quotations). As there is no set minimum size of transaction, trading can even be for a single security.

The monthly settlement (*Règlement Mensuel — RM*) market is the real driving force behind the French bourses. This market opened on October 24 1983, listing 200 French and 76 foreign securities, plus a franc zone security. These securities are the most actively traded on the listing.

The conditions governing trades on the RM market are fixed on the trading day but the settlement and delivery of securities — or rather, the registration of the securities on account — does not take place until a later date, called the account day (*jour de liquidation*). This day is fixed as the seventh trading day before the end of the month. The RM market operates according to the following rules:

Securities are traded in rounds or minimum lots (*quotités*) of five, 10, 25, 50 or 100.[16] If the quantity of securities traded is less than the minimum lot, the deal is treated as a *rompu* or fractional share, which carries an extra charge of 0.3 percent (called the "differential") on top of the broker's commission.

There are two ways of dealing on the RM market, either by deferring payment (80 percent of transactions fall into this category) or by speculating through overdrafts. For investors who request immediate settlement, an extra commission of 1 percent, referred to as the early settlement commission, is charged.

Because of the nature of the monthly settlement market and in order to safeguard a market that is purely speculative, the law requires that when a buy or sell order is placed, an initial covering deposit must be paid to cover the possible payment of debit balances should hedge-buying by investors be turned down by the market. This may be made up of 20 percent liquid assets or Treasury bills, 25 percent fixed-yield French securities or gold, 40 percent variable yield securities.

Reforms of the monthly settlement market were expected to be introduced sometime before 1993. In reality, the RM market plays an important role in ensuring the liquidity of the French market and is considered a French speciality. From the point of view of security, it poses a problem insofar as it has been responsible for a large number of accounts in abeyance. These have hampered the operation of the bourse over the past few years. Several working parties have already been set up by the CBV to look into replacing it with a market capable of guaranteeing liquidity and the continuity of spot trading. If traders were only to deal on the spot market, small-time securities buyers would, in principle, be able to defer settlement by one month in return for interest payments. Such a reform could have the effect of reviving the MONEP market as well as accelerating the growth of warrants.

A second market which is running out of steam
The second market was set up in 1983 with two objectives. The first was to enable medium-sized companies to acclimatise to the financial markets by being initiated into the workings of the bourse. Later, such companies would, in theory, transfer to the official listing.

To encourage family-run companies to seek quotations on the second market without risk of losing control, the stock market authorities put a limit of 10 percent on the portion of capital that they could sell to the public. In addition, the prospectus (stamped by the COB) and the requirement to transfer to the official listing within a certain time limit are no longer required, which partly explains the lack of upward mobility of companies listed on this market.

While the second market experienced phenomenal success in its first few years of operation, a change in fashion since 1987 means that companies are no longer trying to make the leap onto the official market. Moreover, the number of new companies seeking a listing has diminished considerably. In 1990, only 18 new companies were quoted, compared with an average of 40 a year after it was first set up.

The market lists around 300 companies, half of which are Paris-based. With a capitalisation of roughly FF140 billion ($24 billion), trading in 1990 approached FF50 billion ($8.8 billion).

The second market has not succeeded in attracting the bulk of small and medium-sized companies. A survey carried out in September 1990 by market research firm SVP and *Le Monde* among French small and medium-sized enterprises concluded that the second market really only attracts companies that are already successful.

The "marginal" over-the-counter market
The *hors-cote*, or over-the-counter market, is a market which is neither regulated nor supervised by the stock market authorities. It is, in fact, a service available to any shareholder selling securities publicly. But though this market wants to remain unregulated, a basic operating framework was put in place in 1962 based on the following "rules":

* Transactions are handled through *sociétés de bourses*;

* The Société des Bourses Françaises (SBF — the stock market's executive body) is responsible for publicising prices and approves and validates the deals made.

A security may arrive on the hors-cote market either "involuntarily" or "deliberately" — involuntarily, when the minority shareholders in an unlisted company want to sell shares which the majority share-

holders do not wish to or cannot take up; deliberately, when the directors want to value the company by reference to the market.

While the over-the-counter market is not the centre of media attention and trading is low-volume, it answers effectively the needs of certain major companies. Indeed, this market has served as an exit route for the minority shareholders of such well-known names as Bénédictine, Affichages Giraudit, Grand Marnier, Air-Inter, Sudaméris-France, etc. The over-the-counter market allows companies to distribute a limited amount of capital (3 to 4 percent) to the public thereby protecting themselves from any hostile takeover.

The derivative markets
The development of futures markets has enabled French and foreign operators to protect themselves against interest rate risk — something which is an integral part of securities trading, particularly in bonds. Share option contracts and, more recently, warrants have arrived on the scene as additional hedging instruments.

Le Marché à Terme International de France (MATIF — The French Financial Futures Market)
The MATIF began on February 20 1986. The reasons behind its creation are both institutional and technical and are linked to deregulation, monetary policy reforms and the new methods of financing public debt using the markets. The instability of exchange and interest rates were another important consideration. MATIF's attraction for international investors means that the French market now ranks among the world's foremost.

Organisation and supervision of the MATIF
To avoid possible difficulties on the futures market, the French authorities and the market supervisory authority[17] have devised a plan based around the strict separation of market supervision, clearing houses and dealers.

The Conseil du Marché à Terme d'Instruments Financiers (CMT — the Futures Market Financial Instruments Committee) supervises the market. It is made up of 17 members appointed for three years by order of the Ministry of Finance.[18] The CMT draws up ground rules for the MATIF and ensures its proper functioning (admission and de-registering of contracts, monitoring of MATIF SA members). The CMT works in close collaboration with MATIF SA (which has the final say), the COB and the Bank of France. It offers its opinion on contract details (sum of deposit, the underlying value of loans).

Market clearing is handled by MATIF SA, a company registered as an *institution financière spécialisée* (ISF). The function of this body is to accept or reject applications for membership, to guarantee that members' trades are properly carried out, to monitor positions and to order the suspension of dealing for a maximum of two trading days, if need arises.

Following the stock market crash of 1987, two new supervisory bodies were established to back the MATIF's authority. The Comité du Parquet (Official Market Committee) ensures the implementation of the rules, and the Service du Risque was set up to avoid disproportionate risks being taken given the solvency of the principals.

To complement the clearing system, a procedure for outside trading hours registration (*enregistrement hors séance*) makes it possible for members to register and clear transactions negotiated outside official market hours. Almost one-third of MATIF dealing occurs outside market hours.

Members[19] may trade on the MATIF either on their own behalf or on behalf of a third party (ie clients or credit institutions not registered for clearing). They can choose three types of legal status according to the business they intend to conduct (clearing or trading) and the capital backing they can provide. These are i) *adhérents compensateurs généraux* (general clearing members), ii) *adhérents compensateurs individuels* (ACI — individual clearing members) and iii) trader-brokers. A separate special category is the *Négociateurs Individuels du Parquet* (NIP — individual official market traders). The latter are backed by financial institutions and act as independents, adopting speculative positions to increase the liquidity of the market. All members are subject to strict supervision by MATIF SA, the Bank of France, the SBF (the market's executive body) and the Commission Bancaire.

Contracts traded on the MATIF

The number of financial contracts traded on the Paris

MATIF has been growing steadily since it opened. But it is long-term notional bond contracts and options on these contracts that are really pivotal to the market. Other products such as the *Pibor*, the CAC index contract, and Ecu contracts have also grown in importance, while options have increasingly been offered on all types of contract (see Table 8.8).

The notional bond (*le notionnel*) was the first product to be traded on the MATIF and is based on a fictitious bond, using real government bonds as a benchmark. This contract has a duration of between seven and 10 years, and a par value of FF500,000 ($88,464). It is redeemable *in fine* and has a fixed interest rate of 10 percent. There can be no deliveries as it is a fictitious bond. However, when deals are not concluded before settlement date by reverse operations, sellers or purchasers of these contracts must deliver or receive real securities. To facilitate this, the market authorities specify a group of government bonds which constitutes the underlying value of the notional bond. Deals take place on the current quarterly settlement date and on the three following quarterly settlement dates. To buy or sell a notional contract, one must deposit a guarantee (*le déposit*) worth roughly 4 percent of the value of the contract, ie FF20,000 ($3,535).

The notional option contract, launched on January 14 1988, is a US-style option (ie it can be exercised at any time) backed by a MATIF notional bond. It makes use of "calls" (options to buy) and "puts" (options to sell), the prices of which are quoted as a percentage of the nominal value of the notional bond. Quotations are based on at least three different operating prices, set by MATIF SA, and are equal to the nearest whole-par closing price for notional bonds. The option expires on the last Friday of the month proceeding the quarterly settlement date of the corresponding notional contract. The minimum amount by which the price can move — the "tick" — is 0.01 percent of FF500,000 or FF50 ($8.8).

The Pibor (Paris Interbank Offer Rate), launched in September 1988, is one of MATIF's most liquid contracts. With almost 2 million traded each year, it has become a favourite instrument for management of short-term interest rate risk. The introduction of Pibor options on March 1 1990 broadened the range of strategies available for managing interest rates on the Paris market.

Table 8.8

Number of contracts traded, 20.ii.86 - 31.xii.1990

Contracts	1986	1987	1988	1989	1990	Total
Notional bonds	1,663,961	11,911,434	12,357,118	15,004,901	15,996,096	56,933,510
Treasury bonds	50,117	106,856	15,973	—	—	172,946
Pibor	—	—	452,374	2,296,359	1,900,851	4,649,584
CAC 40	—	—	64,688	581,473	1,641,398	2,287,559
Eurodem	—	—	—	613,748	393,850	1,007,598
BTAN	—	—	—	84,628	27,866	112,494
Ecu	—	—	—	—	56,292	56,292
Total Contracts	1,714,078	12,018,290	12,890,153	18,581,109	20,016,353	65,219,983
Option NNN	—	—	3,430,915	7,149,559	7,410,305	17,990,779
Option Pibor	—	—	—	—	709,736	709,736
Option Eurodem	—	—	—	—	109,445	109,445
Total Options	—	—	3,430,915	7,149,559	8,229,486	18,809,960
Total financial	1,714,078	12,018,290	16,321,068	25,730,668	28,245,839	84,029,943
Sugar FRF	—	—	160,441	321,463	255,978	737,882
Sugar USD	—	—	—	—	46,930	46,930
Coffee	—	—	3,383	2,826	1,799	8,008
Cocoa	—	—	2,336	167	—	2,503
PDT 40	—	—	700	606	23	1,329
PDT 50	—	—	7,838	30,983	37,165	75,986
Total commodities	—	—	174,698	356,045	341,895	872,638
MATIF Total	1,714,078	12,018,290	16,495,766	26,086,713	28,587,734	84,902,581

Source: MATIF

The volume of dealing on certain MATIF contracts is negligible (Btan, Eurodem); either that or they belong to the category of dormant contracts (such as Treasury bills). The failure of some of these (in particular international instruments such as the Eurodem (Euro-Deutschemark) which LIFFE, the British futures market, made a greater success of), is due to the cautious attitude which greets new product launches in France. Products initially receive lengthy trials on the over-the-counter market before entering fully onto the MATIF.

In October 1990, the MATIF started offering a futures contract on long-term Ecu rates, attracting competition from LIFFE, which in 1991 launched a similar product. Competition is fierce, especially as LIFFE does not exclude high-quality private issuers with good records. On the other hand, only Ecu OATs figure on the MATIF's underlying value, although figures from 1991 would seem to indicate that the French version has won out with 500,000 blocks changing hands since it was set up.

Considering the spectacular expansion in the Ecu Euro-bond market (almost FF70 billion [$12.3 billion] in 1990 compared to FF8 billion [$1.4 billion] in 1983), the stakes are high. Such competition should result in the creation of a full range of Ecu-derived instruments such as foreign exchange contracts, foreign exchange options, interest rate options, etc.

Proof of the MATIF's effectiveness is underlined by the American Commodities Futures Trading Commission (CFTC)'s agreement to market long-term contracts denominated in Ecus in the US. Competition between LIFFE and the MATIF has intensified even more since they each launched contracts linked to Italian state bonds in September 1991, followed rapidly by options on these contracts in both London and Paris.

Encouraging results

Since it was established, the Paris MATIF has grown enormously. With 16 million contracts changing hands in 1988, the MATIF rose rapidly to occupy second place in the world for long-term interest rate contracts (ahead of London which had 15.5 million contracts). With 28 million contracts in 1990, the MATIF fell to third place just behind LIFFE. However, taken as a whole (financial and commodities markets), the MATIF only occupies eighth position in the world (see Table 8.9).

Table 8.9			
Comparison of forward markets			
Forward market	Volume of transactions		% Change
	1990	1989	
	Contracts (millions)		
Chicago Board of Trade	149.22	138.02	+8.1
Chicago Board Options Exchange	129.49	122.18	+6.0
Chicago Mercantile Exchange	102.99	104.64	-1.6
Sao Paulo Stock Exchange	88.43	33.27	+165.8
New York Mercantile Exchange	42.46	38.49	+10.3
American Stock Exchange	40.89	49.20	-16.9
LIFFE	34.19	24.43	+40.0
MATIF	28.59	26.00	+9.9
Source: EOE- Optiebeurs			

Since its launch, the notional bond has been, and still is, the MATIF's cornerstone. Together with the notional bond option, it accounts for over 80 percent of trading (see Table 8.8). The fact that the authorities stabilised the public debt, plus the increase in

investments from nonresidents in this market, have greatly contributed to the MATIF's present size although it remains a single product market.[20]

Even though there was a fall in the volume of contracts exchanged in 1990, the successor to the "dormant" Treasury bill contract, the "3 months Pibor", has rapidly become the main hedging instrument for corporate treasurers. With decompartmentalisation of the interbank and Eurofranc markets, it is the only instrument providing some protection for nonresidents from sudden fluctuations in interest rates on franc deposits placed with foreign banks.

At the end of 1990, the underlying value of bonds quoted on the MATIF totalled over FF240 billion ($42 billion), which makes it a perfect hedging instrument for investments in Treasury securities. The liquidity of the notional bond, with an average daily trading volume of roughly FF5 billion ($88 million) is similar to that of the secondary market for Treasury securities and is very attractive to non-resident investors who also benefit from tax exemption.

Foreign institutions, mostly British, account for almost one-quarter of MATIF transactions. Since 1988, their presence on the official market has grown thanks to the establishment of broking houses and stakes taken in *sociétés de bourse* (See Chapter 10). Japanese and American institutions are the most active in French government debt securities.

The origin of MATIF orders is difficult to pin-point. According to MATIF SA figures, 30 percent of orders come from members operating on their own behalf (equally divided between the banks and broking firms), 10 percent come from staff, 25 percent from institutions, 25 percent from non-member banks and 10 percent from personal investors and businesses.

The MATIF has not escaped the commissions war which broke out on the financial markets. Since MATIF's establishment, commissions have fallen by four-fifths. The average all inclusive cost of a contract has fallen from FF160 to FF30, and can vary from one category of operator to the next. MATIF commissions can be broken down into three constituent elements:

* The trading commission, which varies from FF5 ($88 cents) — a price which could almost be

termed "dumping" — to FF15 (with the biggest brokers);

- The clearing commission (*commission de compensation*), which goes towards the management of deposits and margin calls and varies greatly from one market operator to the next;

- The stock market commission paid to MATIF SA, which is on average FF7.5 per transaction.[21]

Given the rapid fall in brokers' commissions, the rate of growth in the volume of transactions handled is also decreasing. Growth was 10 percent in 1990 as against 35 and 58 percent for 1988 and 1989 respectively. Consequently, intermediaries are faced with a cut in margins on MATIF activities.

Due to the fact that commissions are stabilising at prices which are considered too low, it is possible that many investors will move away from this market and that there will be a drastic cut in the number of market operators. Already, the two biggest intermediaries on the Paris market, Vendôme (Finacor group) and Staff (Viel group) whose common shareholder is Altus Finance, have a combined market share of between 30 and 40 percent.

The MATIF benefits greatly from the liquidity (and quality) of the Treasury securities market, which goes a long way towards explaining its spectacular success.

Le Marché des Options Négociables de Paris (*MONEP — The Paris Traded Options Market*)

Essential to the spot and futures markets, the Paris Bourse opened a traded options market (MONEP) on September 10 1987. Over-the-counter options had existed for over 20 years on the Paris Bourse but it had not been possible to trade them. They merely "linked" buyers with sellers, who could neither exercise nor relinquish the option. The establishment of the Chambre de Compensation des Marchés Conditionnels (CCMC) broke the contractual link between the seller and buyer and made possible the introduction of traded options to the Paris market.

The MONEP offers call and put options on a certain number of French corporate shares sold on the monthly settlement market and which are the object of continuous trading.

There is no doubt that the privatisation of large companies (manufacturers and services) has facilitated the launch of the share option market. There are currently 27 types of share option plus one CAC 40 Index option. As the CAC 40 Index is made up of 40 securities, as its name suggests, there would still seem to be room for new types of option.[22] Nevertheless, according to the chairman of the SCMC (Société de Compensation des Marchés Conditionnels), Alain Morice, the MONEP's function is not to represent all these securities, and the "ideal" number would be about 30 of the most liquid among them.[23]

Organisation of the MONEP

The MONEP is regulated by the Conseil des Bourses de Valeurs (CBV), which is the sole arbiter in cases involving the introduction of a new category of options. In other words, it may decide to list a category against the opinion of the company concerned. This is seen as one more legal anomaly by some companies opposed to the whole idea, such as Air Liquide, LVMH and Générale des Eaux, which do not operate on the MONEP. In practice, even though the CBV has not made use of its wide prerogatives, a certain amount of pressure is placed on un-cooperative companies.

The responsibility for MONEP's clearing and administration, as well as supervision and control of operations and intermediaries, falls to the SBF. These duties are delegated by the SBF to its 100 percent-owned subsidiary, SCMC. In return for this sizeable undertaking, only members of the SBF can become market traders and are, by law, "clearer members".

Thus, market traders, either directly or indirectly, belong to a *société de bourse*. They have two distinct and mutually exclusive functions: portfolio management and the role of *teneurs de marché* (a distinct type of market maker).

Portfolio managers hold client-order books which they match either with other books they hold or with *contrepartistes* (market makers). The public order-book that the clerks hold has priority over offers and requests from *teneurs de marché*.

The function of the *teneurs de marché* is to help ensure that the market operates smoothly and is sufficiently liquid.[24] They act either as representatives of a broking firm or on behalf of market maker controlled by a broking firm.

The quotation of share or index options is by means of open outcry every day from 10:00 to 17:00, using a system similar to that of the Amsterdam market. Only recently, with the installation of remote computerised management systems for SCMC public orderbooks, have *sociétés de bourse* been able to gain access to this market by traditional routes (transmitting their orders by mail or telephone) or by remote accessing a network of screen terminals for customers' orders on the public orderbook.

Products on offer

Starting in the late 1980s, the MONEP has introduced a range of new categories of options onto the market. There are now 27 types of share options and one CAC 40 Index option traded on the Paris market.

The share options traded in Paris are *à l'américaine*, meaning they can be traded at any time. The underlying securities are among the largest by volume of trades and capitalisation on the monthly settlement market, with a float of at least 5 million securities.

Options may be traded or exercised until the day before settlement date in the month they fall due (March, June, September and December). The contracts consist of options on 100 securities, with the exception of Eurotunnel and EuroDisney (each 500 securities).

When a trading period starts, series are created (call and put) at the four operative prices nearest the closing price of the underlying security: one at par value, one at the closing price and two outside the closing price. When the closing price for the security reaches or exceeds the first operative figure in or outside the price, new series of buy and sell options are created taking distant settlement dates on at least 10 stock markets as a reference.

The exercise of an option leads to the random allocation of a seller and to monthly settlement trading that takes place within the usual procedures and transactional fees. The trading commission (collected by the Chambre de Compensation) is FF12.5 ($2.2) per contract, plus a variable brokers' commission.

Index options are US-style options whose underlying security is the CAC 40. The settlement dates for CAC 40 options are the same as those for share options.

Operating prices are fixed at between 25 and 50 points off the index. The mechanisms for opening trades are the same as for share options but series are not created with reference to the five operating prices nearest the closing price of the support security, but rather to the index value. Trading units are made up of contracts in which each index point is allocated a value of FF200 ($35) (for an operating price of FF1,900, the contract is worth FF380,000 — $67,000). Commissions are the same as for share options.

The MONEP lacks liquidity

The main feature of the MONEP has been the rapid growth in CAC 40 Index contracts and a stagnation in single option deals. In 1990, the overall amount of capital transacted (FF20.5 billion — $3.6 billion) grew by 80 percent.[25] But this growth results solely from the buoyancy of Index transactions, which alone have increased by 300 percent while those on options have decreased by 28 percent. Consequently, capital amounts exchanged for Index contracts currently account for about two-thirds (as against 32 percent the previous year) of all MONEP business. What is more, the bulk of share option operations is concentrated around just four or five securities (see Table 8.10).

The same applies to the number of contracts traded: deals on CAC 40 options have tripled in number while those on single options have decreased by 10 percent (see Table 8.11).

This uneven development is not surprising as the relatively weak liquidity of French equities and the effects of the Gulf War have driven investors to seek forms of "blanket" protection, such as the CAC-40 contract.

Trading has rapidly become concentrated in the hands of a few dealers, due in particular to the high costs of entry and the low level of commissions.[26] At present, three *sociétés de bourse* (Didier Philippe, James Capel and Finacor) handle around 40 percent of sales. Taking the six leading companies together, this figure rises to over 60 percent of sales. This

Table 8.10 Business by class of option (The size of each security as a % of capital amounts exchanged)				
Security	1987	1988	1989	1990
Peugeot	39.2	2.4	19.5	6.1
Elf Acquitaine	2.8	3.0	3.4	2.8
Alcatel Alsthom*	—	7.4	5.0	2.7
Suez	—	—	2.6	2.3
Lafarge Coppée	25.1	11.8	4.6	2.1
Saint Gobain	—	5.0	2.7	1.4
Perrier	—	—	3.9	1.4
Paribas	10.1	8.4	7.7	1.3
Accor	—	1.4	1.9	1.2
Eurotunnel	—	—	5.8	1.1
Others	—	—	—	4.9
Thomson CSF	16.2	7.4	3.9	1.0
Axa	6.6	17.3	2.4	0.7
Michelin	—	6.6	3.3	0.6
Société Générale	—	6.2	1.3	0.6
Havas	—	—	n/a	0.5
Bouygues	—	—	0.2	0.3
Eurodisneyland	—	—	—	0.3
Pernod	—	—	n/a	0.2
Cerus	—	—	—	0.2
Rhône Poulenc	—	—	n/a	0.1
Total	—	—	—	0.1
L'Oréal	—	—	—	0.1
CMB Packaging	—	—	—	n/a
BSN	—	—	—	n/a
Lyonnaise des Eaux-Dumez	—	—	—	n/a
Péchiney International	—	—	—	n/a
CAC 40	—	3.1	31.8	72.7
Market	100.0	100.0	100.0	100.0
Capital amounts exchanged (in millions)	1,878.0	5,745.0	11,349.0	20,426.0

*Ex-CGE

Source: SCMC

concentration is likely to become more pronounced if the monthly settlement system is abolished, which is rumoured for 1993. Indeed, the MONEP would benefit from such a move: it would then be the only market where investors can take up long-term investments.

However, it is accepted that development of new business involving the lending and borrowing of securities, will work in favour of intermediaries backed by large financial groups (banks and insurance companies) considering the underwriting risk attached to this type of operation.

Despite the increase in the overall volume of transactions, the MONEP has not escaped the criticisms and scepticism of market operators. Several problems have led to the efficacy of the market being questioned. First, as the market is insufficiently liquid, it does not allow for "imaginative" management of a specific risk but rather obliges investors to hold options right up until the settlement date. Second, it is the view of certain *teneurs de marché* that the French are not yet used to the principle of "market making" and that price spreads are too wide.

But according to several operators, the illiquidity of certain categories of options determining the market makers' behaviour is simply a reflection of the illiquidity of the underlying securities.[27] Unlike the MATIF which, as we have seen, benefits from the liquidity of the public debt market, the MONEP is linked to a French equity market which has traditionally lacked liquidity. This, in turn, is reflected in the structure of the securities exchanged, with the CAC 40 option finding increasing favour, especially in periods of crisis.

The *société de bourse* monopoly is an obstacle to the entry of single bank-backed market traders, although these could also help to animate the MONEP. One need only consider that *sociétés de bourse* clear 32 percent of blocks traded, credit institutions 14 percent and *teneurs de marché* 54 percent. The latter's share is increasing rapidly because of growth in arbitrage activities and the greater liquidity of index-linked options. Certain problems also arise out of the powers invested in the SBF, which intermediaries consider to be excessive.

In addition, the MONEP is currently faced with

Table 8.11						
MONEP						
	Share options			**CAC40 Index options**		
	1989	1990	1991 (6 mths)	1989	1990	1991 (6 mths)
No. of contracts traded	2,927,804	2,658,139	1,356,663	816,025	2,470,394	1,590,618
Daily average	11,805	10,633	11,120	2,863	9,882	13,037
Source: SCMC						

competition from warrants (option certificates exercisable over a much longer period than the classic MONEP-registered options) and options indexed to stock market indices. Since OAT warrants received authorisation at the beginning of 1990, there have been over 20 warrant issues and everyday trading is growing rapidly: FF1.5 billion ($265 million) in the first quarter of 1991 as against FF700 million in 1990. Crédit Lyonnais has already launched Ecu warrants on the 8.50 percent 1977 OAT French government bond. One of the leaders in this market, Société Générale, in addition to OAT warrants, is quoting warrants on stock market indices, in particular the CAC 40, Dax, Nikkei, etc. In total, by 1991, there were over 100 warrant lines admitted onto the listing.

In 1991, Citicorp issued FF20 million worth ($3.5 million) of calls in two tranches and FF30 million of puts in three tranches indexed to the Paris Bourse CAC 40. These calls are designed with three-year maturities so that investors are not heavily penalised by misjudging market developments. This contrasts with the current MONEP practice whereby, if the market does not develop in the desired direction, investors must hold onto their options for as long as possible before the settlement date.

The SCMC, faced with the possibility that a slice of MONEP business could be diverted from this market, has been forced to follow the US example by launching options with long maturities on the best capitalised French securities. But such measures have been deferred pending the Ministry of Finance's approval of the arrangements for meeting general CBV regulations.

Regulations which discourage *"Offres Publiques d'Achat"* (OPAs — Public takeover bids)
In the second half of the 1980s, the French economy underwent a process of restructuring through a series of mergers and acquisitions. The aim was to build powerful groups which could then increase their presence on world markets. In 1987 alone, the number of M&A deals tripled and the amounts of money involved doubled compared to the previous total.

But though M&A is increasing rapidly, public takeover bids (OPAs) account for only a fraction of these operations. Out of several hundred M&A deals every year in France, only 10 were public takeover bids in 1990 and 13 in 1989. In short, OPAs are not the driving force behind the overhaul of the French economy. In contrast, French corporates are very active in international takeovers. In 1990, they launched acquisition bids (including OPAs) on foreign companies for a total sum of FF80 billion ($14 billion). Consequently, French companies were involved in the 10 largest acquisitions in Europe in the second half of 1990.[28]

Even if there can be no comparison between the level of public takeover bids in France and the US or UK, it is true that the volume of activity has increased considerably over the past few years. Thus, in 1989, the sums involved were huge: one bid was made by Compagnie Financière de Suez for two companies (Compagnie Industrielle and Groupe Victoire), the capitalisation of which was roughly FF25 billion ($4.4 billion).

The rise in takeovers through OPAs, plus the problems associated with some such deals (eg Télémechanique, Holophane, La Providence), have again raised the question of regulation. In any case, France could not remain on the sidelines while new European takeover regulations were being drawn up.

The new regulations governing takeovers
Law No 89-531 of August 2 1989 "pertaining to the security and the transparency of the financial market" determines the legal framework for takeover bids and the acquisition of controlling stakes.

Companies wishing to launch an OPA in France are subject to procedures laid down by the stock market authorities, in particular the CBV and the COB.[29] The Law assigns the CBV the task of setting the parameters for regulation of takeover bids.[30]

CBV regulations hold that any transfer of a controlling stake must take place according to one of the two following procedures: by public bid or by negotiation for the rights to a controlling stake. These regulations do not give a precise definition of a "controlling stake" and each individual case must be submitted to the CBV. The concept generally used is that of "effective control" which is defined as meaning the ability to make strategic decisions regardless of the size of the stake. The legal framework for OPAs has, in fact, been made more rigorous by the addition of various new provisions. Even if this legislation is similar in some respects to EC regulations, there remain at least two points on which they diverge:

a) In France, it is obligatory to launch a public takeover bid for two-thirds of the securities (with voting rights) of the company in question once the threshold of 33.33 percent of capital or voting rights is reached. Under EC regulations, takeover bids must be for the entire capital of the company.

The "100 percent rule" was dismissed by the French authorities who considered that this would make it possible only for those companies with strong liquid assets to make public takeover bids. This rule would, in their view, work in favour of foreign companies whose cash positions are much larger than those of French companies.

However, in order to avoid "stagnation" on the market or possible destabilisation of companies, exceptions are made to the threshold rule. Thus: i) whether a public takeover bid has to be launched or not depends on the speed at which the threshold is reached (purchases of 2 or 3 percent share stakes per year are exempt from the obligation to launch a full takeover bid) and not the total share stake accumulated; ii) the obligation to make a public takeover bid does not apply if the company in which the one-third threshold has been reached was already partially controlled.[31]

b) The EC directive prohibits companies which are the subject of a public takeover bid to increase their capital without prior authorisation from the shareholders' general meeting. French legislation, on the other hand, holds that each year shareholders may vest in the board of directors the necessary powers to increase capital during a takeover bid without prior consultation. This practice allows French companies to react quickly to prevent hostile takeovers.

France is not the only country to have its differences with the European Commission over takeover regulations. In fact, the takeover directive has not been well received by a majority of EC members. France finds itself among the moderates between, on the one hand, the UK, which feels its own code of good conduct (developed by the market itself) is under threat, and countries like Germany, Denmark and the Netherlands on the other, which are opposed to what they perceive as overly liberal takeover rules.

French law is particularly attentive to the need to protect minority shareholders, especially when it comes to declaring when equity thresholds are reached, io the provision of information on the number of shares with long-term access to capital and to the voting rights attached. The law also introduces the concept of "concerted action" in determining the size of shareholders' holdings, with a view to guaranteeing a greater transparency in any distribution of shares designed to "place an obstacle in the way of attempts at covert takeovers".

Systematic purchases
Many takeovers in France are by means of the "systematic purchase" technique when the company is not in the hands of a "hard core" of shareholders. It takes a long time for such purchases to build into a large shareholding, in addition to which excessive purchases can lead to increases in share prices and thereby provoke a counter-attack. There are also at least two legal provisions which restrict this technique:

The COB requires companies to notify the market as soon as they hold blocks of over 5 percent, 10 percent, 20 percent, 33.5 percent and 50 percent of capital. Consequently, the bid does not remain unnoticed.

The Law on Savings of June 17 1989, concerning the requirement to provide additional information on the holding of a percentage of capital in minimum blocks of 0.5 percent over the legal threshold of 5 percent, gives management the right to ask the SICOVAM (the Central Depository Authority) the name of shareholders and the percentage of shares they hold.

The capital of French companies remains under lock and key

Even though the new French law has edged nearer to EC legislation on public takeovers, it is nonetheless still directed towards "safeguarding" control of companies which may be subject to hostile takeover bids. Indeed, several of the new takeover rules impose just as many additional constraints for potential acquirers. Consequently, certain Paris market officials consider that these attempts to render the French market more transparent are paralysing initiators of public takeover bids through the imposition of ever stricter regulations.

Companies have several legal means of defence, in addition to the restrictive elements contained in public takeover regulations. Shareholders have means of defence of their own, such as the allocation of double voting rights on shares held for over two years. This increases the cost of takeovers and develops loyalty among the longest-standing shareholders.

Other means of defence are at the discretion of the Finance Ministry. These are used particularly to provide protection for investments in "sensitive" industries such as defence, health, etc, and other vaguely defined areas.

A *rachat d'une entreprise par ses salariés* (RES — employee buy-outs) is another method of defence which consists of transferring all or part of the capital of the company under attack to its employees. This tactic also provides considerable tax breaks.

Offres publiques d'échange *(OPEs — Takeover bids [for shares]) — an alternative to OPAs*

To protect themselves against possible hostile takeover bids French companies resort largely to the technique of *autocontrôle*, which means placing

voting rights with subsidiaries and subholdings (see Table 8.12).

Table 8.12	
A high level of *autocontrôle* over capital (%)	
Source Perrier	13.8
Bic	10.0
Suez	10.0
Salomon	9.5
Bis	8.6
Chargeurs	7.3
Alcatel-Alsthom	6.5
Saint-Louis	6.5
Société Générale	5.1
Auxiliare d'Enterprises	5.0
Lafarge Coppée	5.0
Générale des Eaux	4.5
Saint-Gobain	4.3
Paribas	4.0
Docks de France	3.8
Source: Option Finance, No.158, April 15 1991	

But since the Dailly amendment to the Law of August 2 1989, *autocontrôle* of voting rights has been abolished. Likewise, to close any loopholes in the new law, limited partnership companies (*sociétés en commandite par action*) — which are not subject to takeovers by their nature — and their subsidiaries are prohibited from exercising voting rights in companies which act as their own sleeping partners.

The aim of this new law is to make the capital of French companies more flexible. While *autocontrôle* gives French companies a means of defence against possible hostile takeovers, it also reduces the effective power of shareholders and leads to managerial "stagnation".

French companies have been displaying great imagination since this law was passed. Although some are retaining *autocontrôle*, others are distributing equity to their employees by means of shareholding funds. But the most effective way of converting from *autocontrôle* is the OPE (takeover bids for shares), the number of which is growing. Indeed, even though the French authorities have poured their energies into controlling OPAs, really it is the OPEs which now occupy centre stage. This is evidenced by the wave of OPEs which has swept through the stock market since mid-1990, including the Paribas OPE at the beginning of 1991.[32] OPEs have quickly established themselves as the main instrument for restructuring alliances and capital in French companies.

OPEs are also increasingly used on the bond market, most notably to give greater liquidity to the quoted lines of the big issuers.

In summary, even though the stock market — long absent from the corporate restructuring process — is playing a more active economic role, the rules governing it are conceived more with the aim of achieving "equitableness" rather than of encouraging corporate restructuring. This seems to indicate that the new takeover regulations will encourage companies to adopt more ingenious means to achieve growth by acquisition, and will force a clearer focusing of activities and stock market operations. This is evidenced by a decrease in the number of public takeover bids together with an increase in other operations aimed at consolidating cross-shareholdings and forms of corporate *autocontrôle*.

Even though Paris has become a fully fledged international market within a few years, it still lags far behind New York, Tokyo and London (and, in some respects, Germany) and finds itself competing fiercely with some countries whose financial and economic strength (Netherlands, Switzerland) is inferior to that of France.

Endnotes

(1) Bond transactions dominate the French financial market with 83 percent of all trades in 1989 compared with 52 percent in 1980.

(2) The payment of dividends in equity allows for the creation of new equity, which from a tax point of view is regarded as reinvested profits. As such they are taxed at a lower rate than distributed profits.

(3) At the present time, an average FF2.5 billion ($441 million) worth of shares are traded daily on the Bourse, with foreign institutions such as JP Morgan and SG Warburg among the main dealers in French shares.

(4) With "variable rate" securities, the rate of interest is calculated over the period to which it applies and is thus not finally known until they fall due. By contrast, with "reviewable rate" securities, the rate of interest is fixed before the period begins. Either money market or bond market rates are used as benchmarks (see Chapter 10).

(5) The decline in issues that include a monetary reference (now less than 15 percent) has been hastened by the abolition of the *obligation de l'obligation* rule for OPCVMs (a rule requiring mutual funds to hold at least 30 percent of their assets in the form of bonds).

(6) OATs make up 20 percent of the portfolio of French stocks held by non-residents.

(7) Compared with 20 percent in the UK and 23 percent in Japan.

(8) More than half of these investors are "domiciled" in Britain, 15.2 percent in the Benelux countries, 8.3 percent in Germany, 5.8 percent in Japan and 3 percent in Switzerland.

(9) The Stock Market Law of January 22 1988 is split into four sections: (i) the *sociétés de bourse*, (ii) the organisation of the market: the Conseil des Bourses de Valeur (CBV) and the Institution Financière Spécialisée (IFS), (iii) the Commission des Opérations de Bourse (COB) and (iv) miscellaneous provisions.

(10) Fleuriot was seconded from the Ministry of Finance.

(11) The COB is made up of a college of nine members: a chairman appointed by decree from the Council of Ministers, members of the Cour des Comptes (public auditor's office), the Council of State, the Court of Appeal, the Conseil des Bourses de Valeur, the Conseil du Marché à Terme (forward market council), the Bank of France and two co-opted members.

(12) Derived from the CATS (Computer-Aided Trading System) software used on the Toronto Stock Exchange.

(13) While this system helps remove arguments over the buying and selling price, it does run counter to the logic of the continuous market.

(14) Under the terms of the Law of November 3 1984, the rights represented by ownership of a certificate were replaced by an entry into a current account. *Dématerialisation,* as this is known, is responsible for a significant cut in administration and commission costs.

(15) The monthly settlement market is highly concentrated. The equities of major corporates and certain bonds (the Caisse Nationale d'Epargne "3 percent" and the "4.5 percent" bond issues) are among the most actively-traded securities.

(16) An extra session, solely for market professionals, is organised in the mornings from 09:30 to 11:00 for around 20 of the most actively-traded securities on the RM market. Securities are traded in lots of upwards of 100.

(17) The MATIF is under the supervision of the Ministry of Finance (the Treasury) and the COB.

(18) The CMT is composed of representatives from the following institutions: credit institutions (4), *sociétés de bourse* (4), insurance companies (2), market officials (1), industrial and trading companies (2) and two qualified people.

(19) Only insurance companies are excluded by law from this business, although they do participate through *sociétés de bourse* in which they are shareholders.

(20) Note, however, that T-bonds on the Chicago Futures Market account for an even higher proportion (85 percent).

(21) Even though this price is lower on the LIFFE (£0.50 [$0.85]), overall commission rates are similar on the two markets.

(22) Twenty of the support shares for options are part of the CAC 40 Index.

(23) The criterion for admission to the MONEP is that the underlying security must be interesting enough from the standpoint of liquidity and volatility to act as a support for options; several securities on the CAC 40 would not meet these requirements.

(24) Even though around 20 *sociétés de bourse* are authorised to function as market makers, only half of them are actually active on the market.

(25) Volume-wise, the MONEP is comparable to the Amsterdam EOE and London's LTOM.

(26) Fixed costs for computerised trading and back-office administration are such that few intermediaries are in a position to deal on this market, much less cut their commissions.

(27) By way of example, every day between 100,000 and 200,000 Peugeot securities are handled on the market, while the number of Royal Dutch shares handled on the Amsterdam stock market is between 2 and 3 million.

(28) In 1990, the low level of acquisitions in France was compensated for by the buoyancy of French purchases abroad.

(29) A public takeover bid must be authorised by the CBV and monitored by the COB which checks the information given to shareholders. In the case of foreign bids (from outside the EC), the Treasury may exercise a veto.

(30) Bidders, however, may have recourse to the Paris Appeal Court to contest CBV decisions.

(31) In 1990, the CBV made 40 exceptions due to pre-existing rulings on thresholds.

(32) First, the OPE against Union de Crédit pour le Bâtiment (UCB) through the intermediary of Compagnie Bancaire and then the double OPE launched against Poliet and Ciments Français. These deals enabled Paribas to reduce its level of *autocontrôle* from 8.5 to 4 percent.

Chapter 9

Financial Market Products and their Issuers

Introduction

Until the Monory Law of July 13 1978, there was a well-defined division between the two main types of transferable securities — equities and bonds. The difference was based on the rights pertaining to each type of security: (i) fixed *droits de créances* (rights of claim) for bonds and (ii) *droits d'associés à revenu variable* (variable interest partnership rights) for equities. But since the end of the 1970s, it has not been so easy to differentiate between products as a result of the proliferation of securities with features common to both equities and bonds. The Delors Law of January 3 1983 reinforced this tendency during a period of nationalisations and fluctuating long-term interest rates. In addition, the 1980s witnessed a deepening of the French budget deficit. To ensure inflation-proof funding for such a deficit, the state had ever greater recourse to the capital markets.

Types of bond

A bond is proof of holding debt. It represents a long-term loan issued by a body (the state, a public or semi-state body, a co-operative, a private company, etc) and confers on its holder the right to receive interest.

There is a standard levy on bonds of 15 percent, to which one must add a further tax of 1 percent, a social security tax of 1 percent and — from 1991 — an across-the-board social security levy of 1.1 percent. The same taxes apply to *titres de créances négociables* (TCN — marketable debt securities).

Variable, floating and revisable rate bonds

Although set up in 1974, these instruments only began to take off in 1979 when interest rates became volatile. Since the indexing of principals was forbidden in 1959, issuers have turned towards the indexing of interest rates.

Indexing allows the issuer to provide against a fall in rates that otherwise leads to heavier interest payments. For the holder of these bonds, it is a means of avoiding a drop in the market price while interest rates are rising.

There are several different categories of indexed bonds, depending on the basis and method of indexing chosen. Most important is the distinction made between "variable rate bonds" in the strict meaning of the term, and "floating" or "renewable rate" bonds. For the former, indexing is calculated over a period that ends shortly before the bond goes ex-coupon. For the latter, the coupon — which is often of six-months duration — is known in advance because the index is calculated over a long period before it goes ex-coupon.

The main variable rate bonds (which may offer a minimal fixed rate of return) are indexed against the *taux moyen obligatoire* (TMO — average bond market rate), the T4M (*taux moyen mensuel du marché monétaire* — the average one-month money market rate) and the *taux annuel monétaire* (TAM — annual monetary rate). Revisable rate bonds generally favour indexation against the *taux revisable annuellement* (TRA — the average rate of return on settlement of loans backed by the government or associate bodies) and the *taux révisable d'obligation d'état* (TRO — revisable interest rates on government loans) respectively.

However, given the growing importance of issues

and transactions revolving around Treasury securities, such indices are tending to be supplanted by the *taux de rendement moyen des emprunts d'Etat* (TME — average rate of return on government loans of over seven years duration) and by TREs (rates revisable on the basis of the return on state loans of over seven years duration).

Zero coupon and single coupon bonds

By definition, zero coupon bonds do not pay interest. Remuneration is, at the time of the final payment, either in the form of a redemption bonus or, more often, in the form of redemption at face value of a loan issued below par.

Zero coupon bonds hold a number of advantages for both borrower and investor. For the borrower, zero coupons avoid the expense associated with servicing a loan annually and often enable loans to be issued at actuarial rates of interest below current ones. For investors, zero coupons hold certain fiscal advantages, ie the absence of compensation allows holders of these certificates to avoid income tax. Only realised capital gains (when the certificate is sold or redeemed) are taxed.

When single coupons are remitted (coinciding with redemption), interest is taxed at the same rate as fixed-interest securities and the person remitting the coupon may benefit from tax relief and a standard rate of deduction of 18 percent. However, a plan has been drawn up to convert this single tax payment into a flat-rate annual charge, the effect of which would be to remove the attraction of this type of bond.

Fonds d'Etat Libérés d'Interêt Nominal (FELIN — Public debt securities with separate trading of principal and of the securities representing each coupon)

These are one of the latest innovations in certificates "derived" from government securities. In these government loan issues, the principal is separated from interest, which means separate quotation for each of the annual coupons on the stock exchange. FELINs, or "dismembered" bonds, result from the separation of a 10 year fixed-rate *Obligation Assimilable du Trésor* (OAT — Treasury-bond equivalent instruments) into one certificate that corresponds to the

OAT's principal and 10 that correspond to the different coupons attached, amounting to a total of 11 certificates quoted separately on the bourse.[1]

Thus, the 1986 9.8 percent loan was split into 11 certificates (Crédit Lyonnais, Caisse des Dépôts et Consignations and Banque Stern were mandated by the French Treasury to place these certificates arising out of the division of 1 million OAT bonds): 10 for each FF196 ($34) coupon and one for the principal of FF2,000 ($3,535). This is the equivalent of transforming this FELIN issue into 11 zero coupon bonds. The return on these certificates is determined by the issue price, in turn made up of its current value at a rate of 10.35 percent of the redemption price. Such division in the loan issue does not preclude the payment of income tax, made through a complicated system of returns based on set terms of references.

FELINs, because they are closely related to zero coupons, present a solution to fluctuations in interest rates. For example, from the investor's point of view, the absence of interest payments eliminates the risk inherent in rate movements when coupons come to be reinvested, as well as the administrative costs attached.

Perpetual and redeemable annuities

These are bonds on which the redemption date is not set, in return for payment of interest over an unlimited period of time. The best examples of redeemable annuities are the "3 percent perpetual" and the "5 percent perpetual", although the number of such certificates in circulation is declining because the state has proposed redemption or conversion on several occasions (the last time being 1987). The 4.5 percent Pinay Loan of 1973 (ex. 1952-1958) is an example of a redeemable annuity, insofar as its original lifespan was some 60 years. The concept of annuity, which was on the way out in the financial world, made a comeback in the 1980s in the form of *titres participatifs* (participating securities) and subordinate bonds of no set duration.

Phased redemption stock

These are fixed-rate bonds on which the subscriber only pays part of the issue price at the time the loan is floated, the rest being paid at an agreed date (generally six months later).

Bonds with a choice of optional clauses

Obligations Renouvelables du Trésor (ORT — Renewable Treasury bond-equivalent instruments)

This is government stock of relatively short duration (from six to eight years), that stands midway between *obligations d'état* — government bonds — and *bons du trésor* — exchequer bills. ORTs can be converted as the bearer decides. He can ask — generally after three years — that his ORTs be exchanged for a new series issued at market rates. Interest is capitalised according to the duration of the bond, making them close relations of zero coupon bonds. Nevertheless, this instrument is gradually falling into disuse.

Obligations Assimilables du Trésor (OAT — Treasury bond-equivalent instruments)

Since the end of 1985, rather than resorting to large loan issues whose very size impacts heavily on the market, the greater part of loans issued by the state (generally on a monthly basis) has been made up of OATs. Thus in 1990, they accounted for 80 percent of marketable long-term debt, 48 percent of total marketable debt and 37 percent of total public debt. In 1987 the figures were 57 percent, 31 percent and 23 percent respectively. Because of their high liquidity, OATs are the most actively traded securities listed.

Each time, to avoid an excessive number of loans being quoted, the state issues a new instalment of an already existing loan. This instalment is immediately absorbed by preceding ones. The main feature of OATs is their maturity dates. At present, there exist four standard maturities for fixed-rate OATs (seven, 10, 15 and 25 years) and a 12-year maturity for variable rate OATs.

OATS — generally placed through "Dutch auctions"[2] — have within a short time become the instrument most favoured for managing long-term public debt. They offer the advantage of progressively reinforcing existing quotations, thereby improving the liquidity of the government securities market. Thus, traditional loans that the state no longer issues and that do not carry an "absorption" clause account for less than 20 percent of loans outstanding, and even this is decreasing as they are redeemed.

Bonds offering the option of redemption before the due date

Emprunts à fenêtres (bonds with an advance redemption option) are also worthy of mention.[3] These are fixed rate, long-term securities that carry the possibility of redemption before the due date, at a pre-determined settlement date and price. There are two methods of redemption. One is as the bearer decides. The bearer then accepts a penalty against his last coupon (it is therefore not in his interest to exercise this option unless rates rise). The other is as the issuer decides. The issuer thus receives a premium on redemption (and will only redeem in advance if rates are falling sharply).

Exchangeable bonds

These instruments allow for the possibility of passing from a fixed rate bond to a variable rate one and vice versa. The issue of contract will state the conditions for such exchanges, stipulating the periods when this is possible, the features of the bond being proposed, etc.

Indexed bonds

These are bonds for which the coupon and/or the redemption of the capital amount varies according to a set index or within parameters of reference, while a minimum is contractually agreed upon.

The main benefit of indexing is that it protects against inflation (eg the 3 percent Caisse Nationale d'Epargne loan, the 1977 8.80 percent loan). Since the beginning of 1990, loan issues linked to the CAC40 index have really taken off (Société Générale, Nord-Est, etc).

Convertible bonds

Since being introduced into France by the Decree of March 3 1953, legislation affecting convertible bonds has steadily become more flexible. The *obligation convertible en action* (OCA — share convertible bond) enables subscribers to choose between holding on to credit in the form of bonds or converting it into shares.

Such an advantage — stipulated in the loan issue contract — allows for a lower return and a conversion bonus. Thus, the idea behind such issues is to attract subscribers interested in good returns and to allow companies command resources at a low rate, the end objective being the strengthening of own funds.

For the issuer, the benefits are three-fold because:

1) Interest paid is deductible from taxes on profits;

2) There is a clearly-stated provision for turning the debt into capital sums. Such a manoeuvre is made all the more favourable thanks to the conversion bonus;

3) The interest rate is lower than for straight bond issues. However the bearer can only exercise this option once.

Obligations à Bon de Souscription (Warrant bonds)

Set up in 1983, warrant bonds are straight, fixed-rate bonds that allow one to acquire shares or bonds of the same company (redeemable shares) over a certain period and at a price stipulated at the time of issue.

After the flotation, the warrant bond is detached from the bond itself. Once they are introduced onto the market, the bond and the warrant bond are quoted separately.

They are issued at rates lower than those prevailing on the market because the warrant bond affords the bearer the right to buy securities at what might turn out to be a very favourable rate. But if stock market rates are lower than this, these securities lose their entire value as maturity nears.

Such certificates do not produce any interest and are quoted separately from the bond. They enable the bearer to benefit from a significant leverage effect at times when the supporting security rises. And as the use of bonds in the case of *Obligations à Bons de Souscription d'Actions* (OBSAs — bonds with equity warrants attached) entail a capital rise, such instruments can forestall hostile takeover bids.

Obligations à Bons de Souscription d'Actions Remboursables (OBSAR — bonds with money-back warrants), issued since 1988, come with an optional component comparable to that for OBSAs and of greater value than that for convertible bonds. Theoretically, the certificate will always hold a minimum value, allowing for its redemption price.

OBSAR certificates are less volatile than OBSAs because they carry less of a leverage effect. Their success over the past two years springs from more advantageous conditions for issues, allowing a company's shareholders to reduce their outlay as much as possible.

Equally, the cost of an OBSAR issue is less than that for an OBSA for the first few years as a result of the free resources such issues procure.

Obligations Remboursables en Actions (ORA — Bonds redeemable in shares) and

Obligations Remboursables en Certificats d'Investissement (ORCI — Bonds redeemable in preferred investment certificates)

Licensed ORAs and ORCIs are a recent creation. Their originality stems from the fact that they must be redeemed as shares, investment certificates or preferred investment certificates at the time of maturity, in accordance with the terms and conditions set out in the issue contract.

Emprunts à Sensibilité Opposée (ESOP — "Bull and bear" bonds)

ESOPs — the French version of "bull and bear" bonds — are divided into two instalments of equal weight. Prices are linked in opposite directions to indices, (for example, a notional loan on the MATIF or the CAC index). The issuer is covered against fluctuations in the index in either direction. Any gain realised on one tranche is compensated by a similar loss on the other. These securities appreciate or depreciate in tandem with movements in the index.

Obligations Spéciales à Coupons à Réinvestir (OSCAR — Special bonds with an option to reinvest the coupon)

What distinguishes these fixed-rate, 10-year securities (redeemable in two instalments), is that in each of the first six years they are held, bearers can allocate the proceeds from the coupon to bonds carrying the same features as the original ones.

These then are products that anticipate downward movements in interest rates. Such special bonds were issued for the first time by the Société Financière de l'Industrie de Gaz in February 1986 for a total of FF300 million ($53 million) and were underwritten by the state electricity company (Eléctricité de France).

Equities

Certificats d'Investissement (*CIs or CIPs — Non-voting shares*)
Conceived mainly as a means of procuring fresh capital for state-owned companies and without the state having to pay out any cash or dilute its control, these are the result of splitting some of the issuing company's shares — up to a maximum of 25 percent of capital — into two separate securities:

A *Certificat d'Investissement* (CI) representing the financial claims attached to the share and termed *privilégié* (hence the *Certificat d'Investissement Privilégié* — CIP) when a preference share is involved;

A *Certificat de Droit de Vote* (CV — a certificate with voting rights) that the original shareholder continues to own if the split involves shares already issued or of which he becomes owner if the split involves the issue of new shares when capital is being raised.

Actions à Dividende Prioritaire sans Droit de Vote (*ADP — Non-voting preference shares*)
These are similar to CIPs, though the issue of one precludes the issue of the other. In addition, issuers can buy back ADPs. They allow family-controlled businesses to raise capital without having to worry about a third party interfering in the company's management.

Actions à Bons de Souscription d'Action (*ABSA — Shares with equity warrants*)
Since the Law of December 14 1985, this form of security has been extremely successful. ABSAs allow large companies to issue new shares with a choice of one or several certificates and enable their holders to subscribe to higher-priced shares at a later date. One should note that such rights issues can take place in isolation without any need for an initial capital increase.

With the launch of the first *Actions avec Bons de Souscription d'Actions à Faculté de Rachat* (ABSAR — shares with equity warrants carrying a buy-back option) (see OBSARs) investors have had a "parachute" at their disposal.

Share dividends
The Law of January 3 1983 permits French companies to propose paying dividends in the form of shares to its shareholders, who may or may not approve the proposal. Such a possibility allows shareholders to increase their participation in the company on favourable terms and for companies to avoid immediate disbursements.

Taken together, ABSAs and dividends in the form of shares represent over 40 percent of capital increases carried out through public offerings — FF27 billion ($4.7 billion) in 1990.

Titres participatifs — *Participating securities*
These make up part of what is known as *dette subordonnée à terme* (forward subordinated debt) which also includes *Titres Subordonnés à Durée Détérminée* (TSDD — dated floating rate notes) and *Titres Subordonnés à Durée Indeterminée* (TSDI — undated floating rate notes). Established under the Law of January 3 1983, participating securities are really a hybrid form of transferable security, midway between bonds and equity. They resemble bonds because the bearer is assured of a regular income and, because returns are index-linked to results, they are also related to equities.

They were created to allow state companies to call on the financial market without undermining the principle of nationalisation. Such flotations are also open to co-operatives and, since 1985, to public industrial and trading companies eg Eléctricité de France, SNCF (the state railway company). Because of their perpetual nature, the proceeds from participating securities are considered own funds.

A participating security can de defined as a perpetual bond remunerated partially by index-linked interest.

Given that they are perpetual, such securities are only redeemable if a company is liquidated or, in certain instances, at the initiative of the company itself — if the conditions of the issue contract allow for this.

On the other hand, participating securities have one important disadvantage. Given the fact that they are perpetual, making them comparable to annuities, such certificates can turn out to be dangerous both for the bearers and for the issuing company in view of the somewhat unpredictable nature of changes in the index over a long period.

Titres Subordonnées à Durée Détérminée (*TSDD — Dated floating rate notes*)

TSDDs are debenture loans with a subordination clause. They have the peculiar feature of a maturity date set by contract. Having first appeared in 1988, their growth is due to the efforts made by banks to strengthen capital funds in preparation for the application of the Cooke ratio from 1992.

But unlike loans and participating securities, the law does not explicitly recognise subordinated stock as own capital. As a result, their assimilation is rather limited. Despite these obstacles, TSDDs allow the issuer to strengthen capital ratios without causing any change in the control of that capital, as they only constitute *droits de créance* (rights of claim). For the nationalised banks, recourse to such securities is a way of increasing capital ratios without having to call on the state shareholder, while at the same retaining their legal standing.

Titres Subordonnées à Durée Indeterminée (*TSDI — Undated floating rate notes*)

TSDIs are more like perpetual annuities than straight bond debt. These are second-order debts, interest on which is only paid if the issuing company's results reach a certain level. However, even if in a given year nothing is paid, interest is still due in principle.

Of no set duration, such securities generally come with an option for the issuer to redeem the principal as he so wishes and are the lowest-ranked form of debt.

Negotiable instruments offered on the money market

Short-term securities issued by companies, financial institutions and the state are all negotiable and have similar characteristics:

Since July 1988, they are all subject to a minimum amount of FF1 million ($176,000); they have a life span of between 10 days and seven years (with the exception of Treasury bonds). Tax is identical for all French economical agents, whether it be applied to interest received or realised capital gains. They are issued at a fixed rate (revisable rates are possible for securities of an initial duration of over one year) with the exception of Treasury bonds.

A feature of such instruments is the narrowness — indeed the non-existence — of a secondary market.

Certificats de Dépôt Négociables (*CDN — Negotiable certificates of deposit*)

These are certificates issued by credit institutions which may receive funds from the public of less than two years duration and then must constitute reserves against payments due. The certificates enable them to pay for liquid assets at rates approaching those available on the money market.

Bons du Trésor Négociables (*BTN — Negotiable Treasury bonds*)

These are certificates issued by the Treasury to the public and to financial institutions. They can be short or medium-term, ranging from four weeks to five years in duration (in practice, 13 weeks is the average). They have become the state's main instrument for short-term refinancing. The share of BTNs in total marketable debt now stands at 40 percent.

Negotiable Treasury bonds are divided into two main categories:

1. *Bons à Taux Fixe et à Intérêts Annuels* (BTAN — interest-bearing medium-term Treasury bills), for which the period of issue can be from two to five years.

2. *Bons à Taux Fixe et à Intérêts Précomptés* (BTF — fixed interest discount Treasury bills

withholding tax on interest), for which the period of issue can be 13, 26 or 52 weeks;

Five-year BTANs predominate with FF310 billion ($54 billion) outstanding, or some 55 to 60 percent of short and medium-term negotiable debt. Two-year BTANs represent 18 percent of the total.

Billets de Trésorerie
(BT — *Commercial paper*)
Issued by companies that have been in existence for at least two years (excluding credit institutions), these enable them to obtain short-term loans without having to go to the banks. They are mostly issued for periods of between 15 days and three months. Since February 1991, industrial and trading companies nonresident in France have been authorised to issue commercial paper on the French market. They must, however, be domiciled in a French credit institution.

Bons des Institutions Financières
(BISF — *Financial institution bonds*)
These are issued by specialist financial institutions (such as Crédit d'Equipement des PMEs (CEPME), Comptoir des Entrepreneurs, Crédit Foncier de France, Crédit Local, etc) as well as by finance companies and institutions featuring in Article 99 of the Banking Law (securities houses).

Endnotes

(1) Each FELIN line has been quoted on the official Paris stock exchange listing since February 3 1986. The issue was over-subscribed as a result of the huge demand from institutional investors.

(2) A "Dutch auction" involves offering the tender for OATs and BTNs to a number of financial institutions which compete for them through bidding. Certificates are issued to tenderers according to the price they are willing to pay, with those willing to pay most being served first until the amount being sought by the Treasury is reached. Thus, each institution whose bid the Treasury is willing to consider acquires certificates at the price it is willing to pay. Having carried out its analysis, the Bank of France announces the average weighted price of certificates issued (Conseil National du Crédit, 1986).

(3) This method affords the possibility of launching debenture loans of quite long duration (between 10 and 15 years), while allowing both issuer and subscriber a certain amount of freedom in case of big changes in market conditions.

Chapter 10

Stock Brokers

The rapid growth in the volume of stock market transactions, the development of new financial techniques and the lack of openness of the Paris Bourse, have all militated in favour of reform and continued modernisation of the financial markets. Institutional reform has aimed to overcome the main handicaps by creating the right conditions for the bourses to prosper before allowing them to extend the range of their activities to compete with other markets (New York, Tokyo and London). Indeed this reform was largely inspired by London's "Big Bang".

Faced with a complete competitive and technological overhaul of their regulatory environment, the stock market intermediaries have had to adapt in order to face the challenge posed by financial market modernisation. But as with New York in 1975 and London in 1986, the adjustment has been painful.

Radical changes in regulations

Law no.88-70 of January 22 1988 introduced radical changes in regulations and in the way the sociétés de bourse operate.

i)   All securities transactions are handled by the *sociétés de bourse*. The new legislation altered the status of the former *agents de change* (stockbrokers) but did not remove their monopoly in handling market transactions. Membership of the stock market was transferred from individuals (legally termed, *personnes physiques*) to companies as defined under commercial law.[1] In 1992, the brokers' "closed shop" system (the "numerus clausus") will disappear.[2] Thereafter, there will be no restriction on the number of new member firms.

ii)   Before the 1988 law, stockbrokers were strictly prohibited from forming partnerships with providers of capital other than individuals of French nationality. But since January 1988, *sociétés de bourse* can open up their capital to French and foreign investors — financial institutions, institutional investors and manufacturing and trading companies. The entire capital of a broking firm can be bought out.

iii)   The *sociétés de bourse* are no longer bound by rules of neutrality, specialisation and independence. The *agents* have become despecialised *sociétés de bourse* entitled to operate over many different lines of business. The *sociétés* which operate under the terms of Article 99 of the Banking Law can now gain access to the interbank market and to businesses that were once specific to *établissements de crédit* (credit institutions).

iv)   The Law defines the scope within which the *sociétés de bourse* may operate. "Securities transactions needing the intervention of a *société de bourse* take place when two persons not knowing each other require the service of an intermediary to be put in contact." This definition, therefore, excludes the case of direct transfers between individuals known to each other. Likewise, in the case of gifts or inheritance, the transfer of ownership is carried out without the intervention of a stockbroker. However, wherever there is a corporate body (legally termed a *personne morale*) involved in a securities transaction, the services of a stockbroker are required except in the specific cases outlined in the legislation, which are (a) transfers between a parent company and its subsidiary; (b) transfers between insurance companies which belong to the same group; (c) transfers between a legal entity and a pension or provident scheme which it manages.

v) Buying orders are transmitted to the *sociétés de bourse*, either directly by the buyer or by an agreed intermediary (banks, securities houses or portfolio managers).[3]

Full intermediaries on the financial market

There are now a total of 55 broking firms in France (as at the end of 1991), of which over a quarter are in the provinces. Before the reforms were introduced, there were 62. They are authorised by the Conseil des Bourses de Valeurs (CBV — the French Stock Market Committee). The new regulations have totally transformed the functions and physionomy of these intermediaries. In effect, the *sociétés de bourse*, which are generally backed by financial institutions, have not only held on to their role as stockbrokers but have been able to extend their operations. The split in the intermediary function has thus gradually been called into question by the interconnection and globalisation of the different markets. The main activities of the *sociétés de bourse* can be grouped under four main headings:

i) Exclusive handling of transactions in listed transferable securities and non-exclusive dealing in futures (on the MATIF market) and options;

ii) Market-making: The long-standing prohibition of market-making has been adapted to allow for the reality of the marketplace and of clients' needs. Market-making, nevertheless, remains strictly regulated and is governed by the CBV's guidelines. The most common type of market-making consists of operations on narrow market segments (fractional shares on the monthly settlement market, high liquidity contracts on the second market);

iii) Providing a service: the broker can look after and keep a record of investment portfolios (listing of securities, statements of account, collection of coupons). It can also manage investment portfolios and offer investment advice;

iv) Originating financial products: the broker can also set up and manage investment funds or unit trusts (SICAVs).

These new departures for the *sociétés de bourse* arise out of the repeal of Article 85 of the Business Code and the possibility now of opting to operate under the terms of Article 99 of the January 1984 Banking Act. This has allowed them to develop new areas of activity such as intermediation on new financial products other than transferable securities, management advice and other assistance to companies, as well as buying equity in companies engaged in businesses other than that in which the *sociétés* had previously been authorised.

By choosing to operate under the terms of Article 99 (of the 1984 Banking Law securities houses[4]), the *sociétés* can now engage in activities traditionally reserved for credit institutions, except those expressly excluded by the same Law (see Chapter 2).

The other side of this is that *sociétés de bourse* which choose to operate under these rules are subject to the same banking regulations and supervision as other credit institutions. However, as far as the Comité de la Réglementation Bancaire (Banking Regulations Committee) is concerned, *sociétés de bourse* are only affected by those rules which explicitly refer to them.

Consequences of the reforms for the *sociétés de bourse*

The legislation enacted to bring about reforms in the financial markets and their institutions succeeded in ending a number of restrictive practices. It paved the way for the broking firms to engage in market-making, to open up their capital to French and foreign financial institutions and to develop new areas of business. The abolition of fixed commissions in July 1989 added one more aspect to the changing face of stock market intermediation.

Nonetheless, these reforms have highlighted a number of problems such as the inadequacy of the *sociétés'* capital base, the over-capacity of intermediaries on the financial market and the consequent financial precariousness and loss of independence of most brokers (a phenomenon repeated in all the other major world stock markets). These problems cannot be ignored as they are a reminder of the twin problem of financial standing and the ability of French stockbrokers to compete with their main foreign competitors (British, US and Japanese).

The "forced march" reforms introduced in the bourse headquarters at the Palais Brongniart have certainly not pleased everyone. Armed with this array of new capital requirements and prudential ratios, the stockbroking authorities have considerably accelerated the link-ups between brokers and banks — and, to a lesser extent, insurance companies. The restructuring of the intermediaries' world has been rapid. By the end of 1988, about 30 Paris brokers and nine provincial firms had already linked up with a French or a foreign partner. Now, only a few brokers are independent or enjoy some degree of autonomy. The web of interests is complex with the banks, both French and foreign, having been especially quick to seize the key intermediary positions (see Table 10.1) Where some *sociétés* still boasted that they were determined to hang on to their independence a short time before (despite the minority shareholdings and alliances being formed), today they are more ambigious and matters have moved in the direction of closer alliances to strengthen capital.

The level of capital required is a double constraint. First, the new regulations require that, to carry on the business of stockbroking alone, the *sociétés* must have a minimum amount of capital (FF25 million [$4.4 million] for Paris firms and FF3 million [$530,000] for provincial firms). Second, the capital requirement needed to deal on the derivative markets, such as the MATIF and MONEP, or to operate as a market-maker, is between 10 and 15 times higher than this again. Consequently, these measures have greatly increased the "entrance fee" into the profession. Now that stockbroking is no longer a closed shop, it will be almost exclusively subsidiaries of French or foreign financial institutions that will want to gain direct access to the stock market.

Foreign institutions which still have no foothold in the marketplace are looking for suitable opportunities before the abolition of the closed shops in 1992. With the present state of market saturation, buying a share in a Paris broking firm is almost impossible, the result being that institutions (UBS, Phillips & Drew, Enskilda Securities) are buying into provincial firms when the opportunity arises.

Are there too many intermediaries?

There are many who question whether there are not too many intermediaries operating on the French market. But too much concentration could result in competition falling into the hands of a small number of dealers (controlled by the French banks, for example). And too great of an involvement by the banks in the capital of intermediaries is liable to lead to a German-style market, restricting the freedom necessary for speculation on the stock market. (At present, the lion's share of bond transactions goes through the banks, not the brokers.)

Given the way in which the *sociétés de bourse* have collapsed, the French banks have been accused, rightly or wrongly, of distorting the market by transforming their brokers into specialised departments of the bank itself. And yet retaining their autonomy seems to be problematic for the *sociétés*. Autonomy implies that they have, in the words of one Paris banker "both the means to achieve their ambition and the ambition to go with their means". The truth is that most of them often have neither the stature, the resources nor the specialist skills needed to survive in the financial marketplace. This is what is

Table 10.1		
The extent of outside party support for *sociétés de bourse*		
	January 1989	September 1991
Number	59	58
Backed by an outside party	52	55
Shareholdings of 80-100%	17	38
Majority control (50-80% shareholdings)	19	13
Shareholdings of 30-50%	15	2
Shareholdings of 10-30%	1	2
Receiving no support from outside parties	7	3
* See appendix for shareholder composition		
Source: ASFB		

Financial Markets

really meant by so-called intermediary "over-capacity".

The quality of intermediation on the French stock markets appears, while not exactly threatened, at least to be left in an uncertain state by the integration of the stockbroking profession within the structures of financial establishments. But the strategy of integrating stockbrokers into the banks could destabilise the market. Merging stockbroking units has the disadvantage of cutting the firm off from its institutional clients, who might not necessarily want to place their orders through the bank. There is also the temptation for a *banque d'affaires* to favour the issuing client (companies) at the expense of the investor.

In December 1990, to reassure what remains of the independent stockbroking profession, the then French Finance Minister, Pierre Bérégovoy, took the stage to remind them that the financial market depends on three types of player — bankers, insurers and stockbrokers. However, the prevailing ideology would prefer to see all intermediaries fit into the banking mould. Caught between the ambiguities of the Anglo-Saxon market and the dream of a Germanic financial market, the independent, autonomous brokers find themselves in the least comfortable position.

To resolve the problems facing stockbroking, a commission was asked to come up with proposals to preserve and develop independent intermediation in France. But the report, presented in July 1991, has not met with unanimous approval. Quite the contrary: the *sociétés de bourse* are contesting the commission's main proposal that the four main functions of trader, clearer, depositor and manager be split up, following the example of the MATIF.

The end of fixed commissions

At the beginning of 1989, there was also a great deal of doubt and fear surrounding the proposed liberalisation of stockbrokers' commissions. Just as in the fees on cheques affair, the most pessimistic sellers of small orders were expecting an overall increase in commission rates and adopted a highly agressive attitude towards banks and brokers.

When commission fees — the method of billing stock exchange orders — were liberalised on July 1

1989, the brokers found themselves again in a precarious position. The change has had a disastrous effect on them. On the bond market, brokers' commissions have practically disappeared and on the equities market, commissions are decreasing at an alarming rate. The main beneficiaries of this liberalisation have been the large institutional investors who, by playing one firm's prices against another's, have brought commission rates down. While the intermediaries had been hoping for a rise in rates they are, in fact, experiencing a dramatic narrowing of margins and while the volume of orders remains flat not all intermediaries are in a position to apply the new standards of remuneration.

In addition, the commissions' crisis has happened at a time when the *sociétés* are having to cope with the challenge created by the restructuring of the Paris Bourse. They must meet an increase in operating expenses as a result of major investments, such as the RELIT settlement and delivery system, carried out during the stock market's heyday in the second half of the 1980s, and the reorganisation of the market (the introduction of a guarantee fund,[5] additional insurance, and a new legal status for stockbrokers' agents). The ending of the fixed commission has once again highlighted the financial precariousness of the French broking houses.

The stockbroking crisis cannot be separated from the sharp fall in the volume of shares being traded. The Gulf War added to the slump in the stock market in 1991 and, compared to the beginning of 1990, the volume of business was halved and commissions continued to fall.

The bulk of *sociétés de bourse*, both in Paris and in the provinces, are in serious difficulties. As a result, there is an acceleration in the trend towards mergers and the liquidation of a number of firms. One of the leading member firms on the Paris Bourse, Tuffier-Ravier-Py, even had to file for bankruptcy. The Tuffier affair quickly became a symbol of the crisis and anxiety affecting French intermediaries. Its closure also served to highlight limitations and gaps in the reform, especially in the area of mutual fund management.

Some of the firms which had so fiercely held onto their independence, like Boscher,[6] have had to seek the backing of credit institutions in haste. In the case of Boscher, this was Banque Nationale de Paris (BNP) following a loss, in the space of a few weeks, of a sizeable number of its clients who feared a serious deterioration in the firm's financial situation. Likewise, the Lyons-based broker firm, Girardet, was bought out just in time by Crédit National[7] which increased its shareholding from 34 percent to 96 percent to reassure the firm's clients. In fact, the bank had to write off losses in the order of FF200 million ($35 million), because of the alleged embezzlement of unit trust funds. Other firms, such as Ferri, have also had to find a partner urgently to save them in their hour of need while Gorgeu, Krucker, Perquel (GKP) decided to sell its seat on the Bourse and implemented massive redundancies. The presence and financial might of the state-owned banks is very much in evidence in the takeover of brokers on the verge of bankruptcy, providing evidence that the state may be endeavouring to protect the reputation of the Paris stock market.

The situation prevailing on the financial markets is hardly conducive to the stability of the intermediary sector. In addition, the reluctance with which the CBV resorted to the guarantee fund at the time of the Tuffier affair has somewhat shaken the public's confidence in the solvency of stockbroking firms. As for the firms which still hold out, the situation is no brighter. In 1990, very few of them, probably no more than five, showed a profit. The prospect for jobs is not much better. Of the 6,000 people working in the stockbroking profession, more than 2,000 were projected to be out of work by the end of 1991.[8]

The stockbrokers' choice of strategy

When the first alliances were being forged, brokers were facing competition from abroad as a result of deregulation and the globalisation of markets. Major investment became necessary.

The fact that the *sociétés de bourse* held on to their monopoly in the buying and selling of securities was reason enough to encourage the financial institutions (banks, insurance companies and insurance brokers) — both French and foreign — either to take over firms or buy shares in them. There were other equally important incentives for investing; namely, the instant acquisition of their expertise, of goodwill, of a list of top quality private clients and an efficient back-office operation.

Synergies generated by closer links between banks and stockbrokers

In the first place, having the backing of major credit institutions has given *sociétés de bourse* the sort of guarantee needed to play a more significant role on the international scene, and particularly on the international marketplace in London.

In this way, one of the leading brokers in the French stock market, Chevreux-de Virieux, (92 percent-owned by Banque Indosuez since 1987) which for many years had a presence in the British market, was able to set up a cell within the confines of London brokers WI Carr (wholly-owned by Indosuez).

Brokers Cholet-Dupont, with its portfolio of UK clients, brought a very considerable volume of extra business to Crédit Lyonnais, which has a shareholding in this firm along with several other institutions. However, generating synergies with its other stockbroking subsidiary, Alexander Laing and Cruickshank, appears to be problematic for Crédit Lyonnais because of the difficulties being experienced in the wake of the drop in securities trading in London.

Crédit Agricole's choice of stockbrokers — Bertrand Michel — is justified by the firm's cross-Channel and US links. As a Treasury bond specialist, Crédit Agricole can offer the stockbroker's clients the benefit of government bonds secured at competitive prices. In addition, the two partners aim to assist US companies in getting a Paris Bourse listing.

Second, apart from the financial analysis they provide, having the backing of (preferably merchant) banks means *sociétés de bourse* have the opportunity to develop financial engineering services and off-balance sheet business.

Broking firm J François-Dufour, J-L Kervern, for example, whose principal shareholder is the Neuflize, Schlumberger, Mallet (NSM) bank, aims mainly to develop financial research-cum-consultancy units. Partners Chevreux de Virieux and Banque Indosuez have formally divided up their roles: Chevreux will look after share analysis and Indosuez industry research.

Synergies between stockbrokers and insurance companies

According to Michel Berthezène, director of investments at UAP, his company's buying of stakes in four major broking firms[9] is aimed solely at preventing all intermediary business coming under the control of the banks as is now the case in Germany. UAP remains, for the time being at any rate, a "sleeping partner" leaving the four stockbrokers relatively independent.

But the involvement of insurance companies also provides the stockbrokers with the opportunity to diversify. Jean-Michel Cedile, managing director of Alphabourse (ex-Lavandeyra) has explained how its 100 percent takeover by Banque de l'Industrie Française (part of the GAN insurance group) is part of his company's strategy to expand into the financial sector. One of the firm's objectives is to build up its financial analysis service to assist the managers of the insurance group's unit trust funds. How these funds perform determines the performance of the insurance products to which they are attached. In the short term, the firm's skills in the area of options and equities on the stock market index also help to support the net asset value of collective investments schemes (OPCVMs). In addition, the plan to group together the GAN-BUE (Banque de l'Union Européenne) group's brokers has gathered steam with the merger of Alphabourse and Magnin.

Banque de l'Industrie Française and Alphabourse have together set up BIF-Lavandeyra Conseil to market insurance products. The establishment of this subsidiary will also enable Alphabourse to play a role on the primary markets when equity in foreign subsidiaries of GAN is being sold.

The decision by Compagnie du Midi (which was taken over by AXA in October 1990) to take a 100 percent stake in Meeschaert-Rousselle arose from their common desire to develop a financial consultancy service for industrial companies. Compagnie du Midi already put this idea into practice by buying a stake in Delmas-Vieljeux, which was threatened by hostile takeover. A joint subsidiary, one-third owned by the stockbroker and called MR Finance, will take on the role of a real investment bank. Operating under the terms of Article 99 of the Banking Law, this subsidiary will be able to issue loans and will have access to the primary market.

Indeed, it is possible that at some time in the future alliances might be forged between some industrial groups and *sociétés de bourse*.

Profile of the link-ups

Based on an analysis of *sociétés de bourse*, one can distinguish six different types of alliance strategy:

Integrated brokers majority-controlled by French financial institutions

These consist of subsidiaries of banks or insurance companies whose strategy is linked to that of the parent company, as for example, du Bouzet with BNP,[10] Delahaye-Ripault with Société Générale, Dynabourse (product of the old Michel and Soulié firms) with Segespar-Titres (a Crédit Agricole subsidiary), Alphabourse with GAN, and Nouailhetas Richard with the Banque Pallas group.

Thus, by acquiring small broking firms, the bank, finance house or insurance company secures an opening on the bourse and makes considerable savings in brokerage costs. Sometimes such small-scale acquisitions can form the germ for larger groupings of intermediaries. The *société de bourse*, for its part, secures a capital injection as well as institutional clients. However, having the backing of a large institution is not enough to guarantee the viability of the new-style stockbrokers. For example, Meunier, a subsidiary of Altus, filed for bankruptcy only months after being acquired. Some experience difficulty in running their business, particularly where the parent company's corporate culture is imposed on them. Others, on the other hand, such as Nouailhetas, make great strides when their business is subsumed into that of the parent company (Pallas).

Integrated brokers majority-controlled by foreign financial institutions

This strategy allows a French stockbroker to take advantage of the foreign (particularly British) institution's expertise and clientele.

The largest orders from Warburg and James Capel already passed through their respective French brokers — Bacot-Allain-Farra[11] and Dufour-Lacarrière-Pouget. In the case of Warburg, London was initially the main market for the listing of French equities. However, a few months ago this business was returned to France where the firm's positions in British and French shares are also managed.

JP Morgan, by taking over the firm of Nivard-Flornoy, has completed its network on the French financial market with Nivard's expertise in equities trading complementing its own expertise in bonds. In addition, JP Morgan took charge of restructuring Nivard-Flornoy's back office which is considered to have performed poorly. Meanwhile, the takeover of the medium-sized broking firm, Ducatel-Duval, by Swiss Bank Corp (SBC) is in response to that bank's desire to specialise in the business of stockbroking in close association with British broker SBCI Savory Milln.

This strategy enables British groups to have a direct opening on the French market and to arbitrate directly between London and Paris.

Brokers majority-controlled by financial institutions but with an autonomous strategy

This strategy involves setting up limited partnerships. For the brokers it gives needed capital without losing autonomy or clients and for the investing company it means establishing preferential contacts needed for large-scale market-making, without the broker risking the loss of its institutional clients.

The relationships established between Chevreux de Virieux and Banque Indosuez, Cholet-Dupont and Crédit Lyonnais, Magnin and Banque de l'Union Européenne, Massonaud-Fontenay and AMRO, Meeschaert-Rousselle and Compagnie du Midi are all examples of this type of strategy.

Brokers with an autonomous strategy and in which financial institutions hold a minority stake

The same motives lie behind this strategy as the previous one but with a desire for even greater autonomy on the part of the broking firm. The distinctive feature of this strategy is that the brokers attract several minority shareholders (banks and/or insurance companies) who themselves want the brokers to retain their identity and their independence. Three brokers, Fauchier-Magnin, Ferri-Ferri-Germe and Oddo et Cie, have deliberately opted for this strategy of full autonomy. While some of these firms, such as Oddo, are successful in their strategy,

others, such as Ferri, are suffering badly as a result of the changes that have taken place in the financial market.

One of the top brokers, Oddo, in which three financial institutions had a 40 percent stake between them, enticed Daiwa, the Japanese securities house, to buy into it. Apart from simply taking a 5 percent stake, Daiwa appears to be motivated by a desire to develop co-operation with Oddo in the area of intermediation, fund management (where it would have the support of Daiwa's Asian expertise) and corporate break-ups. By implication, the broker will be able to hold on to its autonomy and at the same time gain access to the capital of Japanese institutional investors.[12]

Ferri, on the other hand, has not escaped the cloud of suspicion that hangs around some of the autonomous or independent brokers and bank support has become almost indispensable for its survival. It definitely has adequate financial backing but while it produced profits of around FF40 million ($7 million) in 1989, profits for 1990 were only FF4 million ($707,000). It turned in a good performance on the MATIF and MONEP markets, but its commission income on equity transactions fell by a third from the previous year's level (FF240 million — $42 million). The firm has had to reconsider the type of support it receives: Crédit Foncier de France has taken a minority stake of 33.5 percent and UAP has raised its stake from 5 to 6.6 percent, while the CDC has maintained its participation at 10 percent.

Tuffier-Ravier-Py: an example of a strategy which failed

Tuffier-Ravier-Py used to be the only broking firm that based its independence around the setting up of a complex group of companies — growth through acquisitions — specialising in market dealing. These were controlled by holding company Tuffier et Associés SA. However, because of the financial difficulties it was experiencing (suspension of payments), the firm, which had more than 500 employees, was forced to file for bankruptcy.[13] Tuffier's collapse undoubtedly accelerated other link-ups (mergers and increases in capital) with financially-sound institutions to reassure clients.

Under the aegis of Crédit Lyonnais, Altus Finance took control of Tuffier in September 1990. As a result, Altus Finance emerged as one of the two "giants" of the Paris scene (the other being Groupe Pallas) by grouping activities together in order to create *pôles d' intermédiation.*

The Tuffier affair has made the authorities more careful. To protect customers' deposits, the CBV set out rules to encourage the placing of assets in reserve funds. These rules state that a *société de bourse* must limit the extent of its risks to what it is realistically able to bear. Thus, each broking firm must periodically communicate to the SBF the total amount of credit balances held by its customers as well as details of the use to which they have been put.

Independent brokers
In the entire sector, only three brokers had not yet concluded agreements with an outside partner by 1991. These were Leven-Chaussier, Wargny, and Dubus (based in Lille). By avoiding any business that might require substantial amounts of capital such as market-making or MATIF operations, they pursued an independent strategy centered around the traditional activities of broking and asset management. It remains to be seen if they can live up to their ambitions.

The Leven family has a sizeable holding in Leven-Chaussier, and is also closely linked to Groupe Perrier.

By setting up a holding company called Argos Finance, broking firm Pinatton has adapted its legal status to the various activities being carried on by subsidiaries. The group includes a consultancy firm, which provides private clients with tax and legal advice on private assets and securities management, an insurance broker (Patrigest) and other services. In this way, according to Jean-Pierre Pinatton, the group can develop into other areas if the pressures are such that it can no longer hold on to its share of one market. The Petercom (Belgium) group has taken a 21 percent stake in Pinatton, which helps to secure its independence.

The ability of these operators to survive appears in jeopardy, especially as financial as well as psychological pressures mount in a market that is rapidly changing.

The need for the *sociétés de bourse* to restructure is all the more pressing given that the profession is passing through a critical phase with a fall in the volume of business being handled by the brokers, a cut in the size of commissions and consequently a drop in profitability.

Restructuring has taken a heavy toll. The ferocious competition for commissions between brokers has had a disastrous effect on profits. In general, equities business is a loss maker. Everything, therefore, points towards further mergers. We should also note that firms' access to financial information is extremely hazardous.

Redefinition of the competitive environment
What we are witnessing is a redefinition of the competitive environment. The banks and instutional investors — insurance companies and other financial institutions — which have bought into broking firms tend to do business primarily with their own stockbrokers, leading to a considerable fall in the volume of securities traded by autonomous and independent firms.

In an attempt to end the "broking war", intermediaries seem to have come to an informal agreement which limits the passing of business to their banks and their largest customers without waiting for the COB (stock market watchdog) to pronounce on the matter.

This changed environment, coupled with the break-up and diversification taking place within the profession, is likely to lead to the intermediaries concentrating their business in four main areas:

Intermediaries and market makers
Already on the stock and derivative markets (MATIF, MONEP), where they alone are authorised to trade in financial futures and traded options, the *sociétés* will soon also operate as block traders. Not surprisingly, the British are moving into this sector, as are the major French institutions. This type of operation obviously demands substantial amounts of capital. Oddo, which has the largest capital base in the marketplace (around FF200 million — $35 million) is one of the leading brokers to have adopted this strategy.

Integration with enlarged intermediation groups
This strategy has emerged as a result of broking

firms refusing to get directly involved in block trading. The *sociétés* in this group have joined up with brokers already active on the short-term money markets or interbank markets, often with a Treasury bonds specialist within the group (Schelcher, Prince-Compagnie Parisienne de Réescompte; Magnin-Banque de l'Union Européenne; Meunier, de la Fournière-Groupe Viel, Finacor Bourse). This strategy was adopted by Tuffier but instead of joining up with an existing group, it started to build up a "federation" of companies over some years under a joint holding company that would have provided the whole range of instruments required to act as a full intermediary.

Sociétés acting solely as intermediaries

These frequently have the backing of a powerful partner holding a minority shareholding and they operate as intermediaries on the whole range of products and markets (Ferri, Hayaux du Tilly, Fauchier Magnan-Durant des Aulnois, etc). They want to stay independent within the group they are part of and to act as market-makers only insofar as it is part of their duty as intermediary (market-making on the equities market in particular). Pinatton could also be included in this group.

Sociétés with specific strategies

Some broking firms — both those with outside backing and independent ones — prefer to concentrate on a specific side of the business. Elysée Bourse, one of the leading Paris firms and wholly-owned by Crédit Commercial de France (CCF) serves as a model. It receives its orders through the CCF network, and as a secondary line of business, gets involved in institutional investment management. A number of firms, convinced that management's vision can make a big difference, base their strategies around large and respected research departments. At the same time, most firms clearly want to hold on to their own particular clientele.

Possible outcomes

The process of mergers and diversification is likely to continue with the new regroupings entering the market alongside those that already participate. This is part of a process of adjustment by a profession subjected to deregulation and international competition. Such a process has been characterised by a fundamental overhaul of the *sociétés de bourse* both in terms of strategy and business activities.

For most brokers, the situation is critical. Many intermediaries are suffering from these changes in the competitive environment. They are thus faced with rationalisation of their internal structures while at the same time having to deal with the problems of excess staff, operating costs that are too high, etc. And market saturation has dramatically cut margins, particularly for market-making. All this is taking place during a period of general decline in stock market trading. It would therefore seem legitimate to ask how many firms can survive the effect of the stock market reforms begun in 1988. It is highly likely that sometime in the future the system will revolve around just 10 or 15 large firms and a few highly specialised firms of varying size. In the area of pure intermediation, about a dozen groups will share the market between them — some specialising in small orders, others in institutional orders.

With the liberalisation of the profession in 1992, banks will be able to assume the role of negotiators/dealers and will no longer need a broker's services. The disappearance of the closed shop system will, however, lead to fresh debate about right of access to seats on the bourse and the need for change in the legal standing of broking firms so that they resemble those applied to operators on the MATIF. The supervisory authorities seem to favour this solution.

The clash of interests so sharply in evidence since Tuffier's collapse, together with the financial difficulties experienced by other firms, is a cause of increasing concern within the financial community. But despite the storms hitting the "weaker" firms, it is obvious that in the end the Paris financial market gains from these reforms. In truth, the profession had grown in a very haphazard way since 1986. With falling prices and a drop in volumes traded and commissions, an overhaul of the sector was both welcome and inevitable.

Endnotes

(1) Before the new legislation was introduced, stockbrokers had the status of legal officers.

(2) The date set for the creation of new *sociétés de bourse* has been moved forward to 1992 to allow existing firms time to restructure.

(3) Article 29 of the Law of August 2 1989 has eliminated the category of brokers called *remisiers/gérants de portfeuille* (stockbrokers' agents/portfolio managers, formerly auxiliaries of bourse professionals) replacing them with *sociétés anonymes* (limited companies) authorised by the COB.

(4) The Comité des Etablissements de Crédit defines the main business of securities houses (*maisons de titres*) as being to manage stocks and share portfolios for clients and receiving in return the monies and the order to manage that enable them to do so. They may also participate in investing such securities by acting as *agent del credere*. They may also work on the MATIF, issuing short and medium-term bonds, etc (see Appendix for list of securities houses).

(5) In 1990, brokers "emptied" the guarantee fund of FF200 million ($35 million) to indemnify the clients of insolvent firms. Thus, 1991 finds them in a situation of having to "stock up" the fund again, which will mean an additional cost for firms already heavily strained financially.

(6) This firm, which registered profits of around FF35 million ($6 million) in 1989, showed a loss of FF100 million ($17.6 million) in 1990, largely in the market-making end of its business.

(7) Crédit National, a state-owned bank whose role is providing medium and long-term investment financing for industrial companies.

(8) It should be noted that in France, staff redundancy plans are strictly controlled by the terms of the Code du Travail (Work Code). Staff rationalisation could thus prove to be long and costly.

(9) De Cholet, Dupont (5 percent); Fauchier, Magnan (10 percent); Ferri, Germe (5 percent); François-Dufour-Kervern (4 percent).

(10) Du Bouzet took control of Santoin Roulet in the second half of 1991, and then absorbed it into its own operations. BNP itself plans to establish a subsidiary orientated towards asset management services for private clients.

(11) One of the leading French brokers in the equities market and in Treasury bond transactions.

(12) Oddo is set up as a holding company; the firm (a *société en commandite par actions*, a share partnership in which the partners have unlimited personal liability), has five subsidiaries: Le Blan (interbank market brokers), Oddo (market makers), Oddo Finance (deposit, share and fund management activities), Oddo Futures and Oddo MA (mergers and acquisitions).

(13) This was after registering losses of FF60 million ($10.6 million) for the first five months of 1990.

Chapter 11

Collective Investment Schemes (OPCVMs) in France

Collective investment in France can be split into two phases or periods.

From the end of the 1960s to 1988, France experienced a boom in SICAVs (unit trusts). A feature of this period was the rapid growth in OPCVMs under management while other investments stagnated or diminished in relative terms — disintermediation — due largely to inflexible regulations regarding the amount of interest payable on bank deposits.

The second phase of development started with the December 12 1988 Law.[1] From then on, French OPCVMs were exposed to competition from other parts of the European Community and elsewhere. This period also saw a relative slowdown in the value of OPCVMs under management against a backdrop of intense deregulation. There was also the "twisting" of SICAV structures into short-term instruments called *SICAVs monétaires*. Such a development has been keenly felt as it has increased the cost of bank funding for intermediaries on the one hand and posed serious problems for monetary authorities trying to fund the French economy on the other.

France occupies first place in the European mutual fund market

One has to look beyond Europe to find the markets where mutual fund investments have grown most rapidly: the total value of investments per head of population is, in fact, twice as high in the US or Japan as it is in Europe (see Table 11.1), although this disguises the fact that the rate of growth varies considerably from country to country. By way of example, while overall European investment is relatively low, France — with some FF26,000 ($4,595)

Table 12.1			
The Collective investments industry in the world (end-1989)			
	Total assets under management (in ECUs bn)	Growth rate % (1985-1989)	Assets per head (in FF) end-1989
USA	828	51	19,943
Japan	343	206	19,540
Europe	518	164	8,609
France	200	260	26,000
Source: ASFFI, France, 1990 directory; property funds are included under assets per head, but excluded from total assets under management			

invested per inhabitant — out distances both Japan and the US. French OPCVMs accounted for 47.8 percent of the continent's total in 1989, three times as much as the British and five times as much as the Germans (see Table 11.2).

Amounts invested in OPCVMs in France rose from around FF80 billion ($14 billion) in 1980 to over FF2,000 billion ($353 billion) in 1990 — which translates as an average annual increase of 40 percent throughout the 1980s (see Table 11.3).

Regulations encourage the consumption of OPCVMs

The reasons for the success of OPCVMs, and especially for short-term vehicles are many. OPCVMs mainly developed to circumvent the prohibition on interest-bearing sight deposits and the low rate of interest available on term accounts that stemmed from the controls on credit interest rates. They also

Table 12.2

Distribution of net assets held in the form of collective investment schemes around Europe (%)

	End 1988	End 1989
France	48.0	47.8
United Kingdom	15.2	15.4
Luxembourg	11.6	13.5
FRG	10.3	10.1
Italy	7.9	6.3
Netherlands	3.9	3.8
Spain	1.4	1.5
Belgium	0.9	0.8
Denmark	0.6	0.6
Ireland	0.2	0.1
Total	100.0	100.0

Source: ASFFI, France, Directory 1990: Property funds and special funds are not included

prospered because, in the mid-1980s, access to the financial markets was difficult and investment possibilities limited. And the modernisation and subsequent spread of market instruments meant that they became more complicated, and thus less accessible, to non-professionals.

One thing is clear; if the motivations for holding OPCVMs have changed over the years, interest in them has been maintained, thereby ensuring their continuing growth. OPCVM managers, of which the credit institutions are the most important, have themselves directed their customers towards collective investment schemes. These investments have formed the centre piece of competition between credit institutions for a growing proportion of household savings.

OPCVMs, by way of gathering the public's savings, play an important role in the funding of the economy. They fulfil this role either directly, by virtue of the fact that they are significant bond issuers, or indirectly insofar as they help to guarantee the liquidity of financial markets — one of the essential

Table 11.3

French OPCVMs: net global assets (in FF bn)

	SI (Sociétés d'Investissement)	SICAVs	FCP (General)	FCP (Company)	FCP (Risk)	Total	Growth rate
1978	1.9	37.0	—	8.6	—	47.5	—
1979	0.7	47.2	0.6	9.6	—	58.1	+22.30
1980	0.9	62.6	3.9	12.2	—	79.6	+37.00
1981	0.9	72.3	13.9	12.5	—	99.6	+25.10
1982	1.4	104.2	37.5	15.3	—	158.4	+59.00
1983	2.3	190.9	82.9	20.0	0.2	296.3	+87.20
1984	2.3	298.7	137.4	22.0	0.7	461.1	+55.60
1985	2.7	449.6	194.1	31.0	1.4	678.8	+47.20
1986	5.5	701.8	274.1	38.4	2.0	1,021.8	+50.50
1987	7.5	821.6	269.8	36.2	2.7	1,137.8	+11.35
1988	7.0	1,074.5	357.7	44.4	4.2	1,487.8	+30.80
1989	3.8	1,269.6	433.0	61.0	6.0	1,773.4	+19.20

Source: ASFFI

ingredients for ensuring their proper working and their main attraction for the general public.

OPCVM portfolios come to some 20 percent of market capitalisation. These portfolios are largely made up of bonds bought outright or with a repurchase option. SICAVs account for about 23 percent of the capitalisation of French equities, as against 10 percent for French shares. But the proportion of bonds in portfolios is decreasing in tandem with the upgrading of the money market. Thus, the new categories of *titres de créances négociables* (marketable debt securities) made up 31.4 percent of OPCVM assets at the end of 1989 and 45 percent in 1991, compared with just 30 percent in 1988. These are mainly held in short term vehicles, especially the *monétaires* (see Figure 11.1).

Figure 11.1

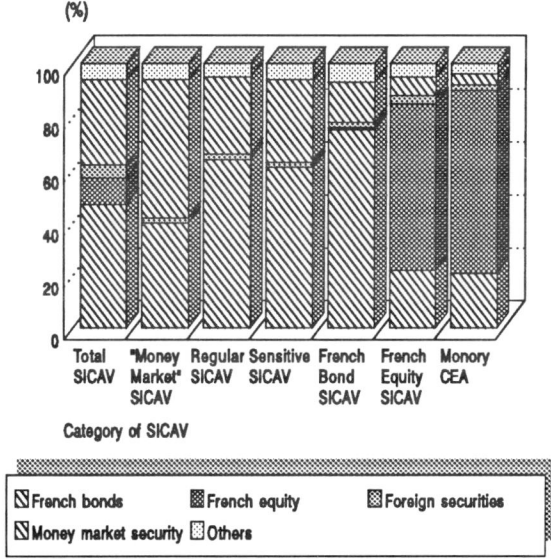

The growth in OPCVMs is in line with the growth of the financial market, including some of its riskiest activities — MATIF, MONEP, *fonds communs de créances* (FCC — mutual credit funds/securitisation), etc.

Given that they jostle for the general public's savings, OPCVMs are subject to a very detailed set of rules designed to ensure the security of the capital amounts entrusted to them. The task of making sure that these rules are respected is that of the Commission des Opérations de Bourse (COB)[2] but, as

we saw in the previous chapter, supervision of OPCVMs poses serious problems in practice as in the cases of the Tuffier and the Girardet stock broking firms. (The latter was taken over by Crédit National, [see Chapter 10]).

Significant variations in the distribution of OPCVMs

In France, SICAVs and *fonds communs de placement* (FCP — opened-ended investment funds/mutual funds) constitute between 12 and 15 percent of personal financial assets and some 30 to 40 percent of personal equity portfolios. At the end of 1990, a quarter of the securities portfolios held by individuals was made up of units and shares in short-term OPCVMs, and another quarter was held in the form of other types of OPCVM security.

Despite these impressive figures, an INSEE study showed that SICAV units — like transferable securities in general — were only present to a significant extent among private assets that were already highly diversified.[3]

This study also gives an idea of the typical holder of SICAVs. They have a markedly different profile to the population at large or even other share or bond holders. For example, *SICAVistes* are older than the general population and shareholders at large, but not as old as bond holders.

The holding of SICAVs seems to increase significantly with income and — to a lesser extent — with total private assets possessed. Likewise, the percentage of OPCVM holders increases with educational attainment (see Appendix 11.1). This proves that the product's apparent simplicity is not sufficient to ensure wide distribution, with some degree of understanding of the underlying market mechanisms still being one of the main conditions for acquisition.

Have OPCVM securities simply been added to other financial investments or rather have they taken the place of some of them? Such "cannibalisation" — which arises with each new investment vehicle — would appear to have been particularly significant in this case, because the rise in SICAV investments has coincided exactly with a drying up in the flow of savings. The rate of personal savings fell from 20 percent in the mid-1980s to 12 percent towards the latter part of the 1980s.

While it is difficult to estimate the extent of substitution against the flow in savings, it is nevertheless possible to examine this phenomenon with regard to the other financial investments with which SICAVs are associated. Thus, one notes that holding a *compte/plan d'épargne-logement* (home savings account/plan) plus the fact that one is repaying a mortgage or the holding of a Livret B passbook savings account are important factors in explaining the presence of SICAVs among the private assets of a given individual. On the other hand, ownership of a life insurance policy, an independent business or a farm holding does not tend to entail subscriptions to SICAVs. The same goes for Plans d'Epargne Populaire (PEP — the people's savings plan), the rise of which appears to account in part for the slowdown in the growth rate of SICAVs under management.

The great variety of OPCVMs

The different types of OPCVM each have their own mechanisms depending on whether they are set up as contracts or corporate bodies, whether they are close or open-ended and depending on their size. The different categories of Organisme de Placement Collectif en Valeurs Mobilières (OPCVMs) are the following: close-ended *sociétés d'investissement* (SI) which account for a negligeable amount of investment, *sociétés d'investissement à capital variable* (SICAV — open-ended investment companies) and *fonds communs de placement* (FCP — mutual funds). There have been two recent additions to this list, the *fonds communs de créances* (FCC — mutual credit funds) which enable the securitisation of bank credits and the *fonds d'intervention sur les marchés à terme* (FIMAT) — which specialise in the forward and optional markets.

The drawing closer together of SICAVs and FCPs

SICAVs were established under the aegis of the then Minister for Finance, Valéry Giscard d'Estaing, to revive the market for transferable securities after the stock market collapse of 1962. They are "open-ended"-type organisations (public companies), obliged to buy back their own shares at any time. They must also issue new shares on a continuous basis at prices fixed with reference to the stock market value of the constituent elements of their portfolios. To facilitate entries and withdrawals, subscription and an acquisition fee are calculated each day. SICAVs vary their capital in line with subscriptions or withdrawals by their shareholders.

A product of the "close-ended" *sociétés d'investissement*, they were regulated by Law No. 79-12 of January 3 1979 and Decree No. 87-544 of July 17 1987, while the Law of December 23 1988 was a means for preparing French OPCVMs for the single European market. Harmonisation measures contained in the EC Directive of December 20 1985 were ratified in French law on October 1 1989.[4]

Assets managed in the form of SICAVs are of the order of FF1,600 billion ($282 billion), or some three quarters of the OPCVM total. It is possible to individualise over 900 SICAVs, each with different objectives and features (see Appendix 11.2). Nevertheless, despite the multitude of companies, three distinct groups can be distinguished based on target customer:

i)   The "general public" SICAV, whose main features are: a low face value and a low net asset value; a large total value of assets; and a large number of units and distribution outlets;

ii) The "mixed" SICAV, of special interest to companies and institutional investors (*zinzins*) have relatively high face and net asset values, moderate distribution and units inferior in number to the "general public" SICAV;

iii) The "reserved" SICAV was created specifically for one or several of the investment company's customers. These have high nominal and net asset values, while total value of assets under management is low and sales distribution limited.

Fonds communs de placement (FCP) are made up of jointly-owned portfolios of transferable securities. Units can be bought either by companies or individuals. They are controlled by the Law of July 13 1979. At the end of 1990, there existed almost 4,000 in France, managing private assets worth almost FF500 billion ($88 billion). A quarter of all assets held in OPCVMs are held in FCP portfolios. It is often the case that FCPs are highly specialised.

Regulatory distinctions are becoming blurred

The regulatory differences between the two types of OPCVM are growing blurred. Decree No. 89-623 of September 6 1989 had the effect of aligning SICAV regulations with those for FCPs. The rule stipulating a FF500 million ($88 million) ceiling on assets managed in the form of FCPs and the obligation imposed on SICAVs that 30 percent of assets should be invested in French bonds (*l' obligation de l' obligation*) were abolished: regulations on investment became identical for both categories of OPCVM.

The same 1989 decree established the frequency of publication of net asset values, which no longer depends on the nature of the OPCVM (whether it be a SICAV or FCP) but rather on total assets.[5]

The only distinctions remaining between SICAVs and FCPs are: i) of a legal nature (the former are *sociétés anonymes* — public liability companies — the latter a joint-ownership of transferable securities); ii) the stipulation of minimum assets of FF50 million ($8.8 million) for SICAVs and FF2.5 million for FCPs).

New rules reinforcing the COB's scope of operation

Minimum capital for fund management companies is set at 0.5 percent of assets under management, or a minimum of FF500,000 ($88,000).[6] Requirements for launching on the French market "co-ordinated" OPCVMs originating in other EC member countries and for the marketing and selling of French OPCVMs in other EC countries falls within the responsibilities of the COB.

Other regulatory and fiscal measures are liable to change the make-up of OPCVMs. The 1991 Finance Law establishes that mergers of OPCVMs are to have a neutral tax effect. Thus, from the bearer's point of view, tax is deferred until he decides to exit from the SICAV or the FCP after the merger has taken place. This measure, which had been widely sought within the profession since the Law of December 23 1988 authorised mergers among OPCVMs, will help accelerate rationalisation of a market that still numbers some 5,000 different OPCVMs. This tax incentive is already encouraging a certain number of institutions to merge the myriad funds (mainly FCPs) they had set up to deal with regulatory constraints.

The drawing together of the two types of OPCVM and the suppression of the requirement to invest in bonds are, over the long term, likely to lead to a certain transfer of funds from SICAVs to FCPs. This move, while broadening the freedom to choose the most suitable legal structure, also facilitates management and leads to economies of scale. Such measures have already led to much consolidation — 388 mergers between OPCVMs — of which 16 were between SICAVs and FCPs — took place in 1990. These operations were, however, tied in with the creation of new OPCVMs. Nonetheless, because of ferocious competition and a drop in the growth rate of capital held in SICAVs, there seem to be problems crystallising such measures.

Fixing prices for OPCVMs

The pricing of French OPCVMs remains competitive. The spread on management fees for funds invested in shares varies from 2 to 4 percent, compared to an average of 6 percent in the UK. In addition, fee charges are rapidly recouped thanks to a system of tapering charges and they fall to almost nothing on short-term or bond funds. The increase, or rather the introduction of management fees for *SICAVs monétaires*, seems necessary to some institutions to stabilise trading accounts.

Fonds communs de créances (mutual credit funds)

A third type of organisation, related to OPCVMs, is much more sophisticated than the preceding and, consequently, less accessible to individuals. These are the *Fonds Communs de Créances* which have given rise to the techniques of securitisation (*titrisation*). Securitisation was introduced to France by the Law of December 23 1988 and is the subject of COB Regulation No. 89-01 of June 20 1989.[7] Securitisation is a financial technique by means of which the backing for customer loans no longer comes from the distributor (a banking institution), but rather directly from the capital markets. Securitisation operations in France are set in motion through the intermediary of a new legal entity (close relatives of OPCVM), called *fonds communs de créances*. These acquire a portfolio of commercial bank debts and provide the equivalent backing by issuing portions of them (securities) on the market.[8]

A difficult start for securitisation

Three years after the passing of the law, securitisation has still not had the success expected of it. Far from it. The number of operations that has taken place has been too small to be able to talk of an actual securitisation market. Since December 1989 when the first FCC was launched, nearly FF11 billion ($1.9 billion) worth of debts have been securitised[9] and around 20 funds (half of them aimed at personal investors) have been placed on the market by six institutions (see Table 11.4 which details the first six FCCs).

To ensure transparency in this market, the OFC2 (the FCC monitoring body) launched a monthly bulletin: *Statistiques sur les FCC*. The OFC2 was set up by the main financial institutions and is directed by the TGF.

Experts remain pessimistic, at least over the short term, insofar as the brakes on the growth of a true market in fund units are still numerous. For a start,

these techniques originated in the US and the UK and remain unrecognised in French law, while the "apprenticeship" of issuers (banks) and FCC subscribers is turning out to be longer than expected. Other structural problems have also arisen; the law only allows credits of two years or over to be securitised, while the inversion in French interest rate curves excludes the possibility of securitising property loans on bank balance sheets. Rates available on the market are too low and so there is no incentive to securitise them.[10]

In short, the securitisation market is inflexible in terms of debt on offer thus severely hampering its growth. And, given that short-term investments give a better return than long-term ones, FCCs are in

Table 12.4

Features of the first six FCC in existence

	CAC-Titrisation		CL FCC 90-1	CB 1	Valora 13,000	Valoratrésor	Premium
Features of the issue:	2 Quarter*	3 Quarter					
Date set up:	15/12/1989	15/12/1989	2/5/1990	7/6/1990	23/7/1990	19/12/1990	31/12/1990
Sum:	160 MF	298 MF	875 MF	900 MF	1,35 MdF	200 MF	400 MF
Vendor:	SBF	SBF	Crédit Lyonnais	Cetelem	CDC	Crédit Local	4 Calsses C. Agric.
Fund manager:	Eurotitrisation	Eurotitrisation	ABC Gestion	France-Titrisation	France-Titres	France-Titres	Segespar Créances
Arranger:	CAR	CAR	CL-Bear Stearns	Sté Gén. M Lynch	TGF	TGF	CNCA
Hedging mechanism:	Stockbroker-ages	Stockbroker-ages	Parts. (prets pers.)	Parts. (prets pers.)	Crédit Local	CDC	Part. (prets pers.)
Grading:	Aaa	Aaa	Aaa	Aaa	Aaa	Aaa	Aaa
Features of "senior shares"							
Nominal value	1 MF	1 MF	10,000 F	20,000 F	10,000	10,000	10,000
Issuing price	100%	99.97%	99.46%	100%	100%	75%	100%
Nominal interest rate	TMM + 0.05%	TMM + 0.04%	10.20%	Pibor + 1/16%	3,000 F le 23/7/93	2,500 F le 21/3/94	2,400 F le 31/12/93
Payments	Quarterly	Quarterly	Monthly	Quarterly	In line	In line	In line
Quotation	No	No	Bourse de Paris	Bourse de Paris	Bourse de Paris	Bourse de Paris	Bourse de Paris
Average planned existence	2 years, 13 days	3 years, 53 days	1.49 year	1.77 year	3 years	3.3 years	3 years

*The first quarter arrived late

Source: Eurostar

competition with the *SICAVs monétaire*. While mortgage loans are the engine that drives the securitisation market in the US, a high-ranking official of the Commission Bancaire maintains that similar growth has been curbed in France for two supplementary reasons: first, as it is a difficult product demanding a high degree of expertise, there is no investment bank in France that has learned to master it; second, pension funds — the cornerstone of the success of this market in the US — do not exist in France.

To stimulate this market, the Treasury is studying the possibility of increasing the supply of FCCs again by allowing them to be recharged by new credits as they come to the end of their lifespans. This is so as to lower fixed costs as well as lengthen their duration.

Fonds d'Intervention sur les Marchés à Terme (FIMAT)

FIMATs are OPCVMs but, unlike SICAVs or FCPs, they specialise in the forward market and the MONEP. Authorised under Law 88-201 of December 23 1989, growth has been limited due in part to the many constraints contained in this Law, of which the most significant are the requirement that 50 percent of assets be held in liquid form, and the formal ban on canvassing and advertising.

Classifying and rating OPCVMs

As a preface to evaluating the performances of OPCVMs, one should attempt to classify them by putting them into homogeneous categories showing similar features. In France, three main yardsticks have been identified: (i) the asset base, (ii) the liabilities and stockholders' equity base, and (iii) the subscribers' aims. In practice, given the difficulty of knowing what actually makes up liabilities and stockholders' equity, classification only takes into account the first and third criteria. Thus, as things stand, classification as a function of the quality of the investor is not very widespread in France.

The classification of SICAVs

The COB separates SICAVs into four groups: short-term SICAVs, share SICAVs, bond SICAVs and international SICAVs. Such classification is the basis for most others in France. It relies primarily on the criterion of asset quality.

As regards the market shares of different "families"

of SICAV, growth in global net assets (while slowing since 1989) is increasingly coming to favour short-term SICAVs, especially the *SICAVs monétaires*. Short-term SICAVs accounted for 68 percent of SICAVs under management in 1990 as opposed to 50 percent in 1987.

Short-term SICAVs

Since the public authorities have restricted the remuneration offered by banks for certificates of deposit (*bons de caisse*) and fixed-term accounts, France has witnessed a proliferation of so-called short-term SICAVs and the repeal of this restriction at the end of 1989 has not really had an impact on this trend. The aim of these is to supply clients with investments that are subject to the minimum fluctuation possible so that they constitute the equivalent of a fixed-income investment. They can be broken down into four categories (*monétaires*, *régulières*, *sensibles* and *première catégorie*), each distinguished by the composition of the securities in their portfolios.

i) The *SICAVs monétaires* consistently hold around 75 percent of their assets in "monetary"-type securities (repurchase options, Treasury bonds, commercial paper, certificates of deposit, mortgage debt and financial institution and finance company bonds) to produce a performance offering rates close to those available on the money market. Normally, these are liquid-asset investments made for periods ranging from eight days to five years. The *monétaires* are far and away the prime cash management instrument around; they account for over 50 percent of all capital invested in SICAVs.

ii) The *SICAVs régulières* prioritise regularity in the growth of net asset values. This type of SICAV portfolio is mainly made up of fixed-rate bonds which are either short-term or hedged by a repurchase option, variable-rate bonds, and money market security contracts.

iii) The *SICAVs sensibles* ("sensitive SICAVs") seek net asset values that are "sensitive" to variations in stock market prices. Such SICAVs can — to a greater or lesser extent — hold securities that are not hedged against interest rate variations. This "sensitivity" means that they can yield capital gains higher than those available on *SICAVs régulières* while carrying the risk for the investor of losing his principal.

iv) The purpose of *SICAVs de première catégorie* (prime category SICAVs) is to manage portfolios of mainly state-guaranteed security loans or those of issuers included on a list drawn up by decree (Decree No. 89.623 of September 6 1989).

The other categories of SICAV

The other types of SICAV are the *SICAV actions*, the *SICAV obligations* and the *SICAV internationales*, with 14, 8 and 10 percent respectively of net global assets.

The SICAV obligations (bond SICAVs)
i) Straight long-term SICAVs. This type of SICAV usually includes 75 percent French bonds among its assets;

ii) Prime category, long-term SICAVs are made up exclusively of "prime category" bonds — government loans or loans guaranteed by the state.

Taxation no longer favours the SICAV actions (equity SICAVs)
i) Up until 1989, *SICAVs Monory-CEA*, which represent three-quarters of investments in this category, provided tax breaks in line with the Law of July 13 1978 on the steering of savings towards certain investments (the Monory Law). Tax breaks are also available under the 1983 Finance Law which set up the *compte d'épargne en actions* (Monory-CEA, the share savings account). To meet the stated requirements, SICAVs have to hold at least 60 percent of their assets in French equities.

ii) Real estate and property SICAVs are directed towards defensive securities, like shares in real estate and property companies, *sociétés d'investissement immobilière* (SII — property investment companies) and SICOMIs (commercial real estate leasing companies).[11] These suit the needs of the most prudent savers and can be integrated into a portfolio fund. In addition, they provide an important support for insurance company investments.

iii) Pension savings SICAVs: these must at any given moment hold 75 percent of their assets in the form of French equity issues.

iv) Diversified SICAVs oriented towards French equities.

International SICAVs
A SICAV is considered "international" if at least 30 percent of net assets is made up of foreign securities. Depending on the composition of the free-standing part of the investment (the remaining 70 percent), one can break international SICAVs down into four categories: predominantly share-oriented,[12] predominantly bond-oriented, diversified and specialised.

Other sources of classification and the introduction of ratings
There are other, generally more subtle, ways of typifying SICAVs, although they all use the COB definitions as a general framework for distinguishing products. The main typologies and classifications belong to the TGF (a subsidiary of the Caisse des Dépôts et Consignations), *Palmarès Paribas,*[13] *Synthèse Financière,* and *La Vie Française*. Since April 1988, French SICAVs have been able to seek ratings. At present, the American rating agency, Standard's and Poor-ADEF rates some 50 SICAVs, most of them short-term. This number should progressively increase: other ratings agencies such as Moody's and Euronotation France are also due to join in. Since the stock market crash and various other accidents concerning *sociétés de bourse*, SICAVs have not enjoyed the same image of invulnerability as before. The rise in risk has led to the "imposition" of ratings.

The different types of FCP and their features
FCPs, like SICAVs, offer many means of diversifying investments and can be grouped together into three main types (see Table 11.3).

General purpose FCPs, also known as *Titre 1*
They offer the same degree of diversification as SICAVs and number 3,872 in all. The difference lies in the tax levied on these companies. Companies are taxed in accordance with the capital gains realised when they sell the units they hold and not in accord-

ance with each transaction carried out within the share portfolio itself. The company thus finds itself in the same position as if it held a security in another corporate: taxation on long-term investments (15 percent) is applied to shares held in FCPs of over two years, and tax on short-term investments (42 percent) if under two years. Tax levied on individual investors is the same, irrespective of whether it is a SICAV or a general purpose FCP.

FCP à risque (Risk FCPs)
This category of FCP was established by the Law of January 3 1983 to open up the capital of unquoted companies. *FCP à risque* possess several features that distinguish them from ordinary FCPs:

(i)   No request to buy back units may be entertained during a period ranging from three to 10 years. However, the investor may sell his units to a third party at any time;

(ii) The fund manager must hold units not exceeding 10 percent of the fund or 1 percent if the fund is reserved for a corporate entity (*personnes morales*).

At the end of 1989, there were 137 *FCP à risques* holding net assets of FF6 billion ($1 billion), 89 of which were managed by credit institutions. This product is intended for the sophisticated investor as it does not provide the same guarantees, particularly in terms of liquidity, as the standard collective fund. It was because of this that an advantageous tax system was devised for *FCP à risque* shareholders. Income from sums invested is tax exempt if the following two conditions are met:

First, the investor must keep his units for a minimum of five years and must systematically reinvest the profits. Second, 40 percent of the fund's assets must consistently be held in the form of securities issued when a new company is formed, when convertible bonds are issued or when the capital of an unlisted company is increased.

Titre 2 FCPs (worker participation, company savings plan)
The FCPs, which manage sums invested in accordance with the Law of July 24 1966 on profit-sharing schemes (*intéressement* and *participation des salariés*), now come within the purview of the October

21 1986 ruling. Theoretically, they can only hold French transferable securities and liquid assets. But they can also, without restriction, invest in SICAV portfolios of which at least 50 percent is made up of French shares or transferable securities issued by the debtor company.

Profits deriving from these FCPs are net of taxes and acquisition of portions of these funds are exempt from income and capital gains tax. Income taken out of funds is also exempt from income tax because it is supposed to be reinvested in other funds. In return, amounts are locked into these funds for a period of five years.

As of December 31 1989, there were 4,123 FCPs. There were 2,186 worker participation schemes, 788 company savings plans schemes and more than 1,000 "mixed" schemes.

The adaptation of French OPCVM legislation to that of the EC
Before the removal of marketing restrictions, the regulatory framework of French OPCVMs placed them at a disadvantage in relation to their European counterparts and, consequently, the legislation needed to be overhauled. This has largely been achieved by the Law of December 23 1988, which radically changed the legal status of both types of unit trust funds (SICAVs and FCPs). This new legal and regulatory framework has made possible the implementation of many management and product changes in a bid to meet the challenge from other European countries and also to prevent an outflow of French savings. However, the problem of OPCVM quotation remains.

Marketing OPCVM co-ordonnés
Since October 1 1989, any OPCVM which has received authorisation from an EC member state and which satisfies the requirements of the EC directives is called *co-ordonné* and may be freely marketed in any other member state on condition that certain local regulations are met.

Thus, the introduction of OPCVMs based in other EC states onto the French market is subject to the prior authorisation of the Commission des Opérations de Bourse (COB).[14] In practice however, the absence of any objections in the two months following lodgement of the application amounts to a tacit authorisation to make public offerings on the French market.

This "semi-automatic" COB authorisation is subject to two conditions. First, the OPCVM must be in line with EC Directive 85/611 on co-ordinated funds. Second, fund managers must publish information documents (in French) which have been passed by the supervisory authority of the country in which the OPCVM is based.

The unrestricted marketing of foreign funds in France sometimes meets with inflexibility, and even suspicion, on the part of authorities faced with practices with which they are unfamiliar. The intensive advertising campaigns run by foreigners is an additional source of conflict which might lead the authorities to making use of bureaucracy to protect the French market.

Yet it is still the case that 200 OPCVMs from other parts of the EC have been authorised to make public offerings in France. According to COB figures, in 1990, of 110 "co-ordinated" OPCVMs, 91 were authorised under Luxembourg law and 19 under British law. One should nonetheless note that 70 out of every 100 foreign *OPCVMs co-ordonnés*, are subsidiaries of French financial institutions — both banks and insurers — set up abroad (mostly in Luxembourg) to operate certain types of OPCVMs excluded or hindered under French law; ie umbrella fund OPCVMs, OPCVMs including distribution and capitalisation shares.

The rules governing OPCVM non-coordonnés

The marketing of other types of foreign OPCVMs in France is subject to two different procedures (Article 14, Decree No. 89-623, September 6 1989). First, funds based in countries outside the EC are subject to prior authorisation by the Ministry of Finance. Second, funds originating in an EC member state, but which do not conform to the directive on co-ordinated funds, must comply with the same COB conditions applying to French OPCVMs.

Finally, the legislation regulating French OPCVMs distinguishes between funds which comply with the EC Directive and which may therefore be marketed outside France, and funds which may not be marketed outside France. The latter include: *FCP d'en-*

treprise (company FCPs), *FCP à risques*, FIMATs and *fonds communs de créances*.

The adaptation of rules pertaining to the spreading of risks

New regulations for the spreading of risks have also been introduced to bring French legislation into line with EC standards.

Henceforth, to lessen the risks associated with endorsement (*risque de signature*), OPCVMs may not invest more than 5 percent of their assets in securities belonging to any one issuer. Exceptions are made in the case of securities issued or guaranteed by the state. Likewise, an OPCVM may not hold more than 10 percent of transferable securities allowing access to the capital of any one issuer or more than 10 percent of the units in any one OPCVM.

Two other significant alterations have been made to SICAV regulations which have led to the easing of restrictions on spreading risk. Thus, the rule known as the *obligation de l'obligation* (requiring SICAVs to hold at least 30 percent of their assets in the form of government stock, bonds, Treasury bonds or French Franc-denominated liquid assets) has been abolished.

Finally, the "code of good conduct" for short-term SICAVs has been gradually eliminated: hitherto they had been obliged to hold at least 30 percent of their portfolio in quoted transferable securities carrying a repurchase option and in variable rate bonds, a maximum of 15 percent in certificates of deposit and 15 percent in commercial paper.

Other rules aimed at improving the competitiveness of OPCVMs

These concern OPCVM accounts which can be held in currencies other than French francs. The same applies to the method used to calculate distributable profits. The *Coupon Couru*[15] rule, established in April 1986, is no longer compulsory. The SICAV or FCP may instead prefer to distribute profits collected during the fiscal year. Likewise, the lending and borrowing of securities or cash within certain limits has also been endorsed.

As for tax, the principle of transparency largely prevails. This decision was made to ensure that there are no differences between direct holdings of securities and securities held through the intermediary of an OPCVM. For example, with MATIF operations or with money market certificates, profits are incorporated at the net asset value of the OPCVM securities and therefore can only be taxed at the rate fixed for capital gains.

Regarding investor protection, the government and professional authorities have been keen to develop a strict professional code of ethics to avoid conflicts of interest arising out of the management of OPCVMs by organisations with multiple interests. The rule is simple: the OPCVM, the depository and the fund manager must act for the sole benefit of the client. This rule is enforced by a special COB investigative team.[16]

In addition, as we have already seen, a number of measures have been taken to amalgamate SICAVs and FCPs. Now, institutions are subject to the same set of regulations and thus are no longer obliged to duplicate funds.

The new legislation also broadens the definition for "transferable securities" which may figure among the assets of an OPCVM: marketable debt securities (such as Treasury bonds, certificates of deposit, commercial paper) now come under the heading of "transferable securities". Figure 11.1, which traces the proportion of money market securities held as SICAV assets at the end of 1990, also shows that the formal separation between financial markets and money market securities is now irrational.

These improvements in OPCVM legislation should give the fund manager greater freedom to invest funds in the market segments of his choice and enable him to offer his clients "straight" products such as *SICAVs actions* which are invested solely in equities and *SICAVs monétaires*, invested in the money market alone (and similar to US money market funds).

Financial innovations and OPCVMs

Law No. 88-1201 of December 23 1988 authorised the development of new products such as the *SICAV de Capitalisation*, the *Fonds des fonds* (managed funds), and the *OPCVM de type indiciel* (index-linked OPCVMs) and also smoothed the way for change in the area of *SICAVs à compartiments* (umbrella funds). The October 1 1989 deadline un-

doubtedly accelerated this process of product innovation. Nevertheless, it is almost certain that these innovations will have built-in limitations which will reduce their effectiveness in one way or another.

i) *OPCVM de capitalisation:*[17]

These make it possible to forego interest distribution, thus allowing the subscriber to transform financial income into capital gains. The tax advantage of such a product concerns the income from bonds and marketable debt securities which is capitalised tax free. The only tax applied is capital gains tax, at 17 percent in the case of annual transfers above FF300,000 ($53,000) — the ceiling as of November 1990. But this tax break does not extend to dividends from equities although fund managers have found a way of circumventing this rule by setting up *SICAVs de capitalisation* consisting of convertible bonds issued by listed companies. These bond certificates offer a facility for conversion into equity. Although this mechanism is complicated, more than half of all OPCVMs had opted for capitalisation by the end of 1990.[18]

ii) Multiproduct, multicurrency *OPCVMs à compartiments* (umbrella funds):

These offer the private investor a large range of products proposing similar flexibility of management and, in particular, the freedom to switch from one compartment to another according to market trends without incurring charges.[19]

The situation in France over this product is quite paradoxical. On the one hand, *SICAVs à compartiments* may not be set up in France, yet on the other all EC OPCVMs, in accordance with the Directive of December 20 1985, may be marketed there. Consequently, as we have seen, French companies have set up OPCVMs under Luxembourg and UK laws that have subsequently been authorised by the COB. However, investors are not exempt from French capital gains tax for sums over about FF300,000.[20]

(iii) *Fonds des fonds* (managed funds):

These are common in the UK and have been developed in France by British institutions. This type of fund makes it possible to hold a variety of lines in the one portfolio. Contrary to the principle behind the "umbrella" where the investor decides on the composition of his portfolio with reference to the market opportunities, with the *fonds des fonds*, it is the fund manager who determines the composition of the fund. Legislation, which precludes *SICAVs à compartiments*, permits the establishment of *fonds des fonds* under French law though they may not be marketed elsewhere in Europe.

(iv) *l'OPCVM de type indiciel* (index-linked OPCVMs):

The aim of these investment schemes is to achieve a performance in line with a benchmark/index (equities or bonds) by simply duplicating this index, or to aim at a slightly higher performance by modifying the respective weighting of securities making up this index. This allows for more rigorous management that aims to separate market risk from that carried by securities, and it makes it possible for the investor to adopt the appropriate stance towards the prevailing market. Such funds (introduced in 1989) have not been taken up in any great numbers and represent only 2 to 3 percent of stock market capitalisation. However, variety in index-linked management has grown considerably and there is now dealing based around all stock market indices, both French and foreign. There are 30 French index-linked OPCVMs for which there is a demand, still difficult to quantify, from Japanese and American institutions.

No consensus over the quotation of SICAVs

The stock market quotation of SICAVs was part of a programme of innovations aimed at providing greater transparency in the OPCVM market. It was thought that a quotation system would facilitate the acquisition of FCP and SICAV securities by institutional investors like insurance companies, most of whose holdings must be in listed securities. But there has been no consensus on this issue.

On the one hand, some top officials at the COB favour quotation, believing that the French OPCVM market — supported as it is by the banks — does not offer investors the all-round "visibility" required of a competitive market. On the other, the Association des Sociétés de Fonds Français d'Investissements (ASFFI) opposes the listing of OPCVMs. It sees listing as only favouring banking institutions (foreign ones in particular) which would see it as a way of compensating for the relative weakness of their placement networks. The ASFFI feels that the bourse's two main functions — determining prices and ensuring the liquidity of the secondary market — would be adequately protected by issuing and purchasing at net asset value. According to the ASFFI, superimposing listing onto the present system would mean splitting the secondary market: purchases without charges through the issuer and issues at reduced charges through the bourse. Lastly, says the ASFFI, if the net asset value which serves as the basis for bourse prices (with a spread of plus or minus 1.5 percent) is known, there would no longer be any risk involved in playing against OPCVMs.

Thus, listing of OPCVMs on the stock market has not yet come about.

The growth in OPCVMs

The total net asset base of OPCVMs has risen from FF680 billion ($120 billion) in 1985 to over FF2,000 billion ($35 billion) in 1990, making them one of the economy's main potential sources of funding. The banks have long been the main beneficiaries of these resources with this rapid expansion largely attributable to short-term SICAVs, in particular *SICAVs monétaires* (see Table 11.5). But this development is beginning to pose problems for the long-term funding of the economy as well as for the big deposit-taking banks. As a result, to compensate for the risks of market-making, a reform in the rules governing the investment of *SICAVs monétaires* was introduced.

Table 11.5			
SICAVs under management (in FF bn)			
SICAV	**End-1985**	**End-1989**	**Nov. 1990**
Monétaires	50	544	797
Régulières	92	153	156
Sensibles	66	33	27
Short-term	208	730	980
French equities	75	151	117
French bonds	86	227	202
Source: Europerformance			

Sales channels and market shares

In France, banks are the dominant sellers of OPCVMs. Moreover, nearly 90 percent of OPCVM sales takes place either through the most powerful of these banking networks or their specialised securities management subsidiaries.[21] The market is largely concentrated around the five main banking groups, which together account for sales of over half of OPCVMs under management. Five banking groups manage, either directly or indirectly, more than half of all SICAVs and Segespar-Titres, a subsidiary of Crédit Agricole, alone holds 16.6 percent of all managed SICAVs. This success can be explained by the fact that it has 35,000 outlets at its disposal in France. In the same way the next four largest institutions (CDC,[22] BNP, Crédit Lyonnais and Société Générale) together manage 35 percent of capital in the form of SICAVs (see Table 11.6).

The level of concentration in the short term SICAV market is even more striking than for OPCVMs. The two leading groups (Crédit Agricole and CDC) hold more than a third of all assets in this category, while the five leading institutions hold nearly 60 percent (see Table 11.7).

The property SICAV[23] market, which is even more concentrated than the above two markets, is exceptional as the second and third largest companies in the market are the insurance companies UAP and

Table 11.6
All SICAVs: The growth in market share of the ten leading credit institutions up to 1989 (as a percentage)

Sponsor	1983	1984	1985	1986	1987	1988	1989
Crédit Agricole	7.6	10.1	12.6	15.1	16.6	16.4	16.6
CDC, Poste, Caisses d'Epargne	9.0	9.6	10.7	11.0	10.8	10.9	11.9
BNP	13.0	12.3	11.5	11.7	11.2	11.8	10.4
Crédit Lyonnais	10.0	9.4	8.9	8.1	8.1	8.1	8.8
Société Générale	11.7	11.6	10.2	9.8	7.6	6.9	6.7
Groupe Paribas	3.4	3.8	3.3	2.7	2.6	2.4	5.1
Banques Populaires	3.3	3.7	4.1	4.2	4.3	4.2	4.1
CIC	3.7	3.6	3.6	3.4	3.5	3.7	3.6
Indosuez	5.8	4.6	3.3	3.4	2.8	2.0	3.5
CCF	4.6	4.1	4.1	2.8	2.8	2.7	3.2
Others	27.9	27.2	27.7	27.8	29.7	30.9	26.1
Total subscriptions (in FF bn)	194.9	300.3	451.8	706.4	819.7	1,072.6	1,271.6

Source: Europerformance

Table 11.7
**SICAVs excluding short-term funds:
The growth in market share of the ten leading institutions up to 1989 (as a percentage)**

Sponsors	1983	1984	1985	1986	1987	1988	1989
Crédit Agricole	7.3	8.5	11.2	15.0	17.9	17.5	17.3
CDC, Poste, Caisses d'Epargne	11.1	11.8	14.4	15.1	15.5	16.7	17.3
Crédit Lyonnais	10.4	10.7	10.0	8.8	8.3	9.0	9.2
BNP	13.6	13.3	12.3	11.9	10.3	9.9	8.7
Société Générale	12.1	12.0	10.3	8.8	7.3	7.2	6.6
Groupe Paribas	2.7	2.5	2.2	1.8	1.9	1.8	4.4
Banques Populaires	2.4	2.4	2.7	3.7	2.9	2.8	2.5
CIC	3.4	2.3	2.5	2.3	2.1	2.0	1.8
Indosuez	7.9	6.7	4.7	3.0	2.2	1.8	4.2
CCF	2.5	2.5	2.5	2.3	2.0	1.8	2.8
Others	26.6	27.3	27.2	27.3	29.6	29.5	25.2
Total subscriptions (in FF bn)	133.6	166.0	243.8	393.9	378.3	461.7	541.3

Source: Europerformance

AGF, whose combined market share is over one-third. An additional feature of this market is the involvement of the *banques de marché* (banks trading on the financial markets) particularly those specialising in private asset management (see Table 11.8).

Table 11.8

The growth in market share of the 5 leading real estate SICAV promoters up to 1989 (% of the total market)

Promoters	1985	1986	1987	1988	1989
Crédit Agricole	17.8	30.9	30.9	28.0	26.2
UAP	15.9	15.1	16.8	16.7	17.6
AGF	18.8	15.7	15.1	15.7	15.8
Indosuez	22.0	13.2	10.1	9.3	8.1
Société Générale	11.6	8.8	7.8	6.9	6.8

Société Générale is the market leader in the general purpose FCP market. Nonetheless, this market which numbers over 1,000 funds and represents 86 percent of all FCPs, is less concentrated than that for SICAVs. The market share of the five leading institutions is less than one-third of the total and more than 100 organisations share 66.7 percent of the market between them (see Table 11.9).

Table 11.9

General Purpose FCPs

The growth in market share of the 5 leading credit institutions up to 1989 (% of the total market)

Institution	1986	1987	1988	1989
Société Générale	16.5	17.0	15.4	16.6
Crédit Lyonnais	5.1	5.1	4.8	5.4
Crédit Agricole	3.9	4.2	3.6	4.0
CCF	3.1	3.0	2.7	3.0
BNP	2.5	3.4	2.5	2.6
Total amount under management (in FF bn)	275.4	271.0	361.8	376.2

Source: TGF

Other sales channels include direct marketing, which is widely used in the Anglo-Saxon countries (35 percent of the total collected in the UK) but still in its infancy in France. Cortal and Robeco are generally considered to be pioneers in this field. Five years after its introduction, sales achieved through direct marketing account for 2 percent of the total but, according to Paris experts, the French are still ill at ease with buying products by correspondence. However, there may well be openings in the richer customer segments of the market.[24]

Finally, it should be noted that the domination of bank outlet-based selling can only be a handicap for foreign companies.[25] But other methods of entering the market can overcome this. For example, Fleming has created a direct sales network with the help of financial advisers (of which Fimagest is the largest). Distribution agreements with the French banks and insurance companies are also used. The same applies to the funds marketed by MIM Britannia of the Britannia Arrow Holdings group, which has joined forces with the French financial advisory group, Cyrus, to distribute its top-of-the-range products. Alliances with property companies (for example, Pelège) have also been set up.

The volatility of equity SICAVs and the consistent performance of the *SICAVs monétaire*

The high average monthly performance of the *SICAV monétaire* is undoubtedly a powerful factor in its astonishingly rapid growth. In addition, this performance is very stable — varying only between 0.7 percent and 0.9 percent per month since 1989. Conversely, the average return from SICAVs invested in French equities has been largely negative and inconsistent (see Appendix 11.3). Yields from bonds vary according to whether they are national or international.

The annual rate of return from short-term SICAVs, particularly *SICAVs monétaires*, approaches that of money market instruments.

These performances are partly explained by the inversion of risk/return ratios at a time of increasing interest rates. In addition, the measures adopted in October 1989 have limited the tax which may be levied on the *monétaire,* with many *SICAVs monétaires* choosing the capitalisation system. As we have seen, these measures exempt from tax capital gains of up to FF300,000 ($53,000). Another feature of *SICAVs monétaires* is the near absence of interest rate risk.

Distortion that favours the short term

Since 1989 net public investment has generally slowed, despite the lasting popularity of high liquidity SICAVs. Indeed, the net asset value of all SICAVs under management grew more slowly in 1989 (18.2 percent) and 1990 (just 15 percent) than in 1988, (30.8 percent). The net 1990 increase at FF141.8 billion ($25 billion), was down FF32.4 billion ($5.7 billion) on the previous year's figures.

However, losses and gains are uneven. Net investment in *SICAVs monétaires* has increased to FF182.2 billion ($32 billion), while that in other categories (equities and bonds) has fallen. But managed *SICAVs monétaires* have increased 16 fold since 1985, reaching FF797 billion ($140 billion) in November 1990, as against FF544 billion ($96 billion) a year earlier — a rise of about 34 percent. *SICAVs monétaires* now represent more than half of all SICAVs and 80 percent of short-term SICAVs. This growth contrasts with the decline in other categories of managed SICAVs like *SICAVs actions* and *SICAVs diversifiées* (down 23.5 percent) and *SICAVs obligations* (bond SICAVs) (down 9.2 percent) in 1990. On the other hand, there has been positive growth of between 12 to 15 percent in international SICAVs.

Growth in French equity SICAVs has slowed. This is explained by divestments following the removal of tax breaks on *comptes d'épargne en actions* (CEA — equity savings accounts).

The growth of *SICAVs monétaires* is worrying the monetary authorities and the banks.

The prevalence and subsequent explosion in the numbers of short-term SICAVs results from a shortcoming in French OPCVMs and poses at least two problems. First, these products are too liquid, weakening equity capitalisation. The spread of this phenomenon has subsequently created problems for the economy's long-term funding. Second, the success of *SICAVs monétaires* is beginning to weigh heavily on the cost of funding for the banks. All in all, the growth of *SICAVs monétaires* has been a cause for concern to the public authorities.

There was a growing desire on the part of the French authorities to monitor the development of *SICAVs monétaires* during 1990. In contrast to previous years, which were marked by a desire to prevent an outflow of institutional and household savings onto foreign markets, the biggest problem now is to find a formula which will limit the volume of investment in *SICAVs monétaires*.

On several occasions, the Finance Minister has stated his intention to correct the "excesses" caused by the *SICAVs monétaires* while at the same time stressing that there would be no new tightening of investment regulations. The solution, it seems, is to be found in applying taxation measures that favour long-term investments, and investments in equities in particular.

The government has taken steps such as launching equity-dominant OPCVMs (or a mixture of money market certificates and bonds) in a bid to modify the structure of OPCVMs which veer too far in the direction of liquidity. However, it is difficult to imagine equity-dominant products (or products integrating bonds)[26] satisfying the current SICAV investors' demands in terms of security, return and liquidity. The task is daunting and must be carried out in an increasingly uncertain stock market climate. Thus, the problem remains of offering an alternative to *SICAVs monétaires* — the only products today which offer relatively high returns with the additional benefit of little exposure to interest rate risk.

The commercial banks are becoming increasingly concerned. In fact, what was until recently considered to be a banking success has now become a dilemma for the credit institutions. Either they must stop promoting *SICAVs monétaires* to private individuals (which in a strongly competitive market would be difficult if not impossible), or they must continue to promote this type of investment which is remunerated at money market rates and, therefore, expose themselves to ever heavier costs of funding.

The banks themselves are responsible for this dilemma. Indeed, the big deposit-taking banks, which had long been protected by tightly controlled rates, compensated for the shift away from intermediation by becoming fiercely competitive on the OPCVM market. Thus, some banks have been offering units in funds at FF100 ($17.6) — with negligable acquisition and disposal charges — to gain wider access to private investors.

According to a Bank of France survey, private investors are at the base of the strong growth in *SICAVs monétaires*. The proportion of *SICAVs monétaires* held by private investors was over 50 percent of the total as against 45 percent in the third quarter of 1989, while holdings by companies fell from 31 percent to 28 percent.

To remedy this situation, as per the government's recommendations, certain banks have begun to impose acquistion and disposal fees on *SICAVs monétaires*. This consists of charging for investment transactions and also discouraging retail customers from using *SICAVs monétaires* as a way of gaining interest on their bank accounts. In practice however, due to the increased competition between financial institutions for market share, these fees remain low and do not seem to be working.

It is clear that the numerous product innovations, such as the combining of *SICAVs de distribution* and *SICAVs de capitalisation*, herald the inevitable payment of interest on current account deposits and general deregulation of deposit interest rates. One might reasonably ask whether the ongoing deregulation on the liabilities side of the banks' business will actually slow down the inordinate growth of OPCVMs, and in particular, put an end to the popularity of *SICAV monétaires*.

The authorities finally decided to reform *SICAVs monétaires* in 1991 (see decree published in the *Journal Officiel* of June 28 1991). Among the measures decided was a change in the spread of risks ratio: henceforth, short-term money market OPCVMs can hold 25 percent of their assets in the form of marketable debt securities (TCNs) that have been issued by the same issuer (as against the present 5 percent) while the overall limit of 40 percent of such securities still applies. But these securities must be rated by a rating agency, although there are no requirements as to the minimum rating acceptable. Naturally, OPCVMs adopting this measure will no longer have the label *co-ordonnables* attached and as a consequence cannot be marketed outside France.

This particular reform has been greeted with less than total enthusiasm. In fact, from the standpoint of those involved in the SICAV market, such a measure represents discrimination against small institutions, the quality of whose endorsements would obviously appear more fragile than those of the larger ones. When it comes to short-term securities, the division of risks is much less important than the quality of its endorsement.

A slowing in overall funds collected in the form of OPCVMs is already evident, partly due to the rise in subscriptions to the PEP (people's savings plan). Nevertheless, growth in *SICAVs monétaires* will continue to worry the banks and financial authorities, although further reregulation of OPCVM activities seems neither likely nor desirable. Nor will it be easy for foreign OPCVMs to compete, particularly because of the domestic banks' powerful distribution networks. However, foreign OPCVMs could make deep inroads in the top-of-the-range market by offering higher performing products than those currently available on the French market. This is because most French OPCVMs are more or less shaped by regulations which favour security of investment over speculation.

Endnotes

(1) This law, which has completly abrogated all previous OPCVM regulations, has three main features: it "confines itself" to deciding the general principles for setting up and operating OPCVMs, gives more power to the COB in the area of OPCVM authorisation and supervision, and has formalised a professional code of conduct.

(2) COB regulation No. 89-02.

(3) According to the INSEE *Actifs Financiers* survey, at the end of 1986 only 13 percent of French people had investments in OPCVMs, 7 percent in equities and 9 percent in bonds.

(4) The aim of these provisions is to regulate the marketing of parts and units of OPCVMs within the EC by member state companies.

(5) If this total is less than FF500 million ($88 million), the OPCVM must publish values at least every two weeks. It must publish values daily if the total is above FF500 million.

(6) Except if the majority of capital is held by a financial institution which itself is monitored by the public authorities.

(7) Before the law on securitisation, French regulations only allowed credit institutions to sell their debts to other credit institutions.

(8) With a minimum nominal value of FF10,000 ($1,760), the units are freely negotiable on the market. But contrary to straight OPCVMs such as the SICAV and FCP, the holder of FCC units may not sell them back to the fund and has no option but to sell them on the secondary market.

(9) The total amount currently securitised is negligible when compared to the FF2,000 billion-worth ($353 billion) of OPCVMs under management.

(10) The special tax treatment of savings banks' funding to finance public housing, as well as the strong competition between commercial banks and savings banks in this market, has the effect of keeping mortgage loan rates artificially low.

(11) The aim of SICOMIs (commercial and industrial real-estate companies) is to rent out or lease property used by trading or manufacturing companies. Generally, they benefit from fiscal transparency and are exempt from corporate tax.

(12) With over 60 percent of the total, international-oriented equity SICAVs are by far the most important in this subdivision.

(13) The ratings agency Europerformance (the product of a link-up between the operations of Paribas and Techniques de Gestion Financières (connected to the CDC) regularly publishes figures on OPCVMs.

(14) Contrary to current practice in other European countries, authorisation (which usually takes an average of one month to obtain), is decided without recourse to legal advisers, thus reducing costs.

(15) *Coupon courus* apply the rate of interest accumulated at a given moment in time in the course of one year.

(16) In 1990, over 150 FCPs and approximately 100 SICAVs were investigated.

(17) This applies to SICAVs and FCPs whose closure date is after September 29 1989 and the entire previous fiscal year.

(18) *SICAVs de capitalisation* have been remarkably successful. Their net asset values quickly overtook those of bond SICAV which distribute income on an annual basis.

(19) This product has many drawbacks: it presupposes "active" funds management because the principle behind umbrella funds is that the markets are closely followed. In addition, it is the investor himself who decides whether to switch funds between markets, not the fund manager, as is the case with *SICAV actions* and *SICAV diversifiées*.

(20) The amount of tax however depends upon how zealous the financial institutions are in passing on information to the French tax authorities.

(21) Other sales networks include: insurance companies (4.8 percent) finance companies (3.5 percent) and stock brokers (1.2 percent).

(22) The CDC has a large sales network in the form of the savings banks and the Post Office.

(23) Property SICAVs represent 1.5 percent of the total market.

(24) According to a Robeco France official, 50 percent of high-income private investors would be prepared to buy a financial product by correspondence.

(25) International OPCVMs represent only 9 percent of French collective investment.

(26) The first attempts to oust money market OPCVMs focused on integrating traditional mechanisms of bonds and warrants into OPCVMs, thus making them more widely available to the public. However, there are difficulties connected with these new products as they are becoming less flexible and generally entail high costs.

Section V

Pensions and Taxation

Chapter 12

Pensions in France

Introduction

In France, the pension system is 95 percent based on *répartition*, or "pay-as-you-go" redistribution, without build up of reserves. The manner in which this system has developed is causing concern, so that pensions by means of capitalisation (pension funds *à la française* and personally-funded pension plans) is a concept which is steadily gaining ground. However, even if the development of pension funds makes economic and financial sense, it is hampered by resistance at political and institutional levels.

The weight of a long-established tradition of state-guaranteed social security is a significant factor in any discussion about the development of pensions through capitalisation.

The social welfare system was indeed considerably altered after the Second World War through the establishment of a widely-accessible system of social security (*la Securité Sociale*). This institution was set up in 1945 to ensure that the public was covered for a wide range of risks like sickness, maternity, industrial accidents and old-age pensions.

For old-age pensions, the main feature of the system is that it operates by a pay-as-you-go mechanism, or as it is often expressed, "the young pay for the old". But the principle behind pay-as-you-go depends on the ratio of beneficiaries to contributors and, as we shall see, this is closely linked to social, economic and demographic changes. Consequently, there has been a rise in the cost of pension schemes (and in problems associated with control of social security costs in general) as well as a decline in the ratio of contributors to beneficiaries. In short, the current pay-as-you-go system raises a number of questions.

- What is the outlook for pension schemes in the light of expected economic and demographic changes?

- How will the pensions of the present working population be financed?

- Should the pay-as-you-go system be reviewed or complemented by funded schemes?

- Finally, what means are available to the French government to encourage pension-savings schemes and, in particular, pension funds?

Both the institutional structure of pension schemes and the contributions system will be addressed in the context of these questions. Also, the problems and prospects for pay-as-you-go-based pension schemes plus some pension instruments (the so-called "third pillar") that may strengthen the role of capitalisation will also be reviewed.

The institutional framework of old-age pensions: a multitude of schemes

In 1945, the aim of the Plan for Social Security was to construct a single old-age pension scheme. But existing schemes for salaried employees, (for managerial staff, etc), and the resistance of non-salaried workers to a single scheme led to the organisation of compulsory old-age pensions along occupational lines. The result has been a highly complex pensions structure.

As most of the occupational groupings wanted to provide themselves with supplementary schemes as well as basic schemes, there were more than 100 compulsory supplementary schemes administered by more than 400 different pension funds by 1991 (see Table 12.1).

Table 12.1

Number of compulsory pension schemes

General scheme	1
Old-age allowances fund	1
Agricultural workers schemes	1
Special schemes (state, local authorities)	130
Complementary employee schemes	387
Farmers schemes	1
Schemes for non-salaried workers in the agricultural industry	17
Total	538

The complexity of the social welfare system is illustrated very clearly in Appendix 12.1 which lists the main institutions. In fact, four levels can be distinguished: the basic old-age pension, statutory schemes, supplementary schemes and additional protection.

The basic old-age pension

General accessibility to old-age pensions has effectively been achieved, but only for people in paid employment. However, there are some exceptions and the system does provide a special scheme for the working population that is not in paid employment (see Appendix 12.2).

The "Assistance" programme entitles (at their request) elderly persons with very limited or no financial means to an income supplement, so that it reaches the level of the basic old-age pension. This is worth more than 60 percent of the SMIC (guaranteed minimum wage). This non-contributory allowance results from the combination of two very different benefits: the basic minimum pension plus the contribution from the *Fonds National de Solidarité* (FNS) (national solidarity fund).

The basic minimum pension, which is provided by the *Allocation aux Vieux Travailleurs Salariés* (AVTS — the old-age pensions paid through the retired salaried workers scheme) is awarded to people who were in paid employment for 25 years or more.

The monies paid out of the FNS are added to the basic minimum pension and to the individual's private means. This contribution is paid to persons aged over 65 years (60 for people who are incapacitated). In 1987, the basic old-age pension was FF31,900

($5,638) per year for a person living alone: FF13,600 by way of the basic allowance and FF18,300 by way of the FNS. However, this minimum can be raised where there is a dependent spouse or children. The number of recipients — that is the number of persons receiving a pension lower than the SMIC — was estimated at 1.4 million in 1988, of whom almost 70 percent were women, for a total cost of FF18 billion ($3.1 billion).

Basic statutory schemes

All working people are members of a statutory pension scheme. However, the 120 basic schemes (including the 90 schemes operating in Alsace-Lorraine[1]) all work through very different methods of contribution and benefits.

They can be divided into four main categories: the *régime général* or general scheme for salaried employees, special schemes for salaried employees, farmers' schemes, and independent schemes for non-salaried persons. Salaried employees in general schemes comprise two-thirds of the working population and account for more than three-quarters of all wage earners.

The Caisse Nationale d'Assurance Vieillesse des Travailleurs Salariés (CNAVTS — the national fund for old-age pensions for salaried employees), which administers the pension funds for insured workers in industry and commerce, has the largest number of contributing members (nearly 13 million, 63 percent of the total) and the largest number of people in receipt of a pension (46 percent). The CNAVTS is managed by a board of directors with equal representation of employees and employers.

The general scheme provides employees who are aged 60 years or over and who have worked for 37 and a half years (150 yearly quarters) with a maximum pension equal to 50 percent of their average earnings over their 10 highest-paid years, up to a ceiling as established by the social security. The employee can, however, retire on a reduced pension after 32.5 years.

Eligibility for a pension ranges from 50 to 65 years: 50 years in the case of the SNCF (the French state railway company) and several other special schemes, and 65 years for employees in industry and commerce who belong to the general scheme. There is, however, a considerable difference between special schemes for salaried employees and other schemes, because the benefits of the former are generally not matched by any additional enhancement — an exception has been made for miners (see Appendix 12.1).

Supplementary (non-contributory) pension schemes

Supplementary pension schemes were made compulsory by the Law of December 29 1972. In fact, they were already well-established:

a) For *cadres*, or managerial staff, since 1947 with the creation of numerous corporate or company pension funds grouped together under the Association Générale des Institutions de Retraite des Cadres (AGIRC — the general association for pension schemes for *cadres*), with 2.5 million contributing members and premium income of some FF40 billion ($7 billion) per year;

b) For non-managerial staff, since 1962 when the ARRCO (the association of supplement retirement pensions) brought together the various supplementary pension schemes for non-managerial employees. It has 13.4 million contributors and annual premimium income of FF40 billion;

c) Various bodies have come into being for other categories of worker, such as the IRCANTEC for non-confirmed officials in the employment of the state and local authorities (17 million subscribers), the CPPOSS for staff of the various branches of the social security and the CRAF for Air France navigation staff, etc.

Supplementary cover for independent professions varies: for some, membership of a supplementary fund is obligatory while for others, membership is optional (see Appendix 12.1).

Additional cover

Other complementary schemes are always optional and generally attract only executives. There are three ways of joining one of these schemes: on a personal basis, collectively or through *Plans d'Epargne des Entreprises* (PEE — company savings schemes). As the following demonstrates, PEEs contain some interesting pensions-savings features and exemplify the trend towards capitalisation.

A PEE is a group savings system which affords employees an opportunity to build a portfolio of transferable securities (Order of October 21 1986 and Decree of July 17 1987). This type of savings plan may be established through the implementation of a staff agreement or at the initiative of management alone. This optional scheme is made available to all employees, sometimes after a minimum period of employment which cannot exceed six months. All contributions enjoy total tax relief.

Such transfers answer a desire to achieve tax efficiency. But despite the substantial tax benefits, company-funded pension plans play only a marginal role in France. They account for FF15 billion ($2.6 billion), as against FF600 billion ($110 billion) in pay-as-you-go schemes. In 1988, about 20 percent of companies had PEE pension plans.

All of the monies paid into a PEE, whether it comes from the employees or the company, must be invested in SICAV securities, FCP units, transferable securities issued by the company or shares in a company set up by the employees to buy out the business.

PEE administration costs are borne by the companies themselves and are assigned to an external body such as an insurer.

Certain features of these company-funded pension plans serve to explain the weakness of the PEE system. First, the market is far from stable. The volume of business varies widely from one year to the next because it consists largely of single-premium operations, essentially orientated towards providing benefits at the end of a career.

Second, some of these company pension plans suffer a serious handicap: in the French system, when somebody dies or resigns, he foregoes his rights entirely, while in certain Anglo-Saxon-style pension funds the employee or his family retains these rights. French-style company pension plans will thus only develop when an employee retains entitlement to a pension, even if he does not remain with the company until his retirement.

Third, the company pension plan is not a standard product. Their marketing and selling demands detailed knowledge of personal and corporate tax as well as the demography of the company, its organisational structure and changes in its wage bill. That corporate pension products are essentially vehicles for achieving optimal tax efficiency is shown by names such as: "Articles 39, 82, 83, etc of the General Taxation Code contracts".

Two special categories

Public sector employees and workers belonging to comparable categories

These benefit from so-called "special" schemes which share a common feature in that they were all set up before the Plan for Social Security (in 1853 for civil servants, in 1894 for miners, in 1937 for clerks and public notaries, etc) and in that they have all wanted to retain their independence. This is because at the outset, these schemes were seen as encouraging staff to stay and protecting the stability of the profession. They incorporate both stages of obligatory cover (general and supplementary schemes) and it is rare to find optional schemes being provided by the employer in this area.

Non-salaried workers

Many categories of working people were fundamentally opposed to the Plan which envisaged a single set of rules for all French people and so they set up independent old-age pension schemes for their respective professions.

Tradespeople

Almost 600,000 investors benefit from three levels of pension, managed by the independent organisation of tradespeople pension schemes of which CANCAVA is the national body: a basic scheme aligned with the *régime générale* since 1973; a supplementary scheme made compulsory since 1978; and an optional pension scheme run on the basis of personal subscriptions since 1987.

Manufacturers and retailers

Cover is provided by the national organisation for industry and commerce and is made up of local or professional pension funds and a national fund (ORGANIC). The 700,000 members pay into a basic scheme aligned with the *régime général* since 1973. The supplementary scheme has been optional since 1978 but is compulsory for spouses.

The professions

There are almost 270,000 people in this sector who contribute to one or other of the occupational branches of the Caisse Nationale d'Assurance Vieillesse des Professions Libérales (CNAVPL — the national old-age pension fund for professional people). Only lawyers are outside this scheme and they subscribe to the Caisse Nationale des Barreaux Français (the national fund for members of the French bar).

Apart from the compulsory basic scheme common to the various professions (including the special one for lawyers), professionals are covered by compulsory supplementary schemes (varying greatly between professions) and other optional supplementary schemes.

Farmers

The old-age pension scheme for farmers and other agricultural workers is managed by the Mutualité Sociale Agricole (the agricultural mutual benefit fund) with just one compulsory basic level of pension. The fund has 1.5 million contributors throughout France.

As can be seen, the French system of compulsory pension schemes is very complex. In particular, it includes supplementary schemes which in other countries like Germany and the US are optional. These supplementary schemes however are established by contract while the basic schemes are established by law.

How old-age pensions work

Old-age pensions in France operate on the basis of pay-as-you-go. In other words, the contributions paid in during the year are theoretically re-distributed in the form of benefits in the same year.

Calculation of contributions

As well as the huge number of schemes, account has to be taken of the extraordinary variety in:

i)   bases of assessment: earned income up to a fixed ceiling for private sector employees; salary with no fixed ceiling (often not including bonuses) for public sector employees; taxable income for tradespeople and retailers; *cadastral* income for farmers;[2] fixed contributions not related to income for members of the professions.

ii) contribution rates (and for salaried workers, the proportion paid by employer and employee, respectively). These are based on the final level of benefits guaranteed, on the basis of assessment, and on the balance between costs and expenditure.[3]

Table 12.2 shows the main elements used in calculating contributions to the general scheme and to supplementary and special schemes.

The benefits

At the end of his working life, the employee receives a retirement pension related to the contributions he has made. There are two main types of scheme:

Annuity schemes which account for almost all basic and special schemes for public sector employees, with three variants:

(i) The general scheme whereby an employee of

60 years of age with 37 1/2 years of credited service is guaranteed a proportion (50 percent) of his average income over the highest-paid years that he was making contributions;

(ii) Public servant schemes which guarantee, under the same conditions as (i) above, a proportion (70 percent) of income earned over the past six months of paying contributions. This scheme serves as a reference (the "pension point") for most special schemes for employees;

(iii) Finally, fixed contribution schemes which guarantee fixed benefits that only vary according to the duration of insurance cover. This scheme applies to members of the professions.

Points-based schemes which account for almost all supplementary schemes, first and foremost that for salaried employees.

Table 12.2

	Basis of assessment	Employer's contribution (%)	Insuered's contribution (%)
General scheme	Salary up to a fixed contribution ceiling	8.20	6.40
Supplementary schemes			
ARRCO	from 0 to 3 times the contribution ceiling	min: 2.76	min: 1.84
		max: 5.16	max: 3.44
AGIRC	from 1 to 4 times the contribution ceiling	min: 6.36	min: 2.12
		max: 10.4	max: 6.36
Civil servants (govt. employees)	graded salaries	25-27	7.70
SNCF (French railway employees)	gross taxable pay	29.00	7.70
Miners	Salaries up to a fixed contribution ceiling	7.75	7.70
Employees of EDF-GDF (French electricity board and French gas board)	Statutory salaries	46.2	7.70
Craftsmen Retailers	Professional income as a basis for personal income tax up to a ceiling	14.6	
Farmers	Fixed *cadastral* contribution set by the Commissaire de la Republique		
Professions	Fixed annual contribution set at national level according to profession		

Each year, total subscriptions paid in are translated into money of account, called "points": thus the worker acquires a certain number of points throughout his working life which determine the size of his pension. The value of each point is established each year with reference to the scheme's outgoings and income.

Unlike annuity schemes, pensions are calculated in proportion to professional income over the entire span of a worker's career instead of just the highest-paying or latest years.

In all, the working population benefits from one or other of these schemes — or rather from two pay-as-you-go pension systems that have different rules and include features specific to each sector of the economy.

Evaluating the pension schemes

In France, evaluation of the strengths and weaknesses of the various pay-as-you-go pension schemes is traditionally made by reference to the criteria of solidarity and economic efficiency.

There are three main pillars of solidarity: between generations, between schemes and at national level.

i) Solidarity between generations is undoubtedly the most important concept. At the outset, only by means of a pay-as-you-go system could a reasonable pension be guaranteed for pensioners who had paid little, if anything, into a contributory scheme.

However, what makes it hard for the insured population to accept is that the future level of their pensions cannot be guaranteed other than by the wealth of the nation and their share in that wealth as pensioners. In addition, contributors to pension schemes consider that they have established inviolable rights, as though the system operated on an individual capitalisation basis, and they do not understand why they must forego these rights as financial circumstances demand.

ii) Solidarity between different schemes: the original pay-as-you-go system has come face-to-face with socio-economic changes and a redistribution of the working population between various occupations, which has trans-

lated into a significant decline in the ratio of beneficiaries to contributors.

In an effort to redress the financial imbalance arising out of demographic changes that threaten the level of benefits obtainable from the different schemes, the legislators have set up a mechanism for transfering funds from over-subscribed schemes to under-subscribed ones.[4]

iii) Finally, the old-age pension system relies upon the solidarity of the government, which, as we have seen with the FNS supplementary allowance, also intervenes to ensure the viability of the most under-subscribed schemes (agricultural workers, railway employees, miners' schemes, merchant seamen, etc).

Thus, in 1987, the cost of the basic old-age pension schemes was 10 percent financed out of the state budget and 5 percent out of taxes.

Amid such a confusion of transfers and subsidies, it is difficult to know who is paying for whom. From the standpoint of solidarity one might be tempted to say that the pay-as-you-go system is viable. Nevertheless, two main planks of the solidarity edifice are regularly called into question:

First, solidarity between pensioners, because the end objective of pay-as-you-go is to guarantee a pension both for those who have not paid any contributions as well as to those who have contributed for 37 1/2 years.

Second, solidarity between the working and non-working population, as the ever-increasing contributions paid in by the working population, coupled with the rise in living standards of retired people, requires that the burden of contributions be shared more equitably.

As for economic efficiency, it is natural for people to want greater security and the various pension schemes have been designed to answer this need. But doubt is regularly cast on a system which is financed on the basis of compulsory contributions and results in economic distorsions.

Funding of the system is obviously linked to employment. Consequently, funding based on a portion of salaries and paid by employers penalises those who take on large numbers of employees.[5] Added to this are the effects of rises in wages and prices.

The debate on the economic efficiency of the French pay-as-you-go system revolves around the basis for determining contributions. But reform in this area raises a number of questions:

Should the employers' social security contributions be increased? This would affect the competitiveness of French companies within the EC.

Should one advocate then that employees' contributions alone be increased? In this case, the community as a whole would have to suffer the consequences that a drop in consumer demand would have on production, investment and employment.

Should contributions to the old-age pension system take the form of a value-added tax imposed on companies? If so, the imbalance between capital-intensive and labour-intensive industries would disappear. But the inevitable cut in companies' profit base would run counter to a policy favouring investment in production.

There remains the solution of a complete overhaul of funding methods, whereby only workers would pay contributions while their income rose proportionately. But to transfer the entire cost to the working population — whose income tax is already index-linked — would do nothing to reduce the ever-increasing cost of running the social welfare system.

The debate on the pros and cons of the pay-as-you-go system is complex and will remain so as the search for a fairer system continues to meet resistance from various quarters.

Moreover, liberalised capital movements since January 1990 and tax cuts on savings — including income from private assets — makes it more difficult to broaden the social security contribution base. While the problem is complicated, it is constantly under review in light of the challenges which the French old-age pension system must meet in the years ahead.

Challenges and outlook for the old-age pension system

According to the Commission des Comptes de la Sécurité Sociale (the social security accounts commission) the total cost of all pension schemes, excluding the cost of disability, amounted to FF683 billion ($120 billion) in 1990. This total includes retirement pensions run under the basic social security pension scheme, the supplementary pension schemes run by ARRCO and AGIRC as well as the special (miners, civil servants, railway employees etc) and professional schemes (banks etc) (see Figure 12.1). Just 11.9 percent of gross domestic product is paid out annually to 9 million pensioners. This portion has increased considerably in the years since the Second World War,[6] particularly during the past 15 years of economic difficulties.

Figure 12.1

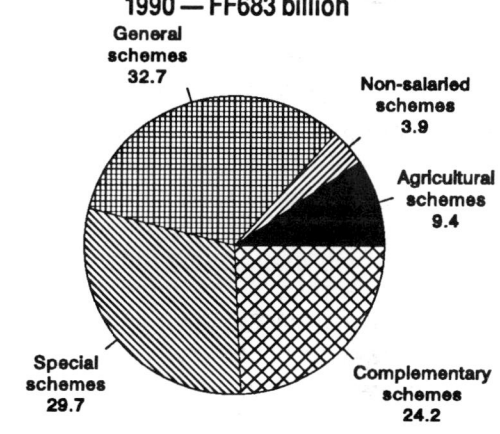

Old-age benefits (excluding disabled allowances) 1990 — FF683 billion

General schemes 32.7
Non-salaried schemes 3.9
Agricultural schemes 9.4
Special schemes 29.7
Complementary schemes 24.2

Source: Comité des Comptes de la Sécurité Sociale, February 1991

In the coming decades, the old-age pension system will come under considerable pressure, not only from an ageing population, but also from the delayed effects of one of the most significant social phenomena of the past 30 years: the increase in the numbers of working women. While a great number of women of retirement age at present only receive the basic old-age pension, in future they will be entitled to a full occupational pension.[7]

Problems with pay-as-you-go systems

Putting aside the financial aspects involving wages

and prices, a balanced pension system depends on the following three factors: the number of contributors, their retirement age and the life expectancy of pensioners and their dependents. While the relationship between demographic factors and old-age pensions is clear, other factors, particularly socio-economic ones, also come into play.

Demographic factors and the old-age pension system

Based on a fertility rate of 1.8 children per woman — the level recorded over the past 10 years — the percentage of people aged 60 years or over will increase from 18.1 percent in 1985 to 20.4 percent in the year 2000, 22.6 percent in 2010 and 26.1 percent in 2020, if the fall in birth and mortality rates continues at today's rate. In the year 2040, 29.9 percent of the population will be over 60 years of age if the birth rate remains at the same level and 26.1 percent if it rises to 2.1 children per woman (the level required to renew generations).

From the year 2010 onwards, demographic factors will be the determining factor in how the pensions system is funded. In fact, the ratio of workers to retired people indicates that from the years 2005 to 2010 onwards, the estimated ratio of working people to pensioners will diminish considerably and consistently; 2.91 in 1985, 2.65 in 2005, 1.96 or 2.04 by the year 2020, depending on the birth rate.

An important factor in considering the increased costs of the pension system at this stage will be the post-war baby-boom generation reaching the age of 60.

Therefore, to maintain a ratio of 2.5 working people to one retired person, as is currently the case, the retirement age in 2010 will have to be raised to 62 1/2 years from the present 60.

Socio-economic factors

The demographic problems will only really begin to take effect around the years 2010 to 2020. However, in the short term, such socio-economic variables as the retirement age, the number of working women and the level of benefits will be more important factors in any increase in charges than demography alone.

The age at which a person is eligible to retire on a full pension after 37 1/2 years of credited service was cut from 65 years to 60 years in 1983. As a result, several generations of the working population can retire at an earlier age, ending their contributions to the old-age pension schemes. Moreover, between 1950 and 1987, life expectancy at 60 increased by three years for men and by 5 1/2 years for women. The average length of time over which a pension is drawn has therefore been extended. Also, people are starting their working lives later and individuals' working lives are increasingly interspersed with non-working periods. There are also greater opportunities for taking early retirement from 55 years onwards.

Besides the age of retirement, the increase in the cost of pensions is linked to their average value. This in turn now depends mainly on the number of women in the workplace.

First, the number of women who have established pension rights by working, and who receive pensions in their own right, is rising. Whereas in 1954 42 percent of women between the ages of 25 and 29 years formed part of the workforce, today that figure is 76 percent. INSEE, the French National Statistical Office, forecasts that over 80 percent of women in this age group will be working at the start of the next century. The percentage of women over 60 years of age in retirement will eventually approach the current level for men (which is 87 percent), as against 62 percent in 1988. Correspondingly, the amount of money paid out in pensions is rising because they are covering longer working lives.

Second, the schemes for salaried workers, which afford higher benefits on average than the schemes for non-salaried people, is taking a growing proportion of pension costs. This is due mainly to the rise in the numbers of women working, most of whom are in salaried employment.

Third, the generosity of the law in granting a variety of additional benefits has contributed to the rise in costs.[8]

Finally, the effect of under-employment on the beneficiary/contributor ratio should be highlighted. The more unemployed people there are, the fewer people there are contributing. Furthermore, the gap is widening as early retirement is encouraged to make way for young people. The replacement of experienced by inexperienced workers is not an ideal solution and as a result the number of people working is falling while the proportion of people in retirement rises. Moreover, the under-employment factor becomes more significant as economic growth slows.

Are the proposed solutions viable?

With a steady cut in the amounts being collected through the various pensions schemes, the problems posed by an ageing population[9] will increase. It is difficult to envisage any solution other than a radical reform of the pension system.

There are three possible ways of balancing the cost of pay-as-you-go pensions schemes: by progressively raising subscription rates as the proportion of pensioners to working people increases, by decreasing the relative value of benefits and by raising the retirement age.

It could be said that this triple solution is doomed in so far as it appears impossible to implement it in its entirety. In each case the measures would involve both an economic and social cost. Increasing contribution rates could create problems of competitiveness in an open economy, as it would add to salary costs. A drop in the relative value of benefits would, without question, meet with strong social and political resistance. Raising the statutory age of retirement could only be contemplated if the economy was close to full employment.

However, the impact of the demographic changes will be such that, all things being equal, there will be no way of avoiding a considerable increase in contribution rates. Consequently, apart from the measures relating to the actual terms of the pay-as-you-go system, it seems essential to examine ways of transferring the purchasing power of an individual's savings today to finance the pensions of tomorrow.

Several solutions have been considered within the framework of capitalisation.

Given the virtues and failings of both pay-as-you-go and capitalisation, it would seem more appropriate to adopt a mixed solution, where pension payments would depend both on contributions deducted directly from wages and from past, capitalised savings. This mix would mean that pensions were based on the two factors of production, namely work and capital, while cutting the risks inherent in each individual system.

The capitalisation option can be applied to pay-as-you-go pension systems through the build-up of reserves, as proposed in a May 1991 government white paper. This can equally operate at company, professional association or individual levels (by recourse to capitalisation). Considering the savings effort required, the optimal solution might be to operate it simultaneously at all three levels. A reform of fiscal and parafiscal deductions would appear to be necessary in this case.

The build up of temporary reserves (based on the US model) has many advantages. As an instrument for managing the demographic changes which the next century holds in store, the reserves could compliment the traditional mechanisms already in use so as to adapt the funding of pay-as-you-go schemes to the constraints imposed by an ageing population. Moreover, a build up of temporary reserves can help cushion the effects of fluctuations in the size of generations and can be used to set up a pension-savings fund (collective schemes) to smooth out the adjustments required and help adapt to a relative drop in numbers of contributors. Nevertheless, the building up of reserve funds could slow down or defer more fundamental long-term reforms, such as increasing the retirement age.

In the light of such negative aspects, the policy of building up reserves can only be regarded as an adjunct to the reforms to be considered. There is always a risk of diversion of reserve funds, as a result of which hard decisions are avoided.

Company pension plans can, as we have seen, act as capitalisation-based pensions to supplement the pay-as-you-go schemes, provided they make the existing system more flexible.

There are several incentives in place to encourage people to invest in private pensions plans. The most traditional type of pension is secured by means of personal savings. However, although the most recent products to come on the market, such as the *SICAV de capitalisation* (capital growth funds), are tax-exempt, they carry certain features — such as the high minimum investment and the risk of loss of capital — that rule these funds out for low-income families.

The creation of the *Plan d'Epargne Populaire* — (PEP — the people's savings plan) in January 1990 was in response to the monetary authorities' desire to encourage long-term savings while indirectly helping individuals build up long-term savings geared towards retirement (see Chapter 3). With state assistance towards payment of the initial premium available for low income families and a considerable freedom of choice left to savers, the PEP is designed in such a way as to appeal to anybody wishing to save.

In contrast to the other financial products currently available to low income families, this plan addresses the specific need of providing a long-term savings mechanism which is both safe and gives a good return, thus offering more security in the face of future risks such as retirement, but also death or unemployment because early tax-free withdrawal of funds is possible.

The second type of pension is secured by means of collectively-managed savings. In contrast to the previous type, collective capitalisation allows for the sharing of risk. This form of pension fund is presently underdeveloped (mainly existing in the form of *caisses de cadres supérieurs* or senior management funds) but more flexible rules and taxation would provide an important stimulus.

Despite some developments in the area of capitalisation, strictly pension-insurance and pension-savings formulas remain largely under-exploited.

Capitalisation: a solution to the problem?

The fact that the pay-as-you-go system is prey to socio-demographic changes has not escaped the notice of those who are most aware of the system's inadequacies — namely, the supporters of capitalisation-type pensions schemes.

But the search for a solution to redress the financial imbalance threatening pension schemes would not seem to lie in a radical substitution of one system by another.

Capitalisation versus pay-as-you-go

In contrast to pay-as-you-go schemes, which offer no definite guarantee, capitalisation by means of personal savings would appear to offer a better way of securing a return on investment. However, like the pay-as-you-go system, the return on savings depends on a number of factors. In addition, this return is linked to the real rate of interest on assets acquired with no guarantee that this will be positive throughout the investment period.

The return on investment effectively depends on supply and demand. Funding a pension via capitalisation is akin to raising a loan on the economy to finance consumption during the period out of work. In a period of growth, the demand for assets will be greater and the rate of interest will be high. However, during an economic downturn the situation will be reversed.

In general, whether through the social partners — by means of pension funds — or through financial mechanisms (by way of the intervention of the financial institutions) all assets acquired today translate into a more or less long-term right to draw on the resources of the community. As to limits on this right, that will depend on what the community is capable of offering when the right is exercised.

The pay-as-you-go system, although it cannot guarantee a predetermined pension like capitalisation schemes, is founded on an unassailable social pact of which the terms of application are under constant review to take account of the interests of the working population and the retired. One point seems accepted by all: capitalisation cannot take the place of pay-as-you-go. The demands that would have be made on one generation in terms of contributions and the size of the financial reserves that would have to be built up render such a radical change impossible.

Capitalisation, like pay-as-you-go, carries no absolute guarantee in the face of the socio-economic and demographic changes that are taking place. The authorities are gradually realising that there is a need to search for some compromise which would satisfy all the interested parties and deal with the problems of both systems.

The future of the pensions system and the advantages and disadvantages respectively of capitalisation and pay-as-you-go are becoming a regular feature of political debate. That debate is taking place between the heads of the various pension funds and the insurers. And although the public authorities have not been particularily assertive, they are steadily drawing closer to those who envisage pensions funds complementing pay-as-you-go schemes. While the social partners continue to cast doubt on capitalisation, increasing sections of the population are questioning the outlook for pay-as-you-go. This leads one to hope that there will be a fresh look at supplementary capitalisation pensions.

While the types of capitalisation scheme operating are likely to develop further, they are limited in scope for the moment, making it unwise to bet on any widescale acceptance among the populace. The setting up of pension funds *à la française* is still the aim of those who advocate capitalisation.

The views of the interested parties

The debate between those who favour capitalisation and those who favour pay-as-you-go has not produced any definite conclusion concerning the future of supplementary retirement schemes through capitalisation. It has, however, provided an opportunity for both sides to present their arguments. Drawn into the discussion, the heads of the two main supplementary retirement schemes (AGIRC and ARRCO) have taken a firm stance and remain resolutely opposed to capitalisation. Their main argument is that capitalisation does not guarantee that the current value of the capital invested will be maintained. Jean-Paul Mouzin, head of AGIRC, believes there are risks involved in funded pension plans that are linked to inflation and financial and monetary uncertainties — in other words, they entail a level of risk that is not compatible with the guarantee of a decent pension for contributors. Taking these uncertainties into consideration, "capitalisation-based pension plans must remain what they are: supplements to pensions," to quote from *Agefi* of March 13 1991.

Thus, the managements of AGIRC and ARRCO remain unmoved in the face of the demographic risks threatening their retirement schemes. The disimprovement in population ratios forecast by the INSEE stikes them as being "alarmist". They think that those who would most benefit from capitalisation are the insurance companies.[10]

The insurance companies, on the other hand, through the medium of their professional body — the FFSA — argue strongly for capitalisation. Nonetheless, their position has changed somewhat. They now appear to be willing to accept a compromise that would leave the pay-as-you-go system in its present form. The capitalisation-type products that the insurers propose would only be complementary to the present pay-as-you-go system. However, it is not easy to see how these capitalisation products could be introduced without also affecting the way the present system is funded.

In principle the FFSA is proposing two categories of capitalisation product: pension funds *à la française* and voluntary personal pension products with built-in tax breaks.

The FFSA also proposes the following criteria for personal policies: premium payments at will; exit exclusively in the form of life annuities with reversion; tax reductions within limits to be decided; benefits identical to those for pensions; policies allowing transfer of rights and provisions.

Certain conditions have now also been laid down by the insurance companies in the area of French-style pension fund management.[11] First, to ensure the transparency of the sums received, funds must be kept separate from the contributing company, because nobody would want them to appear simply as a bank deposit entry on the debit side of a balance sheet. Moreover, while administration of the fund could be entrusted to the social partners, management must be strictly limited to market professionals.[12] Second, the funds must be invested in assets (with a strong emphasis on government securities and blue-chip bonds) that conform to the present regulatory and prudential framework for insurance companies.

The decision currently rests with the government, which published a white paper on pensions in May 1991. It is hoped that this document will serve as a guideline in the debate. In essence, it proposes the development of group savings funds (starting with the PEE) and a build-up of reserves within pay-as-you-go schemes. The latter proposal is particularly worrying insurers. First, they see it as "leading to the concentration of a large degree of financial power within certain bodies". Second, the build-up of reserves "would of necessity have to be achieved by increasing contribution rates". The insurance companies expect the government to introduce a set of rules to replace the rather finicky supervision of fund management (in the area of company pension plans, for example) which characterises the current period. The managers of the pension funds themselves hope to obtain a guarantee that pay-as-you-go will be retained for existing schemes.

Thus, from the insurance companies' point of view, it is no longer a matter of calling for the replacement of pay-as-you-go schemes with capitalisation-run ones. However, it remains to be seen what limit, if any, will be imposed on increases in pension contributions to the former. The establishment of a limit, which is causing great concern to the advocates of pay-as-you-go, now seems to be a pre-condition for getting capitalisation off the ground.[13] So, the establishment of supplementary capitalisation schemes — pension funds — is creating a serious problem for the compulsory one, in the sense that funded pension plans could lead to a freeze on any contribution increases: yet increases are essential if the balance of pay-as-you-go schemes is to be maintained.

Conclusion

The setting-up of a pension system operating by means of capitalisation is a concept which has gained firm support in government circles. However, it is likely that the debate on the establishment of any such scheme will be heated, as the social partners (employee pension funds, unions, etc) are extremly mistrustful of measures which might call into question their hitherto inviolable rights. The supplementary funds (AGIRC in particular and to a lesser extent, ARRCO), do not wish to lose control over this part of their resources.

Pension funds operating by means of capitalisation have a strong chance of success, although it remains to be seen what concrete measures the government will adopt to encourage their development. We might expect to see straightforward tax measures which directly favour the new products.[14] But it is possible that the government will make things easier for capitalisation by limiting the contribution base of pay-as-you-go-type pensions. It is this latter measure which is causing so much concern to the pension funds.

In the present economic climate, and with the in-

creasing sophistication of the financial markets, the solution would seem to lie in a mixture of both systems. This would encourage the contributor to build up providential savings for himself, both personally and as part of a group, in the form of a pension fund. There is no doubt that this transformation would need to be accompanied by sweeping changes in the present pension schemes: these will continually have to take socio-demographic changes into account as well as encourage households to save.

In addition to the anticipated positive effect on household savings rates, pension funds would make the capital markets more dynamic — particularily by lending more liquidity to the equity market, which has been beset by such problems.

Whatever form French pension funds eventually assume, it is imperative that something should be done within the next few years. Consequently, an effort to harmonise the levels of pension the different schemes offer should accompany the proposed reforms. This would simplify administration and cut the large imbalances in some overly-generous schemes.

Finally, it is to be expected that a policy of austerity will bring the allocation of non-contributory benefits under control (particularly those linked to the revaluation of pensions) and that these will be supported to a greater extent by the state — in other words, by taxes.

Endnotes

(1) In Alsace-Lorraine, local authorities run their own statutory schemes, a throwback to the period (1840-1918) when the region was part of Germany. But the number of schemes is dropping steadily.

(2) *Cadastral* income refers to a system whereby a farmer's income is estimated by reference to the quality of the land he owns.

(3) It is estimated that financing pensions accounts for around 20 percent of earned income.

(4) The mechanism operates by comparing the number of pensioners paid out of the fund with the number of pensioners there would have been if the beneficiary/contributor ratio had remained the same as that for all other schemes.

(5) With unemployment running at roughly 10 percent, the effects of such a system could be serious.

(6) In 1959, this portion was 5.3 percent.

(7) Only one in three women has worked all her life which explains the low level of women's pensions. But three-quarters of male pensioners on full pensions over 65 years of age have had a complete working life: in other words, they have worked at least 37 1/2 years and have contributed to one or more of the basic and supplementary old-age pension schemes.

(8) A few figures which give some indication of the situation for French pensioners include: they can draw an average of 2.8 pensions; the value of the pension benefits amounts to FF6,500 ($1,148) per month per pension; half of pensioners are entitled to additional benefits — like bonuses for children or supplementary allowances for a dependent spouse, supplements linked to periods of unemployment or insufficient periods of contribution, etc; 23 percent of women who have worked all their lives are entitled to a surviving spouse's pension on top of their own.

(9) The dependency rate — the ratio of contributors to non-working people over the age of 59 — will increase steadily over the next 15 years. It is at present around 2.5 to 1 and will be less than 2 to 1 the year 2005 — in other words, the cost to the working population will become harder to bear. This statistic alone explains why the future for the French pension system looks so bleak. Added to this, more and more future pensioners will have the maximum number of credited years of service and consequently will be eligible to retire on a full pension.

(10) There is no doubt that opening up the pay-as-you-go system to capitalisation would provide the basis for a very lucrative market for insurers — a market perhaps worth as much as several billion francs.

(11) Group funds directed at workers of similar occupations and at non-salaried workers exercising the same profession.

(12) The resistance of supplementary pension schemes to this plan is understandable. At present, half of ARRCO funds are managed by insurance companies, while AGIRC funds are managed by the pension funds themselves, with the assistance of their banks.

(13) In view of its importance in the reallocation of a portion of savings, the fixing of a legally-set upper limit to contributions to compulsory schemes (general and supplementary) remains an area of much conflict.

(14) The introduction of funded pension plans by way of tax breaks is not "neutral" given the cost to the taxpayer. This is one of the arguments put forward by the opponents of capitalisation who feel that it is the insurance companies that will mainly benefit from the tax breaks allowed.

Chapter 13

Taxation in France

The past 20 years have been marked by a rise in French tax levels that has outstripped growth in gross domestic product. Taxes and social security contributions, which stood at less than 35 percent of GDP before 1973, exceeded 40 percent by 1978. It reached 45 percent in 1984 and has since stabilised. All OECD countries have experienced similar rises in compulsory levies and the increases in France have been about average though there has been a somewhat stronger impact on French GDP since 1980. Such a development is in large part due to the inexorable rise in public spending, especially in the area of social benefits.[1] Numerous improvements concerning the taxation of investments and capital gains are underway to avoid capital flights.

How compulsory levies are structured

Compulsory levies bring together all tax revenue, special levies and national health and insurance contributions collected by local and central public administrations, the social security office and the EC administration.

Table 13.1 highlights the importance of national health and insurance contributions and the relative unimportance of personal income tax. The former make up the greater part of tax revenue (43 percent in 1987, of which 27.2 percent was employers' contributions and 15.8 percent that of employees) while income tax only accounts for 12.7 percent. The pressure exerted by the demands of the social security system has increased relative to that exerted by other forms of tax over the past 30 years (see Table 13.2).

Table 13.1 Tax revenue in France (1987)	In % of GDP	In % of tax revenue
Taxes on personal income	13.9	31.1
of which: income tax	5.7	12.7
national health and insurance contributions levied on employees and independent workers	7.1	15.8
taxes levied on private assets	0.7	1.5
taxes on inheritance	0.3	1.8
recurrent taxes levied on cars	0.1	0.3
Taxes on company profits	2.3	5.2
Taxes on the cost of labour	13.0	29.1
of which: employers' national health and insurance contributions	12.2	27.2
Other taxes on the costs of production	2.1	4.8
Taxes modifying the price of goods	12.7	28.3
of which: VAT	8.7	19.5
excise duty	2.9	6.4
Miscellaneous	0.7	1.5
Total	44.8	100.0

Source: Vers une fiscalité européenne?; CEPII - OFCE (2 Volumes), Paris, 1990

National health and insurance contributions

In France, for a long time the existence of a "ceilings system" meant that contributions from both employers and employees were only due on that portion

Table 13.2

The distribution of national health and insurance levies

	1958	1984	1989
National health and insurance contributions	29.6	43.4	43.5
Taxes	70.4	56.6	56.5
of which:			
The state	61.5	40.2	38.4
Local authorities	8.9	12.6	13.3
The EC	—	1.7	2.6
Others	—	2.0	2.2)

Source: Comptes de la nation

of salary that was beneath a set limit. This system is now on the way out, and only survives for old-age pension contributions where there is a complex system of supplementary schemes.

Contribution rates — both for employers and employees — increased proportionately until 1983. Since then, only the amount paid by employees has tended to rise. Despite this, and because of the serious problems facing the social security system in trying to balance its finances, a new tax, called the *contribution sociale généralisée*, has been introduced. This is a tax on overall private income of 1.1 percent.

Taxes and special levies

Aside from some hybrid taxes, the national accounting system defines three broad tax categories: taxes connected to production and imports, of which the most important are value added tax and excise duties; taxes on income (of individuals and companies) and on fortunes; and capital taxes.

La taxe sur la valeur ajoutée (TVA — value added tax)[2]

France is in line with EC agreements to harmonise VAT rates, the short-term objective being the establishment of a 14 to 20 percent standard tax band and a 4 to 9 percent band for power-rated items. At present, there exist three broad rates:

- A lower rate of 5.5 percent (previously 7 percent) applied to staple products (food), books, pas-

senger transport, water supply and audio recordings;[3]

- A higher rate of 22 percent (28 percent until 1989 and 25 percent until 1990) applied to luxury goods, consumer electronic goods (apart from televisions), cameras and cars. The Law of July 26 1991 provides for the abolition of the 22 percent VAT rate from January 1 1993.

- A standard rate of 18.6 percent which is applied to all other products.

While France is steadily moving into line with European standards, it still applies a number of unusual regulations, for instance:

i)   The existence of a one-month time lag before up-front VAT payments made by companies are deducted. Such a regulation means a cash outlay for companies of the order of FF50 billion ($8.8 billion), or FF5 billion in extra interest charges per annum.

ii) The restriction of the right to VAT allowances on a certain number of items that could also be appropriated for personal use (cars, travel expenses). Fuels are steadily being excluded from such a restriction. Around 12 percent of VAT revenues come from restrictions placed on VAT allowances for intermediate consumption.

Personal income tax

Income tax, in its present guise, was introduced in a 1959 reform. It is a graduated, single[4] and personalised tax levied each year on the income of individuals and affects the overall net income of every taxpayer.

We have seen that income tax plays only a small role in the overall tax system. This is due, on the one hand, to the low rates charged against the first income bracket on the scale (5 percent) and to the narrow tax base on the other.

Income tax assessment

Income tax is calculated against the overall income at the taxpayer's disposal over the course of one year. Valuation of the amount of income to be taxed is carried out in accordance with rules particular to each category of income. There are three such categories:

i) Pay and rewards

Multiple allowances mean that the tax base can be legally cut. Thus the various national health and insurance contributions are entirely deductible, which results in lowering gross pay by around 16 percent. Other allowances — work-related expenses and for pensioners, for example — also cut the tax base.

ii) Income from private assets

Within this category is included income from short-term capital investments, income from property and capital gains (from real estate and personal property).

Rent is taxed as income from property. Since 1965, a standard tax allowance of 10 percent has been applied. Since 1965, fictitious rents[5] are tax-exempt.

iii) Income from the exercise of one's profession

This includes all business income (from manufacturing, trading or small-scale industry); gains from agricultural activity; the remuneration of directors in companies cited in Article 62 of the General Tax Code. All other sources of income not included in the preceding categories are taxed as gains from non-commercial professions and equivalent income.

Calculating tax

Overall net (taxable) income is determined once the allowances set out by law have been deducted and (when the case arises) once deficits for certain income categories have been ascertained. There are, however, exceptions: first, income subject to a separate form of taxation (capital gains, for example) and income subject to a standard tax levy are not counted. Second, to limit tax evasion, the allocation of certain categories of deficit against overall income is not allowed.

Earnings distributed continued to be taxed at the rate of 42 percent until the end of 1991. Since the beginning of 1992, a single tax rate of 34 percent has been in operation, whether earnings are distributed or not.

In addition, only one taxable income is calculated per (fiscal) household. The system of *quotient familial* which consists in dividing overall income into a number of parts depending on the number of children one has, allows taxpayers to counter progressive tax rises.

There are a number of regulatory provisions associated with income tax. There are other allowances designed to provide an incentive for certain types of personal expenditure apart from those available for expenses involved in the acquisition and preservation of income. Such allowances are made either by allocations against taxable income or through means of a tax credit set against one's tax bill. Tax incentives have two main objectives: to encourage housing and to encourage savings.

The narrowness of the tax base and the low rates charged against the first two income brackets, combined with the mechanisms available for tax relief and a system of minimum contributions that exempts low incomes from taxation, have resulted in 12 million households, or 47 percent of the total, being tax-exempt.[6]

L'impôt sur les sociétés (IS — Corporate tax)

This tax affects the profits of manufacturing and trading companies, whatever their form, as well as public bodies engaged in profit-making activities. In principle, and unless there are specific stipulations to the contrary, only profits realised in France are taxed. Profits and losses realised abroad are not taken into consideration.

The law provides for several cost allocations to be made, the most important being tax allowances and credits.

Tax rates (as stipulated under the general rule of law)

Although it had been fixed at 50 percent for a long time, IS (corporate tax) has been steadily decreasing since 1986; it was down to 34 percent for retained profits during the 1991 tax year. Earnings distributed continued to be taxed at the rate of 42 percent until the end of 1991. Since the beginning of 1992, a single tax rate of 34 percent has been in operation, whether earnings are distributed or not.

Long-term capital gains realised from the sale of bonds, of *titres participatifs* (investment certificates) and of units in mutual funds are taxed at a special rate as long as the balance is locked into a special reserve account and thus not distributed. The rate has risen from 15 percent to 19 percent and then to 23 percent (of which 1.1 percent is *contribution sociale généralisée*). To limit the extent of double taxation, distributed profits benefit from a tax credit of 50 percent.

Once account is taken of the tax cut to 37 percent in 1990 (and to 34 percent in 1991), distributed dividends will be subject to a supplementary corporate tax equal to 5/58ths of their net value. This will only affect dividends distributed after fiscal years starting on January 1 1990 and charged against results running over the same period.

Dividends paid out as stock or shares by companies or cooperatives not subject to the Law of July 24 1966 are exempt from paying this supplement.

Corporate tax returns were low throughout the 1980s. They now account for only 9 percent of the public administration's tax revenue. Such mediocre yields cannot but pose real problems for the French tax system, especially given the narrow tax base. While some 700,000 companies are liable for corporate tax, only some 55 percent actually pay it, the others not showing any profit. If one takes out small concerns (with turnover of less than FF2 million — $353,000), the percentage of companies paying corporate tax comes to 63 percent. This figure increases the larger the company and reaches 75 percent of firms with turnover of FF60 to 100 million, but decreases to 64 percent for those with sales of FF1 to 2 billion.[7]

Capital levies

In 1989, *l' impôt de solidarité sur la fortune* (ISF — the solidarity tax on wealth) took the place of *l' impôt sur les grandes fortunes* (IGF — wealth tax). It is presented as a contribution by the most wealthy to those most in need and is the main source of funding for the *revenu minimum d' insertion* (RMI — minimum insertion income). The ISF taxes net personal estates (apart from business equipment and works of art) valued at over FF4.1 million ($724,000) in 1990. (Total amounts taken in under this tax increased from FF4 billion [$706 million] in 1985 to FF6 billion [$1.06 billion] in 1991.) The tax rate levied increases progressively between a minimum of 0.5 and a maximum of 1.5 percent.[8]

Until 1991, taken together with income tax, ISF did not exceed 70 percent of income. Subsequently, this threshold was raised to 85 percent, meaning that the

government should receive an extra FF700 million ($123 million).

The amount taxable is assets net of debts. A surviving spouse and each child benefits from tax relief of FF275,000 ($48,600) on the portion of assets that is bequeathed to them. Inheritance taxes vary from 5 to 40 percent and grow as one moves from direct ancestors to direct descendants.

The taxation of savings

French tax on savings is a mixed bag. More often than not, savings products are not subject to the general rules governing income tax, either because they are entirely exempted or because there is a standard rate of deduction, optional or compulsory (see Appendix 13.1). From 1991, one must add a standard social contribution of 1.1 percent to the standard deduction rate. In addition, many savings incentives, specific to each instrument, exist side by side and come in the form of allowances against taxable income or tax reductions.

Obviously, savings incentives are a burden on the state's budget, as revealed in Table 13.3.

Taxes peculiar to investments

Appendix 13.1 presents a complete panorama of taxation applied to savings products as of 1990. Some remarks are needed to understand this exhaustive table. In the columns "capital gains", "liquidity", and "security", there are scores of between zero and four, representing that product's performance set against these three criteria. For example, the Livret A and the Livret Bleu, available through the mutual banks and offering almost perfect liquidity and maximum security are given a score of four based on these criteria. On the other hand, if the aim is capital gains, such products are of little interest and are given a score of zero.

One column gives observations on the main advantages and disadvantages attached to each product as well as any possible incompatibilities or linkages between products.

Further important points concerning the taxation of savings:

Table 13.3

Cost to the state budget of the main savings incentives in 1988

Every year, the list of tax expenditures contained in an annex to the Finance Act summarises all those legal provisions whose effect is to depress tax revenue. In most instances, this annex gives a detailed account of the amounts involved. Thus, tax expenditure on savings came to FF28 billion in the state budget of 1988.

Main elements of tax expenditure aimed at encouraging savings in 1988 (in FF million)	
1) Cost to the state budget of tax exemption for certain investments	
Livrets A	5,500
Crédit Mutuel-issued Livrets bleus	650
CODEVI	850
Home savings accounts and plans	4,600
People's savings accounts	200
Total	11,800
2) Cost to the state budget of other savings incentives	
Allowances on taxable income from bonds and dividends	3,900
Flat rate tax deductions on yields from fixed income investments	3,900
Interest on the 1973 4.5 percent debt issue and interest on the 1977 8.80 percent debt issue	30
The Monory Law scheme (for persons born before 1932)	230
Tax reductions for the *Compte d'Epargne en Actions* (CEA — Savings accounts in the form of shares)	1,950
Tax reductions for life insurance premiums and survivor annuities (a ceiling on amount available)	2,200
Taxation of 16 percent on net gains realised from the disposal of transferable securities of above a certain value	2,600
Exemption of income arising from long-term savings contracts (not valid after 1981)	60
Exemption of amounts composed of shares held by employees in their company's capital	1,200
Total	16,070
Total 1) and 2)	27,870
Source: OFCE report	

i) Capital gains from the sale of securities

Since 1979, capital gains from the sale of securities are liable to tax once the volume of net sales is above a threshold which is re-evaluated every year. Calculation of capital gains does not take into consideration either how long the security was held or the depreciation of money. They are not subject to the marginal rate of income tax, but to a flat rate of 17 percent.

ii) SICAV de capitalisation (*Capitalisation-based unit trusts*):

Capitalisation-based unit trusts have been authorised since October 1989, thus enabling further reductions in tax payable on investments in bonds. Capitalisation-based unit trusts contain the possibility of redeploying income from bonds and mar-

ketable debt for the acquisition of new securities. Because income is not distributed among bearers, it escapes being taxed. Only dividends from shares have to be distributed and thus are liable to personal income tax.

iii) The Plan d'Epargne Populaire (*PEP— the people's saving plan*):

Set up on January 1 1990, the PEP follows on from the Plan d'Epargne en vue de la Retraite (PER — the retirement savings plan) which dates from 1988. Its aim is to encourage long-term savings, especially among households not liable to tax. Capitalised income is exempt from income tax, such an exemption becoming permanent if one stays with the plan for more than eight years. A 25 percent premium (up to a maximum amount of FF1,500 — $265) is paid for deposits made by savers not liable to tax. Withdrawals are either in the form of annuities or capital amounts (see Table 13.4).

People who have taken out PER investments can transfer them to PEPs. Such transfers are tax-exempt and are looked upon purely and simply as lodgements to PEP accounts.

iv) Life insurance premiums

Life insurance investments were subject to a 5.5 percent tax on annual premiums. This was abolished in 1990, thus putting them on an equal competitive footing to similar investments in other European countries.

Recent tax readjustments

Since the beginning of President Mitterrand's second seven-year term in 1988, France has been busy re-aligning its tax system.

The 1990 and 1991 Finance Acts contained a number of partial reforms and amendments concerning tax on savings, corporate tax, VAT, etc.

In tax terms, the big winners seem to have been stock market investments, thanks to competition and the liberalisation of capital movements. They have benefited from a lowering of standard deductions from January 1 1990.

But such tax relief also has its downside and some sectors — especially real estate — have seen a rise in their tax burden.

Towards a complete reform of the tax system?

Unlike many of its EC partners, France has not yet embarked on a vast tax reform programme. Mitterrand's second seven-year term has thrown up measures that seem more directed towards partial modifications of the present system. However, these modifications pose serious problems as the stated objectives seem irreconcilable: on the one hand, greater social justice is sought at a national level, while on the other greater economic efficiency is the goal (when European unity is under discussion).

Still at an early stage is the plan for reform of the taxation of private estates as set out by former Prime Minister Michel Rocard: "Both to simplify and make more equitable levies placed on private assets that, at present, are both numerous and contradictory, stretching from land tax to the solidarity tax on fortunes (ISF), from inheritance tax to levies on savings".

In addition, a real struggle is now taking place over tax. The dispute centres around the proposals for tax reform contained in the Hollande Report.[9] This re-

---

Table 13.4

How the 'Plan d'Epargne Populaire' works

	First 8 years		From 8-10 years	After 10 years
	Up to 4 years	From 4 to 8 years		
Instalments	For a total of up to FF600,000 per plan (FF1.2m for a couple), whatever the plan's duration, with a minimum instalment of FF2,400 per year			
Withdrawals	Yields from capitalisation is integrated into taxable income, or there is a withholding tax of:		Total exemption for savings accumulated (with withdrawal from the plan possible either in the form of annuities or as a capital amount)	
	35%	15%		
	Leads to the closing of the plan			Prolongation is possible, but without any further instalments being paid in
Bonuses (persons not liable to tax)	No	No	Yes, maximum amount of FF1,500 per year after first payment instalment	No additional bonus

Source: L'Express, 24/12/89 (???CHECK WITH AUTHOR)

---

port starts with the premise that the 1980s were marked by a continuous rise in the value of private estates, net improvements in returns on capital and a lowering of tax on financial savings. This has resulted in widening inequalities. To rectify this, the Hollande report advocates heavy taxation of capital gains arising from real estate and share transactions for companies, as well as an overhaul of inheritance tax.

The Ministry of Finance has reacted negatively to these proposals by pointing out that, if such measures were adopted, they would lead to capital flight. This, in turn, would have repercussions on the stability of the Franc, the defence of which remains one of the government's main objectives.

The government finally decided on a further cut in corporate tax (34 percent) payable on profits reinvested in the course of the 1991 tax year. Moreover, in the budget proposals for 1991, tax on the capital gains from financial operations realised by companies goes up from 19 to 23 percent (lower than proposed in the Hollande Report). This measure is retroactive from January 1 1990.

The lifting of exchange controls

Since January 1 1990 exchange controls have been abolished, the Ministry for Finance having decided to bring forward the date for liberalisation from July 1 1990.

Individuals now have the right to open accounts abroad and to hold foreign currency accounts in France. To avoid fraud and tax evasion, Article 60 of the 1990 Finance Act sets out very precisely the rules that have to be respected.

All individual entities transferring sums of money, stocks or bonds to or from France without the intermediary of a banking or financial organisation must sign a declaration, except in cases where the value of the transfer is less than FF50,000 ($8,800). Such a measure allows the authorities to monitor the source of expatriate funds and to place levies on amounts liable under wealth tax.

Upon request, each organisation subject to the Banking Law must communicate to the tax or custom authorities the date and total amount transferred abroad. They must also supply the identities of the persons who carried out the transfer and who deposited the amount in question.

Organisations that do not comply with these obligations are liable to a tax fine equal to 80 percent of the total amounts not communicated to the tax and customs authorities.

Finally, as the sums transferred are considered one single amount of taxable income, tax reminders are accompanied by a surcharge of 40 percent in instances where tax declarations are proven to be erroneous. This is quite aside from surcharges for overdue payment.

In practice, the lifting of exchange controls has not caused a major change in habits. The private estates of French households contain very few foreign assets and are mostly made up of transferable securities and property. In any case, the soundness of the franc represents the best defence against the flight of savings.

Endnotes

(1) In 1987, France had the highest amount of income as a percentage of gross domestic product collected by the social security system of any of the OECD countries.

(2) VAT is a French invention, dating from 1954.

(3) An "extra-reduced" tax rate of 2.1 percent is applied to medicines.

(4) It bears on the algebraic sum of the various income categories, net of any allowances and deductions particular to each income category and deducting the burden from overall income.

(5) "Ficticious rents" is a method of calculating tax due on a property even if that property is not rented.

(6) In 1987, households exempted from income tax received 21 percent of total declared income, as against 11 percent in 1983. Tax on income is thus a progressive one, concentrating on a limited number of contributors. In 1986, 1 percent of households declaring incomes paid 27 percent of taxes, while 10 percent paid 64 percent.

(7) Around 1 percent of profit-making concerns (2,000 companies) pay 60 percent of corporate tax.

(8) The 1.5 percent ceiling is applied to estates worth more than FF40 million ($7 million).

(9) Socialist member of parliament.

Appendices

Appendix 1.1

The demographic situation in France

Changes in population

Year	Population on Jan.1 ('000)	Births	Deaths	Natural increase	Net migration	Overall increase	Birth rate	Death rate	Infant mortality
1964	48,059	874	516	358	185	543	18.1	10.7	23.4
1970	50,528	848	540	308	180	488	16.7	10.6	18.2
1975	52,600	745	560	185	14	198	14.1	10.6	13.8
1980	53,731	800	547	253	44	297	14.9	10.2	10.0
1985	55,062	768	552	216	0	216	14.0	10.0	8.3
1986	55,278	778	547	232	0	232	14.1	9.9	8.0
1987	55,510	768	527	240	0	240	13.8	9.5	7.85
1988	55,750	770	524	246	0	246	13.8	9.4	7.7
1989*	56,303	765	529	236	0	236	13.6	9.4	7.5
1990*	56,536	762	529	233	0	233	13.5	9.4	7.2

Source: INSEE

Appendix 1.2

Breakdown of the French population by age group

Age group	1980	1985	1986	1987	1988	1989
0-19 yrs	30.6	29.1	28.8	28.5	28.2	27.9
20-59 yrs	52.4	52.8	52.9	53.0	53.1	53.1
60 yrs+	17.0	18.1	18.3	18.5	18.7	19.0
	100.0	100.0	100.0	100.0	100.0	100.0

Source: INSEE

Appendix 1.3

France - Demographic indicators, 1981-1990 (*)

	1981	1982	1983	1984	1985	1986	1987	1988	1989	1990 (p)
Births ('000)	805.00	797.00	749.00	760.00	768.00	778.00	768.00	771.00	765.00	762.00
Deaths ('000)	555.00	543.00	560.00	542.00	552.00	547.00	527.00	525.00	529.00	529.00
Natural increase ('000)	251.00	254.00	189.00	217.00	216.00	232.00	240.00	247.00	236.00	233.00
Net migration ('000)	56.00	37.00	16.00	14.00	0	0	0	20.00	50.00	—
Overall change ('000)	306.00	291.00	205.00	232.00	216.00	232.00	240.00	267.00	287.00	233.00
Birth rate (per 1,000 inhabitants)	14.90	14.70	13.70	13.90	14.00	14.10	13.80	13.80	13.60	13.50
Death rate (per 1,000 inhabitants)	10.30	10.00	10.20	9.90	10.00	9.90	9.50	9.40	9.40	9.40
Infant mortality rate (per 1,000 live births)	9.70	9.50	9.10	8.30	8.30	8.00	7.80	7.80	7.50	7.20
Fertility rate (per female)	1.94	1.91	1.79	1.81	1.82	1.84	1.82	1.82	1.81	1.80
Life expectancy (male)	70.40	70.70	70.70	71.20	71.30	71.50	72.00	72.30	72.40	72.70
Life expectancy (female)	78.50	78.90	78.80	79.30	79.40	79.70	80.30	80.50	80.60	80.90
Marriages ('000)	315.00	312.00	301.00	281.00	269.00	266.00	265.00	271.00	280.00	288.00
Marriage rate (per 1,000 inhabitants)	5.80	5.70	5.50	5.10	4.90	4.80	4.80	4.90	5.00	5.00
Population (at year-end) ('000)	54,335.00	54,626.00	54,831.00	55,062.00	55,278.00	55,510.00	55,750.00	56,017.00	56,303.00	56,536.00
Under-20s (at year-end) (%)	30.00	29.80	29.40	29.10	28.80	28.50	28.20	27.90	27.70	27.40
65 years or over (at year-end) (%)	13.50	13.20	12.90	12.80	13.10	13.30	13.60	13.80	14.00	14.20

(*) Estimates based on the 1982 census. This proviso mainly applicable to the entries 'net migration', 'overall change,' and 'total population'.

Appendix 1.3 b

Year of
Birth

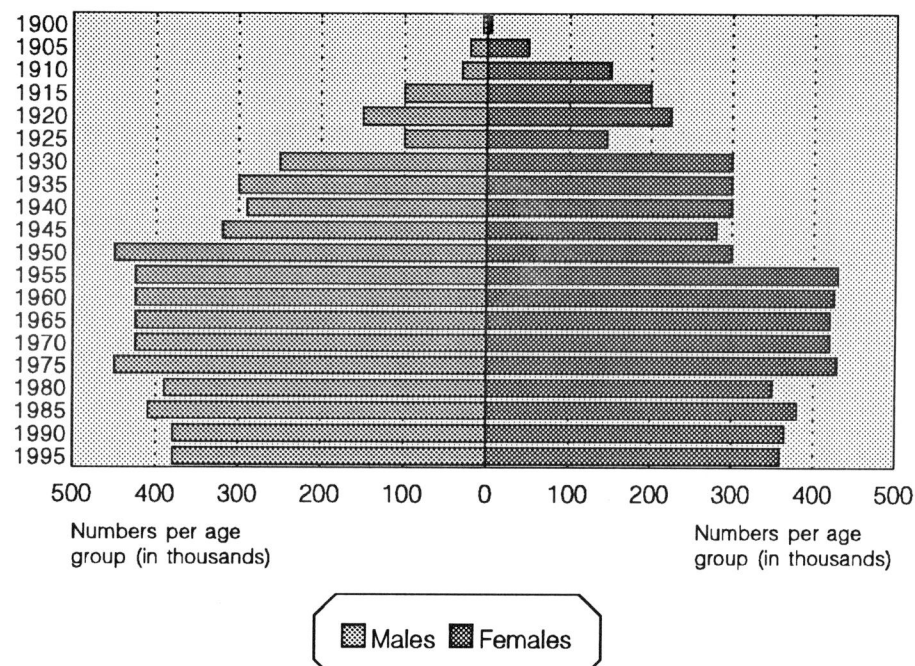

Numbers per age
group (in thousands)

Numbers per age
group (in thousands)

■ Males ■ Females

Appendix 1.4					
Privatisations — results of the public offerings					
Asset	Date of public offering	Price of public offering	No. of shareholders[1]	Total value of shares subscribed to by the public[2] (in FF m)	No. of shares per person
Saint-Gobain	02/11/86	310	1,547,044	6,249.6	10.0
Paribas	19/01/87	405	3,804,834	5,961.8	4.0
Sogenal	09/03/87	125	853,176	618.8	6.0
BTP	06/04/87	130	1,030,305	133.9	1.0
BIMP	21/04/87	140	523,640	116.7	1.5
CCF	27/04/87	107	1,650,000	1,693.2	10.0
CGE[3]	11/05/87	290	2,237,000	8,265	10.0
Havas	25/05/87	500	730,000	1,147.2	3.0
Société Générale	15/06/87	407	2,298,630	9,100	10.0
TF1	25/06/87	165	415,741	1,260	10.0

[1] *Individuals only (ordres A)*

[2] *Shares subscribed to by individuals multiplied by the price of the public offering*

[3] *Capital increase included*

Source: J.J. Burgard, 'La Banque en France', 1989

Appendix 3.1

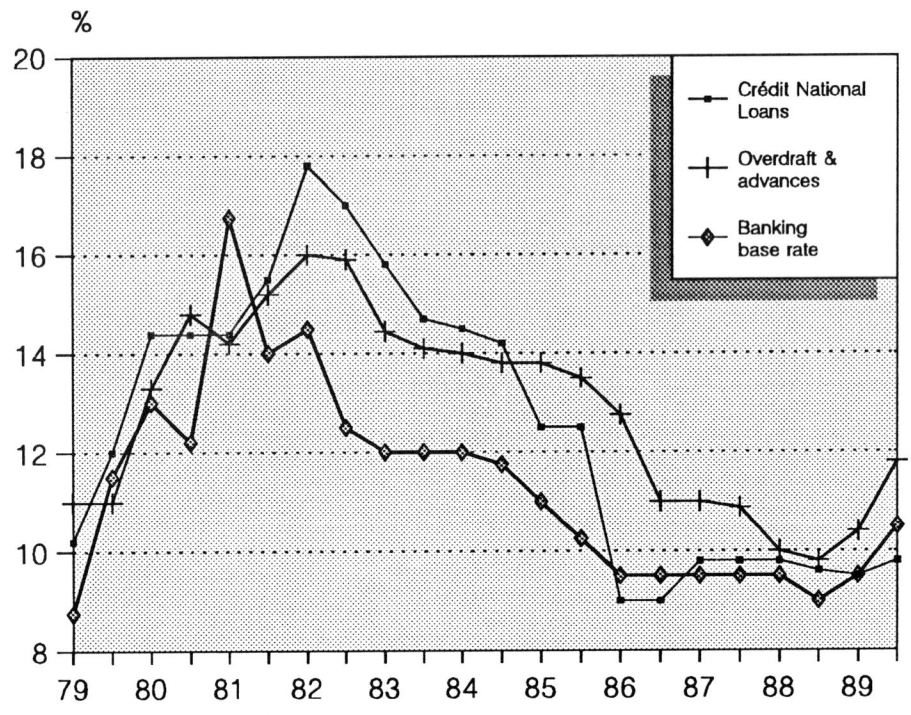

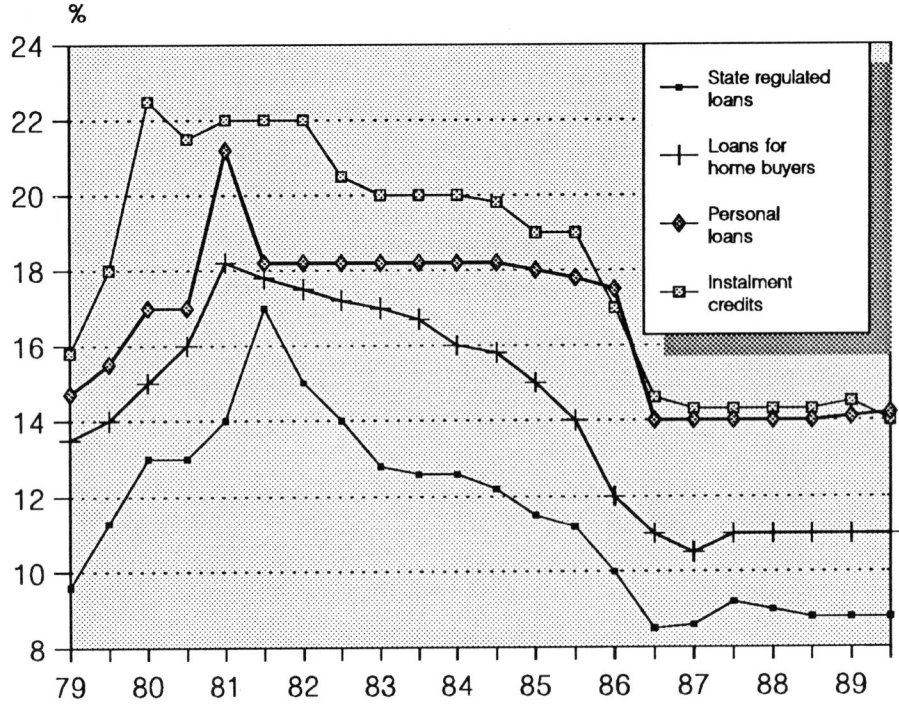

Appendix 4.1

Changes in the funding structure of AFB-member banks (in %)

	1980	1989
Customer funds	76	52
Interbank funding (net)	17	7
Certificates of deposit	—	15
Bonds	3	15
Own funds and reserves	4	11
Total	100	100

Source: Commission Bancaire

Appendix 4.2

Top ten leader managers to French issuers in 1990

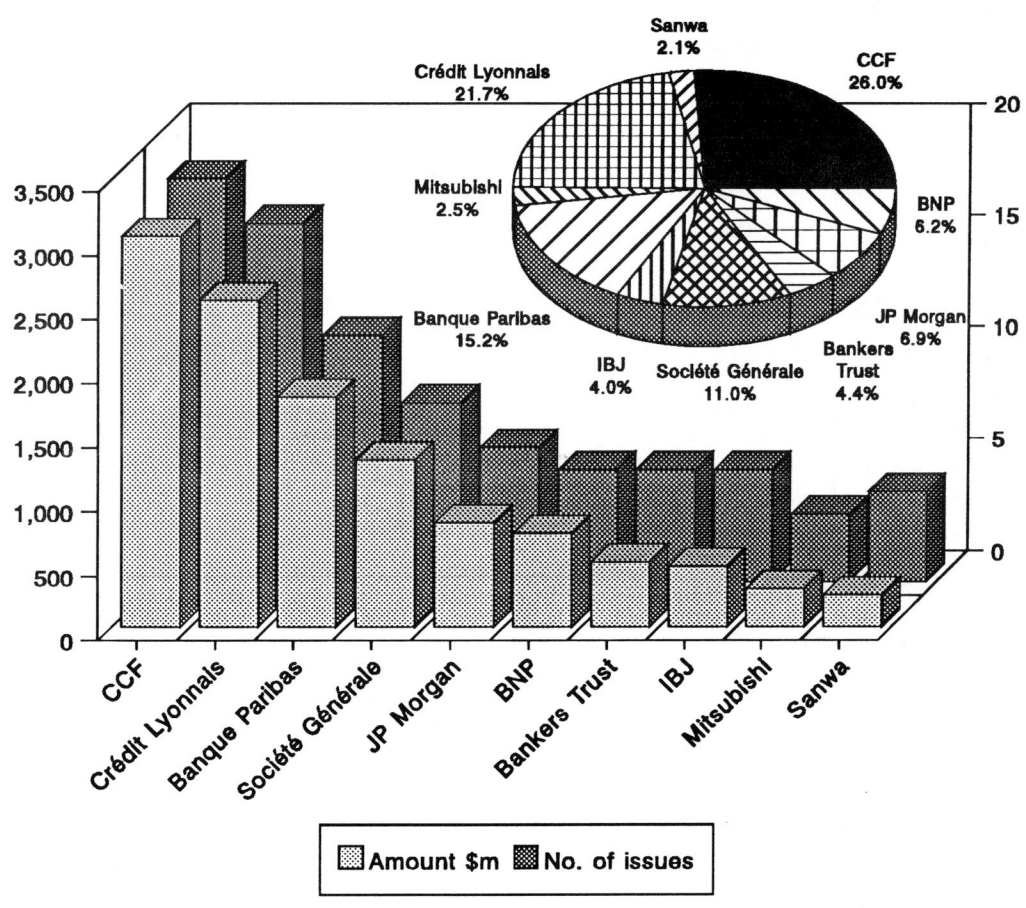

Source: European Bondware

Appendices

Appendix 4.3

World ranking of French banks by euro-bond issues

1989	1990		Amount ($ m)	No. of issues	Share (%)
10	10	Banque Paribas	5,562.7	24	3.2
13	24	CCF	4,538.1	25	2.6
19	17	Crédit Lyonnais	3,289.6	20	1.9
31	31	Société Générale	1,687.2	10	1.0
36	26	BNP	1,538.9	9	0.9

Source: European Bondware

Appendix 4.4

Mergers and acquisitions

Ranking		Adviser	No. of deals(2)	Value(1) (in FF bn)	Average (1)/(2) (in FF bn)
1990	1989				
1	1	Lazard Frères	38	120.7	3.17
2	9	Banexi (BNP)	84	49.6	0.59
3	6	Crédit Lyonnais	61	33.2	0.54
4	2	Paribas	54	31.7	0.58
5	4	Goldman Sachs	11	28.6	2.60
6	12	J.P. Morgan	12	25.7	2.14
7	—	Crédit Suisse*	24	22.1	0.92
8	10	Salomon Brothers	12	21.9	1.82
9	—	Lehman Brothers	6	20.7	3.45
10	7	CCF	22	16.2	0.73
11	5	Morgan Stanley	5	15.4	3.08
12	14	Demachy Worms	10	14.5	1.45
13	3	SG Warburg	6	13.4	2.23
14	—	Rothschild & Cie.	11	10.5	0.95
15	—	James Capel (CF)	7	10.5	1.50
16	—	BGP-SIB	24	10.1	0.42

Source: Fusions et Acquisitions magazine

* = Crédit Suisse First Boston

Appendix 5.1

Some legal considerations concerning companies with differing statutes.

1. The state-owned sector includes first, the Caisse Nationale de Prévoyance (which is linked to the Caisse des Dépôts et Consignations) and second, three state-controlled companies, UAP, AGF and GAN.

2. *Sociétés Anonymes* are public companies and as such are subject to Company Law as well as to the requirements set out in the Insurance Code (L.III Articles R322, 5 to 11).

3. The mutuals must set up a capital fund whose amount is fixed by government decree. Since 1989, they have all been subject to the same statute.

4. Foreign companies must be licensed to underwrite risks in France. They are subject to French law for all their activities there. They can adopt various statutory forms but generally they retain the statute of the parent company and operate as branches in France.

5. "1945 Mutual Benefit Insurance Companies" are organisations subject to the *Code de la Mutualité* and are supervised by the minister responsible for social security.

6. Finally, *tontines* are subject to Articles R322, 139 to 159 of the Insurance Code. Only two *tontines*[1] remain and their income is not significant.

Appendix 5.2

How the profession is organised

As of 1991, the Fédération Française des Sociétés d'Assurance (FFSA) which represents the profession included 332 insurance companies that accounted for 80 percent of the overall insurance market. The remaining 20 percent is split between the Groupement des Entreprises Mutuelles d'Assurances (GEMA) (whose 17 non-intermediary mutual company members are particularly strong in car insurance with some 43 percent of the market) and the Mutualité Agricole. There is also a Syndicat National des Sociétés d'Assistance. Some companies do not adhere to any professional organisation.

Numerous technical groups and specialised associations have also grown up around the profession (See alphabetical list in general appendix).

About 100 foreign companies (branches) are represented by the Union des Sociétés Etrangères d'Assurances.

---

[1] *Tontines* are associations of savers with a common insurance objective. Membership is restricted.

Appendix 7.1a					
The top 20 life insurance companies in 1989					
1989 Ranking	Group	Direct business in France (in FF m)	Of which:		Group's market share(%)
1	UAP	23,563.3	UAP Vie,	23,552.2	12.1
			Vigilance Vie	11.1	
2	Prédica	21,625.4	—		11.1
3	CNP	19,694.1 (22,752.3)	CNP	13,665.9 (13,665.9)	10.1 (11.7)
			Préviposte	2,865.0	
			Ecureuil Vie	2,126.3	
			Investissement Trésor Vie	1,046.9	
4	AGF	14,187.7	AGF	14,187.3	7.3
			Arcalis	1.4	
5	Abeille Vie	13.187.7	Abeille Vie	11,729.2	6.8
			La Hénin Vie	1,227.4	
			ACEP	230.8	
6	GAN	12,422.1	GAN Vie	7,168.2	6.4
			GAN Capitalisation	1,492.7	
			SOCAPI	3,127.4	
			Caisse Fraternelle d'Epargne	124.7	
			Caisse Fraternelle Vie	52.6	
			Cofassur Vie	6.5	
7	AXA-Midi	11,286.2	Vie Nouvelle	3,821.2	5.8
			Mutuelles Unies Vie	2,039.3	
			Axiva	1,735.1	
			Paternelle Vie	1,155.0	
			Trans Expansion Vie (TEV)	1,393.8	
			Présence Vie	1,141.8	
8	Ass. Fédérales Vie	5,944.7	—		3.1

1989 Ranking	Group	Direct business in France (in FF m)	Of which:		Group's market share(%)
9	Cardif	5,575.3	Cardif	5,161.1	2.9
			Hélios	414.2	
10	Natio Vie	5,088.1	—		2.6
11	Soravie (Groupama)	4,599.2	—		2.4
12	Sogécap	4,471.6	Sogécap	4,402.2	2.3
			Sogénal Vie	269.4	2.3
13	Mut. du Mans Ass.	3,691.8	Mutuelles du Mans. Ass. Vie	3,690.1	1.9
			Télévie	1.7	1.9
14	Generali	3,540.3	Generali France	1,648.0	1.8
			Fédération Continentale	1,892.3	
15	ACM Vie	3,532.9	—		1.8
16	Athéna	3,296.4	GPA Vie	1,922.3	1.7
			PFA Vie	1,123.7	
			Coparc	185.3	
			Proxima	65.1	
17	Allianz	3,108.8	RM VIA	1,636.4	1.6
			Rhin et Moselle Vie	104.1	
			VIA Assurances Vie	334.5	
			Allianz France Vie	155.0	
			Cie. Générale de Prévoyance	872.5	
			Cie. de Gestion et de Prévoyance	1.3	
18	Fructivie	3,089.6	Fructivie	2,838.1	1.6
			Prospérité	103.4	
			Fructuavie	148.1	
19	La Mondiale	2,352.4	—		1.2
20	GMF Vie	2,247.6	—		1.2
	Total	169,559.4			87.3

Source: L'Argus

Appendix 7.1b

Profitability and solvency of life insurance companies (1989)

Groups	Balance sheet results/total premiums (%)	Own funds/mathematical reserves (%)
UAP	+2.3	4.1
Predica	+1.7	3.4
CNP	+2.9	7.6
AGF	+9.9	6.9
Abeille Vie	+2.1	3.3
GAN	+6.0	6.9
AXA-Midi Assurances	+1.8	6.4
Assurances Fédérales Vie	+1.6	3.1
Cardif	+1.4	3.2
Natio Vie	+2.9	3.9
Soravie	+2.6	4.4
Sogécap	+2.1	4.7
Mutuelles du Mans Ass.	+11.1	10.5
Generali	+6.4	7.9
ACM Vie	+1.3	2.4
Athéna	+9.6	8.4
Allianz	+4.2	8.9
Fructivie	+1.2	2.0
La Mondiale	+10.9	8.7
GMF Vie	+4.5	3.9
Total	+3.7	5.5

Source: L'Argus

Appendix 7.1c

The 20 largest general insurers in 1989

1989 Ranking	Group	Direct business in France (FF/m)	Of which:				1989 Market share %
1	AXA-Midi Assurances	17613.0	Mutuelles Unies MPG Mut. St-Christophe Mut. Générale RD Drouot Ass. Nouvelle Mutuelle Présence Ass.	2584.3 816.6 127.3 35.6 5198.2 147.8 4112.3	Paternelle RD Prévoyance Mut. Seine et Rhone Mut. de Marseille Défense Civile Mut. de l'Est Mut. de l'Ouest	2321.5 1896.4 225.0 56.7 45.2 43.1 3.0	10.3
2	Groupama	16737.4	CCMA	12471.7	SAMDA	4265.7	9.8
3	UAP	16414.9	UAP IARD Avenir	16247.7 68.3	Navigation et Transp.	98.9	9.6
4	AGF	11632.7	AGF IART	11632.7	CAP	0.0	6.8
5	MACIF	8474.2	MACIF	8474.2			5.0
6	GAN	8445.4	GAN IA GAN Santé	7807.8 461.1	Contingency SFPJ	138.0 38.5	5.0
7	Mut. du Mans Ass.	8416.6	Mut. du Mans Ass. DAS Finistere	7676.7 478.1 52.7	SACREN Norman Ins.	144.1 65.0	4.9
8	GMF	6250.9	GMF GMF Prot. Jurid.	5691.6 30.2	Sauvegarde	529.1	3.7
9	MAAF	5970.3	MAAF	5970.3			3.5
10	Athéna	5869.6	PFA Soc. Lilloise d'Ass.	3768.7 1146.1	GPA Soc. Franc. de Recours	939.4 15.4	3.4
11	Allianz	5638.5	Allianz France VIA Ass. IARD Rurale	1443.9 2339.6 48.7	Rhin et Moselle AF CIAM 2 Languedoc	1288.2 62.8 255.3	3.3
12	Groupe Victoire	5499.6	Abeille Ass. AMIS La Paix Nieuw Rotterdam	4913.4 141.5 22.5 81.4	Colonia Nordstern Assurop	212.9 55.2 72.7	3.2
13	MAIF	4952.1	MAIF	4769.1	Filia MAIF	183.0	2.9
14	Generali	4127.9	Concorde Equité Européenne de PJ	2939.3 565.4 20.5	La Lutece Cie Cont. de'Ass.	451.1 151.5	2.4
15	Matmut	3039.8	Matmut	3039.8			1.8
16	Groupe Azur	2910.6	GAMF Céres Occidentale de PJ	2595.1 20.8 13.4	Strasbourgeoise SOCAD	281.2 0.1	1.7
17	La France Ass.	2637.2	La France Ass.	2637.2			1.5
18	SMABTP	2364.6	SMABTP	2184.0	SAGENA	180.6	1.4
19	Le Continent Ass.	1690.9	Le Continent Ass.	1426.8	Union Gén. du Nord	250.4	1.0
20	Winterthur	1499.6	Winterthur	1499.6			0.9
	Total	140185.8					82.1

Source: L'Argus

Appendix 7.1d

Profitability and solvency in general insurance (1989)

Group	Balance sheet income/total premiums (%)	Own funds/total premiums (%)
AXA-Midi Assurance	+10.7	81.7
Groupama	+11.0	91.5
UAP	+3.0	16.8
AGF	+5.2	29.0
MACIF	+2.8	18.8
GAN	+6.8	25.5
Mutuelles du Mans Ass.	+7.4	36.4
GMF	+5.3	35.9
MAAF	+0.8	25.4
Athéna	+7.0	36.9
Allianz	+4.7	35.3
Groupe Victoire	+11.8	62.0
MAIF	+5.3	36.3
Generali	+1.9	20.2
MatMut	+8.0	50.8
Groupe Azur	+10.1	58.0
La France Assurances	+1.4	13.9
SMABTP	+1.3	104.1
Le Continent Ass.	+8.0	34.3
Winterthur	-122.5	9.1
Total	+6.3	44.5

Source: L'Argus

Appendix 7.2

Market shares (per product)

Total life insurance (market share in % of premiums)

	1989	1990
CNP	12.0	11.2
AGF	8.9	8.6
UAP	7.5	8.0
Abeille Paix Vie	8.2	6.9
GAN	5.5	5.8
Prédica	5.9	4.8
Natio Vie	2.4	2.9
Soravie	3.0	2.6
Mutuelles du Mans	2.7	2.5
Assurances Fédérales	2.3	2.5
Cardif	2.3	2.2
Total premiums in FF bn	145.2	167.4

Source: Direction des Assurances, Commission de Contrôle des Assurances

Appendix 7.2 a

Personal life insurance

(market share in % of premiums)

	1985	1988	1989	1990
UAP Vie	13.8	12.7	12.6	13.9
AGF	19.7	16.3	15.2	12.4
CNP	16.9	16.1	14.5	11.5
GAN Vie	7.6	7.1	8.1	8.5
Ecureuil Vie	—	—	2.0	5.9
Préviposte	—	—	n/a	4.5
Mutuelles du Mans Vie	3.2	3.6	2.8	2.8
Abeille Vie	—	—	5.1	2.7
GPA Vie	1.7	4.1	3.4	2.5
GMF Vie	7.4	4.2	4.0	2.3
Vie Nouvelle (AXA)	—	—	3.0	2.6
Société Suisse	3.2	2.6	2.5	2.0
Total premiums (in FF bn)	24.7	33.3	37.9	50.4

Source: Direction des Assurances, Commission de Contrôle des Assurances

Appendix 7.2 b

Wholesale life insurance
(market share in % of premiums)

	1985	1988	1989	1990
Abeille Vie*	5.9	7.2	10.2	9.4
CNP	12.6	9.3	8.0	8.3
Prédica	—	4.8	9.1	7.8
AGF Vie	8.1	6.5	6.5	6.9
UAP Vie	5.9	5.2	4.8	5.1
Natio Vie	—	4.8	3.8	4.6
Soravie	7.6	7.0	4.3	3.9
Assurances Fédérales	—	3.5	4.0	—
GAN Vie	6.8	4.0	3.6	3.5
Sogécap	4.1	3.5	2.9	3.5
Axiva	n/a	n/a	5.1	n/a
Total premiums	30.3	71.9	93.9	103.1

Called Abeille-Paix Vie since 1989

Source: Direction des Assurances, Commission de Contrôle des Assurances

Appendix 7.2 c

Capitalisation (market share in % of premiums)

	1985	1988	1989	1990
UAP Vie	45.0	27.6	25.7	34.0
Prédica	—	32.5	24.0	13.2
Préviposte	—	—	5.2	7.3
GAN Capi	8.2	3.3	2.7	4.5
Assurances Fédérales	—	4.7	4.6	3.9
AGF Vie	6.1	3.3	3.1	3.9
Epargne de France	6.1	2.4	2.6	3.5
Ecureuil Vie	—	—	2.5	3.3
Cardif	13.9	5.1	3.7	3.2
Socapi	1.6	1.1	2.6	2.4
Fructivie	4.8	3.8	2.8	1.6
Natio Vie	—	2.5	2.8	1.2
Total premiums in FF bn	9.3	42.4	55.4	39.1

Source: Direction des Assurances, Commission de Contrôle des Assurances

Appendix 7.2 d

Car insurance (market share in % of premiums)

	1988	1989	1990
MACIF*	9.3	10.1	10.6
UAP lard	7.7	7.3	7.1
MAAF*	6.3	6.5	6.7
GMF*	6.5	6.5	6.2
AXA	—	—	5.9
MAIF*	5.1	4.9	5.4
Groupama**	n/a	5.7	5.4
GAN	4.4	—	—
AGF lard	4.1	4.2	4.2
Mutuelles du Mans lard	3.9	3.9	4.0
Samda	3.7	3.7	3.6
MatMut*	3.7	3.8	3.8
Total premiums in FFbn	64.0	66.6	69.4

* Non-intermediary mutual companies

** Caisse Centrale des Mutuelles Agricoles

Appendix 7.2 e

Damage to property (market share in % of premiums)

	1988	1989	1990
UAP lard	10.2	10.1	10.0
Groupama	5.9	7.9	7.9
AGF lard	7.9	7.8	7.8
Drouot	3.2	3.3	7.0*
Présence	2.8	2.8	—
GAN lard	4.9	5.1	5.0
Mutuelles du Mans lard	4.3	4.2	4.0
Abeille Assurances	3.5	3.7	3.7
MACIF	n/a	2.5	2.9
Samda	2.6	2.7	2.8
MAIF	2.8	2.8	2.7
Total premiums in FF bn	41.62	43.41	45.20

* AXA Assurances lard

Source: Direction des Assurances, Commission de Contrôle des Assurances

Appendix 7.2 f

Bodily injury (market share in % of premiums)

	1988	1989	1990
UAP	13.4	13.4	13.7
AGF	12.7	12.6	12.5
Groupama	7.8	12.3	12.0
AXA Assurances Iard	—	7.5	n/a
Mutuelles du Mans	6.4	6.1	6.0
GAN	5.6	5.3	5.7
Abeille	3.5	3.4	3.6
La France	4.5	4.3	3.0
Lloyd Continental (France)	2.6	2.4	2.5
Drouot*	3.3	3.2	3.1
Mutuelles Unies*	2.3	2.3	2.3
Total premiums in FF bn	28.92	31.83	34.40

* Companies integrated into AXA Assurances Iard

Source: Direction des Assurances, Commission de Contrôle des Assurances

Appendix 7.3

The workforce and tied agents employed by the main French and foreign groups

	Salaried employees*	Tied agents
UAP	17,000	1,600
AGF	12,805	1,600
AXA	8,300	4,000
Victoire	12,600	1,240
Groupama	11,950	0
GAN	8,555	1,400
Groupe Athéna	8,092	950
MACIF	5,200	0
Mutuelles du Mans	4,989	1,200
GMF	4,368	0
Via-Rhin et Moselle	2,381	1,500
CNP	1,800	0
Prédica	93	0
Generali France	360	2,500
Allianz	463	315
Norwich	432	791

* Insurance business within France

Source: Annual reports

Appendix 7.4

Real estate holdings of some French companies (estimates)

	UAP	GAN	AGF	AXA	Victoire	Groupe Athéna	Mutuelles du Mans
Estimated value of holdings (in FF bn)	40-50	30	22-28	40	12.5	12-15	4.2
Balance sheet value of holdings (in FF bn)	23	13	13	n/a	5.0	4	2.6
Total square metres owned (in '000)	3,560	1,200	1,575	2,200	465.5	n/a	410.0
Geographical breakdown (%):							
Paris	34	—	56	—	58.0	—	—
Paris region	41	86	29	94	29.0	92	55.0
Provinces	25	14	15	6	13.0	8	45.0

Source: Le Journal de l'Assurance

Appendix 9.1 a

	Fixed rate (in FF bn)	Variable or revisable rate (in FF bn)	Total	Fixed rate (in %)	Variable or revisable rate (in %)	Total
Convertible loans:						
in equities	18.9	0.3	19.2	98.4	1.6	100
Straight	12.2	0.3	12.5	97.6	2.4	100
With equity warrants attached OCABSA and OCABSAR	6.7	—	6.7	100.0	—	100
In *certificats d'investisse-ment*(CI) with CI warrants	—	—	—	—	100.0	100
Loans redeemable in shares (ORA)	1.4	—	1.4	100.0	—	100
Loans with warrants						
With equity warrants:	7.8	—	7.8	1000	—	100
(Non-redeemable (OBSA and OCABSA):	5.3	—	5.3	100.0	—	100
Buy-back option (OCABSAR)	2.5	—	2.5	100.0	—	100

With *certificat d'investissement* warrants					
Loans with a redemption premium	0.1	—	0.1	100.0	—	100
Loans with an exchange option	1.0	7.1	8.1	12.3	87.7	100
Issues of floating rate notes					
Undated (TSDI)	0.2	5.9	6.1	3.3	96.7	100
Redeemable (TSR)	14.4	2.3	16.7	86.2	13.8	100
State loans	107.5	10.2	117.7	91.3	8.7	100
Other loans	147.2	21.4	168.6	87.3	12.7	100
Exercise of bond warrants	—	0.2	0.2	—	100.0	100
Total	291.8	47.1	338.9	86.1	13.9	100
Total (excluding state loans)	184.3	36.9	221.2	83.3	16.7	100

Source: Commission des Opérations de Bourse

Appendix 9.1 b

Bond issues (gross)

	1986	1987	1988	1989	1990
Convertible or redeemable as shares	0.3	0.4	6.0	4.3	6.1
With equity warrants attached	2.4	2.9	0.4	1.6	0.3
With bond warrants attached	2.8	4.5	3.7	0.9	—
Others	94.5	92.2	89.9	93.2	93.6
of which are state loans	40.7	27.4	28.7	29.2	34.6
Total (in %)	100.0	100.0	100.0	100.0	100.0

Source: Commission des Opérations de Bourse

Appendix 9.1 c

Breakdown by beneficiary sector of straight bond, convertible bond, bond with warrants and *titres participatifs* issues (structure in %)

	1986	1987	1988	1989	1990
Public utilities	13.7	12.4	11.5	10.6	15.2
Industrial and trading sectors	14.1	16.6	12.8	16.0	16.8
Other financial institutions	24.3	32.8	37.0	38.4	41.1
Administration	47.5	36.8	37.0	38.4	41.1
State	40.2	27.3	28.5	29.1	34.1
Local authorities	7.3	9.5	8.5	9.3	6.4)
Foreign	0.4	1.4	1.1	1.8	1.1
Total (in %)	100.0	100.0	100.0	100.0	100.0
Total (in FF bn)	351.5	296.4	346.5	329.8	339.0

Source: Commission des Opérations de Bourse

Appendix 9.1 d

Changes in money market securities

	1986		1987		1988		1989		1990	
	(1)	(2)	(1)	(2)	(1)	(2)	(1)	(2)	(1)	(2)
Exchequer bills	374	24	434	90	450	104	520	151	550	137
(Jumbo) Certificates of deposit	59	37	193	154	330	254	515	393	862	680
Commercial paper	24	22	41	39	63	61	129	124	159	156
Specialist financial institution and finance company bonds	28	2	35	8	58	18	73	27	104	37
Total	485	85	703	291	901	437	1,237	695	1,675	1,010

(1) Total under management in FF bn

(2) Held under management by resident non-financial agents (including OPCVMs)

Source: Monetary statistics, Banque de France

Appendix 10.1

Big Bang in Paris broker-dealers (September 1991)

Broker-Dealers	Shareholders	Participations (%)
Alphabourse	Banque pour l'Industrie Francaise (GAN)	100.00
Alboyneau, Labouret, Ollivier	Banque Bruxelles Lambert France — France BBL (ex Banque Louis Dreyfus)	90.00
Bacot, Allain	Warburg Group	99.50
Purex de Bouzet	Banque Nationale de Paris	75.00
Chevreux de Virieu	Banque Indosuez	92.00
De Cholet, Dupont	Crédit Lyonnais	40.00
	Nippon Life	5.00
	UAP	5.00
	Commerzbank AG	5.00
De Compiegne	Banque Parisienne d'Investissement et d'Arbitrage	85.00
Courcoux, Bouvet	Paribas UK Holding Ltd	100.00
Delahaye, Ripault	Genefinance (Société Générale)	99.91
DG Bourse	DG Finance	100.00
Paris et Province:		
Ducatel Duval	Société de Banque Suisse	89.46
Pouget	James Capel International	100.00
Dupont Denant	Domibourse (Crédit National)	51.00
Dynabourse	Segespar Titres	99.92
Elysées Bourse	Crédit Commercial de France	100.00
Fauchier-Magnan	Caisse des Dépôts et Consignations	35.00
Durant des Aulnois (holding company)	Union des Assurances de Paris	15.00
	Kleinwort-Benson Ltd	10.00
Ferri, Germe	Crédit Foncier de France	35.50
	Caisse des Dépôts et Consignations	10.00
	Union des Assurances de Paris	6.60
Finacor Bourse	Finacor	24.50
	Altus Finance	51.00
	Viel	24.30
FIP Bourse	Premium (BIP subsidiary)	59.40
Francois-Dufour-Kervern	Banque de Neuflize, Schlumberger, Mallet	67.40
	Caisse des Dépôts et Consignations	4.00

Broker-Dealers	Shareholders	Participations (%)
	Union des Assurances de Paris	4.00
	Nomura International Ltd	8.00
Coy, Hauvette	Bred	100.00
(Hamant) NMB Bourse	NMB Bank	100.00
Hayaux du Tilly	Segespar Titres	10.00
	SA des Vallées de Brunoy	20.00
Magnin	Omnium Industriel et Financier (Filiale BUE)	100.00
Massonaud, Fontenay	Amsterdam Rotterdam Bank	76.40
Meeschaert, Rousselle	Compagnie du Midi	100.00
Melendes	Banque Oppenheim	50.00
	Banque Pierson	50.00
Meunier de la Fournière		
Michelez le Febre	Groupe VIEL	43.25
Bertrand Michel	Segespar Titres	87.11
J.P. Morgan	Morgan Guaranty International Finance Corporation	100.00
Nouailhetas	Groupe Pallas	95.00
Oddo	Compagnie Financière du Phénix	25.00
	Instituto Bancario San Paolo di Torino	8.80
	Caisse des Dépôts et Consignations (& Daiwa: 5%)	7.00
Didier Philippe	Bankers Trust	49.00
Puget Mahe	Barclays de Zoete Wedd Holding	97.00
Richard	Banque Pallas France	59.95
Paris and provincial:	Société Lyonnaise de Banque	10.00
	SDR du SUD EST	8.60
	SDR Centrest	8.20
	SDR Sodecco	8.20
	Marusan	5.00
Schelcher Prince	Compagnie Parisienne de Réescompte	100.00
Sellier	National Westminster Bank	99.80
Soulie Tellier	Via Banque Société de Banque et de Financement*	16.30
Pinatton	Petercom	21.00
Independents: Leven-Chaussier, Wargny.		
* plus Navigation Mixte 51 percent		
Source: Société des bourses françaises		

Appendix 10.2

Sociétés de bourse / brokers

Alphabourse SA	10 boulevard Haussmann, Paris, 75009	(1) 42 47 70 00
Auboyneau, Labouret, Ollivier SA	23 boulevard Poissonnière, Paris, 75002	(1) 42 33 21 80
Bacot, Allain, Warburg SA	65 rue de Courcelles, Paris, 75008	(1) 48 88 30 30
Boscher SA	28 rue Drouot, Paris, 75009	(1) 40 22 15 15
P. du Bouzet SA	15 boulevard Poissonnière, Paris, 75002	(1) 40 22 19 92
BZW Puget Mahe SA	7 rue Drouot, Paris, 75009	(1) 40 22 85 85
CCF Elysées Bourse SA	10 Cité Paradis, Paris, 75010	(1) 40 22 66 66
Cheuvreux de Virieu SA	2 rue de Choissui, Paris, 75002	(1) 42 86 18 18
Courcoux, Dupont SA	3 rue de Gramont, Paris, 75002	(1) 44 77 15 15
B. de Compiègne SA	92 rue de Richelieu, Paris, 75002	(1) 42 96 66 16
Delahaye Ripault SA	178 rue Montmartre, Paris, 75008	(1) 40 41 38 00
Ducatel, Duval SA	178 rue de Peninièvre, Paris, 75002	(1) 40 17 68 68
Dufour, Lacarrière, Pouget SA [1]	8 rue Lavoisier, Paris, 75008	(1) 49 24 16 00
Dupont, Denant SA	42 rue Notre Dame des Victoires, Paris, 75002	(1) 40 2125 25
Dynabourse SA	3 rue Rossini, Paris, 75009	(1) 48 00 11 00
Fauchier Magnan, Durant des Aulnois SA	75 rue de Richelieu, Paris, 75002	(1) 40 15 25 25
Ferri, Ferri, Ferme SA	53 rue Vivienne, Paris, 75002	(1) 40 41 42 43
France Compensation Bourse [2]	52 Avenue des Champs-Elysées, Paris, 75008	(1) 40 74 15 15
FIP Bourse [3]	7 rue Bergère, Paris, 75009	(1) 40 22 14 15
François Dufour, Kervern SA	116 rue Réaumur, Paris, 75002	(1) 40 41 85 00

Gorgeu, Perquel, Krucker SA	11 rue des Filles Saint Thomas, Paris, 75002	(1) 40 20 67 67
Goy, Hauvette SA	142 rue Montmartre, Paris, 75002	(1) 42 33 44 56
Hayaux de Tilly et Cie	19 rue de Provence, Paris, 75009	(1) 42 46 82 76
J.P. Morgan SA	27 boulevard des Capucines, Paris, 75002	(1) 40 15 48 00
Leven, Chaussier SA	63 rue Sainte Anne, Paris, 75002	(1) 40 20 74 74
Magnin SA	89 rue de la Boetie, 75381, Paris Cédex 08	(1) 45 63 13 13
Massonaud, de Fontenay SA	8 rue du Sentier, Paris, 75002	(1) 40 39 56 00
Meeschaert, Rousselle SA	16 boulevard Montmartre, Paris, 75009	(1) 42 46 72 64
Melendes SA	10 rue du 4 septembre, Paris, 75002	(1) 42 86 30 00
Meunier, de La Fournière, Michelez, Le Febvre SA	46 rue de l'Echiquier, Paris, 75010	(1) 48 00 25 25
NMB Bourse SA [4]	20-22 rue de la Ville-l'Echiquier, Paris, 75008	(1) 42 66 01 57
Nouailhetas, Richard SA	8 rue Vivienne, Paris, 75002	(1) 42 61 53 62
Oddo et Cie	31 rue Saint Augustin, Paris, 75002	(1) 40 17 58 00
Dider Philippe SA	3 rue Taitbout, Paris, 75009	(1) 42 46 72 95
Pinatton et Cie	8 rue Auber, Paris, 75009	(1) 40 17 52 02
Saintoin, Roulet SA	36 rue de Louvre, Paris, 75001	(1) 40 39 17 17
Schelcher, Prince SA	10 rue du Faubourg Montmartre, Paris, 75002	(1) 48 01 16 16
Sellier SA	12 rue d'Uzes, Paris, 75002	(1) 42 33 51 01
Soulie, Tellier SA	3 rue Rossini, Paris, 75009	(1) 42 46 46 95
Wargny SA	9 rue du 4 septembre, Paris, 75002	(1) 42 86 14 14

[1] *JLP James Capel,* [2] *Finacor,* [3] *Ex Legrand-Legrand,* [4] *Ex Hamant.*

Appendix 11.1

Financial and property assets held by individuals

Age (of person being referred to)?	Current account	Payment card	Savings account ("A" or "Bleu")	Savings account ("B" or bank passbook)	Codevi: The industrial savings account	LEP: The people's savings account	Savings account (Total)	Home savings plan	Home savings account	Home savings (total)	Government stocks and bonds	SICAV — FCP	Equity (excluding SICAV)	Transferable securities (total)	Life assurance (valid)	Ownership of main residence	Ownership of another residence (second or other)	Housing (total)
less than 30 years	96	59	73	9	16	3	82	22	13	30	—	6	6	8	28	16	4	20
from 30 to 39	98	59	75	10	17	1	82	22	20	35	5	10	7	17	39	49	10	56
from 40 to 49	97	55	72	11	20	2	81	25	17	35	6	13	8	21	46	53	21	67
from 50 to 59	96	40	69	12	25	3	79	26	12	35	11	16	7	23	40	65	30	73
from 60 to 69	95	30	72	16	29	7	82	21	9	27	15	19	9	26	22	65	25	70
70 and over	86	15	76	21	23	10	83	10	3	13	16	13	7	22	11	55	18	60
Socio-professional category																		
Farmers	99	43	63	31	30	6	83	35	20	47	8	10	5	16	38	77	27	80
Craftsmen, retailers, company directors	97	43	71	12	24	1	78	28	21	42	11	17	13	25	53	66	32	74
Cadres	100	75	76	17	29	1	85	38	27	54	20	36	22	49	45	58	36	75
% of liberal professions included in Cadres	99	65	72	20	29	0	80	47	31	58	27	43	27	54	60	58	38	74
Middle professions	99	63	79	10	25	2	88	28	21	43	8	18	9	27	40	55	19	53
Employees	99	49	70	7	15	1	79	20	12	25	3	5	3	9	33	37	11	43
Workers	94	46	71	8	13	3	78	16	11	25	2	3	3	7	39	44	10	49
Retired	91	23	74	17	26	8	83	15	5	19	14	15	7	23	16	60	19	54
Others not working	86	26	69	13	19	9	77	12	5	15	12	10	5	17	13	38	15	44

Income of household (in 1985)																		
less than 30,000F	80	15	60	11	11	69	8	5	3	8	2	2	2	5	3	35	7	37
from 30,000 to under 50,000	87	20	65	12	15	76	7	9	4	12	4	2	1	7	12	41	10	45
from 50,000 to under 75,000	92	32	69	12	20	79	7	15	7	20	6	5	3	12	21	41	11	46
from 75,000 to under 100,000	96	40	74	13	21	83	5	19	10	27	5	9	3	13	32	50	15	56
from 100,000 to under 130,000	99	53	79	11	21	86	3	23	15	34	8	12	6	19	41	54	16	60
from 130,000 to under 200,000	100	60	80	13	25	87	2	23	20	42	12	19	11	29	41	66	24	74
from 200,000 to under 300,000	100	65	78	20	34	88	1	38	25	51	23	37	21	49	51	73	36	95
300,000 and over	100	75	76	22	37	83	0	41	31	67	34	52	34	58	56	74	57	92
Community of residence																		
Rural communities	94	41	72	16	23	83	6	19	16	31	7	8	4	15	31	72	16	76
Urban units 20,000	95	42	74	14	22	82	5	22	10	29	7	13	5	18	35	57	17	61
Urban units from 20,000 to 100,000	92	44	73	12	19	82	3	17	10	25	8	12	6	18	29	47	17	53
Urban units of over 100,000 (excluding Paris region)	94	44	75	11	20	82	3	22	12	29	10	14	9	23	31	43	18	49
Paris region 1 — City of Paris	97	43	69	13	25	77	2	23	15	32	10	18	9	24	30	44	21	54
City of Paris	97	45	67	12	25	78	4	22	8	26	17	20	15	30	24	26	30	46
Composition of household																		
Single person	89	28	66	15	22	77	7	15	6	19	9	10	6	16	13	38	13	43
Couple without children	95	40	73	13	27	82	4	21	11	28	13	18	9	26	30	61	24	67
Couple with 1 child	99	57	78	11	20	84	2	28	17	40	8	13	7	19	46	55	20	62
Couple with 2 children	99	62	81	9	15	87	1	23	21	39	6	13	9	21	49	61	19	69
Couple with 3 or more children	95	49	74	11	16	81	3	18	18	30	5	9	7	15	44	65	15	72
One parent families	96	42	67	10	16	78	2	13	8	20	4	6	2	11	25	29	11	37
Other households	96	38	74	20	27	83	10	29	11	36	12	15	8	22	29	56	22	62
Total	94	43	73	13	22	82	4	21	12	29	9	13	7	20	31	52	18	59

Source: Donnees Sociales, 1990

Appendix 11.2

Number of SICAVs in operation (at year end)

SICAV in operation	1989	1990
Total SIVAC	873	916
Short-term priority given to regularity of the liquidative value	107	105
Short-term, LY sensitive to fluctuations in price	64	62
Short-term money market	139	167
French bonds	186	186
Foreign bonds	7	7
French and foreign bonds	78	80
French equity	51	54
Foreign equity	9	14
French and foreign equity	70	78
Diversified French equity and bonds	26	26
Diversified foreign equity and bonds	2	2
Diversified French and foreign equity and bonds	134	135
of which — Monory or CEA	31	33
of which pension schemes	64	48
Credit institutions	697	734
Stock brokers	51	54
Sociétés de bourse	35	36
Specialised financial institutions	9	9
Insurance companies	75	78
Other management companies	6	5

Appendix 11.3

SICAVs in Operation

SICAVs in Operation	Year	1st Term	2nd Term	3rd Term	4th Term
SICAV Total	1988	663	696	724	772
	1989	793	822	841	872
Short-term, priority given to regularity of net asset value	1988	89	94	96	100
	1989	104	108	108	111
Short-term net asset value sensitive to fluctuations	1988	57	57	60	61
	1989	59	60	60	63
Short-term money market	1988	87	96	103	116
	1989	118	125	130	137
French bonds	1988	138	144	146	160
	1989	167	175	183	185
Foreign bonds	1988	6	6	6	7
	1989	8	7	7	7
French and foreign bonds	1988	49	51	53	58
	1989	63	65	69	76
French equities	1988	46	51	51	51
	1989	53	53	52	52
Foreign equities	1988	8	8	8	8
	1989	8	8	8	8
French and foreign equities	1988	54	55	60	61
	1989	64	64	65	68
Diversified French equities and bonds	1988	18	20	23	26
	1989	25	26	28	28
Diversified foreign equities and bonds	1988	2	2	2	2
	1989	2	2	2	2
French and foreign diversified	1988	109	112	116	122
	1989	122	129	129	135
of which: Monory law and CEAs	1988	30	31	31	32
	1989	34	34	33	33
of which: *Plans d'épargne retraite* (PER)	1988	64	73	76	82
	1989	83	86	85	86
Credit institutions	1988	495	525	547	581
	1989	593	618	628	650
Stock broking firms	1989	25	27	29	34
	1989	34	35	36	39
Special status institutions	1988	35	35	37	39
	1989	41	41	44	47
Specialist financial institutions	1988	—	—	—	—
	1989	—	1	5	5
Insurance companies	1988	61	62	64	71
	1989	71	73	73	75
Finance companies	1988	44	44	44	45
	1989	44	43	43	43
Other fund management companies	1988	3	3	3	2
	1989	10	11	12	13

Appendix 13.1 a — The Taxation of Savings

Products	Return	Capital gains	Liquidity	Security	Taxation	Observations
'Livret A' and 'Livret bleu' savings accounts	4.50%	0	4	4	Earnings net of tax.	Accounts cannot run concurrently. A ceiling of FF90,000 on deposits. One account per member of fiscal household. Attractive from the liquidity point of view.
'Livrets bancaires' and 'Livret B' savings accounts	4.50%	0	4	4	Personal income tax or standard deduction of 47%. Reduced to 38 percent as and from 1.1.90.	Can run concurrently with other accounts. No ceilings on deposits. Given the rate of return, the tax burden is heavy.
'Codevi', (the industrial savings account)	4.50%	0	4	4	Earnings net of tax.	Can run concurrently with other savings accounts. Ceiling on deposits of FF15,000 for a single person and FF30,000 for a married couple using two accounts. Same observation as for 'Livret A'.
'Livret d'Épargne Populaire', (The people's savings account)	4.50%+ bonus	0	4	4	Earnings net of tax.	Minimum annual return guaranteed, sometimes accompanied by a State bonus (at the moment 1%, giving a total net return of 5.50%). Aimed at those who are only lightly taxed. Ceiling on deposits of FF30,000. Can run concurrently with other savings accounts.
'Livret d'Épargne Entreprise', (The company savings account)	See observations	0	0	4	Earnings net of tax.	Returns are fixed at 75% of the rate offered on 'Livrets A'. It gives savers access to loans at a special rate. If no such loan is applied for, there is an extra remuneration equivalent to 30% of interest received. The account can only be closed after 2 years.
'Plan d'Épargne Logement', (The home savings plan)	6% with bonus	0	0	4	Earnings net of tax.	An attractive product for those wishing to apply for the loan part of this savings plan. A ceiling of FF400,000 on deposits. Otherwise of little appeal (see later).
'Compte d'Épargne Logement', (The home savings account)	2.75% + 5/11th of interest received	0	4	4	Earnings net of tax.	Exclusively aimed at those seeking a loan (see later). A ceiling of FF100,000 on deposits.
Fixed term accounts	Varies according to duration and amount (4.5-8.5%)	0	1	4	Personal income tax (IRPP) or standard deduction of 38 percent.	Relatively unattractive given taxation, even if the standard rate was brought down to 38%.
Bons de Caisse	See fixed term accounts	0	0	3	See fixed term accounts If the borrowing is anonymous, standard. deduction of 50% plus 3% of the nominal value of the certificate per annum.	See fixed-term accounts. Possibility of opting to stay anonymous, though taxation is structured to dissuade this.
Bonds offering graduated interest rates	The rate increases with duration	0	0	3	See fixed term accounts. Anonymity is possible, with the same consequences as for deposit receipts.	As earnings are dependent on duration, only 5 year certificates offer a positive net interest rate, though below those available on 'Livrets A' or 'Livrets Bleus.' If the standard rates of deduction are reduced, returns will be slightly better. But our conclusions remain unchanged.
Negotiable debt instruments	Close to the interbank rate	0	4	3	A withholding tax rate of 10%. Personal income tax or standard deduction rates of 34% reduced to 18% as and from 1.1.90.	Marketable debt instruments bring together certificates of deposit, treasury bills, marketable current account Treasury bonds, marketable securities issued by financial institutions and other authorised parties. These products are for the most part available to the public through SICAVs (unit trusts) and short-term FCPs (investment funds).

Appendix 13.1 b

Products	Return	Capital gains	Liquidity	Security	Taxation	Observations
Individual loans	Cannot exceed the usury rate	0	0	0 to 3	Income tax or standard deduction of 38%.	The interest rate on a loan is negotiated between the parties concerned. Can be dangerous if not covered by a mortgage.
Loans among business associates	Cannot exceed the usury rate	0	0	0 to 3	If the company is the lender, company taxation applies. If the business associate is the lender, taxation is as for individuals.	Care should be taken of the amounts lent and to the risk that the loan is considered an abuse of company assets.
Transferable securities	variable (see below)	4	4	0 to 4	The first franc of capital gains is taxable at a rate of 17% when above a certain threshold for annual sales of shares in SICAVs and FCP. In 1989 this threshold was FF298,000. The first FF8,000 of income for single individuals (FF16,000 for couples) coming either from shares and bonds is tax-exempted.	The conditions set out opposite apply to income and capital gains realised within the framework of a managed portfolio of shares, bonds, portions of SICAVs or FCPs. Whatever its source, this income or the volume of sales that trigger capital gains tax are merged together.
Fixed rate French bonds	Around 9%	2	4	3	See 'transferable securities'. For amounts above allowances ceilings, coupons are presently subject to a personal income tax or standard deduction rate of 8%. Withholding tax rate of 12% for securities issued before January 1st 1965, and of 10% for those issued since January 1965. Tax credits available.	Debt issued to the public by corporates. The level of security depends on the quality of the issuer. The best are issued by the state or guaranteed by the state. Beware the difficulties involved in managing a bond portfolio. While securities can be redeemed at par value at the agreed settlement date, they can in the meantime fluctuate depending on interest raes and their life-times.
Variable rate bonds	Vary according to market rates	1	4	3	See 'Fixed rate bonds'.	Prices do not change in accordance with rates, but rather with the going rate of interest. Prices are thus relatively stable. One should note that a great number of variable rate bonds rely on different parameters. See elsewhere.
Convertible bonds	See under Bonds	0 to 4	4	2 to 4	See 'Fixed rate bonds'.	Such bonds can be exchanged for equity from a set date. This possibility means investors can hope to realise capital gains that are much higher than those available on ordinary bonds.

Appendix 13.1 c

Product	Return	Capital gains	Liquidity	Security	Taxation	Observations
1977 8.8% loan	8.80% on nominal amount (FF88)	2	4	4	A special allowance of FF1,000 on loan coupons. Can run concurrently with FF8,000 and FF16,000 coupons.	See bonds.
Foreign bonds	Vary depending on the origin of the security	3	4	2	Income subject to personal income tax and no allowances. Capital gains come under taxes on transferable securities.	The same considerations valid as for French bonds, with in addition a currency risk.
French equities	Vary according to the security in question, averaging 3% in October	4	4	2	See transferable securities. Once tax allowances have been made, income is subject to personal income tax. Tax credit of 50%.	Shares in the capital of a company giving right to a share (dividend) in profits. Income depends on the company's results. Share prices governed by the laws of supply and demand contain a large potential for gains or drops in value.
Sociétés d'Investissement Immobilièr (SII — Property Investment Companies)	Variable	4	4	3	SIIs are exempt from corporate tax. There is little or no tax credit attached. Aside from these particularities, taxation is as per other French equities.	Real estate company shares, of which 3/4 of the total value must be devoted to housing. SIIs are required to distribute at least 85% of profits.
SICOMI (Commercial real estate leasing companies)	6-9% at the end of October	4	4	3	Exempted from corporate tax on renting activities. Same legislation applied as for SIIs.	Shares in real estate companies with a stock of industrial and commercial property letting is within the framework of a straight lease or other leasing arrangements. The latter is a purely financial transaction and has a leverage effect on results. As with SIIs, SICOMIs distribute at least 85% of their profits.
Foreign equities	Variable	4	4	2	Income tax. Apart from exceptions, no tax credits. No annual allowances. Same taxation as capital gains on transferable securities.	More speculative than French equities because of the currency risk. Because of the excessive costs involved, equities not quoted on the French markets should be avoided.
SICAV — Unit trust companies	Variable	3	4	3	Tax regulations specific to each of them is applied to income from equities, bonds or other securities arising from the management of a portfolio and distributed to bearers of parts of these trusts after allowances (FF8,000-FF16,000). Capital gains arising from the management of a SICAV are not taxable. Capital gains from the sale of portions of SICAVs are taxed as transferable securities.	The goal of SICAVs is to manage a portfolio of transferable securities. SICAVs can be specialised or diversified. The requirement to hold at least 30% of their assets in bonds or liquid assets has been abolished since 1/10/89. SICAVs publish their net asset value on a daily basis and may be quoted.

Appendix 13.1 d						
Product	Return	Capital gains	Liquidity	Security	Taxation	Observations
Diversified SICAVs	Variable	4	4	3	See SICAVs.	Managers of this type of SICAV operate under no constraints as to how they build up their portfolios They can buy and sell bonds and shares (French and foreign) as they wish.
Specialist SICAVs	Variable	4	4	2-4	See SICAVs.	SICAVs can be specialised by product (shares or bonds), by industrial category (technology, mines etc) or by geography (US, Europe, Japan, France etc). Managers are required to respect the goal of the SICAV in their choice of investment.
'SICAV de capitalisation' (Capital growth funds)	Weak (see Observations)	4	4	3-4	Income arising from bond coupons or from marketable debt instruments is not distributed and escapes tax. Such income is capitalised. Other income and capital gains is treated in the same way as ordinary SICAVs.	A new and attractive product. Such SICAVs are due to benefit from other advantages in the course of the coming years. Helps in preparing retirement.
Monthly or Quarterly income SICAVs	Variable	2	4	3	See SICAVs.	Income is distributed on a monthly or quarterly basis. Up to the time of writing, the measure of protection they provide against the depreciation of money is debatable. Rather, they tend to favour returns over protection against losses in purchasing power.
Regular, sensitive ('sensibles') or short term ('monétaires') SICAVs	Near to market rates	2	4	4	See SICAVs.	Special SICAVs for cash investments. According to how they are defined, they are concerned with products that are more or less sensitive to market variations (variable rate bonds, repurchase option certificates, debts, marketable debt instruments etc). 'SICAV monétaires' can be used over a period of days or weeks. 'Regular' ones run from a period of 1 to 6 months and 'sensitive' ones from 6 months to 1 year.
Fonds communs de placement (FCP — Mutual funds/investment trusts)	See SICAVs	See SICAVs	3		See SICAVs.	Nowadays, what most distinguishes FCPs from SICAVs is the frequency with which the former publish their net asset values (every week or fortnight) and their legal status. FCPs are no longer the concern of *sociétés anonymes* (limited companies) but of joint share portfolios. What is more, FCPs share the same characteristics or specialisations as SICAVs.
Risk FCPs	0-4	0-4	1	2	Capital gains are not liable to tax if the funds invested in the acquiring of portions are blocked for at least 5 years; likewise if income is reinvested over 5 years.	These funds differ from straight FCPs insofar as they can hold stakes of over 10% in a company but have to have over 40% of their assets tied up in the stock of companies not quoted on the official or second market. Their net asset value need only be published once a month.

Appendix 13.1 e

Products	Return	Capital gains	Liquidity	Security	Taxation	Observations
Futures markets operations (MATIF or MONEP)	0	0-4	0-4	0	Capital gains are liable at a rate of tax that varies with their origin.	See under 'Stock market'. Mostly aimed at market professionals or the 'initiated'.
Off-shore Luxembourg funds	0	0-4	4	2	Only portions of funds sold are subject to taxation in Luxembourg. All operations carried out within the fund benefit from fiscal transparency. French taxpayers are required to declare every transfer of capital carried out from one compartment to another within an umbrella fund and these transfers are subject to taxation.	Such funds operate like umbrella funds (see below). They thus contain a portfolio of specialist funds. The investment manager or the investor can shift capital from one fund to another as market opportunities arise, without such operations being considered transfers. In the same way, income from bonds and equities can be capitalised.
Umbrella (SICAV) funds	0	0-4	4	2	Apart from off-shore funds (see above), these do not offer any particular tax advantage. The relocation of capital from one compartment to another is considered a transfer in each country.	Made up of a portfolio of specialised funds. Investors can shift from one specialist fund to another (equities, bonds, American or Japanese securities etc) according to market opportunities and without the operation incurring the normal transfer costs.
Gold, quoted metals	0	3	4	4	Flat rate of tax of 8% at sale.	Gilt-edged securities. Gold always beats inflation in the long-term. Held to provide protection in the medium to long term. (See other entries).
Quoted gold coins	0	3	4	4	See above.	Much French and foreign gold coinage is quoted on the stock market. What sets them apart from ingots is that they can produce a positive or negative premium. Such premiums correspond to the difference between the official price of the coin and the value of its gold content (expressed in percentage terms). This value is itself calculated using as a basis the official spot rate per kilo for ingots.
Non-quoted gold	0	2	2	3	Choice between a flat rate of taxation and taxation as per the general rule of law: exemption when the sales price is less than FF20,000. In other cases, 4% of the sale price at auctions and 6% elsewhere. It should be noted that there is tax relief when the value of the sale is FF20,000-30,000.	Taxation as per the general rule of law applies. There is an allowance of FF6,000 on capital gains after revaluation of the acquisition price using money depreciation ratios and an allowance of 5% on capital gains for each year of ownership. The taxation alluded to here does not apply to quoted gold (bars, ingots, coinage accepted in official transactions). It covers jewels, objets d'art, art collections or items of antiquity.

Appendix 13.1f

Products	Returns	Capital gains	Liquidity	Security	Taxation	Observations
Objets d'art, art collections, items of antiquity	0	3	2	3	See taxation described above.	A gilt-edged investment. Particularly secure if the objects are internationally recognised or are the work of a well-known name. Otherwise, they become more speculative.
Diamonds and precious stones	0	2	1	2	VAT rate of 28% and taxation that applies to objets d'art.	Over the long term, and if they were acquired under normal conditions, diamonds and coloured stones (rubies, sapphires, emeralds) ought to count as gilt-edged investments and act as a precaution against.
Life insurance	0	3	2	4	Exemption from income tax and capital gains for policies of over eight years. For lesser periods: standard deductions based the depreciation of money. A long-term investment, given VAT and intermediary charges on a sliding scale (see capitalisation bonds). Exemption from sales duties if the subscriber was less than 60 years of age at the time the policy was taken out. Tax credits against paid premiums (see elsewhere).	Often presented as excellent savings products, life insurance policies are first and foremost investments made in preparation for retirement. Made particularly attractive by satisfactory performances, a high level of security and a special, low rate of taxation.
Capitalisation bonds	0	3	2	4	Exemption of income for bonds issued after 1.1.90 and capital gains for contracts lasting beyond 10 years. For bonds of lesser duration, standard deduction on a sliding scale identical to those for life insurance: 38% if less than 4 years, 18% if between 4 and 8 years. Possibility to subscribe to bearer bonds. Standard deduction is then 50 + 3% on income and capital gains.	It can be a tempting product if nominal, but much less so if made out to the bearer because of the taxation applied.
Life annuities	3	0	0	4	Tax allowances according to the age of the annuity's recipient at the time of first instalment payments. The portion of the annuity that escapes tax is: 30% if the beneficiary is under 50 years of age; 50% if between 50 and 59; 60% if between 60 and 65; 70% if over 70.	There are many types of life annuity on offer. No two offer the same interest or guarantees.

Appendix 13.1 g

Products	Return	Capital gains	Liquidity	Security	Taxation	Observations
Plan d'Epargne en vue de la Retraite (PER — Retirement savings plan)	0	2-4	0	2-4	Very complicated from a taxation perspective, especially when one decides to withdraw from the plan. Lodgements of up to FF8,210 for single individuals and FF16,420 for a married couple are deductible from taxable income. A further amount of FF4,110 is granted for each child in one's guardianship. Interest and capital gains received as part of the PER package are capitalised and are not liable to tax.	It has not been possible to open a PER account or to make any further lodgements to an existing account since January 1st, 1990. Those who held PER accounts before 20th July 1989 are allowed to convert them into PEPs.
Plan d'Epargne Populaire (PEP — People's saving plan)	0	2-4	0	2-4	No tax advantages at the time of opening one of these accounts. Tax relief and capitalisation of income and capital gains arising from the PEP. There is total exemption from taxation if there is no withdrawal in the 8 year period.	Encourages the building up of long term savings, especially among non-taxable households.
Real estate						
Main residence	3	3	2	4	Tax relief for interest on loans taken out for acquisition, construction or major repairs. Reduction in cost of loans for restoration work and major repairs. As a general rule, no taxation of capital gains. Domestic rates ('taxes d'habitation' and 'taxes fonciers') apply.	One of the best investments. It protects and increases the value of personal estates and eliminate rents.
Secondary residence	0	3	2	3	Same taxes and rates as for main residences. Exemption from capital gains at the time of the first transfer of ownership if certain conditions are respected. No tax relief for loan interest or for repairs.	More advantageous from the point of view of allocating resources than a strictly financial one. Attention should be paid to the charges that accompany this investment.

Appendix 13.1 h

Product	Return	Capital gains	Liquidity	Security	Taxation	Observations
Rental accommodation	2	3	2	3	Capital gains are taxable as income deriving from the ownership of property after an allowance (presently 15% but due to be reduced in the Finance Act to 10%). Income from the rental of furnished property is liable to tax as 'bénéfices industriels et commerciaux' (BIC — profit from trading or industrial activities) (see the Mehaignerie property scheme).	Deficits on property are only deductible from income from the same source, an exception being Malraux scheme operations.
The Mehaignerie property scheme	2	3	2	3	10% tax relief on investments of up to FF200,000 for individuals and FF400,000 for couples. These ceilings are due to be raised to FF300,000 and FF600,000 respectively in the Finance Act. These reductions should be spread over two years. The allowance of 35% on rental income over 10 years has been reduced to 25%.	'Mehaignerie real estate' refers exclusively to the purchase of new rental accommodation that is intended to be the tenant's main place of residence for at least six years. Taxpayers can still purchase such real estate under the old Mehaignerie scheme conditions from now until the end of the year. From the 1st January 1990, one sole operation will be authorised.
The Malraux property scheme	2	3	2	2	The interest on mortgage repayments is offset against income liable to tax, as is money spent on renovation. Same taxation as applied to rental property.	Within a very strict legal framework, an amalgamation of restoration works allows investors to deduct all connected expenses from their overall taxable income (apart from income arising out of the acquisition of the property). Apartments have to be rented as main residences. Special attention should be paid to the legal framework. Any sign that the rules as set down are not being respected will lead to the advantages associated with this scheme being terminated. Likewise, one should be careful not to pay for apartments above their real value.
Tourist residences	2	3	2	3	VAT refunds. At the end of its term as tourist accommodation, rent is taxed as BIC (profits from industrial and commercial activities).	In exchange for delegating management and giving up rents for 10-12 years, the investor recuperates VAT. Doing this, and announcing the residence's availability for rental allows investors to reduce the cost of acquisition by around 30%. Be careful of problems in reselling and of wear and tear to the property.
Parking lots	3	3	3	3	Normal taxation.	Good returns if the site is chosen carefully.

Appendix 13.1 i

Product	Return	Capital gains	Liquidity	Security	Taxation	Observations
Agricultural land and 'groupements fonciers agricoles' (GFA — Grouping of agricultural properties)	1	2-3	1	4	Relief available on capital gains if the land has a value below a range of FF5-30 per square metre (varying with the type of cultivation). Transfers of land ownership entail registration fees of 4.80%, 14.60% or 5.40%. Revenue taxable as per income from property. Relief on 3/4 of inheritance taxes if certain conditions are met.	A very long term investment. Returns are excessively low, but there is hope that there will be capital gains after 10 years of falling values as expressed in constant French francs. An advisable investment for large fortunes, given partial exemption from inheritance taxes on the first transfer in ownership. Resale problems for portions of GFAs.
Forests and groupings of forest	1	2-3	1	4	In the overwhelming majority of cases, such land investments avoid taxation on capital gains. Tax relief on capital gains for tree planting. Low tax on income (cadastral basis). Relief on 3/4 of the amount owed in inheritance taxes and wealth tax if certain conditions are met.	Mainly attractive from a taxation point of view. Care should be taken that the proposed price is not above the real value of the property.

Miscellaneous

Product	Return	Capital gains	Liquidity	Security	Taxation	Observations
Sociétés de financement du cinéma et de l'audiovisuel (SOFICA — Film and audiovisual financing companies)	2	2	0	1	Subscription to this scheme allows investors a reduction in taxable income of up to 25% of one's overall net income provided that stakes are held for a minimum of 5 years. Income: taxation as for transferable securities. Capital gains: taxation as per the general rule of law.	SOFICAs invest in audiovisual and cinematic productions. Attention should be paid to the risks involved and the problems that can arise when it comes to reselling shares.
The Pons property scheme	2	3	2	1	Reductions in tax spread across five years based on 20% of the overall cost of the operation. In 1989, the reduction was still 50% for the basic investment. From 1990, this will fall to 25%.	Investments have to be in new apartments or buildings destined for rental as the tenant's main place of residence. Given that such property has to be in France's overseas 'départements' and 'territoires' (the DOM-TOM), there are risks associated with the political situation and climate. Care should also be taken of the quality and actual costs associated with this investment.

Appendix 13.1 j

Product	Return	Capital gains	Liquidity	Security	Taxation	Observations
'Sociétés civiles de placement immobilier d'entreprise' (SCPI — Company property investment trusts)	3	3	3	3	Taxation on real estate.	Shares in SCPIs can be had for a few thousand Francs. The aim of SCPIs is to manage a portfolio of industrial and commercial properties and ensure a return that is better than that available on the housing market. Income is distributed every quarter and shares are revalued regularly. Good supply and demand on the secondary market. No portfolio management problems. Diversification of risks.
The Mehaignerie SCPI scheme	2	3	1	3	Taxation as for previous Mehaignerie scheme. However, only 75% of the investment is deductible from tax.	These SCPIs buy new apartments that are intended as the tenants' main place of residence. In order to improve returns, 25% of the property portfolio can be made up of industrial or commercial property. When there was the risk that the secondary market would quieten down, SCPI managers decided to sell property after holding it for ten to twelve years and to wind up SCPIs after dividing the fruits of the sales among partners.
The Malraux SCPI scheme	2	3	1	3	Taxation as for previous Malraux scheme.	These SCPIs buy property that has been restored under the Malraux Law The investment offers the same advantages as the other Malraux scheme, but is rather less risky. After ten years of existence, SCPIs have been wound up and the fruits of sales have been divided among the partners.
Time-shares	2	2-3	2	3	Capital gains are subject to the taxation applicable to capital gains on real estate. Income is subject to tax as BIC (industrial or trading profits).	Time sharing allows one to buy an amount of time in a property that is connected to one's share in the company that owns the property. This scheme holds many advantages, particularly the use of the property for life, and the possibility of exchanging one's allotted time-share with other owners of the same property. The investment is small. Only consider offers made by well-known and reputable companies.
Containers	1-3	0	1	1	Depreciation possible. BIC taxation applies.	High-risk investment that some companies have been able to manage very well during times of crisis. Duration limited to 12-15 years. Beware of high storage charges.
Train carriages	2-3	0	1	2	Depreciation possible. BIC taxation applies.	Less risky than containers if long-term rental agreements are taken out with the French State Railways (SNCF) or big foreign railway companies.
Dairy cows	3	3	3	3	Income subject to taxation on profits from agriculture.	Heifers ready to calve are bought by an investor and an investment company entrusts them to a breeder. His responsibility is to ensure that the herd renews itself. The returns come from the sale of cows born to the herd. Once the age of the herd is held constant, its value and thus the value of the investment follows changes in the market for cows. A tempting and amusing product for those who wish to diversify their assets.

Lafferty Management Reports

Financial Services in the United Kingdom
Financial Services in Ireland
Financial Services in Denmark
Financial Services in the Netherlands
Financial Services in South Africa

The pace of cross-border activity in financial services is increasing dramatically. To what can busy executives refer, though, for detailed factual information and analysis of the financial services markets? This series of reports fills the gap with comprehensive, well-informed intelligence at a moderate rate.

If you are a senior executive or corporate planner considering an investment or an acquisition overseas, or if you are a consultant, adviser or other commercial professional, you will find these reports invaluable to show how the industry in each country evolved to its present state; to give details of the main operators in each of the markets; to highlight market gaps and acquisition opportunities; to help identify feasible partners; to provide sources for obtaining further information; to assess the future of the markets; and to provide product development ideas.

Financial Revolution in Europe II
The Revolution Deepens and Widens

This report examines how the financial revolution affecting European banking, insurance and financial services has been greatly intensified. Bankers and insurers must now examine how the emergence of two powerful factors will affect their strategies for Europe in the 1990s

- political change in Central and Eastern Europe and the new will to create market-based economies; and

- the increased likelihood that the EC member states will develop closer economic and political links and that a single currency will be in circulation issued and controlled by a single European central bank.

Financial Revolution in Europe II examines the changes that these factors have exerted on the European banking and financial services market and analyses their longer-term significance for the future evolution of the European financial services market. Published 1992.

The Allfinanz Revolution
Winning Strategies for the 1990s

This report looks at the changing regulatory environment and the opening up of markets throughout the past decade and how these have effected the behaviour of financial institutions. Through case studies and country surveys, the report demonstrates how bankers are increasing profits through their branch networks by using them as cost-effective distribution channels for life insruance, while at the same time preserving their deposit base and cultivating a closer relationship with customers. The book also looks at the entry methods used by banks and insurance companies to blur the line between the two previously distinct industries. Successful and unsuccessful ventures alike are covered in the report. Published 1991.

Lafferty Newsletters

Banking and Life Insurance:

Retail Banker International, the flagship of the Lafferty Group, is a worldwide business intelligence service for the consumer financial services industry. Every two weeks *RBI* covers a broad range of important issues encompassing the whole consumer financial services sector — not only traditional retail banking, but also cards, life insurance, mortgages and mutual funds — making it the industry's premier sources of intelligence.

Electronic Payments International provides business intelligence for all those involved in electronic payments. *EPI* is unique in that it offers objective global coverage of the entire scope of electronic banking, with in-depth analysis of the important topics and issues. The information is presented in a concise format for busy executives who can ill afford to wade through reams of material to get to the heart of a particular issue.

Cards International is the worldwide briefing on the plastic card industry. Published twice monthly, *Cards International* is designed to provide a complete information service for senior executives involved in card operations in banks and retailing organisations, technology suppliers, other issuers, card processors and payment systems companies.

Private Banker International is an independent monthly publication designed to meet the needs of all who service the high net worth banking customer. It is an informative mix of news, comment, analysis, case studies, interviews, country surveys and statistics. *PBI* analyses the strategies, products and services, marketing techniques and organisational structure of successful providers and new entrants in this profitable — and difficult — area of banking.

Bank Marketing International is designed to provide market intelligence for the financial services industry. To guide you through the marketing maze, Lafferty Publications brings you *BMI,* a monthly intelligence bulletin scanning the globe to bring readers the best and brightest marketing ideas, techniques and strategies.

European Banker, published every two weeks, is targeted to senior executives of banks and other financial institutions involved in Europe. *EB* monitors the news and analyses the impact of emerging trends. In addition, *EB* looks at strategies, mergers, bids, alliances, regulation, legislation, profiles key figures and provides crucial statistics on Europe's national markets.

East European Banker, the newest Lafferty newsletter, provides vital intelligence on the fast-developing East European financial services market. Each month *EEB* provides sharp and penetrating insights into major developments in Eastern and Central Europe. Its scope covers East/West joint ventures, strategic moves by key players, the establishment of new financial institutions and appointments to senior posts. A vital intelligence source for any organisation seeking to maximise opportunities in this expanding market.

Life Insurance International is the monthly bulletin for senior executives in financial institutions that provide life insurance and other forms of contractual savings. *LII* examines the life insurance industry as a whole — encompassing life institutions, banks and building societies, pension funds, and the major intermediaries. This broad industry overview enables you to put your organisation and its plans into context.

Insurance Industry International reports on corporate performance and strategy in the insurance industry worldwide. It evaluates competitive strategies and performance among general, life, corporate, marine, aviation, fire and accident insurance companies and reinsurance and broking companies — worldwide.

Accounting:

Corporate Accounting International, a must for CFOs, finance directors, auditors, regulators and standard-setters. *CAI* provides a comprehensive and sophisticated briefing on developments and trends in corporate reporting standards, requirements and practices worldwide. It incorporates *Bank Financial Management International*, a special monthly supplement focusing specifically on reporting issues for the financial services industry.

The Accountant reports on news and developments in the advanced accounting world — notably the UK, the US, Canada and Australia. It covers the issues and developments affecting finance directors and chief accountants as well as partners in accounting firms.

International Accounting Bulletin was launched in 1983 and is now read by the world's leading accountants. *IAB* provides the necessary intelligence so that crucial business decisions can be made from an internationally-informed standpoint. Every month, readers of *IAB* can follow the competition and jockeying for position in the world's established and emerging markets for audit, tax, consulting and other advisory services.

European Accountant assesses, monitors and reports on the emerging European market for accounting services. It offers informative, in-depth coverage of the European accounting profession from both a European and regional perspective.

Professional Services:

Management Consultant International brings you news of the developments in the consultancy industry worldwide. Find out what your competitors are thinking and doing, what new areas of business are opening up, the latest trends and the latest news of new contracts, mergers and acquisitions.

Lawyer International provides intelligence on the most significant developments in the international market for legal services. News and features will cover corporate performance and recession, diversifying practice areas, international networks and mergers, restrictive practices and competition and international harmonisation of legal qualifications.

Practice Marketing International covers international news and developments in the marketing of law, accounting and consulting services and other professional services. News and features include coverage of pricing, regulation, promotion, branding, cross-selling and markets and services around the world.